SOUTHAMPTON'S

CULT HEROES

JEREMY WILSON

Know The Score Books Limited

www.knowthescorebooks.com

KNOW THE SCORE BOOKS PUBLICATIONS

CULT HEROES	Author	ISBN
CHELSEA	Leo Moynihan	1-905449-00-3
NEWCASTLE	Dylan Younger	1-905449-03-8
SOUTHAMPTON	Jeremy Wilson	1-905449-01-1
WEST BROM	Simon Wright	1-905449-02-X

MATCH OF MY LIFE	Editor	ISBN
ENGLAND WORLD CUP	Louis Massarella & Leo Moynihan	1-905449-52-6
EUROPEAN CUP FINALS	Ben Lyttleton	1-905449-57-7
FA CUP FINALS (1953-1969)	David Saffer	1-905449-53-4
FULHAM	Michael Heatley	1-905449-51-8
LEEDS	David Saffer	1-905449-54-2
LIVERPOOL	Leo Moynihan	1-905449-50-X
MANCHESTER UNITED	Sam Pilger	1-905449-59-3
SHEFFIELD UNITED	Nick Johnson	1-905449-62-3
STOKE CITY	Simon Lowe	1-905449-55-0
SUNDERLAND	Rob Mason	1-905449-60-7
SPURS	Matt Allen & Louis Massarella	1-905449-58-5
WOLVES	Simon Lowe	1-905449-56-9

HARRY HARRIS	Author	ISBN
HARRY HARRIS WORLD CUP DIARY	Harry Harris	1-905449-90-9
HOLD THE BACK PAGE	Harry Harris	1-905449-91-7

AUTOBIOGRAPHY	Author	ISBN
TACKLES LIKE A FERRET (England Cover)	Paul Parker	1-905449-47-X
TACKLES LIKE A FERRET (Manchester United Cover)	Paul Parker	1-905449-46-1

FOOTBALL FICTION	Author	ISBN
BURKSEY The Autobiography of a Football God	Peter Morfoot	1-905449-49-6

CRICKET	Author	ISBN
MOML: THE ASHES	Sam Pilger & Rob Wightman	1-905449-63-1
LINES AND LENGTHS	Paul Smith	1-905449-45-3

FORTHCOMING PUBLICATIONS IN 2007

CULT HEROES	Author	ISBN
DERBY	David McVay	978-1-905449-06-4
MANCHESTER CITY	David Clayton	978-1-905449-05-7
RANGERS	Paul Smith	978-1-905449-07-1

MATCH OF MY LIFE	Editor	ISBN
BOLTON WANDERERS	David Saffer	978-1-905449-64-4
FA CUP FINALS (1970-1989)	David Saffer	978-1-905449-65-1
HULL	Grahame Lloyd	978-1-905449-66-8

GENERAL FOOTBALL	Author	ISBN
BELIEVE IN THE SIGN A Football Life	Mark Hodkinson	978-1-905449-32-3
OUTCASTS The Lands FIFA Forgot	Steve Menary	978-1-905449-31-6
PARISH TO PLANET A History of Football	Dr Eric Midwinter	978-1-905449-30-9
MY PREMIERSHIP DIARY Reading's Season in the Premiership	Marcus Hahnemann	978-1-905449-33-0

PUB BORE: 1001 facts to bore your mates with	ISBN
MANCHESTER UNITED	978-1-905449-80-4
NEWCASTLE UNITED	978-1-905449-81-1
SUNDERLAND	978-1-905449-82-8

CRICKET	Author	ISBN
THE 2006/7 ASHES IN PICTURES	Andrew Searle	978-1-905449-44-6
GROVEL! The 1976 West Indies Tour of England	David Tossell	978-1-905449-43-9
MY AUTOBIOGRAPHY	Shaun Udal	978-1-905449-42-2

SOUTHAMPTON'S
CULT HEROES

JEREMY WILSON

Series Editor: Simon Lowe

www.knowthescorebooks.com

First published in the United Kingdom
by Know The Score Books Limited, 2006

First published in the United Kingdom by Know The Score Books Limited, 2006
Copyright © Jeremy Wilson, 2006

Know The Score Books Limited
118 Alcester Road, Studley, Warwicxkshire, B80 7NT
www.knowthescorebooks.com

A CIP catalogue record is available for this book from the British Library
ISBN-10: 1-905449-01-1   ISBN-13: 978-1-905449-01-9

Jacket and book design by Lisa David

Printed and bound in Great Britain
By Cromwell Press, Trowbridge, Wiltshire

Photographs reproduced by kind permission of Southern Daily Echo, Southampton FC and Duncan Holley

Jacket Photographs
Front centre: Matthew Le Tissier transcended mere legendary status with his genius, ball skills and incredible array of long range goals
Left: Mick Channon soaks in the Wembley bath after helping Saints to win the 1976 FA Cup
Right: Terry Paine made himself a legend at The Dell with his wing play and now has attained similar status as South Africa's answer to Alan Hansen!
Inset: Bobby Stokes hugs the FA Cup which made him a hero, but arguably killed him
Background: Saints fans liven up the Millennium Stadium for the 2003 FA Cup Final

Rear
Left: Ted Bates and Lawrie McMenemy set the tone for the longevity of Southampton managers with over 80 years service to the club between them
Right: Francis Benali became a Cult Hero in one magic moment, whacking Wimbledon's John Fashanu, but then maintained his status with 21 years of sterling service

Author's Acknowledgements

I would like to thank my publisher, Simon Lowe, for his constant enthusiasm and encouragement over the past year.

Numerous people have given their time generously. Thank-you to: Clare Balding, Alan Ball, Mary Bates, Jo Bates, Francis Benali, Bob Brunskell, Denis Bundy, Jimmy Case, Jim Chamberlain, Mick Channon, Michael Channon Jnr, Richard Cody, David Coles, Ron Davies, Chris Davies, Paul Davies, Mark Dennis, Jason Dodd, Paul Doswell, Jonathan Fry, Ivan Golac, Rob Holley, Denis Hollywood, Nick Holmes, Cliff Huxford, John at SuperSport, George Lawrence, Matthew Le Tissier, Claus Lundekvam, Kevin McMahon, Lawrie McMenemy, Dave Merrington, John Mortimore, Antti Niemi, George O'Brien, Peter Osgood, James Smith, Jim Smith, John Sydenham, Daniel Taylor, Danny Wallace, Paul Wayman, Bernard Wickham and Iain Wilton. Past interviews with David Armstrong, James Beattie, Iain Dowie, Sir Alex Ferguson, Matthew Oakley, Brett Ormerod and Jeff Stelling have also proved helpful, while my brother, Ben, has been a constant sounding-board.

Special thanks to Hilly and Terry Paine for their generous hospitality in South Africa, Gordon Strachan for his foreword and Brian O'Neil for both the interview and taking me to visit Mick Channon. Southampton Football Club have been very supportive of this project – thanks to Jo Dalton, Graham Hiley and Leighton Mitchell for their help.

Three further sources have been invaluable. I am very grateful to my old boss Ian Murray for allowing me to delve at leisure into the archives of the Southern Daily Echo and utlilise their coverage of more than a century of Saints' ups and downs. Adam Leitch, Jez Gale, Simon Carter, James Rose and Ian 'Merse' Crump have also all provided additional help.

Secondly, a big thank-you to the team of official Southampton historians known as the 'Hagiologists' – David Bull, Dave Juson, Duncan Holley and Gary Chalk – whose knowledge of all things Saints is encyclopaedic. Between them, they have checked the text for factual errors; any lingering mistakes are mine. Their publication In That Number has provided the basis for the majority of my statistical information. David Bull kindly made available his previously unpublished interview with Charlie Wayman while Dave Juson, along with Iain Wilton's biography, were invaluable for the CB Fry chapter. Duncan Holley was also a big help with locating photographs.

The other vital source has been the Southampton fans. Many helped with ideas, anecdotes and memories and I am grateful to Keith Legg of SaintsForever and Nick Illingsworth who runs the Ugly Inside webzine. Thanks to Saints fanatic Javier Igeno Cano for permitting me to use some extracts from his DvD.

Last, but most importantly, my fiancée Clare has been an unwavering support – I'm now out of excuses for not doing the washing up...

Jeremy Wilson
August 2006

Contents

Introduction

The crowd are as much a part of the atmosphere as the air, the rain, the sun and the mist...

Bernard Joy

Being a Cult Hero is not as easy as you might think. The adulation, the chanting of your name, the cheering and the sheer excitement that comes with being the focal point of worship for tens of thousands of people must be some buzz. It can disappear quite quickly or it can last years, decades even. But eventually it stops. The tap is turned off. Yet there is still a life to lead after stepping from the main stage. And, whatever comes next, it is never going to match what went before. However much we might envy, as well as revere, our Cult Heroes, that cannot be easy. Paul Kimmage, of the *Sunday Times*, describes the experience of coping with life after football as 'the bang'.

"The bang is loud, the bang is cruel, the bang is the hardest thing any footballer will ever face in life," he says. "The bang is what awaits Beckham, Rooney, Owen and Gerrard and the other England stars a few years from now when they return to the real world after a life on planet football." And 'the bang' excludes nobody, as Geoff Hurst testifies. "It doesn't matter what they're doing today or how much money they've earned, when they are 35 years of age and stop playing they will still have to go and live and work and be part of society," he says.

In their different ways and to varying extents, all 20 of my all-time Cult Heroes have had to face challenges after leaving Southampton. They are now scattered across the globe. Terry Paine is in South Africa, Chris Marsden is enjoying life in Cyprus, Ivan Golac goes between Vienna and Belgrade while Ron Davies lives in a residential vehicle in New Mexico. The change in earnings and the lifestyle of foot-ballers is evident in what they are doing now. Those who played in more recent times appear to have greater financial security, while players from earlier eras are often still working hard well into their 60s and sometimes even their 70s.

George O'Brien, the great inside-right, now drives a taxi. He narrowly missed out on my final 20 – mostly because there have been so many prolific goal-scorers down the years – but was honest enough to admit that he does often wish he had been born about 40 or 50 years later. When I spoke to him, it was on the day that Michael Ballack joined Chelsea on wages in excess of £100,000 a week. "There must have been a couple of hours last week when I didn't think about what they earn now compared to us," he said. O'Brien continues to be recognised in and around Southampton, although he's not sure whether that's a good thing. "I was in a pub the other day and someone pointed over and said, 'that's George O'Brien'," he laughed, "and the guy he was with looked at him and just said, 'no, he must be dead by now'."

The change in the life of footballers has had a knock-on consequence for the fans. It seems there are fewer Cult Heroes. A generalisation perhaps, but none other than Pelé summed up this trend when he gave an interview to the *Guardian* about the state of modern football. "One season they play with one team and the next season they play with another team," he said. "They play more for money than love. I think for the fans it's very tough. There used to be a good relation between the star and the team but no more . . . I worry about this lack of loyalty."

Yes, fans love the skilful players, the tough tacklers, the characters and the real workers, but the quality they appreciate above all others – especially in Southampton – is loyalty. They want to know that their club means as much to the players on the pitch as it does to those all around them in the stands. When I started work on this book in the summer of 2005, I tried to forecast who the next Southampton Cult Hero might be. Theo Walcott was the obvious choice and yet he was soon bound for Arsenal in a £12m deal signed before he was even 17, and after just 13 starts. Pelé's words seemed to be ringing true. Increases in wages, transfer fees and, most importantly, player freedom following the Bosman ruling have made it increasingly difficult for clubs like Southampton to keep players of the very highest calibre. The likes of Charlie Wayman, Terry Paine, Mick Channon, Ron Davies, Kevin Keegan and Matthew Le Tissier are so special precisely because they are unusual in giving some or all of their prime years to Southampton despite being sought after by richer clubs.

And yet, despite the changes in football, there will always be another Cult Hero. Supporters demand them and they create them. Who knows what storylines and heroes will emerge at the start of each new season? Essentially, though, this is a book which wallows in Southampton's sometimes glorious past. Nostalgia, after all, is the one constant shining light for fans during those gloomy days which all clubs suffer.

The most difficult aspect of this project was selecting my 20 greatest Cult Heroes. It's probable that no two fans would come up with the same list and it genuinely pained me to leave out so many great candidates. It would undoubtedly be possible to bring out further volumes of other deserving players. O'Brien, Dodd, Sydenham, Ellerington, Drake, Lundekvam, Day, Traynor, Williams, Moran, Armstrong, Steele, Fisher, Boyer, MacDougall, Hurlock, Worthington, Shilton, Rawlings, Walker, Gabriel, Dominy, Watson, Wimshurst, Osgood, Shearer, Cockerill, Peach, Martin, Wright, Nicholl, Mills, Hollywood, McGrath, Chivers, Reeves, Rodrigues, Pahars, Beattie, Bridge and Ekelund, I really could go on and on and on with a justifiable cast of alternatives.

The difficulty in narrowing the list down is a happy reflection on the calibre of the players who have represented Southampton down the years. I'm sure I've probably offended someone who has not made the list, but at least they have the consolation of being in the company of a World Cup-winning manager and player in Sir Alf Ramsey and Alan Ball. When I told him about the book, Ball began licking his lips at the thought of all the great players Southampton have had down the years. "We could talk for hours about all the players and the teams and the great games we have had down here," he said. Ball, of course, was among the finest midfielders in Southampton's history and, shamefully, I didn't have the courage to tell him he hadn't quite made the final cut.

Many supporters also kindly came forward with suggestions and anecdotes about their favourite players. Aside from the predictable choices, there were several original selections. For example, Peter Seddon wrote: "I've got someone for you who had the 'onomatopoeic' name of Billy Wrigglesworth. He only played a dozen or so games for the Saints in the 1950s. My reason for nominating him? Well he would entertain the crowd by trapping the ball with his backside! The crowd loved him. Just imagine someone doing that trick today...oh the memories."

It has been wonderful to meet so many men who brought such joy to generations of Saints fans. Ivan Golac was the most entertaining and, largely due to my timing, Mick Channon was the most difficult to interview. Visiting Terry Paine in South Africa was the best experience, while my one-on-one audience with an extremely candid Matthew Le Tissier was also a real treat. The hardest challenge was locating Ron Davies and persuading him to give his first interview for around eight years. Almost without exception, though, my Cult Heroes were generous with their time. What's more, they collectively reassured me that Southampton is a unique club which has attracted genuinely nice people as well as great players and managers. The former manager Dave Merrington talks about Saints as a "tightly knit family", while Jason Dodd simply says, "the city is superb, the supporters are fantastic and you get the best weather".

In choosing my final 20, I have aimed for a spread of players which reflect the best years in the club's history. A representative from the early and successful Southern League days, therefore, was a must and, while CB Fry was not the club's best footballer during that period, he was certainly the most remarkable. I have also tried to select people from a variety of positions. It would have been easy to stack the book with strikers (mostly those from the late 1970s and early 1980s), so I'm pleased to have finished with a reasonable balance of two managers, six defenders (including a goalkeeper), six midfielders and six forwards. For me, the only automatic choices were Ted Bates, Terry Paine, Mick Channon, Lawrie McMenemy, Bobby Stokes and Matthew Le Tissier. After that, I simply tried to find players with a blend of those characteristics which Southampton fans most enjoy. Accordingly, doses of charisma, class, commitment, fun, loyalty – and even a little controversy – flow from the stories which follow.

Jeremy Wilson
September 2006

Dedication

To George, Joyce and Jean

Foreword

Southampton seemed like a long way from Dundee and Aberdeen, the clubs where I started out as a footballer. But, even from a distance, you could sense that it would be a fun place to play football. We achieved against the odds at Aberdeen during the late 1970s and early 1980s and Southampton were doing something similar in England at the same time. To consistently finish so high in the league was some going. And, as I say, with the likes of Mick Channon, Kevin Keegan and Alan Ball, it was a football club you always associated with fun. It came across in the way they performed and this book is a reminder that Southampton has been blessed with many special players.

The first time I played at The Dell would have been in the mid-1980s and it was a ground I really liked visiting. People used to say that it was an intimidating place for the away team, but I didn't find that. I found it a place where you could enjoy yourself. I liked the fact that the crowd were close-by. You could almost feel them breathing on you and there would always be a bit of banter. You could have fun and interact with the Southampton supporters. I thought it was a great place to play football and I looked forward to matches there. You would think, 'this is what football used to be like all the time with the atmosphere and the crowd close to you'. It was old-fashioned, but it was a real footballing ground with a lot of history.

I know other players liked visiting The Dell as well and sometimes that didn't help Southampton. If you look at the club's record in the Premier League, Southampton had a few defeats at The Dell and that was partly because people liked going there. Having said that, the compact nature of the ground was perfect for Tiss (Matthew Le Tissier). He didn't need to run about too far on that pitch…maybe he wouldn't have stayed so long if the pitch had been ten yards longer or wider and he'd have had to run about a bit more! The Southampton supporters saw genius with Tiss, but they do also enjoy the people who have stuck with them and that is reflected in this book. They might have had sticky periods, but the likes of (Francis) Benali and (Jason) Dodd are big, big names when you meet Southampton fans and Tiss is obviously a superstar.

Of course, the club had moved to St. Mary's by the time I arrived as manager. It was a fabulous experience – everything about it was great and the people were always friendly to me. I kept my house in the area and lived in Southampton when I had a break from football and it was a lovely place to be. It is something you find with a lot of the people who have been managers or players at Southampton. You speak to them and they say, 'I'm keeping my house there, I love it there'. It's a place where you can enjoy life and football at the same time because the south coast is such a relaxed area. I found that people were generally laid back during the week, but then they would change on a Saturday and be right up for their football. In Glasgow, it's different because nothing changes and they are fanatical throughout the week about football wherever they are. That was a nice thing about being in Southampton because you had your football fever on a Saturday but you got a bit of peace and quiet as well.

From my time as manager, I think that getting to eighth in the league in 2002/03, and then up to fourth at Christmas was the best achievement from a football point of view. Lots of things came together, but basically we had a good set of players who worked hard and wanted to improve. The other thing is that they were all good lads and they loved playing for the club. Paul Telfer has come with me to Celtic, but I know he loved his time in Southampton.

The run to the FA Cup final in 2003 was obviously great. They say you can't enjoy the Cup final if you lose, but that's not strictly true. It's if you don't compete and you have regrets, that you can't enjoy it. Living with regrets is a horrible thing and I don't think we had any reason to have regrets at the way we prepared and performed. It was an absolutely fantastic day and a special one for me personally. For us as a family, from my dad to my grandson, it was the first time we had all got together at a football match.

People ask me what I remember most about the Cup final. Apart from the job of speaking to those players who were not going to be starting, the overriding memory is of the supporters. As I walked out, I didn't look up at the stands to begin with. Then, when we lined up, I turned around and had a glance. I was next to Antti Niemi and I remember saying to him, 'turn around and just have a look at this'. You can never be certain with Antti, but I'm pretty sure he got excited at that point. I've been fortunate to be a part of some great occasions in football, but that sea of yellow in the Millennium Stadium was one of the best things I have ever seen. It really was awe-inspiring and it is something that will live with me forever.

Gordon Strachan
May 2006

CB FRY

1900-1902

SAINTS CAREER

Games	25
Goals	0
Caps	2

MAGIC MOMENT

An outstanding performance in the 1902 FA Cup semi-final against Nottingham Forest, which took Saints to a second final in just three years

'ALMIGHTY'

AS the new Millennium turned, a footballer known as 'Le God' had won the hearts and minds of the Southampton faithful. A century earlier, the crowd at The Dell fell for another whose nickname suggested he had been blessed by a higher place. Charles Burgess Fry is, by common consent, the finest all-round sportsman who has ever lived. Nicknamed 'Almighty', he is the one former Southampton player who could claim justifiably to have been blessed with more natural sporting talent than Matthew Le Tissier.

The list of Fry's accomplishments is incredible. As well as a Southampton footballer during one of the club's greatest eras, he was – now take a deep breath – the England cricket captain, an England footballer, holder of the world long-jump record and an accomplished rugby union player. What's more, Fry was also a fine boxer, a reasonable golfer, swimmer, sculler, tennis player and javelin thrower. A man of prodigious versatility, he once lamented never having been involved in the Derby, apparently prompting a friend to say: "What as Charles? Trainer, jockey or horse?"

Away from sport, he was a writer, a poet, a politician and an academic. He was also an associate of people as prominent and diverse as Winston Churchill, Louis Mounbatten and even Adolf Hitler. Oh, and he was approached by delegates from Albania looking to recruit him as king. Having retired when he was 40 from first-class cricket, Fry then patented the formula of celebrity sports journalism which continues to this day. He was a master of self-promotion, but there was also plenty of substance. "There is a lot of myth, things got exaggerated and he exaggerated things himself – he was quite a boastful man," admits his grandson Jonathan Fry.

Boastful or not, his accomplishments were remarkable in any era. While it has not been uncommon for people to excel in both football and cricket over the years, it is unheard of to reach international standard in one discipline (in Fry's case football) and be among the best in the world in two other sports (athletics and cricket).

Comparisons are extremely difficult. The likes of Daley Thompson and Ian Botham are considered 'all-rounders' for excelling in different elements within their own sports and both also played a decent standard of football. Others have tried to master different sports. They include the tennis great Ivan Lendl who failed in an attempt to make any impact on the European golf tour, the former Southampton defender and manager Chris Nicholl who did make it into the top 50 on the world senior tennis circuit and the basketball legend Michael Jordan who took up baseball, but failed to reach the highest level.

Yet none of this comes even close to Fry. As a complete sportsman, with his fantastic physical capabilities, allied to his ball-playing skills, dedication and a forensic mind for self-improvement, he was simply unique.

Of course, he was helped by the era in which he lived. As an amateur, it was easier to take part in numerous different sports and the demands were clearly very different than today. After all, who's to say that Theo Walcott or Thierry Henry could never have been Olympic standard sprinters, or that Gary and Phil Neville could not have made their mark as international cricketers as well as footballers? We shall never know, yet this should not detract from Fry's achievements. Even in the late 19th century, he was exceptional and a figure whose national and even international prominence was to transcend his sport. As Jeremy Paxman wrote: "Here, surely, is an English hero."

Jonathan Fry says it first dawned just how famous his grandfather was when he spoke at a memorial service for him. "I suppose growing up and talking to your elderly grandfather you don't have that appreciation," he says, "but the range of people that attended his service brought it home to me how well known he actually was. He had a wonderfully natural physique for sport, but what seemed to set him apart was that he could also make an intellectual analysis of a game. He wrote a book on cricket called *Batsmanship* which is a real technical treatise. The current Sri Lankan player Kumar Sangakkara says that he has studied it."

FRY'S footballing debut for Southampton came on Boxing Day 1900 against Tottenham Hotspur and was greeted with wild enthusiasm from supporters. Immaculately turned out and possessing a physique which was compared to that of a "Greek God", his popularity was such that his breakdown from cramp late in the game was greeted by a spontaneous rendition of "for he's a jolly good fellow" from the 14,000 supporters present.

Somewhat different from the chants of the modern day, but, in an era when crowd participation was less developed, it was an unusually enthusiastic show of affection. The excitement locally over Fry was summed up by the *Echo* which said: "A player of Fry's stamp would be a distinct gain for the best club in the kingdom; he is, without doubt, the finest amateur back playing, a player who shines conspicuously in a constellation of football stars."

The paper also went on to praise his, "physical perfectness, grace and power". That Saints could attract a player of such huge fame may appear surprising. But even more surprising to the contemporary fan is probably the news that their club could once have been described as the very best in the land. Looking back, it really does appear to be the most unlikely of marriages. At the time, however, it was not unexpected.

The lofty status of Saints meant that the club was regularly able to attract some of the best players in the country, as well as the most celebrated and famous sportsman of his time in Fry. Indeed, the late 1890s and early 1900s stand comparison with the 1960s, 1970s and 1980s as the club's finest era. Dave Juson, the author of *Full-Time at The Dell,* says: "People looking back might think 'it's only the Southern League', but, at that time, it was a competition to rival the Football League. In eight years, Saints won six championships and reached two FA Cup finals. The Southern League was getting better crowds than the Second Division and Saints and Pompey were bigger clubs than any of those based in London. Without question, Saints were among the ten biggest clubs in the country at that time."

SAINTS' rapid ascent to success is impressive considering the area's history. Indeed, for the most part of the 19th century, Southampton was not the footballing area it has become today. The foundations of the modern docks in 1838, however, combined with a functioning railway to London by 1840, meant that the area was being crowded out by labourers, seamen and tradesmen from all over the country and was transformed from the Spa town it had been prior to the 1820s. The main organised sports at this time, though, were bowls, yachting, annual horse racing events on the Common, cricket and probably boxing. Rugby union was not introduced until Trojans formed in 1874 and the first known local association club, Southampton Rangers, emerged in the late 1870s, and was dominated by Scottish marine engineers.

The population increased from 27,000 in 1841 to 60,051 in 1881, rising to 100,061 if you include the growth in outlying suburbs. The parish of St. Mary's, by then encompassing the area northwards from what would now be Ocean Village to just south of the St. Mary's Stadium, was one of the town's most densely populated suburbs with 8,000 of its poorest inhabitants crammed into sub-standard housing. But St. Mary's, being Southampton's "mother church" also had a host of rich, highly respectable patrons. Many of the younger, more affluent and better educated churchgoers found themselves in the St. Mary's Church of England Young Men's Association, a grouping of the choristers, Sunday school teachers and parochial volunteers, which, in 1885, formed a football club.

The first match was against Freemantle on November 21 on an area that was part of Hampshire Cricket Club's former County Ground at Northlands Road and the new team ran out 5-1 winners. The *Hampshire Independent* report correctly predicted that they had, "the material to form a fairly strong club". They quickly became known as 'The Saints'. Interest in football exploded as Saints played their first competitive matches. This came with the formation of the Hampshire Football Association in 1887/88. Saints were to win the Hampshire Junior Cup for their first three seasons, before immediately winning the Senior Cup on two occasions to make it five successive cup wins. Saints had quickly established themselves as the top side in the area and demonstrated their wider potential with a 7-0 thrashing of Reading in the FA Cup of 1891/92, only to have the result overturned for fielding two ineligible players.

With the formation of the Football League in 1888, a professional era was born for what was quickly becoming the nation's favourite sport. Even for such a relatively young club as Saints, crowds of around 5,000 were not uncommon for local derbies against Freemantle, with gate receipts providing the income for the club to pay their players. The Southern League was formed in 1894, meaning Saints, now re-named Southampton St. Mary's, would play fixtures against teams from much further afield with Millwall, Luton and Swindon also in the division. Two consecutive third place finishes followed, as well as qualification for the first round proper of the FA Cup. There then arrived a period of sustained success, with Saints winning three consecutive Southern League titles and making the FA Cup semi-final of 1898 and then the final in 1900. Within the space of less than 15 years, football had firmly taken over as the number one sport in Southampton and Saints were the town's leading club.

That grip on the public imagination was demonstrated on the final day of the 1899 season when a dramatic 4-3 victory at Bristol City clinched the title. The scenes at the Dock Station were reportedly, "without parallel in the history of southern football. Long before ten o'clock the streets at the lower end of the town were almost impassable, and joy triumphant reigned. The procession through the streets reminded one of the conclusion of a great electoral campaign". The template for supporting Southampton, as fans who revelled in each of the club's most significant moments, was set.

The year before, the FA Cup quarter-final win against Bolton Wanderers demonstrated that the predominantly midland and northern clubs which comprised the Football League could no longer claim to be the very best in the country. Saints defeated Bolton 4-0 in a replay in front of some 15,000 supporters at the County Ground. The *Daily Mail* reported: "Southampton's success against Bolton Wanderers marks the dawning of a new era for professional football in the south and it is now becoming more and more evident that absolutely first-class football is not to be forever monopolised by northern organisations."

The semi-final was lost 2-0 in a replay with Nottingham Forest at Crystal Palace amid controversial circumstances, with Saints playing into a blizzard in the second-half. They protested to the FA that the goalkeeper George Clawley was blinded by the snow and insisted the game should have been abandoned. There were no complaints, however, two years later when they became the first Southern League team to reach an FA Cup final, losing 4-0 to Bury in front of some 75,000 supporters after disposing of Football League clubs Everton, Newcastle and West Bromwich Albion in the earlier rounds.

SO JUST why had Saints become the first southern club to shake the Football League citadel? Crucial in their progress at the time and the eventual signing of Fry was their forward-thinking chairman Dr Ernest Stancomb and the manager/secretary Mr Arnfield. They publicly stated their ambition was to build a side equal to Aston Villa and there was little doubt that the established order had taken notice. *Athletic News* said: "As a representative southern club it cannot be said that the Arsenal have made so remarkable impression on the public as Southampton. The last named are undoubtedly in a better class."

The boys' magazine *Chums* agreed: "No team can boast of having fought their way to the front with such lightening-like rapidity as the champions of the south, and if the opinions of experienced judges are worth anything, the Southampton men have absolutely no superiors."

Significant developments off the field included the decision in 1897 to form a limited liability company and change the club's name to Southampton Football and Athletic Company Limited, although the tag 'Saints' continued to stick. Next came the move to The Dell, which was considered among the very best grounds in Victorian Britain. The Dell held 24,500 and was the first in the country to boast stands on both sides of the pitch.

The land had been a dell, a wooded valley with a stream running through it, until it had been excavated to accommodate a goods siding for an aborted section of the Didcot, Newbury & Southampton Railway. Club director George Thomas purchased it and transformed it into a football ground on his own initiative and at his own expense. The pitch was actually laid over a stream and, after a good deal of draining and work, The Dell was ready for the 1898/99 season. The first visitors were Brighton United and Saints, captained by Harry Wood, ran out 4-1 winners.

Most important, however, in explaining Saints' rise was the ambitious transfer policy of the chairman Stancomb. "The success of Saints at this time was primarily because they spent a lot of money and went into a lot of debt," says Juson, "they bought most of the Stoke team, although it was still hard to compete with the big city clubs like Everton and Aston Villa. Saints also had an exceptional trainer at that time called Bill Dawson, who had also been at Stoke and he kept the players very fit."

After the "Stoke invasion" when top players like Charles Baker, 'Lachie' Thomson, Alfred Littlehales, Jack Farrell, 'Chippy' Naughton and Sam Meston arrived from the Potteries, there were further significant recruits in 1897 when Bob Buchanan came from Arsenal, Harry Haynes from Small Heath, George Clawley from Stoke, Arthur Chadwick from Burton Swifts, Thomas Nicol from Blackburn, Robert Petrie from Sheffield Wednesday and James Yates from Sheffield United. It led to a letter in the *Morning Leader,* which, in keeping with Victorian principles of a distaste over receiving money for sporting prowess, described Saints as, "an imported team of mercenaries".

Undeterred, Stancomb and Arnfield continued to sign top players. This was most evident the season Saints moved to The Dell with four internationals arriving. Scots John Robertson and Peter Meehan came from Everton, while there were shades of the Peter Shilton signing more than 80 years later when the England goalkeeper John Robinson, who was registered with Derby County, arrived from New Brighton Tower for an eventual fee of £400.

Yet even that was over-shadowed by the capture of the England and Wolves inside-forward Harry Wood. His signing is an illustration of the lengths Saints were prepared to go to improve their team. Trainer Bill Dawson happened to be in the midlands on a short holiday when he read in a local newspaper that Wood had not signed a new contract and was in dispute with the club's directors. After meeting Wood in a Walsall pub, Dawson used his powers of persuasion to secure a deal the following day, which, legend has it, was concluded in the waiting room of Birmingham railway station. Another example of Saints' aggressive transfer strategy came when the goalkeeper Robinson was reported to the FA in 1900 for allegedly trying to poach former team-mate and then the England record goal-scorer Steve Bloomer from Derby County.

"Saints were a bit like Chelsea under Ken Bates," says Juson, "they spent money, but were living above their means." It was certainly a different philosophy from the generally well-managed and frugal outfit the club became throughout the latter half of the 20th century. At this time, the Southern League was standing shoulder to shoulder with the Football League. This was confirmed when Tottenham Hotspur and not, as had been expected, Saints became the first Southern League team to win the FA Cup.

Money was tight and the ambitious transfer policy had been funded almost completely by the series of FA Cup runs. When the FA introduced a maximum wage of £4 a week in 1901, Saints had at least five players equal or above this. Yet the manager/secretary Arnfield maintained a footballing philosophy which placed emphasis very simply on recruiting the best quality of players.

He said: "In the main, our bold forward policy is to engage only tip-top players. No man is good enough for us who isn't good enough to take his place in any team in England. We shouldn't dream of engaging a player who wasn't worthy of inclusion in the Aston Villa eleven, for instance. This is our standard." It was this expansive thinking which led to the idea of looking within a still flourishing amateur game and pulling off arguably the most celebrated transfer coup of all.

WHILE Saints were going from strength to strength, CB Fry had by 1900 become a national institution. Born in Croydon in 1872, his early achievements were remarkable.

Fry first displayed a natural and instinctive ability for sports at the age of seven, which originally manifested itself in cricket and athletics. It was while at school at Hornbrook House near Orpington that he first played football, although the rules were still not fully developed. Fry soon became the school's soccer captain and by the age of 12, he had appeared for the local West Kent football team. He was then to move to Repton School and forced his way into the first team as a 15-year-old right-back.

It was a significant achievement. In his biography, *CB Fry: King of Sport*, Iain Wilton explains: "Proof of Repton's strength came in the 1888/89 season when the first team drew with Derby County in one match. Fry received fulsome praise and well-earned recognition for his contribution to the side's success…the *Football Annual* was unambiguous in its assessment of CB's record at Repton. He was, quite simply, 'the most brilliant back the school has ever had'. It went on to praise his exceptional pace, the strength of his kicking, and quality of his captaincy."

Fry continued to be a part of the Repton team which, in future years, was regarded as the best in the school's history. He also excelled in athletics as a sprinter, a hurdler, a high-jumper and a long-jumper. His long-jump record of 21 feet was only beaten decades later by Harold Abrahams, a future Olympic champion. Fry's breakthrough in cricket came later, but was also developed at Repton and he gained entry to Oxford University after winning a scholarship in 1891.

He made his way into the Oxford football team and was a surprise selection for the England team which beat Canada 6-1. It meant that by the age of 19, Fry was not only a leading scholar at one of the world's best universities, but also a county cricketer (initially with Surrey) and an international footballer. He was later to play rugby for Oxford, Blackheath and the Barbarians as a wing three-quarter. Fry was also timed at 10.2secs for a 100-yard sprint, but earned his place in athletics history in March 1893 in the Oxford trials when he leaped 23ft 6ins to equal the world record held by American Charles Reber. Had he been fully aware of the Athens Olympics of 1896 (the first of the modern era), he would almost certainly have added Olympic medals to that list of achievements. He was also to score a century at Lord's in the Varsity match. The *Oxford Magazine* said: "In Fry, we have undoubtedly the best all-round man seen in Oxford for many years."

With his good looks, sporting achievements and academic abilities, he was a complete celebrity in and around the university. Central to his status, however, as a Cult Hero was the element of show in what he did. Examples of this come in his non-sporting pursuits; he could also act, skate and, in his final year at Oxford, indulged in some naked modelling. A party-piece which displayed his natural spring was described in Arthur Wallis Myers' biography, *The Man and His Methods*: "He would take up a position in front of an arm-chair and clear it with one spring; or, more dramatically, would sometimes face the mantelpiece, crouch down, take a leap upwards, turn in the air, and bow to the gallery with his feet planted on the shelf."

After leaving Oxford in 1895, Fry's attention switched to cricket and he made his England Test debut in 1896 and, playing for Sussex, was to replace WG Grace as the best batsmen in England. He began one season for Sussex with consecutive scores of 135, 125, 229, 110, 96 and 105 and was to follow this up with the world record landmark of six consecutive first-class centuries.

Despite such success in cricket, his interest in football continued. He spent several years playing as an amateur for Corinthians, a devoutly amateur club who attracted some of the country's greatest sporting talent due to their ideals and were good enough to compete with the best teams in the Football League. In the mid-1880s they defeated the FA Cup winners Blackburn Rovers 8-1 and then the league champions Preston North End 5-0.

Fry revived his Corinthians career after graduating, playing regularly in the latter part of the 1890s. Style was king for the amateurs, whereas, of course, results were everything for professionals and Fry was critical of the foul play of the 'northern pro'. He even argued that having a penalty area was an affront to the integrity of footballers. "It is a standing insult to sportsmen to have to play under a rule which assumes that players intend to trip, hack and push their opponents, and to behave like cads of the most unscrupulous kidney. I say that the lines marking the penalty area are a disgrace to the playing field of the public school."

Despite Fry's comments about the style of professionals, he had already established a reputation for a sometimes over-zealous style of play and that was evident on the first occasion that he played against Southampton in 1899, when he broke a cheekbone after a clash with the Saints' goalkeeper John Robinson. It was said that he had "needlessly charged" Robinson.

THREE factors, however, secured Fry's eventual union with Saints. Firstly, The Dell was just a few miles from his West End home, Glenbourne Manor. Secondly, Saints' status among the best teams in the country and their ambition to capture some of the biggest names in the game. Thirdly, being adept in the art of self-promotion, Fry was well aware that his England ambitions would be given more coverage from the platform of a professional team.

He made that clear in an article for *Athletic News* just a month before he signed. "I wonder why it is that so many papers and periodicals which devote attention and space to football news and criticism are so deeply impressed with the *a priori* superiority of professional players," he said.

Fry was always going to be a little different to the rest of his Southampton team-mates. University educated footballers have never been common and Jonathan Fry smiles at the thought of his grandfather in a footballing dressing room. "God knows what they would have made of him," he says, "I have a picture of the team – he looks a bit different from the rest."

Fry's arrival certainly provoked huge additional interest in Saints. Following the 3-2 win against West Ham, the *Hampshire Independent* said that Fry had, "affected several smart clearances to the delight of the crowd, with whom 'CB' is extremely popular". Saints went on to win the Southern League for a fourth time in 1900/01 with Fry playing a particularly influential part in a crucial draw at closest challengers Bristol City. Fry did, however, take a little time to adapt to the demands of the more physical professional game. One initial deficiency was his heading. But, in a story which explains Fry's general success, he went to impressive lengths to tackle this weakness.

JAH Catton was quoted in Wilton's biography saying: "The late Mr Charles J Hughes, of Northwich…stated that after an important match he stated to Fry: 'Charles, you would greatly strengthen your game as a back if you would learn to head the ball properly. You can't head properly'. The Oxonian replied that he would see what he could do. The next time Mr Hughes saw Fry on the field his heading was excellent. After the match he went to see Fry and congratulated him, asking him at the time how he had acquired such accuracy. 'Oh, it's all practice,' answered CB, 'for my wife was good enough to go out into the garden and throw the ball at me until I could always meet it properly and put it in the direction desired. That's all; nothing but practice'." Fry also attributed the precision of his kicking to time spent with a tennis ball on a tarmac yard.

The clamour for Fry's England recall grew. In February 1901, he played for the South against the North and was then chosen alongside Saints team-mates Arthur Turner and John Robinson to face Ireland in an international staged at The Dell.

Fry, though, did not shine particularly in a 3-0 win and never played for England again. In his account of the contest for *Athletic News*, he wrote: "It was one of those games which, without any obvious reason, are aimless and vague and watery; nothing in the atmosphere of play to buck one up or incite one to effort." According to the *Athletic News Football Annual* of 1901/02, Fry was "a very strong tackler but rather erratic".

His back-passes were also notorious. It was reported that he, "struck his back-passes to [John] Robinson with such ferocity that opposing forwards would have been content to claim them as shots". Describing his style, *English Sport* said: "His excessive speed, his dauntless kicking, and his sturdy tackling have won for him a reputation second to none among the great full-backs of the day. He runs risks, but always with a successful termination; he often wanders afield, but is always back again should any emergency arise." His biographer, Iain Wilton, has studied the match reports from Fry's football career and says: "The impression I got was that he was somewhat erratic, although he obviously made up for it with his speed."

His standing in Southampton, however, was clear. The *Tatler* described Fry as: "The most remarkable cricketer in England" and "probably the most popular footballer".

Because of his many other commitments, he tended to pick and choose his matches. His availability for local derbies, 'prestige' matches on Boxing Day and in the FA Cup, however, was generally assured. He played most of his games for Saints during the 1901/02 season. Of a 2-2 derby draw against Portsmouth at Fratton Park, the *Football Mail* reported that: "Time after time the Pompey forwards swept clean up the goalmouth, only to be either forced back by Fry or [his defensive partner] Molyneux."

THE priority of the season, however, was clear: the FA Cup. Fry was an ever-present in all of Saints' eight matches on their run to the final of 1902. An extremely difficult first round tie loomed against the Cup holders Tottenham at White Hart Lane, but Spurs were fortunate to escape the match with a 1-1 draw.

The replay was held at The Dell the following Wednesday and was, according to Fry, a "ding-dong affair". Spurs led twice before Saints came back. A second replay was held two days later on neutral territory at Reading's Elm Park on a snowy night. The touchlines were marked out with blue paint and the surface was, in the words of Fry, "like a skating rink". A late winner from Albert Brown secured a 2-1 victory.

The second round saw Saints see off Liverpool in impressive fashion with a 4-1 win at Anfield. The match had been billed as 'Champions of the South' against 'the Champions of the North'. Trainer Dawson described it as "the finest exhibition of football put up by the Saints". It set up a quarter-final at Bury – the team which had denied them in the Cup final two years previously. Pitch conditions were again a problem and Saints were, by common consent, extremely fortunate to come away with a 3-2 victory, thanks to a late Brown goal. The *Bury Times* was particularly scathing in its assessment of Fry: "Everyone expected to see one of the finest backs yet played on the Bury ground; but though he is speedy and recovers quickly, the fact that he has to recover so often bespeaks faulty play."

Fry, however, performed well in the semi-final against Nottingham Forest at White Hart Lane as Saints ran out 3-1 victors in front of 30,000 spectators. The final opponents Sheffield United had been in three of the last four finals and contained some of the biggest names in football. In legendary goalkeeper William 'Fatty' Foulkes they also possessed a player whose stature matched his frame. Foulkes was 6ft 2ins tall and weighed more than 21 stone. He used his size to intimidate opponents and it was famously known that he would pick up rival players and dangle them by their ankles in pools of mud. He was perhaps the one footballer in this era to rival Fry in the nation's minds for the tag of greatest living player.

A crowd of around 75,000 assembled at Crystal Palace for the 1902 FA Cup final, including WG Grace and some of Fry's other colleagues from the England cricket team. The *Hampshire Independent* described the scene: "The surrounding trees shook as though whipped by a gale, denoting the enthusiasm of adventurous individuals who were in their branches." Alf Common, who was to become the first £1,000 footballer, opened the scoring for Sheffield United. Saints, however, eventually equalised late in the game in controversial fashion through Harry Wood. This incident is explained by Duncan Holley in *Match of the Millennium:*

> "The referee consulted his linesman about the possibility of offside before he allowed the equaliser. It seems that Wood was tying his boot-lace in what he himself considered to be an offside position, when the ball reached him. The officials decided, though, that the ball had struck a Sheffield defender and that Wood had been 'played on'. Their goalkeeper was not impressed. Described by Fry in his auto-biography as 'the burliest, the heaviest, and the most rubber-like goalkeeper known to history' when he [Foulkes] left the dressing room, unclothed, in angry pursuit of the referee, Mr Kirkham took refuge in a broom cupboard. It required a posse of FA officials to dissuade his huge, naked assailant from wrenching the door from its hinges."

The replay also took place at Crystal Palace. But the match started badly and Saints fell behind before assuming control. The equaliser came from Albert Brown – the former Aston Villa forward known as the 'Tamworth sprinter' – and it looked as if Saints would be victorious. The *Hampshire Independent* described the action: "The Saints again pressed, and Foulkes had all his work cut out to stop shots by Chadwick, Wood and Lee." But Sheffield struck with a winner against the run of play in the 88th minute, meaning Fry had missed out on what would have been the crowning moment in his footballing career. By way of small consolation, two days later Fry was opening the batting against Surrey at the Oval and putting on 130 for the first wicket with WG Grace.

Fry's relatively brief Saints career came to an end the following year, as he made just two appearances for the 1902/03 Southern League winning team. His availability had become sporadic and an attempt to become a centre-forward was unsuccessful. After capturing a sixth Southern League title in only eight seasons the following year, Saints were to gradually fade as a strong force.

FRY continued to assume huge prominence on the national stage after leaving Saints, playing cricket for Hampshire until 1921 and scoring 94 first-class centuries with an average of 50.22. He still boasts the highest batting average in Hampshire's history.

He went on to stand as a Liberal candidate for parliament, edited a popular publication called *Fry's Magazine* and was a delegate to the League of Nations. He also flirted with a career in Hollywood – with no more success than Ian Botham, and a lot less than fellow Corinthian and cricketer, Sir C Aubrey Smith. For some 42 years he and his wife (formerly Miss Beatrice Holme-Sumner) directed the training ship Mercury at Hamble, which developed less fortunate young men into good, solid stock. Prior to the Second World War with Germany, Fry's reputation was somewhat affected by an association in the 1930s with Adolf Hitler. It stemmed from Hitler's hopes of increasing the contact between German and British youth organisations and their meeting is recorded in Fry's autobiography. Fry felt Germany, under Hitler's rule, genuinely wanted a friendly relationship with Britain.

Fry had previously disappeared from public view having suffered bouts of paranoia. His mental condition, which was treated with electric shock therapy, was largely caused by his relationship with his wife who, by various accounts, was both domineering and fearsome. Yet he returned to the public eye with his superb cricket column 'CB Fry says' in the *Standard*. He was present at the 1936 FA Cup final and remained a keen watcher of cricket until his death in 1956 at the age of 84. That interest has continued in his family. His grandson Charles is the chairman of the MCC, while Jonathan hopes to be in Australia for the Ashes tour of 2006.

The attendance list at CB Fry's memorial service demonstrated the diversity of his life. JW Grant attended on behalf of Southampton Football Club and he joined representatives from the FA, Surrey, Sussex, Hampshire, the MCC, five former England cricket captains, several former Olympic champions including Harold Abrahams, as well as numerous contacts from the literary and political worlds.

The *News Chronicle* concluded that he was the "perfect human being". That, of course, went too far. His true greatness came as a cricketer and as an all-rounder. This alone generated a presence that absolutely radiated through the terraces during his time with Saints. Judged simply as a footballer, however, he would struggle to be included in a list of Saints' best 100 players – although he'd probably be among the fastest. His main asset was that exceptional pace allied to a willingness to improve, but he was prone to mistakes. Indeed, in an era of great Southampton footballers, he falls behind the likes of John Robinson, Albert Brown and Harry Wood.

Yet he remains surely the most remarkable personality to ever pull on the red and white stripes. As his grandson Jonathan remarks: "He had a fantastic aura about him and, back then just as now, people wanted heroes." CB Fry certainly gave Saints fans someone to worship.

TED BATES

1937-2003

SAINTS CAREER

As player

Games	216
Goals	64
Caps	0

As manager

Games	865

MAGIC MOMENT

Guiding Southampton into the top-flight of English football in 1966 for the first time in the club's entire history

'MR SOUTHAMPTON'

'He was our Shankly.'

Denis Hollywood

THE picture on the wall shows a smiling Ted Bates meeting the Queen while collecting his MBE. Facing it is a large certificate which provides confirmation of his status as a Freeman of the city of Southampton. I'm not sure exactly what else there should be, but, other than a few other family photographs, you would hardly know that you were in the home of one of British football's greatest servants. It's all rather normal. Except, that is, on a match-day.

Although she no longer attends the games, Bates' widow Mary will tune into BBC Radio Solent to listen to the action. Daughter Jo, meanwhile, will be at St. Mary's watching the game in person. Old habits die hard and the Bates family still avidly follow the fortunes of a club to which husband and father devoted his entire adult life.

"We were completely smothered in football, there's no two ways about that," says Mary. "He [Ted] always had football on his mind, he was always lining things up and he never wanted to miss out on anything. I suppose when you have been at a club as long as he was you do become a bit of an institution.

"If he wasn't out playing football somewhere he was out coaching or watching other matches. It was lucky I liked football too and I still follow it now. We have football on the television most nights, but I don't go to the stadium anymore. They said I was the longest serving person in the directors' box, but I'm a bit too doddery now for all that."

It is almost three years since the passing of Ted Bates, but his impact lives on. For the family, Saturdays are obviously still dominated by their interest in football. For supporters, the campaign to build a statue of the man known simply as 'Mr Southampton' is almost complete. The Ted Bates Trust has raised a sum of £45,000, which has been matched by the club, for the tribute which is due to be erected outside the reception of St. Mary's early in 2007. It will serve as a lasting and fitting memory to a contribution to Saints which is unique in its longevity, style and accomplishments.

Indeed, if the best indication of an employee's effect on a football club is a comparison between where the club was when he arrived and when he departed, then Bates certainly stands alongside any of the great names in British football history. He first arrived at The Dell as a player in 1937 with the team flirting with the possibility of dropping into the Third Division. By the time of his death on November 26, 2003, Saints were about to move into the top four of the Premiership, having just appeared in the FA Cup final and qualified for that season's Uefa Cup.

Credit, of course, for successes over the final three decades of an incredible span at one club of 66 years lies overwhelmingly with those managers and players who succeeded him. Yet it is indisputable that the change in the expectations of a football club which had previously spent its life in the Southern League or the second and third tiers of English football was predominantly down to Bates.

Lawrie McMenemy's overall record as manager is superior. But could subsequent achievements like three Wembley finals, 27 consecutive years in the top-flight and regular European football have been achieved as quickly without those foundations which Bates so meticulously laid?

Bates spent 15 seasons with Southampton as a player and then another 30 as chief executive, director, vice president and president, but he achieved true greatness as manager. It was in 1955 that Bates took control of a first team that were down in Division Three (South) of the Football League. When he retired as manager 18 years later, Saints were well established in the top-flight of English football and poised to enjoy their greatest era.

One player, Terry Paine, was with Bates for just about the entire ride and is in no doubt that Bates sits with the best in the pantheon of legendary managers. "They say Bill Shankly, Matt Busby and Bob Paisley are the greatest, but what Ted did for Southampton on next to no money is equal to that for me," he says. "Just look at his achievements. He got us from the Third Division to the First Division, into Europe and the semi-final of the FA Cup."

THE position of manager rarely means universal popularity in the dressing room, yet Bates' style and commitment to Southampton Football Club ensured he commanded a much more important commodity: respect. Even players like Ron Davies, who was denied the opportunity to move to Manchester United or Denis Hollywood, who was unexpectedly released from his contract, speak only of their admiration for Bates.

A complete infatuation with football is what most remember although, according to Terry Paine, that is not quite right. "It wasn't so much football that was his obsession, but Southampton Football Club," he says. "It's as simple as that. All he thought about was what was best for his club. He really was quite a character."

Cliff Huxford, who captained Bates' Division Three Championship-winning team, remembers how he would go looking for the manager in his office and often find him standing up and seemingly in a trance. "The offices were under the stands and you would go into the entrance and turn left for the office and the boardroom and the gymnasium," says Huxford, "I would walk past Ted's office and he would be stood facing against the wall with his hands resting against it. I used to wonder if he was okay, but I soon realised he was just thinking. He would just stand there trying to work out the team he was going to put out and how it would play."

The great goal-scorer George O'Brien remembers that Bates would often be "lost in the job". He says: "I wouldn't say it was too much for him, but it was all that he lived for. I remember we would be lapping the training ground and he would be stood pulling his jacket zip up and down thinking about the game. He was just staring in front of him, oblivious to what was going on. It would be unbelievable." Bates' priorities were highlighted in his treatment of O'Brien. The Dunfermline-born inside-right averaged 29 goals a season during just over six years at The Dell and, despite being approached by other clubs, was not allowed to leave. Then, when he became ill during the 1965/66 season, he was swiftly transferred just as Saints were on the threshold of finally reaching Division One. O'Brien also believes that a rather surprising absence of international opportunities was down to Bates. "Ted never put me forward for Scotland," says O'Brien, "in those days the managers would put players' names forward, but he was too worried about me getting injured or tapped up by another team."

Nick Holmes was signed as a schoolboy by Bates and remembers that, in later years, he was blown away by his footballing expertise. "Ted was very, very quiet," he says, "he would quite often not be around for training sessions and he'd let other people take them. If he came, he would just stand around the edges and watch. But his knowledge of the game when you had one-on-ones with him was just phenomenal.

"He could talk with you and explain things to you, but football was pretty much the only conversation – there was no general chit-chat. That was the one thing I remembered about Ted – he only ever talked about football. I used to think, 'there can't be anything else in his life except football because he doesn't talk about anything else'. But then, one day, completely out of the blue, he started talking to me about strawberry fields.

"He was very friendly with a strawberry grower out where I lived in Warsash. I didn't think he even knew where I lived. He said, 'I was over your way. You know Rodney don't you?' All of a sudden we had a five minute chat about strawberries. In all the time we were both at the club together [17 years], I think it was the only occasion we ever talked about anything except football."

The club president John Mortimore and the former manager Lawrie McMenemy agree that Bates' constant preoccupation with football made driving with him a nerve-racking experience. "You would be in the car with him and he would just talk football," says Mortimore, who was Bates' assistant manager from 1969 until 1972. "We would be driving up to the midlands or something and he would be, 'how are we going to play on Saturday, what do you think of him, we've got to get someone going forward' and when he mentioned forwards, the old gear-stick would go forward!"

McMenemy talks of Bates' "single-mindedness" when it came to football and confirms that being behind the wheel of a car rarely interfered with his thought process. "He didn't seem to notice anyone else on the road," says McMenemy. "My two best, or possibly worst, recollections are after a long trip to Blackpool for a midweek scouting mission. He took a turn behind the wheel coming down the M6, suddenly braked hard, realised he had missed a turn and proceeded to reverse up the motorway! Another time we were going to Wembley to watch an international. Being new to the south, Ted was showing me a shortcut he knew. He missed his way in a built-up area and did a three point turn which, in itself, may have got him through a driving test the way he performed it. Unfortunately, we were on a zebra crossing."

There was, however, one incident from a pre-season tour where Bates' total focus on football led to him suffering a rather short, sharp shock. Southampton were facing a Stoke City team containing Stanley Matthews at the old Victoria Ground and a rather rowdy crowd was dishing out the abuse in the direction of the Southampton dugout. "It was a little dugout with an iron roof," says Denis Hollywood, "all the fans are banging on the roof and the noise inside is horrendous, so Jimmy Gallagher [the trainer] kept shouting, 'pack it in'.

"Batesy said to him, 'if you keep quiet Jimmy they might stop, all you have done is make them worse'. So Jimmy goes on to treat someone, and on his way back he has sprayed a couple of the fans who have been shouting at him with his sponge. A couple of seconds later this great big guy jumps over the wall and picks up the bucket of water on the side. I'm in the dugout between them. Me and Jimmy saw what was going on, but Batesy is sat in his suit, watching the game, totally engrossed as ever. The guy picks up the water and points at Jimmy and says, 'you bastard, you sprayed my wife'. He lobs the water, Jimmy ducks, I duck and Batesy got the whole lot. He was like a drowned rat."

TED BATES' passion for football began during a childhood spent in Norfolk and he was initially spotted by Tom Parker, the former Southampton full-back, who was managing Norwich City. Parker took over at The Dell in March 1937 and duly signed the 19-year-old inside forward.

A somewhat difficult time in Southampton's history had followed the successes of the Southern League days at the turn of the century, but another good period during the 1920s arrived when Saints entered the new Football League Division Three (South). In the aftermath of the First World War, with the emergence of influential players like Parker, Bill Rawlings, Arthur Dominy, Fred Titmuss and Bert Shelley, who became the first Saints player to reach 400 Football League appearances, the club rediscovered the sort of form which had made them so feared around the turn of the century. The Division Three (South) championship of 1921/22 was duly secured largely thanks to a return of 30 goals in 38 league games from Rawlings.

In 1923/24 Saints came within three points of promotion to the First Division and then reached two FA Cup semi-finals in 1925 and then 1927. By the early 1930s, Ted Drake had emerged as Rawlings' replacement as The Dell's main Cult Hero and he admitted that watching his predecessor as a schoolboy growing up in Southampton had fuelled his dream to play centre-forward for England.

Saints fan Joan Moody, who is now into her 90s, remembers that it would be a tradition of the players and directors to have a meal at the Quilter's Hotel in the Lower High Street at around 1pm before walking up to The Dell for their match. Her parents, Beatrice and Sidney Osborne, were season-ticket holders at the time and Joan collected the autographs of all the stars. She recalls that the players would have boiled chicken and toast while the directors would get roast chicken. "They would arrive dressed in suits and they were all real gentlemen," she says, "there was never any rowdiness. Saturday was football day, people would be talking about the football all over town. The players were very much part of the community, very popular and would be recognised wherever they went."

Saints were moving into a rebuilding process and the signing of Bates was very much part of that strategy. He was, though, to appear only 30 times before the Second World War. The players heard Neville Chamberlain's broadcast that the nation was at War with Germany in the dressing room of The Dell on September 3, 1939. Bates, who was then known as 'Eddie', found employment locally in the Police War Reserve and played almost 200 times for Saints in unofficial matches from 1939 until 1946. The timing of the War was not kind and he missed playing league football in what would almost certainly have been his prime footballing years between the age of 21 and 27.

After the War, Bates enjoyed some happy playing seasons, with Saints particularly thriving under the management of Bill Dodgin, who enticed Charlie Wayman – one of the finest players to ever grace The Dell – to the club. Bates was noted for his heading ability and, while his footballing abilities did not command cult status, he draws praise from those who appeared alongside him. "He would walk up people's backs to get the ball," says the former England and Saints full-back Bill Ellerington. "He was an honest, honest player – not great in terms of ability, but he had it in here [points to chest]. He was a worker and you have got to have workers and finishers."

Wayman is also generous about a player who crafted many of his goals. "Ted was a good passer of the ball, I fitted in with him great, I could read him and knew where he was going to go to put the ball," he says. "Ted was also really likeable, when I went down to Southampton he was always talking to me."

By this time, Bates' wife, Mary, had also begun working at The Dell as the assistant secretary. Given her husband's love for the game, it was ideal she shared that interest. Mary was unusual in being a woman working in football and she remained in her post from 1945 until 1958. "It was after the War, there had been a general election in May and I went to work for the Labour Party as a secretary," she says. "I had no permanent job after that, but I had sat with the chairman Mr Sarjantson at Don Roper's wedding and he said, 'would I come and have a look and see if I would like to be assistant secretary' and that's just what I did.

"A woman couldn't be called club secretary, but I still did all the work. I was a one-off which didn't worry me, I was trying to put the men in their place and I did that eventually! I worked all day and I was overworked. We lived in 64 Archers Road which was right next to The Dell and we had a garden gate which led us into the West Stand and all the offices through there. But I always took work home with me and worked in the evening. I was well and truly into football and I always thoroughly enjoyed it even though it took over our lives completely."

BATES played his last game for Saints in December 1952. The team suffered relegation into Division Three later that season and he was duly appointed as reserve team manager. His enthusiasm shone quickly and, after guiding the reserves to victory in the 1954 Combination Cup, he succeeded Sid Cann as manager on September 7, 1955, at a salary of £1,000 a year. His promotion surprised many in the club, including his former team-mate Bill Ellerington, who had never imagined Bates to be a natural leader. "I knew him as well as anyone and I wasn't certain when he was made manager, but he proved me wrong and thank God he was made manager – he did a remarkable job," he says. "He was always so calm, he never blew his own trumpet, but you would follow him."

The type of teams that Bates produced had one common factor: they were deadly going forward. His planning was invariably shaped around scoring goals and, although he had the considerable advantage of the master creator in Terry Paine playing regularly in all but his first one-and-a-half seasons at the helm, it is worth noting that the team still scored a total of 167 times in the league campaigns of 1955/56 and 1956/57.

Under Bates, The Dell crowd were to be treated to wave upon wave of creative talent as the likes of Paine, John Sydenham, Derek Reeves, Brian Clifton, Ken Wimshurst, Eric Day and George O'Brien flourished before the arrival of players of the calibre of Stuart Williams, Martin Chivers, Jimmy Melia, Mick Channon and Ron Davies. Bates' teams generally scored more than they let in, although the defensive frailties meant that promotion into Division Two took longer than hoped, finally arriving in his fifth season at the helm in 1959/60. He would, of course, have been unlikely to be granted so much time in the world of modern football with its demands for instantaneous success.

Crucial in Saints' progress under Bates was the recruitment policy. In that regard, Ellerington, who moved into coaching and scouting, was vital and helped identify several Southampton greats such as Cliff Huxford, George O'Brien and Mick Channon. Ellerington remembers how Bates would study the lists of players who were on free transfers and was always alive to what was available and what he specifically needed in his team. "We were very careful who we brought in," remembers the former assistant manager John Mortimore, "Ted always said that if we are going to take a player, we must watch him three times. We would watch him twice at home and once away, or twice away and once at home. But it would be three times we watched him and then we would make a decision."

Bates rarely had significant money to spend, but his canniness in the transfer market and the blossoming of local players John Sydenham and Terry Paine meant he continually strengthened the team. His dealings prior to the 1959 season when he managed to recruit Huxford, O'Brien and Dick Conner for the sale of Charles Livesey is one such example, but he says his best piece of business was the £55,000 spent on Ron Davies following promotion to Division One in 1966. Bates identified the devastating aerial potential of Davies in a team with wingers like Sydenham and Paine. It was a plan which allowed the club to establish themselves in Division One and ultimately qualify for Europe.

Bates' care over spending money was legendary. In later years, he would even refuse formally to register schoolboys with the FA at a cost of £5 – something nobody knew until McMenemy discovered a drawer which was stuffed full of unsent forms. "He would go cap in hand to the supporters' club for money to sign a player," says Ellerington. Mary remembers how he was constantly attempting to raise money for the club. "Life was always hard – they certainly didn't throw millions at you, like they do today," she says, "he would go to the supporters' clubs to try to get players. He never had an evening off. He would be, 'I'm at the ladies' section of the supporters' club tonight' and he would toddle off or he would be going to speak at something and he'd say, 'there'll be a fee so that can go into the kitty'. He'd always be following somebody and hoping to take them on if we could get the wages covered."

Another good addition was the midfielder Brian O'Neil, who says: "Ted had to beg for money in the early days from the women's club and supporters' club. That's what he used to do. You look at what he had and look at it now at St. Mary's. But I'll tell you one thing, Ted always got it right on the pitch – that's what mattered, that's what came first."

Bates could also be cunning when it came to signing players. That much is evident when considering perhaps the two best players he recruited in Terry Paine and Mick Channon.

Arsenal were also in the hunt for Paine, who was playing locally in Hampshire for Winchester City, and were impressed enough after a first trial to invite him back to Highbury. Paine was 17 and working at Eastleigh's British Rail Depot and mentioned to a colleague that he was heading back to Arsenal for a second trial. "The guy was a Southampton supporter and he phoned Ted and tipped him off that me and Colin Holmes were going back," says Paine. "Ted got us straight back to the club, locked the door and wouldn't let us go until we had signed. I still went back to Arsenal for the final trial, but I'd already signed the forms for Southampton."

To get Channon, Bates was happy to break FA rules, as Bill Ellerington testifies. "One of the teachers from Mick Channon's school let us know he was playing at the Andover ground for Wiltshire against Hampshire Under-15s," he says, "I went to watch and the next day Ted asked me if there was anything there and I mentioned Channon to him. He said, 'what do you think about signing him'. I said, 'well, it won't cost us anything, we've got nothing to lose have we?'

"So off Ted goes to Mick Channon's house near Shrewton on the Sunday. Now Swindon had been keeping a close eye on him and, as he was a Wiltshire player, expected to sign him. On the Tuesday or Wednesday, we were at Swindon and we walked into the boardroom and if their manager had had a gun he would have shot us. He said, 'you bastards! You signed Channon on a Sunday'. Ted was 'c'mon, no it was a Saturday'. But it was Sunday! In those days you couldn't sign a pro on a Sunday."

LIKE all successful managers, Bates had a style which inspired players to perform for him. Most testify that he was not a strong, imposing or sometimes frightening character like a Brian Clough, Sir Alex Ferguson or Lawrie McMenemy, but a quiet and unassuming person. He brought people in who were strong personalities and, while there are numerous stories of alleged player power and unruly behaviour off the pitch, Bates largely turned a blind eye to any shenanigans or mickey-taking providing the players did the business for him on a Saturday. That he was able to handle the pressures of football management for 18 years also says much for his character.

"Ted was very good in that he didn't allow his worries, of which there are many as a football manager, to come into his home," says Mary. "The family didn't suffer. He was very even tempered. We never heard him swear although someone once said, 'you want to hear him in the dressing room'." Daughter Jo adds: "He would never shout or get cross even though the pressures were 24/7 really."

Bates' style was non-confrontational and, although some players were occasionally disrespectful on the surface, it was an approach which encouraged a deep bond of loyalty. When it really mattered, few let him down. John Sydenham, who now lives in Australia and returned to Southampton in 2005 to speak at a dinner in honour of his former manager, played some 402 times under Bates. "He was my manager for the whole of my career," he said, "he knew the game inside out, I don't think there has ever been a manager who would totally live for the game as Ted did. He had great insight and could always see a player. He was a manager we all wanted to play for and that's what makes a good manager."

John Mortimore remembers how Bates would be deliberately vague when dealing with the inevitable visits to his office from disgruntled players. "He was so wonderful at dealing with players," says his former assistant, "there would be a knock at the door and a player would come in. I was nearly always in Ted's office. He used to say to me, 'when they come in, as long as they forget what they came in for, they can go'. He would just talk to them and try to get them to forget what they had come in for."

Bates had a close relationship with his captain, Terry Paine, and it was a common remark in the dressing room that the manager was not picking the team. Paine refutes this accusation, saying Bates would be just as elusive with him whenever he was trying to make his point. "All I ever got out of him if I had a complaint or went in was 'um, um, um, pardon son'," says Paine, "I used to say, 'I'm wasting my time' and he would be, 'pardon son, um, um'. He never answered. In all the time I was there Ted Bates never ever said to me, 'do you think we should play this player this week?' He may have asked me what a player was like to be playing against. But never on selection. Because I was close, the players used to say that it was me who was selecting the team. But that's all part and parcel of it."

When I tell Hollywood of Paine's claim that he had no influence on selection, he grins and says, "Painey was never out of the office," before adding, "we used to say that Batesy's office was the only office you had to knock to come out of because if you were in talking, there was usually about three people outside listening to what he was saying".

BATES faced a constant battle to keep his players out of mischief whenever they were on trips away from Southampton, but seemed to handle any misdemeanours in a way that meant he never lost the players' respect. "We were on a tour in Bermuda and we were invited to a banquet with the police," remembers Hollywood, "and Frank Saul wandered off and had found a police uniform – helmet, truncheon and everything. So next thing he is stood next to us in a full police uniform. We were killing ourselves laughing and a couple of the coppers came up to him and said, 'you're impersonating a police officer and you're under arrest'. They were winking at us, but Frank was getting really worried. They took him downstairs and put him in a cell for half an hour, so we rang Ted up and said, 'Frank's in prison, can you come down and bail him out?' Batesy just said, 'no it's too late for that, but look after him, he's a nice lad'.

"Then we'd get back to the hotel and we would find out Batesy's room number and put the drinks on there. He'd get the whole bill. One time we were somewhere and his bill was astronomical because we had done it for a few nights and he got to reception and he turned round and said, 'you crowd better pay for this' and he just stormed off. It was a £500 bar bill, but most of the time he just used to laugh."

Although Bates had a deft touch in his dealings with players, he would never shy away from tough choices. "He would make a decision about things," says Mortimore, "not necessarily immediately, but he would do. He would think about things and have an answer. He was quiet in the dressing room, I don't remember any cups flying around. You just left it to him at half-time, you accepted his way of dealing with things. His pre-match and half-time talks were good. He would hit the problem on the head. He knew what was happening and he could say it to the players and they knew that he was right.

"He would listen to players. He was very good at that. People like [John] McGrath, [Jimmy] Gabriel, [Terry] Paine and [Jimmy] Melia were strong characters. You couldn't kid them, you had to convince them. They wanted to win, they were leaders and Ted was terrific at handling them."

Bates could also be tough with his players, as Hollywood found to his cost when he was told that he would not be going on a pre-season tour to Japan because he was not fit enough. "I stood up and swore at him and slammed the door and the walls were still shaking as I walked up the corridor, I think I called him a big nosed so and so," he recalls, "he ran after me and he shouted up the corridor, 'I'll tell you another thing, every day we are on tour, you are in'.

"I turned and said, 'you must be joking' and he said, 'every day you don't come in, I'll fine you and every day it will go up'. I did go in every day because the fine would have been astronomical. He was a football man, a nice bloke and he handled the strong characters very well."

BATES' finest moments, of course, were guiding the team into the top-flight of English football and then Europe. Both were firsts for Saints. "What he did for the club was unbelievable," says Hollywood, "I thought personally the promotion was a better achievement than the FA Cup [win in 1976]. Don't get me wrong, the Cup is fabulous, but it was a tremendous achievement to get into what is the equivalent of the Premiership for the first time in the club's history. The club had never done it and I don't know if Ted got the credit he deserved."

Paine scored the goal at Leyton Orient in front of an estimated 14,000 travelling Saints fans which, barring a 6-0 defeat the following week against Manchester City, guaranteed promotion to Division One in 1966. "We were all celebrating, the champagne was open and it was a great, great moment," says Paine, "but I remember he [Ted] turned to me and said, 'I'm drinking Champagne, but I'm not celebrating, because it's not all over yet'."

Saints' venture into the Inter City Fairs Cup in 1969/70 saw them beaten in the third round against Newcastle and they lost in the first round against Athletico Bilbao in the 1971/72 Uefa Cup. His team were, however, more than capable of holding their own domestically, peaking at seventh in 1969 and 1971 before Bates stood down as manager in 1973. Given Bates' success, it was inevitable that other clubs were interested in him. According to Mary, he gave greatest consideration to a job with Bermuda which came when he had no managerial experience just before he finished playing back in 1952. "He had lots of offers and some very nice ones and we turned down a very tempting offer to Bermuda," she says. "It would have been a very good job, we considered it, but decided to stay. In our day, people didn't move around as much as they do today – they seemed to stick a bit better. He would have felt very disloyal if we decided to up sticks and work for someone else, so it never really entered into our lives that we should do that."

At the time of his retirement from management, he was the longest-serving manager in the entire Football League. Having been at the club so long, it was great credit to both Lawrie McMenemy, his successor, and Bates that he was subsequently able to move seamlessly into the position of chief executive. It was McMenemy who later suggested Bates should take a role on the board, calculating that it would be good for all concerned. "Ted said to me, 'that's not me, what am I going to do on the board'," remembers McMenemy, "and I told him, 'you sit next to me and whenever I kick you, raise your hand'."

Bates' personality meant that he was never likely to be a threat to McMenemy, who appreciated having such a knowledgeable sounding-board alongside him. "You have to remember there hadn't been any change for 18 years," says McMenemy, "Ted was a wonderful man and a good friend of mine, but there were one or two players ruling the dressing room. I didn't mind Ted staying on. He didn't come in every day, I put him in charge of looking after the schoolkids' forms and he would come with me to games, he loved all that. He used to like to come and jog around the pitch in the afternoon. On a Friday afternoon when everybody had gone, him and me would go in the gym and kick a ball at each other. He knew that was me getting my frustrations out. He didn't have any day-to-day input, but he was a good pal."

Saints, of course, were relegated in McMenemy's first season as manager, but Bates showed his class by never wavering in support of the new man. "Ted always held his counsel and never interfered," says Paine, "and to see it cave in to a certain extent must have been hard. He could have come in and said, 'this guy is not doing it', but he supported Lawrie. That was remarkable."

As time passed, Bates' position became more ambassadorial, but the likes of Francis Benali, Jason Dodd and Matthew Le Tissier can still recall him doing his laps around The Dell when he was well into his 60s. And, even after McMenemy had departed, future managers like Chris Nicholl, Ian Branfoot, Alan Ball, Dave Merrington and Dave Jones recall how he would talk football with them, though never in any sort of demonstrative fashion. "He always stayed involved," says Mary, "but not too interfering, he would feel that wouldn't be right. They respected his opinions and they would ask him, but he would never thrust his ideas on anyone at all."

SO COULD Bates' quiet approach to football have proved successful in today's multi-million pound era when television cameras are everywhere? In an interview in 2001, he was in no doubt. "I don't see why not," said Bates. "You either have what it takes to be a manager or you don't. You have to make decisions in pressure situations and you can stand or fall by them. I like to think that I got a few right. You have to know your players, you have to have the right people working around you on the coaching and scouting side. It all boils down to your judgement. Those principles applied when I was manager; they still apply today.

"What has changed is the nature of the game. It's much quicker and it's much more of a team game. In my day there were more skilful players around. Today it is knocked out of them a bit by team work. But extra talent will never go amiss. It should always be harnessed for the benefit of the team. Of course there is a lot more money in the game now. It's a much more serious business. That's not to say that we didn't take it very seriously, but we did what we wanted to do. There was perhaps more fun in the game."

Bates was to became a vice president of the club and then, in 1998, it was unanimously agreed that he would become club president following the passing of John Corbett. In the years that followed he was to receive many awards and accolades. The publication of his biography *Dell Diamond* in 1998 brought his story to a new generation of Southampton fans and he was awarded the MBE in the 2001 New Year's Honours list. Later that year he was made a Freeman of the City of Southampton and was the man to close the gates on The Dell in June 2001 for the final time.

At the time, he stressed his pleasure at seeing the club take such a giant step forward, even if it meant seeing his spiritual home of the past 64 years crushed under the weight of several bulldozers. "I'll be sad when The Dell shuts down, of course I will, but don't expect me to a shed a tear," he said. "I'm especially pleased for the supporters that they have something new and better to go to, somewhere with good facilities where they can have a bite to eat and something to drink in nice surroundings – something which was lacking at The Dell. With a bigger ground and a bigger crowd, the club will have more cash to improve the team. I would like to see staying in the middle ground in the Premier Division from now on and building from there. I don't think that's asking too much of the present set up."

Later in 2001, Bates was joined by Matthew Le Tissier to perform the opening ceremony at St. Mary's. His health was gradually to deteriorate, although he continued to attend home games until the sixth round of the 2003 FA Cup against Wolverhampton Wanderers. He returned to the club for the last time just two days after the final in Cardiff. There, he was welcomed by Terry Paine and John Sydenham as Paine presented his first England cap to the club. It was fitting that two players to whom he had given so much and who had played well over 1,000 games for him should be present at that ceremony.

I covered that event for the *Echo* and, while Bates' presence clearly crowned the occasion for both Paine and Sydenham as well as the manager Gordon Strachan and the chairman Rupert Lowe, it was clear that just being there had required considerable effort. It was, in fact, his last public appearance and he passed away later that year.

The tributes poured in from players, fellow managers and supporters alike. "I respected Ted as much as I respected anyone," said Cliff Huxford, "his record of 66 years with one club will never be beaten. The word 'legend' is bandied around too often these days – but Ted is worthy of that word." Lowe said: "Ted's years with us stand out as a monument to everyone in the game. Ted stood for three principle values – service, loyalty and integrity. The position of football's curator for honesty and decency is now vacant."

Bates' funeral, fittingly, was held at St. Mary's Church, where Saints were formed back in 1885. Speakers included Mick Channon, who talked movingly about a man who, quite simply, gave more of his life to Southampton Football Club than anyone before or since.

"He was a man of few words," said Channon. "Often he pretended he hadn't heard what you'd said, but when he spoke you listened. We called him Mr Indestructible because he hated losing. Sometimes when we were really up against it, he'd play a 1-9-1 formation with me the one up the pitch. We'd win 1-0 and he'd clench his fist and cry 'indestructible!' I will also remember his enthusiasm for football – his life was Southampton Football Club. He was the person who gave Southampton Football Club a heart. The rest of us who come along are mere side salads – players, managers, coaches, directors, fans – who just keep the heartbeat ticking over."

And, of the man christened Edric Thornton Bates, Channon added: "He was the original ET. On winter days for the rest of this season and ever more, there will only be one ET phoning down to see how his beloved Saints have got on."

CHARLIE WAYMAN

1947-1950

SAINTS CAREER

Games	107
Goals	77
Caps	0

MAGIC MOMENT

Scoring a dramatic winner at White Hart Lane during the infamously unsuccessful 1949 promotion campaign, despite being barely able to stand because of a torn thigh muscle

'CHAMPAGNE CHARLIE'

'30 goals a season was my target. I wouldn't sleep if I didn't get it.'

Charlie Wayman

IT was Charlie Wayman's fifth outing in a Southampton shirt. He had recently arrived at The Dell from Newcastle United as a club record £10,000 signing with a reputation for remarkable goal-scoring feats. The Southampton crowd and players were waiting to see what it was all about. Luton Town were the opponents. It was the 43rd minute of the match when Wayman collected the ball through the middle.

"I'll never forget it," says Bill Ellerington, his team-mate and the right-back of the team, "he had broken clear and was right in the centre of the goal and suddenly, for no apparent reason, he veered off to the left. I thought, 'what the hell is he doing?' He had created a tight angle for himself, but he looked up and...bang! His shot crept just inside the far post. I thought, 'you lucky bugger'. But then he did it again and again and again. He would veer left and then stick it in the far corner with amazing regularity. Absolutely brilliant!"

Tom Finney later played alongside Wayman at Preston North End and, in his autobiography, describes Wayman as "the goal poacher supreme" and a "scoring superman". Eddy Brown tried in vain to replace Wayman when his Dell career came to an end and says simply: "He could shell peas with that left foot." Not surprisingly, The Dell fans loved Wayman and the cry of "up the middle for Charlie" is fondly remembered to this day. He played with a smile on his face and his personality, as well as the timing of his arrival at Southampton, were large factors in explaining his huge popularity. The fundamental reason, though, was simple: everyone loves a goal-scorer. As Rick Broadbent wrote in his book, *Looking For Eric:* "The one immutable element [of football] is the status of the goal-scorer. He is king."

Wayman died during the writing of this book at the age of 84 in February 2006, but the reaction to his passing demonstrated the depth of feeling for a player up there with the very best to have ever appeared for the club. A minute's applause was held in his and Peter Osgood's honour prior to the match against Coventry on 4 March 2006, after the Southampton and Chelsea FA Cup winner had died in the same week. Wayman's son, Paul, said the response to his father's death surprised even the family. "Lots of lovely bits were written about him," he says, "my son printed them all out and he just said, 'I didn't realise granddad was so famous'. I was not quite so taken aback because he used to get recognised quite a lot. He didn't really change much as he got older and people would always recognise him on holiday or wherever.

"He would always stand talking – and he just loved it all. I would say, 'who's that, dad?' and he would be, 'I don't know, someone who recognised me from football'. He was always happy to do anything for anyone. I met someone once and he asked if I was Charlie Wayman's son and then he told me a story about how he was stood at the players' entrance and how dad invited him and his mates back to his house for sandwiches and a cup of tea. He was that type of man. I know he loved his time in Southampton, but, as is quite well known, my mum didn't settle and they went back to the north."

WAYMAN'S death came after he had fought illness for a number of years. It was most commonly thought that he was suffering with Alzheimer's, although his family and some medical experts were not so certain. "It began to affect his speech. You could see he wanted to say something, but would have difficulty getting it out and he gradually deteriorated, but it wasn't like the usual symptoms of Alzheimer's," says Paul. "The consultant said he thought it could have come as a result of heading those old footballs. Dad used to say to me that they could never score the goals they do now and kick them the way they do with the balls they used, especially when it got wet."

There is conflicting medical evidence on the issue, although some studies have shown a link between dementia and repeated heading of a football. The risk was magnified for those players from Wayman's era when they used the old leather balls, which are estimated to have doubled in weight to around 2lb when conditions were wet. The former West Bromwich Albion centre-forward Jeff Astle died at the age of just 59 and the coroner recorded a verdict of industrial disease, caused by the repeated heading of a ball. Unlike Astle, however, Wayman was not noted for his heading ability and the majority of his goals came from the trusty left foot. He is part of a great tradition of forwards at Southampton. Yet, of all the legendary figures over the past century, including Arthur Dominy, Bill Rawlings, Derek Reeves, George O'Brien, Mick Channon, Ted MacDougall, Kevin Keegan, Steve Moran and Matthew Le Tissier, it is Wayman who has the best goals to games ratio. In 107 appearances between 1947 and 1950, he scored 77 times.

That works out at almost three goals in every four games. The likes of Moran, Le Tissier, Channon and recent heroes like Marian Pahars or James Beattie average less than two. As an out and out goal-scorer, Wayman's record stands comparison with the very best in post-war British football and his prolific period at Southampton ranks alongside the likes of Jimmy Greaves at Chelsea and Tottenham Hotspur, Brian Clough at Sunderland, Gary Lineker at Tottenham and Alan Shearer during his most fruitful spell at Blackburn Rovers.

Wayman did not score particularly spectacular goals like a Matthew Le Tissier, but no Saint before or since converted their chances with greater regularity. In terms of his style of play and an almost telepathic knack of being in the right place at the right time, the best comparison is probably with a Greaves, Lineker or even Michael Owen.

In an article in 1948, 'Observer' from the *Echo* tried to explain what made Wayman such a star. He wrote: "Watch him only once to know the answers. Wayman scores where others would miss because he is so quick on the turn. He is small. He can twist and hit the ball from angles impossible to bigger or clumsier players. Whenever he is in the penalty box he is dangerous. Opposing centre-halves don't know which way he will swerve. Wayman has another advantage. He seldom shoots over the cross-bar. That is because he keeps his body over the ball. Like all good centre-forwards he can shoot hard with both feet."

Supporters who watched Wayman recount how he was masterful with the ball at his mercy. He developed a trademark trick, which involved flicking the ball over the head of a bemused opponent, sprinting around the other side before shooting for goal.

At just 5ft 6ins tall, less than ten stone and with feet that were only a size six-and-a-half, Wayman guested for Portsmouth in several games while serving with the Navy during the Second World War and his small feet meant that he would carry his boots with him wherever he went on trips all over the world. His son, Paul, recounts a story about how Charlie had come to play football against a tribe on an island just off Mombasa on the Kenyan coast.

"They heard he played for Newcastle and he scored a few goals past their chief of the island who was apparently about 7ft tall," he says. "They found out who he was and he was taken out of the boat and they invited him to spend an evening with them. He said there were women with grass-skirts and dancing and that it was a great evening – and all because he could play football!"

BORN IN 1921, Wayman had signed as a professional with Newcastle in 1941 after writing to the manager Stan Seymour while playing for Chilton Colliery where he was a miner from the age of 14. "I was knee deep in water for 12/6d a week, I soon decided I wanted out," he would later tell the *Northern Echo*. "I went down the road to Bishop Auckland, and caught the local bus in and I was so excited, I forgot my boots."

Wayman started out as an inside-left with an eye for goal, scoring 11 times in his first three home matches for Newcastle. During the 1944/45 season, he scored 14 goals in 28 matches before taking his tally to 17 in 33 and then 30 in 41 when he moved for the first time to centre-forward after the departure of the Geordie legend Albert Stubbins to Liverpool. By the time of the 1946/47 season Wayman was Newcastle's leading striker and he topped the Division Two goal-scoring charts with 32 goals in 37 matches.

Wayman was also on sparkling form that season in the FA Cup and new Southampton manager Bill Dodgin was given a first-hand exhibition of his talent when he scored a second half hat-trick for the Magpies at St. James' Park in a 3-1 victory. Nine months later when Dodgin persuaded Wayman to head south and sign for Saints, many assumed it was this match that had convinced him. Dodgin, though, maintained that he had remembered him since September 1944 when, as a Southampton defender, he was given what he described as "a hard time" while Wayman was guesting for rivals Portsmouth.

The decisive moment in Wayman's transfer to Saints, however, was the rather mysterious decision to leave him out of the Newcastle team which reached the 1947 FA Cup semi-final. Newcastle lost that match 4-0 against Charlton Athletic and Wayman was soon on his way. His record at Newcastle stood at 36 goals in 53 games, although including war-time appearances, those figures were 71 in 124 matches. It was a superior strike-rate to many of the great Newcastle 'number nines', including his contemporary Jackie Milburn and more recent stars like Malcolm MacDonald, Peter Beardsley and even the all-time goal-scoring record-holder Alan Shearer. Had he stayed, Wayman may well have put that record out of Shearer's reach, for he was to be the top-scorer wherever he went for seven consecutive seasons.

Wayman's son, Paul, says that his father had never really wanted to leave Newcastle. Paul remembers helping on a school trip to St. James' Park with his own son. "We went in the dressing room and on the pitch and we were walking up a corridor and there was a picture on the wall of my dad and a few other players," he says, "I asked them why and they said it was for the players who had scored more than 30 in the league in a season. There were only about seven players and it did not include Malcolm MacDonald or Alan Shearer."

The FA Cup omission, though, clearly cut deep. In a previously unpublished interview with the Southampton historian David Bull in 1995, Wayman outlined the extent of his disappointment. "I couldn't understand that they dropped me – and nobody told me," he said, "Stan Seymour was manager. I was top goal-scorer. I had won the Golden Boot. I just wanted to get away. In my heart I knew I had been let down."

NEWS OF Wayman's unhappiness at Newcastle reached Dodgin, who was rebuilding Southampton in some style following the War. Nicknamed 'Daddy Dodgin', he was an excellent man-manager. Of future incumbents, his charismatic style had the most similarities with Lawrie McMenemy and he had the ability to sell the club to potential signings, being known for having "a Cinderella touch to his transfers".

"Technically Bill didn't know that much about the game, but he had something about him and we would roll our sleeves up to play for him," says Bill Ellerington. "He also got us some very good players. Not only Charlie Wayman, but other great players like Bill Rochford and Joe Mallett as well." Wayman was in agreement over Dodgin's managerial style: "He was such a good manager, he was one of the lads and just really popular. I enjoyed the years at Saints, everyone was nice to me. Bill was a Geordie and I liked him."

He certainly pulled off a master-stroke in persuading Wayman to sign, particularly as there was plenty of interest from other clubs. Wayman had just played in a reserve team match for Newcastle at Hillsborough when Dodgin met him off the late train at Newcastle station from Sheffield shortly before midnight on a cold October night. He took him to the adjacent Station Hotel where the deal was concluded.

Wayman recalled: "Bill Dodgin came in and he said, 'Charlie, I want a word with you, why don't you come to Southampton?' And I said, 'I'll show these lot' [Newcastle]. It was pitch dark, right where the railway station was. The wife didn't want to go, but at the finish I said, 'no, I'm going to Southampton'. Bill Rochford was there, he said 'c'mon Charlie' and in the end I said, 'I might as well go'." Wayman also admitted that the manager's persuasiveness and the promise of a "strawberries and cream" lifestyle in Southampton was enough to convince him to move. "He buttered me up well and truly – I was sold on becoming a Saint." Sheffield Wednesday had come in with a late offer of £12,000 to Saints' £10,000, but the deal was done, apparently thanks to a good relationship at boardroom level between Newcastle and Southampton. Mary Bates (Ted's wife), who was assistant secretary for Saints at the time, remembers that £1,000 towards Wayman's transfer fee had to be "scrounged" from the supporters' club.

Dodgin, though, had got his man and, over the next two-and-a-half years, Wayman reached the prime of his footballing life and treated The Dell faithful to an instinctive exhibition of pure finishing skills. Wayman has always been quick to describe his time at Saints as "some of the happiest days of my career".

"They were grand days," he said, "the supporters thought the world of me, and I of them. I can still hear them singing, 'up the middle for Charlie'. I had a priceless gift. I knew where the winger was going to put the ball, and I was always ready for it. So many players would just stand and watch the ball. The chances are there if you are willing to move about and get into open spaces. That's the art of the game.

"A lot of centre-forwards stay too deep and others are not mobile enough. I was always looking for the ball, waiting for the half chance. Eric Day was a very good winger and I just seemed to fit in, we had good players, passing the ball up to feet and I would turn the man. Mainly the goals were with my left foot."

WAYMAN'S impact on the Southampton team was fairly immediate and it is probable that the club would have been promoted to the First Division in 1947/48 had he arrived at the beginning of the season rather than in time to make his debut early in November. Saints were ninth in the league at the time, but climbed to third by the end of the season largely thanks to 17 goals in 27 games from Wayman.

At the time, it was the highest Football League finish in Saints' history, yet in those days, there were no play-offs and only the top two clubs were promoted, so Saints remained in the Second Division. Dodgin had constructed the best Saints team since the days of Arthur Dominy and Bill Rawlings in the late 1920s and probably since the Southern League glory era at the turn of the century. That was underlined by the FA Cup exploits of 1948 with a quarter-final berth for the first time since 1927.

Wayman scored twice en route to a meeting with Tottenham in the last eight, although the star of the Cup run was the winger Eric Day who scored the decisive goal in a 1-0 third round win over Sunderland and then twice in a memorable 3-2 fourth round defeat of Blackburn. It was dubbed 'Day's Match'. Like Wayman, Day stood at only 5ft 6ins tall and, with the likes of Ellerington, Alf Ramsey, Bill Rochford, Eric Webber and Joe Mallett, was a player of great popularity at the time. Day and Ellerington also showed an impeccable loyalty and service to Saints by each playing for over a decade. In most eras, they would have been the outstanding Cult Heroes, yet Wayman's goal-scoring was so exceptionally prolific and his impact on the team so obviously crucial, that he captured the hearts of the man on the terrace above all others.

Harold Wallace vividly recalls watching this particular team. "It was one of the finest Saints teams, no doubt about that," he says. "Ellerington, Ramsey and Rochford were the equal of any full-backs I have seen since, but the catalyst for everything was little Charlie Wayman. He just had the midas touch in front of goal. Ron Davies was superior in many respects and he didn't have the flamboyance of a Le Tissier or the energy of Mick Channon, but there was no-one I have ever felt more sure of in a one-on-one situation than Wayman."

That feeling was to be further underlined during the 1948/49 season, but first Saints were to embark on a remarkable six-week summer tour to Brazil for what many have since described as a 'trip of a lifetime'. According to *Dell Diamond,* the biography of Ted Bates, the original idea had been to tour the United States, but these plans fell through and it was arranged to travel to South America as guests of Botafogo FC. The key to the tour was the strong relationship between the City Council and the Brazilian Consulate in Southampton. A fitting destination, though, since it was the former Saint Charles Miller who famously introduced football to Brazil as a 19-year-old in 1894.

Saints travelled to Brazil by sea with a squad of 16, manager Bill Dodgin, trainer Sam Warhurst and travelling referee George Reader, who was to officiate in the matches. Wayman, naturally, was to lead the line, but there were several surprises in store. The first was a pleasant one. After leaving a country where rationing was still in place following the War, the Saints players found themselves treated like kings both at sea and upon arrival in Brazil where they stayed as guests in the lavish Luxor Hotel in Rio.

"It was a wonderful trip," remembers Ellerington. "We trained on the ship every morning from 6am till 9am and then we arrived in Rio." The poverty shocked members of the Southampton squad, but so too did the skills and work ethic of their hosts. "We were on Copacabana Beach," says Ellerington, "on the hill at the back there were 100,000 people in shanty-towns, bits of tin and wood. They had tremendous skills and many didn't have a job, so people worked their guts out to be footballers."

Saints went under the assumption that they would show their hosts how to play football. Brazil had not yet emerged as a serious player on the world football stage, but those days were not very far away. "I wasn't surprised when they came through and won the World Cup in 1958 – what a side they were," says Ellerington. "They were light years ahead of us then. On a Sunday they had beach leagues on soft sand and you should have seen the skills from the youngsters. We used to look at each other and think, 'my God'. Absolutely unbelievable. Even their goalkeeper could keep the ball up about 150 times on his shoulders."

Saints were battered 4-0 in the first match against Fluminense, with the Brazilians light of foot in their slipper style shoes against the old-fashioned 'boot' still used by the Southampton players. Saints lost their opening four matches and Wayman was somewhat bemused. "I was running here, I was running there, wondering why the ball wasn't coming to me," he said. "I'd been all over the world, but it was something else. They were good players. I learnt by the way they passed the ball."

Wayman struggled with the Brazilian sweeper system, but his quality was genuine at any level and in any continent and he adjusted by the end of the trip to score twice in a 3-1 win over Flamengo. "It was like we had won the World Cup!" smiles Ellerington.

SAINTS HAD returned a better team from their Brazilian experience and set about the task of finally winning promotion from Division Two. Wayman scored five times in the first four matches to quickly underline Saints' credentials before setting a club record in the league which still stands with five goals in the 6-0 win against Leicester City. Bill Rawlings scored four against Northampton Town and Millwall, while Charles Livesey, George O'Brien, Derek Reeves, Ron Davies and Martin Chivers have all since matched that feat, yet only Wayman has ever managed five.

It happened at The Dell almost exactly a year after he had arrived from Newcastle and cemented his status as the most celebrated footballer in Southampton. Wayman was given a deafening ovation as he left the pitch, although he was again thankful for the wonderful service of Eric Day who had made three of his goals and also supplied the cross for Ted Bates' strike.

Saints had moved to second in the table by Christmas and a run of 12 Wayman goals in the next 12 games seemed to have settled the destination of the title. Following a 3-1 win at Leicester, the team-bus broke its journey to stop at a London hotel. AE Jukes, the Southampton chairman, called for champagne and the group drank a toast to Wayman, who had reached 30 goals in the league that afternoon. By Easter, Wayman had scored 32 goals in 35 games and Saints looked unstoppable. He was already the highest league scorer in a single season at Saints and the talk was of whether he could reach 40 for the season. Preparations were being made to celebrate promotion and there were plans afoot for a souvenir programme.

Saints faced Tottenham at White Hart Lane on April 2, 1949, in front of a crowd of some 69,265, of which around 15,000 had travelled from Southampton. The match-day programme said "only a series of unlikely disasters" could deny Saints from reaching Division One and added that they were in "what appears to be an unassailable position". Sadly, it took only one disaster – injury to the talisman.

At the time, it appeared that Wayman had been rewarded for his decision to stay on the field at White Hart Lane when, despite suffering a torn thigh muscle early in the second half, he popped up with a dramatic 82nd minute winner which stretched the lead at the top of the table to some eight points with only seven matches remaining. It was described as a moment of "sheer pluck...straight out of the highest dramatic pages of football". One reporter added that the goal was "one of the most remarkable of his career" and described the build up. "How he ever got there will always remain a mystery to me. The last previous glimpse I had of Wayman was of him as a limping, hobbling figure near the touchline obviously feeling pain at every step. Yet there he was in the goal-mouth.

"Bates, battling against odds and close tackles by two opponents, forced the ball across to Wayman who swung his injured leg at the ball. It was desperate and it seemed hopeless gallantry when the ball was pushed out by Ditchburn. But then, ignoring what must have been crippling pain in his left leg, Wayman shifted his weight to that foot, used his right leg, the uninjured one, this time and swept the ball into the net.

"That was as much as human muscles could withstand. Wayman fell under the strain...was almost smothered by elated colleagues and carried off the pitch. That dramatic moment was worth all the miles spectators had travelled; all the hours they had spent queuing." Rob Holley began watching Saints in 1945 and idolised Wayman. "I can still see Charlie scoring that Tottenham goal. It is fixed in my brain," he says.

Wayman, himself, recalled the moment in the *Daily Mirror* series of 1995 entitled 'My Greatest Goal'. "I don't know how I got to that ball...I hit it and it came back off the goalkeeper and I hit it with my other foot – the one that worked...then they carried me off," he said. Wayman and the rest of the Saints team spent the evening at the London Palladium, prompting a cartoon in the Monday edition of the *Echo* with a picture of a deserted Southampton. "Anybody in Town?" asks one man. "All gone to Tottenham, mate," replies the other. Below, there is a picture of Leicester Square with the name 'Champagne Charlie' up in lights and Saints fans with banners saying 'up the middle!' According to Saints legend, that evening was the first night after the War that all the lights were working in Leicester Square.

Promotion appeared to be a certainty. Of course there was the injury to Wayman to contend with, but the initial prognosis from physio Sid Cann was that he should recover after only two weeks out of action. And anyway, Saints were not that much of a one man team. Were they? Former players remain at a loss to understand how they won just one of their last seven games, especially as they dominated so much of the play. But the goals had dried up and only Ellerington and Day scored in those final matches.

Wayman tried in vain to return prematurely from his injury and featured twice, but it was not to be as Saints were pipped by Fulham and West Brom. "Charlie was half the team," admitted Dodgin.

That missed promotion remained a painful memory even decades later. In an interview in 1980, Wayman said: "Even now, I just can't believe we didn't go up. Everything went against us. If only. But that's football isn't it?" He later admitted that he had still been injured when, in sheer desperation, Saints drafted him back for matches against Grimsby Town and Chesterfield. Speaking some 57 years after that fateful season, Bill Ellerington said: "It was crazy, I still sometimes think about it when I'm sat around."

DESPITE the disappointment, Wayman was clearly established as Saints' leading player and he was to have a football café named after him during the summer of 1949 in Southampton with more than 300 people attending the grand opening. Many people in the city assumed Wayman had some commercial interest in the café. In fact, it was the idea of a fan who simply used the name of the club's star striker in order to gain publicity. More than 50 years later, another Southampton supporter decided to name a pub after Matthew Le Tissier. Perhaps the trappings of hero worship haven't changed that much.

"People always used to come up to me and say, 'you are the greatest'," chuckled Wayman in that 1995 interview. His son, Paul adds: "I remember he told me about the chap who opened the place called 'Charlie Wayman's Café'. But dad didn't work there or get any money from them using his name, although he used to say that the butchers and bakers would come around and deliver things to his house for free.

"His brother, my uncle Jack, stayed with him at Southampton and was working at the docks. He's five years younger and he would go out to the pubs and clubs. They looked identical and, on one occasion, it was in the paper that Charlie Wayman had been out drinking before a game. But it was Jack! They had to explain the misunderstanding to the manager."

The likes of Terry Paine and John Sydenham were just schoolboys at the time, but both regard Wayman as the club's first big superstar. A man universally adored by supporters.

THEORETICALLY, Saints were well placed for a third successive promotion push in 1949/50, but they again missed out by a whisker as they were denied on goal average by Sheffield United and Sheffield Wednesday. This time, however, they were never in the top three throughout the season and had to pay for a slow start which saw them take just one point from the opening four games.

The club, though, had been rocked during the summer by the departure of Dodgin to Fulham and the promotion of Sid Cann to manager, rather than the expected elevation of the full-back Bill Rochford. Many of the players have since referred to a different atmosphere without Dodgin around the place. Yet with Wayman scoring another 24 league goals in 36 games, including his 100th post-war goal in 137 league games in February 1950, results on the pitch remained fairly encouraging.

Off it, though, problems were brewing. Wayman was coming under pressure from his wife, who had not settled in Southampton and was now desperate to return back north. By the summer of 1950, Wayman's mind had been made up, despite the best efforts of staff at Southampton. Saints fan Terry O'Farrell recalls a family story. "I was born in 1947 and soon after my eldest sister got a job as a receptionist at The Dell," he says. "However, there were fears that Charlie Wayman would be seeking a transfer because his wife couldn't settle in the south. Apparently, my mother, Daisy O'Farrell and her toddler [me] were sent around to visit her in the hope that she would be captivated by the 'sweet child' and would want to stay in the area – the cunning plan did not work..."

Unfortunately Wayman was forced to leave. In his words: "I have no grievance with the club, but my wife wants to go back to the north of England. She has never really been comfortable away from the north, and the time has come to meet her wishes. I should prefer to go to some club in the north east, but I must wait and see."

Wayman eventually was on the train to Preston North End for a fee of £10,000 as well as Eddy Brown. 'Champagne Charlie' was to prove literally irreplaceable as, without their star striker, the team struggled for goals and it was not until Eric Day moved to the centre and then Derek Reeves arrived that Saints began to recover almost a decade later. Yet that was not before they had been relegated to Division Three (South) in 1953.

THE CHANGE of scenery did little to harm Wayman's predatory instincts and Saints could only look on at what they were missing as his goals helped Preston take the Division Two title in 1950/51. He had finally won a cherished promotion. Wayman was to remain at Preston for four seasons, scoring an incredible 119 times in that period, to remain for many years the leading post-war goal-scorer in English football. He helped them to an FA Cup final in 1954 and they missed out on the Division One championship only on goal average to Arsenal in 1952/53.

"Wayman's arrival was a turning point, catapulting Preston North End back into the big time," says his former team-mate Tom Finney who points to Wayman's consistency at Newcastle, Southampton and Preston in response to suggestions that his goals were somehow fortuitous. "To score 20 goals or more every season for four seasons in a row required a bit more than luck," he says.

Despite Wayman's goal-scoring exploits in the 1954 FA Cup, Preston were beaten 3-2 by West Brom in the final and Wayman was surprisingly sold to Middlesbrough later that year for £9,000. A certain Brian Clough eventually succeeded Wayman as the top striker at Middlesbrough and Charlie concluded his career at Darlington before retiring to work as sales manager for the Scottish & Newcastle brewery.

"He loved that job," says son Paul. "He would basically go all around pubs and clubs selling beer. I would sometimes go with him and everybody would be all over him, asking about the football. His life was still football and he loved talking football to people. He used to still get invited to open things and present trophies.

"I remember I was in Preston once and I went to look around Deepdale and there was an old chap outside and he said, 'are you one of the new signings?' I explained that my dad used to play for the club. He said, 'who is he?' I told him and he just looked gobsmacked."

Although Wayman retired to his native north east, his popularity remained undiminished among Southampton supporters. They could not forget the goals, nor his ear to ear grin. That was evident when he received a touching and rousing reception in 1995 when he returned for a dinner in Ted Bates' honour at The Dell. "He would often get requests for autographs and he was pleased that people remembered him," said Paul.

They still most certainly do and his huge popularity at each of his previous clubs is testament to his quality on the pitch. With 255 goals in 388 Football League appearances, it remains an anomaly that he was never selected for England.

In an obituary for the *Independent,* Ivan Ponting suggests that England's rather archaic selection procedure may have been to blame. "Many knowledgeable observers deemed the affable north easterner a world-class finisher, and it was an outrage to them that he didn't win a single England cap," he said.

"The most obvious explanation for the omission was that Wayman was in competition for his country's number nine shirt with the stellar likes of Tommy Lawton, Nat Lofthouse and Roy Bentley. A more contentious theory was that he couldn't find favour with members of the selection committee with which the team coach Walter Winterbottom was required to work – a group often derided by professionals for its collective lack of knowledge about the game – because they believed that, at 5ft 6ins, he was too short for the international arena. Such a stance was risible, as anyone would testify who had witnessed the quicksilver left footer making buffoons out of towering defenders."

England's performances at the two World Cups during Wayman's halcyon days, 1950 and 1954, hardly lit up the competition and it is arguable that they lacked a striker of the mobility of Wayman and stuck rigidly to the 'English' method of wingers crossing the ball for big centre-forwards to head home – a tactic which has been employed by remarkably few successful sides on the world stage.

At Saints, however, Wayman's talents were always appreciated and he is revered by an older generation of fans as the best striker the club ever had. Yes, better than Le Tissier, Beattie, Keegan, Channon or Davies. That particular debate, of course, will rage on and on. Advocates of Charlie Wayman, though, have a powerful argument. They can simply point to the statistics.

CLIFF HUXFORD

1959-1967

SAINTS CAREER

Games	320
Goals	4
Caps	0

MAGIC MOMENT

A crunching tackle and then a 25-yard shot to open the scoring in a 5-1 rout of Portsmouth

'THE TANK'

CLIFF Huxford against Denis Hollywood in a 50-50 tackle? It's a thought to send shivers down the spine of most Saints fans from the 1950s and 1960s. These two Saints greats never went head-to-head of course. Well, not in public anyway. The back garden of Huxford's Southampton home, however, was a different matter.

As a 15-year-old apprentice from the Govan ship-building region of Glasgow which spawned Sir Alex Ferguson, Hollywood spent four years living with the Huxfords when he joined Southampton. And, when he was not training, he would drag his older colleague outside and the duo would have tackling competitions. "Denis was more of a kicker than myself to be honest, but we had a good laugh," says Huxford. "It used to sometimes get serious. It could be a Friday afternoon and I've got a game the next day and it would be 'okay Den, one more and that's enough'." The smile-cum-grimace on Huxford's face suggests the younger man rarely got the better of him. But then again, who did?

"He was the hardest player I ever came across," admits Hollywood, "he was tremendous for me, a terrific example. He went to bed at 9pm and the lights were off. He didn't drink, he never went out and he was a fitness fanatic. He never argued with referees, if the decision was given that was it. He never threatened other players, he would just pick himself up, look at them, walk off and make a mental note.

"But he was as hard as nails. He would block tackle me in the back garden. The club owned the house next door as well. There was a 12-foot fence between them and we would also chip balls to each other over the fence."

Saints became famed for their no-nonsense defending during the late 1960s and early 1970s, yet the man who set the standard played in the preceding generation. When the legendary hard man Ron 'Chopper' Harris once compiled a list of the top ten footballing 'iron men', he placed himself below Huxford. And, anyone who came across him while he was at Saints, testifies that Huxford was the toughest footballer to play for the club.

"People talk about that team of the early 1970s with [Denis] Hollywood, [John] McGrath, [Brian] O'Neil and [Dave] Walker," says Terry Paine, "but no-one was tougher than Cliff. I remember he was involved in a tackle which broke someone's leg. Cliff didn't realise and he was just busy taking the throw-in while this guy was lying there in agony. I remember him colliding with Davies of Derby and he [Davies] went off on a stretcher needing 20 or 30 stitches."

To the supporters on The Dell terraces, Huxford was known simply as 'The Tank'. To this day, Huxford needs some convincing that it was a compliment. "There was a crowd of dockers who shouted that at me and I wasn't too sure about it, but I guess I'd rather be called something than nothing," he says. "I suppose it was either because nothing went through me or because I steamrollered everything in front of me." In all probability, it was both.

Trevor Baker never missed a game from the East Stand during that period. "Huxford was a hero because no-one went through him," he says, "they might occasionally have passed it or ran around him, but no-one ever got through him. The phrase 110% could have been invented for him." It's an assessment shared by the former Saints and England full-back Bill Ellerington, who was part of the scouting team that brought Huxford to The Dell in 1959. "He was what I would call a do or dier," says Ellerington. "He would go through a brick wall for the team and he used to. I spent more than 35 years at the club and he was the hardest player I've ever come across and as honest as the day is long. He would literally run his guts into the floor for you and was the most solid tackler I've ever seen. He was similar to Dave Mackay or Tommy Smith. Those three frightened people. Cliff had the most tremendous pair of thigh muscles I have ever seen in my life."

CLIFF HUXFORD still lives just outside Southampton and, as he opens his front door, it seems apt that the first thing you see and hear is his dog, which is a boxer. 'Murphy', however, is a big softie with an insatiable desire to be patted on the forehead. Huxford beckons me in. He is now approaching 70 and, although only 5ft 9ins tall, there is something in his sturdy build and slightly crouched posture that suggests he would remain a fearsome opponent in any tackle.

Photographs of him in his prime show he indeed had the sort of muscular definition on his legs which would make a body-builder jealous. The long scar on his arm is a reminder of an accident in 1985 which nearly killed him. Huxford worked as a painter and decorator after retiring from football. He was doing a job at Southampton's Red Lodge School and thought he could just reach to a wall rather than move his ladder. The ladder toppled over and he fell straight through a greenhouse beneath him and bounced off a table. As a footballer, Huxford always played through the pain barrier and this occasion proved no different. With blood pouring from a deep laceration, he calmly got to his feet and walked around the corner to tell his work-mate that he had cut himself.

"The policeman who was first on the scene after it had happened said he thought I was a goner and I think a few other people did too," he says, before adding with typical understatement, "and I was a bit worried too." Huxford was in hospital for the next three weeks and required 40 stitches and transfusions which amounted to 20 pints of blood. He laughs at the story until his wife Jill reminds him that he nearly died and he concedes, "I was a lucky man".

Huxford grew up in Stroud and began his career with Chelsea after being recommended for the club following his performances as a 15-year-old with a works team called Hoffmans. He spent the next six years at Chelsea, first as an apprentice and then as a professional during one of the most successful periods in the club's history. An affiliation with The Blues remains and he was delighted to be invited to the centenary dinner in 2005.

"I was there when they won the league [in 1954/55]," he says, "although I was mostly in the youth side and the reserves at the time." Huxford had to do his national service while in London and his love for football meant that nothing would stop him from playing. That much was clear from the fact that he was prepared to risk the certainty of several weeks confinement in the 'Glasshouse' – a military prison – in order to play every Saturday.

"I never missed playing for Chelsea reserves or Chelsea's youth team in all that time and, if you know the army, that takes some doing," he says. Huxford was based at Netley, just outside Southampton, and would climb over the wall on a Saturday morning and take the train to London before returning in the evening in the hope that he hadn't been missed. People would cover for me and every Saturday morning they would line up and call out your names. But they never looked up. So there would be '649 Huxford!' and my mate would say, 'yes sir!' I never got caught."

By 1959, Huxford was captaining the reserve team at Chelsea, but he was well aware that first team opportunities at Stamford Bridge might be limited. At Saints, Ted Bates had been manager for four years and had established a strong scouting network. "Ted said, 'why don't you go to Chelsea?'" remembers Bill Ellerington. "I was there to watch their wingers which I did four or five times, but I went back and said to Ted, 'there's not a bad wing-half who plays for them – he never stops running'. He was strong, keen, workmanlike and very destructive.

"At the time, we had a guy called Charlie Livesey. Ted Drake was the manager at Chelsea and they wanted Charlie, so we did a deal. I think Charlie ended up on the treatment table more than he did playing and Cliff was a great buy for us. Cliff was a great, great lad. An honest player – the sort who you would notice when you were struggling and hanging on."

The deal that brought Huxford to The Dell also saw Bates get £12,000 in exchange for Livesey, who had scored 15 goals that season for Saints. "One of the shrewdest signings Ted ever made," agrees Terry Paine. "You knew Cliff would be there fighting for you through thick and thin."

Huxford was delighted at the chance of first team football, even if it meant dropping two divisions, and was instantly sold on Southampton as he walked down across the parks from the old station to The Dell. "I was happy to move because I was more or less guaranteed first team football," he says. "I was on the fringes at Chelsea and I don't think I would have held a regular first team place."

The great hallmark of Saints teams under Bates was goals. With the arrival of the prolific Derek Reeves and the emergence of Terry Paine and John Sydenham, the manager had quickly constructed a team that was capable of hurting any defence. Entertainment was always high. In the four seasons from 1955/56 to 1958/59, the team scored 91, 76, 112 and then 88 league goals.

Bates knew where he had to strengthen and, remarkably, even though he had never played for the club, Huxford was instantly made Saints' youngest captain at the age of just 22 for the 1959/60 season. It was another good choice. Finesse might not have been part of his game, but for out and out defending there were few braver or stronger. Supporters love a never-say-die attitude and this was what Huxford brought to the team at a time when it was most needed. "I gave my all and the fans could see that," he says. "Even if you are having a bad game, there is no reason why you shouldn't be trying. Everyone makes mistakes, but as long as your head doesn't go down, they will forgive you."

Bates was to describe his summer transfer dealing in 1959 as "amazing" and admitted that he acquired Huxford "as a captain rather than a player". There were eight new arrivals before the start of the season with Huxford, George O'Brien and Dick Conner later described as Bates' 'three card trick'. Of the trio, O'Brien also ranks among the club's most popular ever players. Indeed, with an outstanding goal-scoring record of 180 goals in 281 games as an attacking midfielder at inside-right, O'Brien was a far more accomplished footballer than the more limited Huxford. Yet he was perhaps not such a talismanic or iconic figure with the fans.

"I was an organiser, I opened my mouth," says Huxford. "Apart from being a defender, I would organise defensively. If you are captain you have got to open your mouth. I was a physical defender, an out and out defender. The main reason I was captain was because I was volatile, verbal and I organised players."

Huxford certainly needed all his powers of leadership to encourage the Saints team of 1959/60 to remember their defensive duties. He sighs, smiles and shakes his head as he remembers how often he would be left stranded as an opposition team surged forward on the counter-attack. "With George O'Brien, Derek Reeves, Terry Paine, Dave Burnside, George Kirby and John Sydenham, we were a very attacking side in those days. We were okay coming forward, but coming back! If they didn't have the ball, you didn't really see a lot of our players. But if they had it, we were okay.

"I used to shout at them when the opposition got the ball to come back and defend. George O'Brien and Derek Reeves were great goal-scorers, but lazy buggers when they weren't on the ball. They weren't interested in defending, they were looking to get forward, so we were exposed time and time again on the counter-attack. But there were always goals to be had."

O'Brien agrees that he did not chase back, but simply points to the statistics in suggesting that the defence was what prevented Saints from progressing more quickly from Division Three to Division One. "I must admit that I didn't do much tackling," says O'Brien, "but having said that, if you are scoring 100 goals a year and not winning the league, it's not hard to see where the problem in the team was. It felt like we would regularly go away from home and go two up and then we would lose 3-2."

Huxford's arrival added the necessary steel and organisation to harness the attacking prowess into a team disciplined enough to challenge for promotion. Indeed, with Huxford captaining the team, 1959/60 proved to be a record-breaking season in more ways than one. Reeves scored 39 league goals in 46 games, beating his own tally of 31 from the 1957/58 season. As a whole, the team scored 106 goals and conceded 75. Most importantly, though, they were promoted to the Second Division as Division Three champions. It was the first silverware since Bill Rawlings inspired promotion from the Third Division (South) to Division Two back in 1921/22.

After the 1922 triumph, it also remains only the second Football League trophy that Saints have ever won. Huxford was presented with the cup at The Dell having been an ever present in defence throughout all of the 46 league games. Saints' promotion was fuelled by a run of 15 wins from 19 games between October and March, but the title was not clinched until the final day of the season with a 2-0 win over Bradford City.

It was a young side with Tommy Traynor and John Page the only regular survivors from the squad which had been relegated in 1953. The great potential was quickly shown the following August with a 4-1 demolition of Liverpool in the first home match of the season. It was a game which many felt stirred Bill Shankly's apparent antipathy towards Saints which lasted throughout his tenure at Anfield. Reeves, O'Brien, Paine and Sydenham were the goal-scorers.

Saints took the scalp of local rivals Portsmouth the following week in the first south coast derby in a Football League game for 33 years with a 5-1 victory. This time Huxford provided inspiration rather than perspiration, opening the scoring in front of a crowd of 28,845 with what was described as a "splendid opportunist" goal. In fact it was much better than that. Huxford won a typically crunching challenge in the middle of the pitch and sprinted through to crash a 25-yard shot home. Saints had the wind in their sails and momentum behind them as Bates' young team matured into one of the most promising in the entire country. The club were on the cusp of their best period since the Southern League days of CB Fry.

THE DELL was a place guaranteed to generate excitement. Electricity, however, was a problem on one famous night in December 1960 for a League Cup clash against Leeds United. The lights twice failed, meaning that 62 minutes of play were lost and the match did not finish until almost 10.30pm after kicking off at 7.30pm. Events on the pitch were just as extraordinary with Derek Reeves scoring all five in a dramatic 5-4 win.

What's more, after just 21 minutes, goalkeeper Ron Reynolds was stretchered off. No substitutes then, of course, meant Terry Paine was the designated stand-in goalkeeper, but Bates decided that Huxford should take a goalkeeper's sweater that was several sizes too large. According to one report, "Huxford stopped one or two dangerous shots". It concluded that it was, "one of the most fantastic matches in the history of football…a cup tie that will be talked about for years".

"I think the less said about that the better," laughs Huxford as he recalls conceding four goals. "I think I made a few saves, but I remember Jack Charlton scored a penalty against me when I dived over the ball."

Huxford was called into emergency duty between the posts again in his Saints career. In 1963, he kept what he calls a "clean sheet" after taking over with the score already at 2-0 against Portsmouth and then again in a 6-4 win over Derby County later that same season. Terry Paine (3), Martin Chivers (2) and John Sydenham were the goal-scorers but the *Echo* labelled the stand-in goalkeeper as "hero Huxford", who pulled off a save which "any goalkeeper would have been proud… he showed quite an aptitude for the position".

That Huxford was prepared to go in goal underlines his constant willingness to take responsibility. "Why did I volunteer to go in goal?" he says, "I wanted to be on the pitch and I think people must have thought I was brave – or stupid." The early 1960s were outwardly a happy period for the club. Huxford, though, admits there was friction between himself and Terry Paine. It was a problem which led to him giving up the captaincy.

His admiration of Bates is total, as is his assessment of the attacking quality of Paine, but Huxford says: "To put it mildly, Terry Paine was Ted Bates' right-hand man – his blue-eyed boy. I could understand it because he had been with him from the early days, but it caused a little bit of bad feeling and I felt it affected my job as captain. One of the parts of being captain is that you represent the players to the manager. I was doing that, but after Christmas and towards the end of the 1960/61 season, Terry was going in and that wasn't on to me. That was the main reason I packed in the captaincy to be honest. Generally, though, it was a decent atmosphere at the time. We were mainly on the same money. The basic wage when I came from Chelsea to Southampton was £18 a week in the summer and £20 a week in the winter and it would be £6 bonus for a win and £3 for a draw. The national average wage then was about £7 or £8 a week."

Paine is nothing but complimentary about Huxford. "He was involved in a lot of what was happening at the club," he says. "He would give you 150% in every game, whether you were playing against Chelsea or it was a kick around in the car park. I remember Cliff punching me on the jaw on Christmas Day in a six-a-side because I went around him.

"He thought I was taking the mickey. He turned around and whacked me and said, 'don't you ever do that again'. He took training as seriously as an FA Cup final. But it just made you realise how much you wanted him in your side. He was a winner, absolutely brilliant and he gave us a massive lift in terms of defensive duties."

THE LIKES of Terry Paine and Mick Channon still vividly remember those six-a-side or five-a-sides that Ted Bates introduced which would take place in the club car park and later in The Dell's gym. "It couldn't happen today," says Paine. "It was a tradition every Friday morning. To start with it was in the car park and then in the gym. It wasn't a big gym and you had the confines of a tight space.

"People would be cracking up against the wall, all kinds of things went on which, looking back on it, were horrendous. It was just a free-for-all. I've seen George O'Brien fly over the top of Tommy Traynor's head. I've seen Cliff Huxford clatter Tony Knapp, sparks were flying, unbelievable, but that's how it was. It was frightening, but we survived. Cliff was always on my side. I always made sure I had Cliff on my side because I could wind him up to get stuck in."

After Huxford, the player that most frightened team-mates and opposition players was his protégé, Denis Hollywood, who became infamous for his sliding tackles inside the gym. "I remember him being butted in a match," says Paine. "His nose was spread across his face and there was blood everywhere – but he merely smiled at the bloke who'd done it. And that fellow turned white." Brian O'Neil adds: "Denis was hard, cold even."

In his autobiography, *Man on the Run*, Mick Channon says: "Southampton had two of the hardest men I've ever played against in my life, Cliff Huxford and Denis Hollywood. Their motto was 'you can go past me; the ball can go past – but you won't both bloody go past me together!' That was their law – break it, and they'd have your legs off. Those two gave some terrible kickings…Cliff and Dennis hurt me physically, and mentally it made an impression."

Training sessions would often break out into brawls. Bates, though, would later say that his team would win the European Cup if it was played in the gym. "I fought with 'Big' Ron Davies once," says Hollywood, "every day there were fights. Not just pushing and shoving, but real fights. If you are fighting somebody, you end up the best of pals and you laugh and joke about it. But it was deadly serious – especially the Scotland and England games."

Huxford says the drinking culture which came into football from the late 1960s was not prevalent at Saints at the time. "The social side of it wasn't so much until the next decade," he says, "we would get in about 9.20am, start training at 10am and then finish at about 12 noon and the rest of the day was your own. I had a boxer dog then as well and I would go and walk in the New Forest every day."

IN THE league, Saints established themselves as a team which regularly finished in the top half of the Division Two table and the goals continued to flow freely at both ends as Derek Reeves was succeeded by the likes of George Kirby, Martin Chivers and Norman Dean as the grateful recipient of the outstanding wide service offered by Terry Paine and John Sydenham. Yet it was in the FA Cup of 1963 that Saints once again announced themselves as a real force to the wider football world. Their best previous performance had been reaching the finals of 1900 and 1902 more than 60 years earlier, but victories over York City, Watford and Sheffield United set up a quarter-final meeting with First Division Nottingham Forest.

Saints drew 1-1 at the City Ground and appeared to be on their way out of the competition after falling three goals behind in front of 29,479 at The Dell. But the support was magnificent, with thousands swarming outside the old ground – including some who watched from the top of trees overlooking the Archers end – and Saints fought back in an amazing finale for a 3-3 draw. 'Observer' wrote for the *Echo:* "I have never seen nor heard a crowd at

The Dell so enthusiastic as they were in those closing minutes." It meant a second replay, this time at the neutral ground of White Hart Lane, with an estimated 25,000 fans making their way up the old A30 to north London. At the time, it was said to be the largest peacetime exodus from Southampton.

The support was again matched by the display on the pitch with Saints running out 5-0 winners as George O'Brien and David Burnside both scored twice. The star of the night, however, was the right-half Ken Wimshurst, who also scored. "The 5-0 win was one of those days when everything came off and Ken Wimshurst had a brilliant game," says Huxford. "But what I remember most was coming back in the coach. All we could see for miles in front of us was the red lights of all the cars going back to Southampton. The kick-off had been delayed a quarter of an hour because they couldn't get all the people from Southampton in the ground. The support that night was fantastic. You saw all the scarves and you thought, 'I can't let them down'. They had paid good money and put in the time and effort to support us."

The semi-final, though, against Manchester United at Villa Park proved to be something of an anti-climax with Saints losing 1-0 to a Denis Law goal. On the Monday before the game, Bates had taken the team to a secluded base at Droitwich. Huxford said that boredom was a problem. "It was a brilliant hotel, but it was in the middle of nowhere," he says. "We would train at one of the local non-league clubs and then have the rest of the day. That was where I was table-tennis champion! The game itself went quick and I really can't remember too much about it." Huxford does, however, recall travelling back to the village of Whitchurch in Hampshire where the team watched highlights of their defeat on television.

In the league, Saints were getting closer and closer to reaching the top division for the first time in the club's history. In 1963/64 they were fifth and then fourth in 1964/65, with Huxford firmly established in the team. Yet the end wasn't so very far away and he was dropped in 1965 for the first time since joining the club. Huxford, though, remained a regular during the 1965/66 season as Saints finally achieved promotion to Division One.

The emergence of Dave Walker, however, meant Huxford was no longer in Bates' best eleven and he started just one game in the First Division, although he was a substitute in the 3-2 win against Blackpool – Saints' first top-flight victory. Huxford handed in a transfer request in 1966, but stayed on to the end of the season to help the club's younger players in the reserve team matches.

AN ERA at Southampton came to an end when Huxford joined Exeter City the following year. "I probably just wasn't good enough for the First Division – simple as that," he says. Huxford continued to live in Southampton and trained twice a week at The Dell, but admitted that all the travelling to Exeter meant that it could never really work out.

"It was a big mistake because you are not involved," he says, "I remember we played Hartlepool away for a midweek game. I would meet them at Gloucester which was 100 miles, then went up to Hartlepool, got stuffed 3-0, had fish and chips on the coach and I got back to Southampton at about 6.30am! For what?"

"Because you loved it," interrupts wife Jill.

"True," he says. "I loved it. I love football."

And that's why supporters loved him. Dedication, determination and desire; wherever Huxford went he gave in spades and received adulation in sackfuls.

That love of football took him to play at Worcester City, Basingstoke Town and Stevenage, before a range of coaching and management roles at Basingstoke, Aldershot, AC Delco, Bashley, Totton, Fareham Town, Brockenhurst, Thatcham Town, Swanmore and the director of coaching job at Eastleigh as recently as 2002. Even now, he will regularly watch football, whether it is Saints, the reserve team or Colden Common, just down the road from where he lives.

CLIFF HUXFORD was from an era where pride, loyalty and hard tackling were part and parcel of the game. "Men were men," he says, "you gave it and you took it. I enjoyed the physical side of the game when the ball was there to be won. Today you get yellow carded for those kind of tackles, but physical contact has always been in the game. I would tackle hard, but I would never argue with the referee and I was never sent-off.

"I'm proud to have been a professional footballer, that's why I can't stand this cheating in the game now and this win at all costs attitude. There are many talented players, but the way they throw themselves on the floor for the slightest touch is embarrassing."

Huxford, though, has no regrets and says he feels privileged to have played during such a historic era in Saints' history. "Eight out of ten young lads would wish to be a professional footballer and I was one of them," he says. "I was lucky. I used to look at the people stood in the stands and think 'I'm playing and they wish they were'. I used to love those crowds."

TERRY PAINE

1956-1974

SAINTS CAREER

Games	815
Goals	187
Caps	19

MAGIC MOMENT

A rare headed goal at Leyton Orient – which all but clinched promotion to Division One in 1966

'POGO'

> 'I've played with some greats like Bobby Moore, Alan Ball and Kevin Keegan and I've faced Franz Beckenbauer and Johan Cruyff and George Best. But Terry Paine comes out on top for me.'
>
> "Man on the Run" Mick Channon

I'M like a missionary," says Terry Paine as he slopes back on the sofa in his Johannesburg home. "I came here to help bring their soccer on." The glint in his eye suggests that the climate and lifestyle may also have been factors in his decision to move to South Africa, but there is no doubting that he has played his part in popularising football across another continent.

Paine was arguably the finest footballer to don the red and white stripes, something he did a staggering 815 times, yet he has become as much a Cult Hero in South Africa as he is 6,000 miles away in Southampton. That much becomes crystal clear just minutes after I step off the plane at the Johannesburg International Airport to be met by the familiar face of a true Saints legend. Paine is now 67, but he really does not seem a day over 60. Apart from a greying of the hair, he looks pretty much exactly the same as he did when he trudged off the pitch in disappointment at Lawrie McMenemy's decision to substitute him more than 30 years ago in his last match as a Southampton player. Tanned, trim and immaculately turned out, Paine is mobbed by a group of excited airport workers as we walk to his car and he stops to shake all their hands. Just about every other person we pass exchanges a 'hello' with a man who has become one of the faces of what they call 'soccer' in South Africa.

"It goes to show the power of television," he says, as we climb into a car with the words 'Terry Paine MBE' on its side. The power of television, certainly. Mnet SuperSport, the station on which Paine has been an expert analyst for the past decade, is the third biggest sports network in the world and broadcasts to some 53 countries across the African continent.

Yet Paine's celebrity status also underlines the global explosion of interest in football. Rugby union and cricket are traditionally perceived to be the two leading sports in South Africa, but their popularity is actually dwarfed by football which is the number one activity amongst the black population and is increasingly popular across the entire country. Paine was one of the ambassadors who successfully lobbied for the football World Cup to come to South Africa in 2010 and it is obvious that the entire continent is already bubbling over with excitement. It should be some tournament. In Africa, football truly is the people's game and the fervour among 60,000 sell-out crowds at club matches between leading teams like the Orlando Pirates and Kaizer Chiefs has to be seen to be believed.

PAINE LIVES in Rivonia, a northern suburb of Johannesburg where ANC leaders were famously arrested in 1963, leading to the 'Rivonia trial' which saw Nelson Mandela eventually imprisoned for 27 years. He points to a building that was once the Liliesleaf Farm and says: "They've knocked down the old building because they didn't want it to become some sort of shrine, but that's where Mandela was arrested." There are groups of black people along the road-sides selling everything from fruit to replica football shirts and, as we turn into the road which leads to Paine's house, it is obvious that crime continues to be a major problem in South Africa. We must go through two security gates before entering the cul de sac where Paine lives and the high walls are all covered by electric wires.

"It's the way it is," says Paine, who is quick to point out the transformation that has taken place in South Africa since the early 1980s when he began to spend a significant amount of time in the country. "It just had to change, it couldn't continue the way it was, not if South Africa ever wanted to return to the world fold," he says of the apartheid system which openly discriminated against the black majority and lasted until 1990. "When the change came, it was a great moment for the majority of people in this country and it's gone pretty smoothly," he says, "I think people have accepted what it is now. If you are not going to accept it, you will have to move.

"One was worried that there might be a civil war and it never materialised largely thanks to Mandela. He [Mandela] is a magnificent man, he's man of the century, no doubt about that with the way he went about it. He is so well loved in this country and quite rightly so. The World Cup [in 2010] will be a turning point for soccer in this country and the whole of Africa – it is the first time it will be held in this continent and it is a great achievement. It will be a huge boost to the whole continent."

Paine is friends with many of the most prominent people in South African sport and is proud to say that he once lunched with Mandela. A photograph with the man known affection-ately as 'Madiba' takes pride of place at the top of the stairs in his house alongside a picture with golfing great Gary Player. Paine, who plays off a handicap of six, matched Player through the opening seven holes of a recent pro-am event and he also shows me the certificate for a hole-in-one at a tournament earlier in the year. "Just chuck your bags down and we'll take the dog out for a walk and go for some lunch," he says.

Cassie, a friendly dachshund with a weight problem, is, according to Paine's partner Hilly, the most spoiled dog in South Africa. I soon discover this to be the case as I have to give up the front passenger's seat for the benefit of the dog. We head for a local Italian restaurant owned by a big, bald chap called Georgio and the topic of the conversation immediately switches to football, horses and betting. Paine was the consummate wind-up merchant in a Southampton dressing room which his personality dominated between 1957 and 1974 and nothing, it seems, has changed. Georgio has forgotten to place their accumulator bet for the previous weekend's football action and is mercilessly barracked by Paine throughout our meal for costing them a few hundred South African rand. Paine had correctly selected the outcome of all but one of the ten weekend Premier League matches and winks at me as he manages to convince Georgio that Liverpool and Arsenal drew – the one result he got wrong – even though it was actually a 2-1 win for the Gunners.

Paine is a larger than life personality wherever he goes and it is quickly easy to under-stand how he clashed with Lawrie McMenemy as his Southampton career was brought to a somewhat acrimonious end at the age of 35. As much as he has sometimes annoyed people in the past – it was once said that he was 'wanted' by every defender in the First Division – it is clear that Paine lives only in the present and holds no grudges from his football career.

"I love it out here," he says, "South Africa is similar in many ways to England, it's English speaking, there are a lot of Poms out here and there is a massive following for the English game. Also the way of life, the climate is brilliant, the cost of living is good and it's a magnificent country in terms of the scenery. You can go to many different parts of the world but we have got it all here – it's stunning. And I've found a niche for myself with the television.

"I was manager of Cheltenham, but you get to the stage where you think, do you want to go back to manage a Third Division side where you know you will have two years unless you win something or get promotion? You have to move on, you can't live on your reputation all the time. Mnet was growing with the satellite business and it was an ideal opportunity. Now we have our own soccer channel 24 hours a day, seven sports channels and we are as big as any television company in the world."

The studios of Mnet – the company which owns SuperSport and a host of other channels – are vast and cover an entire street. As we enter, we immediately bump into the South African rugby union great Joost van der Westhuizen and an enormous former second-row forward by the name of Kobus Wiese who was also in the 1995 team which lifted the World Cup in such unifying circumstances at the nearby Ellis Park. Paine, though, is no respecter of reputations and an exchange of friendly insults ends with him telling them to follow a "proper sport".

The calls flood in for the evening's phone-in show from Nigeria, Uganda, Angola, Egypt, Tanzania and St Helena, as well as South Africa, and there are even emails from Vietnam, China and London. Illegal satellite decoders mean that Mnet SuperSport is actually broadcast far beyond Africa. Much of the chat surrounds Peter Crouch – "not international class, but can do a job as a sub", according to Paine – and David Beckham. Paine – loud, passionate and opinionated – and who was among England's best outside-rights, was adamant that Beckham should no longer be an automatic selection in the international team long before he was dropped after the 2006 World Cup. "He's been a brilliant player but all he can do now is ping balls around when he is stood at the half-way line and I can still do that," he says.

Paine has developed a sizeable following among SuperSport's viewers. Every week he sits down and replies to fan mail and, while he still gets many autograph requests from Southampton, his post comes from across Africa. There is obviously a knack to punditry and Paine has it – his timing and delivery is not too far behind what he displayed in his prime as a footballer. He often watches more than ten matches every week in various competitions. "I know every single Premiership player and I must see more Premiership matches than any manager in England," he says.

Yet for all his knowledge of the likes of Frank Lampard, Steven Gerrard and Wayne Rooney, I haven't come to South Africa to hear Paine's views on the current crop of football stars. I'm here to find out about a Southampton winger who inspired Saints from Division Three to Division One, helped England to World Cup glory in 1966, yet seems to have antagonised numerous team-mates and opponents, and whose exit from The Dell was not the dignified send off which such a great career merited.

PAINE WAS born in Winchester and he grew up in Highcliffe, which at the time possessed one of the leading amateur clubs in the county. He progressed from the Highcliffe Corinthians into the Winchester City team and the manager Harry Osman, who was a former Southampton outside-left, soon informed his Saints counterpart Ted Bates that the club had a talent good enough to be playing in the senior Hampshire League by the age of 16. Despite competition from Arsenal, Bates' determination meant he got his man. It was a time when Bates was strengthening the Southampton youth team and Paine still remembers the players being congratulated by Sir Matt Busby after they had beaten Manchester United at Old Trafford in the second leg of the 1957 FA Youth Cup semi-final. "We had good exposure with the youth team, we had beaten some decent First Division sides like Spurs," says Paine, "I'd played one [A-team] game in the Isle of Wight against Cowes, then one reserve game against Bristol Rovers and then I remember phoning Ted to find out what was happening at the weekend and he just said, 'you're in the first team on Saturday'. It all happened very quickly."

Paine's debut came on March 16, 1957, against Brentford in a 3-3 draw. Paine then scored in his next two games and he never looked back. Indeed, over the next 17 league seasons, he missed just 22 league games. Or, to put it another way, from the start of the 1957/58 season, he played in 704 of the club's next 726 league matches. It is a breathtaking record and one which no-one in the history of Saints comes close to matching. Paine eventually surpassed Jimmy Dickinson's all-time record for league appearances when he moved to Hereford United. His final figure of 824 was eventually beaten by Peter Shilton, although Tony Ford is the only outfield player to have also gone past that tally. Ford, though, played less in the top-flight and moved around between clubs, particularly towards the end of his career. To put Paine's playing longevity into perspective, it is perhaps enough simply to say that if you added together the number of league matches that Francis Benali and Matthew Le Tissier started in their entire careers you would still be short of Paine's final total.

That Saints were down in Division Three when Paine first broke into the team probably suited him and allowed a gradual process of establishment in senior football. Yet it did not take long before his class shone through. Those who watched Paine regularly comment particularly on two of his qualities. The first was a vision and mesmerising ability to see the correct pass, but perhaps more important was the fact that he had the touch to deliver the ball with unerring accuracy and consistency whether playing it long, short, high or low.

The Southampton journalist John Hughes remembers it was a saying at The Dell during this time that no-one had ever seen Paine cross the ball into the crowd during his 17 seasons at the club. The Southampton inside-right George O'Brien agrees, saying that guesswork was often necessary to predict the crosses of John Sydenham, but that Paine had the ability to place the ball exactly where he wanted.

As Paine sips his cup of tea, he looks almost lost for words as he tries to explain his touch and vision. "There is so much coaching can give you, but it can't give you the natural feel for the game," he says, "and I was lucky because I had a perception of how the game should be played. We didn't have too many training facilities at Southampton, but one thing we did have which I think really helped me was a shooting box in the car park.

"It was concrete walls with a cage on the top and at the end of it there was a bit of wood and the ball would come off at different angles. It was a case of hitting that, left foot, right foot. It was a simple training gadget, but it proved to be very effective from my point of view in being able to play the ball with both feet. It was a case of practice, but my strength was picking out players in small areas. They said I could drop the ball on a six-pence and it stood me in good stead throughout my career."

Paine likens his awareness on the pitch to playing with a constantly evolving photograph in his head of what was going on around him. "I could take a picture of what was happening on the field before the ball got to me," he says. "I had that at every level, even stepping up to internationals, which meant I was always able to pick players out before the ball came to me. There's one thing seeing it, but it's another delivering it and I was lucky to have that combination."

Team-mates, managers, opponents and supporters are unified in their respect of Paine's attributes as a footballer. Ted Bates rated Paine as "easily" the best player in his 66 years at The Dell. "He had two good feet and mentally he was as sharp as a pin," he said in an interview in 2000. In his biography, he also praises Paine's vision. "Terry Paine could see a train coming out of the tunnel before it had gone in the other end," he said.

John Mortimore was assistant manager to Bates for three years before going on to manage Benfica and then returning to Saints. He had previously played for Chelsea and says that Paine and Matthew Le Tissier possessed an ability to strike a football as cleanly as Bobby Charlton and the Portuguese great Eusebio. "Painey's crossing of the ball and passing was superb, he could hang them up there and see things early." Sir Alf Ramsey described Paine as "the thinking foot-baller", while Don Revie said, "he was one of the finest users of the ball there has ever been and, even in full flight, could give crosses of exactly the right weight and accuracy". Bill Shankly was another huge admirer. "Terry Paine had it all – ability, cunning and skill," he said. "He was very aware of all that went on around him and in some respects had the ability of Tom Finney – and he had eyes in the back of his head. Without doubt he was one of the best players since the War and his 19 England caps should have been doubled."

Brian O'Neil says that Paine's crossing was superior to David Beckham. "He was the best crosser of the ball Southampton will ever have. Beckham is a great crosser and passer, but Painey was better than that and he did it with a big, heavy wet ball – not like the balls used now."

PAINE produced many virtuoso performances, but he particularly recalls a 5-1 FA Cup destruction of Manchester City at Maine Road in 1960 when Saints were down in Division Three and City were among the leading teams in Division One. With Paine, as well as the electrifyingly quick John Sydenham, on the wings and George O'Brien and Derek Reeves getting into the penalty area, Bates had constructed a team with real firepower.

"That team was as good a team as I played in," says Paine, "it was much, much better than a Third Division side, we were head and shoulders above that. The performance I turned on that day was as good a performance away from home as I ever played. After that game Manchester City sent their coach Jimmy Meadows down to my house in Winchester and he said, 'I'm just coming through on holiday and I thought I'd come in and say hello'. Obviously he wanted to poach me. We tore their full-backs to ribbons."

Reeves scored four that day and he was first in a line of Southampton strikers to benefit from playing in the same team as Paine. The club unquestionably produced a great conveyor-belt of classy forwards during this era, but it was no happy accident that they all had the same provider in Paine and, to a lesser extent, the Southampton-born Sydenham. Reeves topped 30 goals in a season twice alongside Paine, while George O'Brien scored over 20 on five occasions. Martin Chivers matched that feat twice, Ron Davies three times and Mick Channon once in 1973/74 when he was the division's top goal-scorer. It is also interesting to note that while Jimmy Greaves scored 44 goals in 57 England internationals, 17 of those goals came in only 14 matches alongside Paine. Even in his last two seasons at Hereford United, Paine was helping Dixie McNeil score more than 30 goals in 1974/75 and again in 1975/76. Basically, wherever Paine played in almost 20 years as a professional footballer, there was always an unusually prolific striker in his team. It simply could not be a coincidence. The number of goals Saints scored while Paine was at the club is consequently phenomenal. In his first ten seasons, they surpassed 100 goals on three occasions and averaged just over 88 per year in the league.

Paine's greatness as a footballer also stemmed from his ability to adjust the way he played according to the striker he was feeding. "It doesn't matter what system you play, there is only three ways of getting around the defence, ever," he says. "It's around the outside, over the top or through the middle. All the strikers at Southampton had different strengths and the main one was that they could score goals. Derek Reeves was quick, you could lay it over the top for him. Martin Chivers was a big, strong and powerful individual, quick as well. For George O'Brien you would play a short ball into the box. If you got to the by-line and he was running on to it, it was all over. Ron [Davies] was obviously good in the air and Micky [Channon] was such a willing runner that you could just play balls over the top and he was gone. There were some great combinations."

ENGLAND recognition arrived in 1963 and Paine appeared established in the team as he notched up 19 caps and seven goals, including a memorable winner at Wembley in the Centenary international against a Rest of the World XI which included the likes of Puskas, Eusebio, Di Stefano and Law. He also scored the first hat-trick under floodlights by an England number seven in the 8-3 defeat of Northern Ireland.

Despite his never having played in the top division of English football, Ramsey selected Paine in his squad for the 1966 World Cup finals. "Alf Ramsey obviously saw me and fancied what I could do," he says, "once you got in that squad, he was never interested in how you played for your club, it was how you played when he selected you that mattered. You might be having a bad time for your club, but if you were having a good time for England you were in that squad. He never worried too much about your current form, all he was interested in was how you performed for him which was nice. He ran it almost like a club side.

"We were moving forward under Alf and it was a great experience. He was focused on what he wanted to do and he didn't suffer fools. He really believed in his England team and also what it would mean for the country to win a World Cup. When the call came in 1966 to leave Nobby Stiles out because of his rough play, he said, 'I select the team, Nobby Stiles is playing and if you want to change that I will resign'. Alf was very strict in many ways, but had a very dry sense of humour at the same time."

Paine has no complaints despite being somewhat unfortunate to lose his place for the latter stages of the tournament to Alan Ball as Ramsey moved away from the use of wingers. After England had drawn the first game against Uruguay, Paine came into the team and performed well in the 2-0 win against Mexico, but ended the game concussed following a nasty clash of heads. "The geezer headed me in the back of the head and I played all the game and then I woke up on the treatment table," he says, "I didn't even know I'd played the game and I was groggy for four or five days. I was okay, but Alf left me out and they beat France and next thing they were in the quarter-finals.

"It would have been interesting to see if I had stayed 100 per cent what would have happened and whether he would have still brought Alan [Ball] in. He might have had the idea to bring Alan back in anyway. I don't know, but whatever the situation was, he got it right because they won the World Cup and I've never complained about my time with England. I really appreciate the fact that he brought me on board when I was a Second Division player."

Ball believes that his inclusion ahead of Paine was because it suited the system Ramsey wanted. "Painey was a terrific crosser of the ball, he made goals for people and was a clever player," says Ball, "mainly he was a right-sided winger in the old days. Alf wanted somebody who could roam around a little bit more. We were the wingless wonders after all."

Cliff Huxford felt the freedom Paine was granted at club level to create havoc in attack meant that he was not disciplined enough at tracking back. "Terry Paine didn't play as many games for England as he should have done," says Huxford, "going forward he was as good as gold, but when he played for England, he had to work back. And you cannot change your game just like that."

At the time, Paine was sometimes concerned that playing in the Second Division might adversely affect his international opportunities, largely because it could be holding back his development as a player. "Maybe I wasn't getting that competition – if I'd been playing against the Manchester Uniteds, the Arsenals that could have made my game possibly even sharper, I don't know," he says, "but whenever I got itchy feet we seemed to get promotion. In 1966 [when Saints went up], it was 'well I've waited all this time, so there is no reason to move on, because we are there'."

PAINE, who briefly held Saints' all-time league goal-scoring record and still only stands behind Mick Channon and Matthew Le Tissier in that list, finished his Southampton career with some 187 league and cup goals. His loyalty to Saints in the decade preceding that achievement is notable. It was, however, an era when players had less power and Bates held firm. "He wouldn't sell you if you were any good," says George O'Brien.

Indeed, it was not until 1967, when Saints were in the First Division that Bates admitted that "many top clubs have been angling for him [Paine]", adding, "his perception for the game is brilliant and the accuracy and penetration of his passing devastating. I have never seen him short at any level of the game". Paine has no regrets at not moving on in the early 1960s, although he says this interest was never something which Bates discussed with him.

"I was never, ever taken into Ted's office to say someone wanted me, even to say they had turned it down," he says, "so I never really knew who was coming in. I know Tottenham were chasing me for a long time – I know that for a fact. They had an assistant manager called Harry Evans [a war-time team-mate of Ted Bates] who would wait for me outside grounds and he would be, 'how are you going, you are playing well'. If I had moved, Tottenham would have been my choice because Jimmy Greaves was there. But who knows how it would have gone? I could have made the move and it could have been a disaster or I might have been a great success. I certainly wouldn't have had the affinity with another club that I had with Southampton and a manager who truly believed in me."

Paine grins and then lets me in on a scam he had going with a friend in the press at the time. "We had a guy called John Tudor and he used to work a little bit for the *People*," he remembers, "he used to come to me to and say, '£25 or £50 and we'll say you put in a transfer request, tell me you have and then you can deny it on Monday'. He used to give me the £50 and then on the Monday the *Echo* would phone up and I would be 'no, what a load of rubbish'."

It is a tale which sums up another facet to Paine's character – and one which almost certainly helped him throughout his career. 'Mischievous' and 'crafty' are adjectives that former team-mates have all used to me when describing Paine. For all their appreciation of his footballing qualities, Paine was not liable to win any popularity contests in the dressing room. But he had supreme confidence in his own ability and wasn't scared to show it. Denis Hollywood says that Paine would always make a point of telling the opposing winger to be careful because "we have a head-case at left-back [meaning Hollywood]". "I used to think 'that's nice'," says Hollywood, "but it probably worked to put them off."

Former team-mates concur that Paine can be good company, but that he is also adept at getting under people's skin. Frank Saul once roomed with him and was so fed-up that he apparently put all his clothes and golf clubs outside the room and locked the door. "Terry came down and was laughing about it and he said, 'do you think he's trying to tell me something?'" remembers Hollywood, "and we all said, 'yeah'. But he didn't care, it didn't bother him whatsoever."

Paine accepts he had a reputation in the game for kicking out at full-backs. "I never used to worry about the full-backs, especially in the early days. I got a reputation, but what I never understood was, why is it only defenders who are allowed to kick? I might have kicked a full-back if he had kicked me, although I mostly got George Kirby to do that. 'Big' George would come over and look after me and sort out the full-back. There were players who would kick you – they would kick the grass if it moved.

"The first thing if you go and watch a defender as a scout at the top of the form is, 'did he impose himself on the opposition?' And that means, 'did he sort them out?' I wasn't going to let anyone sort me out."

Another of his gifts, however, was an instinct for self-preservation. It was a quality which probably infuriated opposition defenders more than the verbal and physical niggling he could dish out. "Terry was brilliant at that," says Hollywood, "he might kick someone or say something and the next moment he would have switched wings and he would be away from it." Brian O'Neil concurs. "Opposition players didn't have a good word to say about him," he says. "He had a nasty streak, he could set out to hurt you and if you thought, 'I've got him now' he would jump out of the way.

"I saw 'Chopper' Harris at Peter Osgood's funeral and he told me that he didn't like playing Terry because he had done him in a tackle. With a lot of wingers if you hammered them you could think you had got them, but Painey would be straight back after you." This characteristic in his temperament, however, only enhanced his popularity. As well as being an outstanding player, Paine was a fierce competitor.

That he played for so many years with so few injuries is a testament to his knack for recognising danger as well as his fitness and bravery. "I was lucky, but I was sharp, I could see what was happening quickly," he says, "There is a skill in not being caught with the ball, although the majority of it has to be down to luck. You try not to do silly things and leave yourself exposed to be kicked. If you have got good awareness and position your body correctly on a field when you receive a ball it makes a difference. I would get my body right on the touchline when I received the ball and they can't tackle you from behind then. They could only come at one angle." Team-mates used to call him 'Pogo' for his knack of hurdling trouble.

A MEASURE of the longevity of Paine's stature at Saints came when he returned to Southampton in 2003 for the FA Cup final and was still recognised by hundreds of Saints fans around the Millennium Stadium. Back in 1966, his popularity was such that a fan club was set up for him and he was even elected onto the city council in 1969, topping the poll in the Bargate ward. Paine continues to take a strong interest in politics, although his experience as a local Conservative councillor was marred by criticisms that he did not attend enough meetings.

He says: "We were canvassing and I went down to a restaurant at Below Bar which was run by a Greek-Cypriot guy and he said, 'Terry, you have all the votes. They will all vote for you' and I topped the poll. It was a bit of fun, it was different. I took a bit of flak. I was called a playboy councillor and this, that and the other." Paine's foray into politics is typical of someone who has dabbled in most things at different times in his life. He has also run a restaurant, a fruit and vegetable shop, two pubs and owned several racehorses. Indeed, he has an interest in several horses in Johannesburg and was delighted to see one of them secure its first victory while I was staying with him. But, of course, there is always a time for any player when football ends.

The arrival as manager in 1973 of Lawrie McMenemy signalled a completely new approach. McMenemy felt there were discipline problems in the dressing room which needed tackling and Paine was to be the first big casualty. The clash was, perhaps, inevitable, particularly at the respective stages of their careers. Although McMenemy proved himself adept at handling other big personalities in his career, it was clear that he would be sensitive to any possible threat to his own position. Paine's unique status and previously close relationship with Bates ensured that he would be perceived as a danger, especially in the early days when McMenemy was unproven as a manager at the highest level. "They simply couldn't stand each other," says Mick Channon in his autobiography, Man on the Run. "They both had dominating personalities and wanted to be top man." Partly it was due to the timing, but there is a certain irony in the incompatibility between men who enjoyed such success at Saints in their different capacities.

Paine was disappointed at the way it all ended and he believes that he could have had a better send-off. Yet his whole outlook means that he does not dwell particularly on the past. "It probably was right for change at the time, it probably was right for Ted [Bates] to stand down and for me to move on," he says. "Obviously it becomes hard when it happens and at the time I didn't agree, but you move on and forget it. You can't hold grudges.

"I think he [McMenemy] probably did see me as a threat. He is one of these people that would want to do it his way. There's nothing wrong with that, but you have casualties and I never really felt he gave me a chance. He never sat down and said, 'this is how I think it's going to be, your personality is all over the club, maybe there could be a parting of the ways'. Just to call me in after all that time and say, 'I'm giving you a free transfer'. I hadn't even had a testimonial at that stage and, although I came back for one, it was affected hugely as I was trying to do a job at Hereford at the same time. I made £8,000 for 18 years' service." After Southampton, Paine helped Hereford into the Second Division under John Sillett and then had a stint as Cheltenham manager and coached at Coventry and various multi-racial clubs in South Africa.

HE MAY be only three years short of his seventieth birthday, but Paine's zest for life remains undiminished. After a two hour interview, we are out to another of his favourite restaurants where he is again given the full red-carpet treatment as we feast on a huge bucketful of prawns. He does not go to bed until gone midnight, but a knock on my door just after 6am signals that the weather is fine and we will be heading for the golf course.

He is playing a four-ball with two friends from SuperSport and a local professional who apparently supplies all of his golf shirts. A person's character is stripped open on the golf course and it is interesting to watch Paine. He obviously has an outstanding temperament for sport. Hugely competitive (there are a fair few expletives), yet he always keeps his emotions under control and has the ability to give every shot his maximum attention. He takes few risks, occasionally makes a few remarks which wind up the opposition and rolls in a birdie three at the last for a round of 79 as he and his partner run out comfortable winners. As he goes to put his card in, he grins, "okay, so what was that? 82". The other players laugh. "What? I'm getting old," he protests.

The professional he is playing golf with also gives him a tip for a horse running in a race later that afternoon and there are whoops of delight as 'West in the Wind' canters to victory in the 3.15 at Newmarket. Its price at the start of the race was 7/2, but Paine had somehow negotiated odds of 7/1 with his regular bookie.

On the following day (my last staying with him in South Africa), Paine takes me to a shopping centre in Johannesburg and he seems to know about every third person that we pass. They include the former Leeds defender Lucas Radebe, who helped South Africa win the African Nations Cup in 1996 and Dave King, a director at Glasgow Rangers, who was about to head out to Augusta to caddy for Gary Player in the US Masters.

Before I leave, the final job is to ask Paine to sign some Saints shirts which already have the squiggles of the likes of Francis Benali, Ivan Golac, Nick Holmes, Jimmy Case and Cliff Huxford. A search in my suitcase proves fruitless and it suddenly becomes evident that the baggage handlers at the airport have helped themselves. Paine then disappears upstairs and offers me several signed photographs, three golf caps and the SuperSport shirt which all the presenters wear. As energetic as ever, he is back in the television studio later that evening for a match between Liverpool and Fulham and is then playing in a pro-am golf tournament the following day.

TERRY PAINE, the sometimes abrasive and ebullient personality, stirs mixed assessments among former players, but my own experience was of a generous and charismatic man who is as sharp as a needle and interested in everything around him. His quality as a footballer, however, sparks no debate and he was a justifiable inclusion when the Football League announced its list of 100 legends in 1998.

Matthew Le Tissier might have been the most breathtaking and Mick Channon the most fun, but researching this book and interviewing so many former players and supporters leaves me satisfied that Terry Paine was Southampton's best ever footballer.

As I make my way into the airport for my return flight to Heathrow, Paine asks who else I have been interviewing. Amongst others, I tell him that I am seeing Denis Hollwood the following Friday. Paine has only occasionally seen Hollwood in the past 35 years, but smirks as he instantly remembers a pre-season tour to Japan which his team-mate was devastated to miss because Ted Bates did not think him fit enough. "Can you give Denis a message for me," laughs Paine. "Ask him one thing. Just say to him, 'how's your weight?'"

RON DAVIES

1966-1973

SAINTS CAREER

Games	281
Goals	153
Caps	29

MAGIC MOMENT

All four goals at Old Trafford in the 1969 4-1 demolition of Manchester United, whose team contained Best, Law and Charlton

'HEAD OF GOD'

'The finest centre-forward in Europe.'

Sir Matt Busby

IT is getting on for ten years since Ron Davies has given an interview and five years since he has even talked about football. It shows.

"So what about this Wayne Rooney," he says. "I saw something about him on the news a few weeks ago and I'd never heard of him. Who's he? Does he play for Chelsea?

"And what's happening at Southampton? Where are they nowadays?

"Who won the league last year then? I heard Chelsea have got all the money.

"And how are Manchester United getting on?"

Many ex-players have difficulty leaving the game behind. Like addicts, they find it impossible to look away, even though each reminder of past glories may cause a certain pain. The sight of comparatively average players becoming financially secure must be like having sand-paper scraped across those wounds. Either Ron Davies couldn't give a stuff, or he has decided that the best therapy is one of complete withdrawal. How else could one of Britain's finest strikers have not heard of the star player at the most famous club in the world? Still, Wayne Rooney probably doesn't know who Ron Davies is either.

Yet it is Davies, not Rooney, who has been twice top-scorer in English football's top division. What's more, his tally of 37 league goals in the 1966/67 season has not been bettered by anyone – not even Rush, Dalglish, Keegan, Lineker, Cole, Shearer, Henry or Van Nistelrooy – in the 39 seasons since.

With Thierry Henry gliding around, Wayne Rooney has probably never been described as the best centre-forward in Europe either. The legendary former Manchester United manager Sir Matt Busby thought Ron Davies was and wanted to smash the British transfer record of £110,000 for Alan Ball in 1966 by paying £200,000 to bring Davies to Old Trafford during the late 1960s.

Fortunately for Saints fans, the Welsh striker was kept at The Dell for the best years of his football career between 1966 and 1973. He played in a team which was often struggling for survival in the old First Division, all the more incredible then that, in just over three years, Davies amassed 90 goals in 123 league games. In that period his phenomenal strike-rate saw him scoring with greater regularity than any player in Southampton's history and, unlike his predecessors, he was doing it at the highest level in English football. Regular visitors to The Dell are convinced that he could head a football better than anyone who ever lived.

Yet while Rooney enjoys an estimated basic income of £60,000 a week before sponsorship deals and endorsements, Davies is short of money and in poor health. He is 64 and lives in a mobile residential vehicle (an RV) on a site in New Mexico. His body has been wrecked by football. He feels the game probably owes him something, but insists that he is not bitter. "Southampton gave me a chance and I think I repaid them," he says, "it was a wonderful life, but when it's over, it's over and you have to move on. I was loyal to Southampton, I gave it my best and suddenly you are out." He laughs and adds: "In my day, the players were treated like cattle – if they could have shot you, they would have probably shot you."

TRACKING RON DAVIES down and persuading him to give an interview has been among the more bizarre experiences of my journalistic career. As you might expect of a former footballer who appears uncertain which division his former clubs now play in, he is cut off from the English game.

Davies has not been back to England since 1998, when he was coaching football in Florida. On that occasion he returned with his wife Chris for a dinner held in honour of his former manager Ted Bates. Davies looked in good health and, even in the company of many other Southampton legends, he was the star attraction among supporters. They flocked to get his autograph and, when he was introduced, he received a standing ovation. Davies is also a talented artist and had sketched caricatures of his team-mates and managers throughout his career. The climax of the evening was his presentation of a wonderful drawing of Bates which he had spent a week crafting.

Yet after that appearance, Davies seemed to disappear and no-one heard from him for several years. Former team-mates assumed that he was continuing to enjoy life in the Sunshine State. But then an article appeared in a national newspaper in 2003 claiming he was living in some sort of hostel. Various friends and media attempted to follow the story up, but the source for the report remained anonymous and no-one actually discovered the truth.

The two most recent addresses which people seemed to have for Davies were both in Casselberry, Florida. It so happened that I was spending a week in Florida just a few miles from Casselberry in June 2005, and so I decided to look these addresses up. It was of no great surprise to hear that the present occupants did not know of a Ron Davies.

Over the months which followed, some worrying news (and gossip) continued to seep out regarding his health and general state. In an interview, his former team-mate John Sydenham said: "The last news I have of Ron was not good. Terry Paine told me last year he'd heard Ron was living in Mexico and had fallen on hard times." Within a few weeks of this information, a group of supporters had written to Southampton Football Club and several other organisations in a bid to find Davies with the suggestion of holding some sort of benefit match.

The Welsh Football Association replied, saying the last address they had was in Florida and their information was that he had moved west and was "down on his luck". They added: "Naturally our current manager, John Toshack, would be very keen to help, given that he played in many of his early internationals alongside Ron."

The help of various media was also enlisted, including the BBC, whose football writer John May contacted the corporation's Los Angeles Bureau. He had heard reports that Davies had been seen in Albuquerque and Phoenix. One rumour was that he had separated from his wife and had moved into the 'underclass' of society.

Staff at Southampton Football Club, meanwhile, had heard that Davies was in extremely poor health. I also contacted Norwich City, another former club, and was told that they also only had his Florida address. They said that they did not receive a reply when they invited him for their centenary dinner in 2002. The search appeared to have ended, however, when the Southampton club secretary Liz Coley issued the following letter to Saints fan Jim Smith:

Dear Mr Smith
Thank you for your letter addressed to various members of staff regarding the welfare of Ron Davies.

We have been making some inquiries regarding Ron and can clarify that our understanding of the situation is that he is unfortunately in a nursing home in America. We have not had any contact for a number of years now, but we believe he is being well cared for; we did used to forward mail to an address that we had in Florida, but some time ago we received a compliment slip from the nursing home requesting that we stopped forwarding any letters as Ron was not in a position to read or reply to the correspondence.

Thank you for your concern regarding Ron Davies, we are sorry this is not the news you were hoping for.

Yours sincerely,
Liz Coley
Club Secretary

The news came as a hammer blow to a generation of supporters who idolised Davies. For this book, however, I still wanted to find a family member to verify what really had happened to Davies since 1998. He was an almost unanimous choice as one of the club's greatest players and Cult Heroes. For there to be so little information about his recent life all seemed rather strange. Apparently he and his wife had stayed with friends near Winchester while they were last back in England in 1998, and I managed to get hold of them. The mixed messages continued when I spoke with his friend who seemed rather surprised to hear what the club had been told.

"That's not right," he said, "I spoke to Ron a few months ago and he was fine. He's still with Chris [his wife] and they have moved from Florida, but they are in New Mexico and both working. They moved recently and haven't been in touch with a new telephone number, but we still hear from them every so often and I'm sure they will contact us soon. We had a wonderful week when they came to stay for Ted Bates' dinner. Ron drank us out of house and home! It was a fantastic evening and he got a wonderful ovation and the queue to his table was huge all night long."

Given that Davies had lost touch with friends as well as team-mates and past football clubs, it was clear that I needed to contact a family member to find out the truth. Davies' rather common surname made tracing his sisters almost impossible, but he does also have a brother who played professionally for both Arsenal and Charlton Athletic. Most clubs have contact details for ex-players, so the next logical step was contacting the respective press offices. At Arsenal, they are clearly well trained in the art of fobbing people off and, before I could explain exactly what I wanted, I was rather robotically advised to send my request via email. Sensing this would be futile, I telephoned Charlton and was immediately given a number for Bernard Wickham who is chairman of the Charlton Athletic Former Players' Association. He could not have been more helpful and, within a week, he had replied with a telephone number and the news that Paul Davies (Ron's brother) would be happy to talk.

When I got hold of Paul, it was difficult to know exactly where to start. I explained my project and why Ron was an overwhelming choice for a book which paid tribute to the great players in Southampton's history, but also that I understood he might not be in the best of health. "It's true that he is not having the best of times at the moment," said Paul, "he and Chris had to sell their house in Florida because they couldn't afford it. It was a shame because he loved it out there and he was having a good time. But they have moved to New Mexico where it is better for him.

"Since then, they had been moving from place to place and staying in different motels until they got hold of this mobile home recently. He has had arthritis and an infection in his knee. He is also having trouble with his hip. He just does manual work. It is a bit of a come down from when he was as a footballer, but he was never one to push himself and he maybe let things slide. He also got taken to the cleaners a few times and lost his money. He is very trusting. He won't come home. I've asked him about coming back and he just says, 'there's nothing for me there'. He can be a bit stubborn."

Paul duly passed on Ron's address as well as a contact number for his wife's work as they do not have a telephone in their home. When I then spoke with Chris Davies, she pretty much repeated what Paul had said. Ron stopped his football coaching about five years ago and they have been living in Albuquerque for the past three years. They left Florida because Chris lost her job, and it was also possible for them to get a better health plan in New Mexico. Unlike England, there is no National Health Service in the United States. Their health policy, however, only covers 'necessities', meaning Ron must wait for a new hip.

"I worked for the government in Florida and they laid everyone off," said Chris, "Ron still works for a construction company doing tiling, but it is about time that he retired. He will be 65 next year. He still looks in great shape, his heart is good, he is slim – he is 6ft and 190lbs – but he has had real problems with his knee and his hips. At one point he was in hospital every day with his knee and they thought they might have to amputate his leg.

"Now he really needs a hip transplant otherwise he will be crippled. I would like him to get his hip done, retire and get his social security. He gave his all to soccer, but he has got nothing now. What would he be worth if he was playing today? About £2m?" I don't like to say it, but it would probably be seven or eight times that.

AS A FOOTBALLER, Ron Davies was something of a freak. When he was bought from Norwich City in 1966, he cost a Saints club record £55,000 and, if I had a pound for every time someone has told me over the past year that he was "the best header of a ball I saw in my life", I think I would be close to pocketing that transfer fee myself. It was, of course, true and most seasoned observers of Saints regard Davies as the finest 'number nine' in the club's history.

Davies' ability to jump and hang in the air was almost supernatural. He was 6ft in height, but he would regularly out-leap much taller defenders and even goalkeepers. Photographs and old videos of his playing days provide evidence for this talent and the distance between his feet and the ground while he hangs in the air is quite incredible. His head was often as high as the cross-bar when he jumped for a header. It was also not uncommon for him to out-jump goalkeepers when meeting crosses. To do this, there was no need for any Maradona-style 'hand of God'. Davies simply had the 'head of God'.

So how was he able to jump so high? It was a subject Davies remained quiet on until an interview in 1998 when he explained that, during his three years with Chester City, he would be taken through a gruelling training routine with an army instructor. Each and every day, he would be made to wear huge, heavy boots weighing several kilograms and would exhaust himself by jumping over hurdles. When he changed into football boots, the transformation was dramatic – it was as if he had wings attached to his feet. "Bill Lambton was a tough old character, who took us training at Chester and I owe him such a lot," he revealed. "It was bloody hard – but when I took those boots off – I felt I could jump over the moon."

The benefit to Saints was obvious. Terry Paine, John Sydenham and later Tommy Jenkins were the club's wingers at the time and they knew that any cross in the direction of the back-post was almost inevitably a goal. Manager Ted Bates, who also brought Terry Paine and Mick Channon to The Dell, regards Davies as his best signing. "I'd seen him play and when I saw Painey and Sydenham working I thought, 'my goodness, if I can get Davies in the middle of those two, he's going to get a lot of goals and we are going to get a lot of goals'," he said. Bates was proved right and both Paine and Sydenham agree that Davies was a very special footballer.

"We used to play golf at Stoneham and there was a clock miles up on the wall and I bet all the club members that Ron could jump up and reach it," says Paine. "They all said, 'don't be daft, that's impossible'. But Ron could do it and, for a round of drinks, I used to get him to jump up and reach the clock. On the field, Ron had that perception. His timing was so good that he appeared to hang in mid-air. He could just hang there and still deliver. I saw him score two goals for Wales against Scotland and he headed one that hit the stanchion and then came out before anyone realised that he had scored. He was extraordinary – a great player.

"Just imagine having someone who could out-jump anyone in any defence. The timing of his running and jumping was absolute perfection. He could score on the floor, but it got to the stage where I said, 'bugger this, I'm not going to play it on the floor, I'm going to chip it'. I knew I could trust his head more than his feet."

Sydenham added: "He was also a lot better on the ground than people gave him credit for. He also had the ability to make ordinary crosses good ones which was very handy at times."

John Mortimore became the assistant manager while Davies was at the club. "When he headed the ball, it was like kicking it because of the power he got," he says, "he was bulky, strong and difficult to play against. He scored some great goals and was just an outstanding player. Ted knew exactly what he wanted when he went to get him."

Saints fan Andy Leitch can testify to that power as he vividly recalled being knocked clean off his feet by one of his headers as he stood in the Archers end. He said of his boyhood hero: "To the supporters at the time, he was as popular as Mick Channon or Matthew Le Tissier. He was a bit like a Le Tissier with his head because he scored all different types of goals. He could score glancing headers, lay the ball off or power them in. When I was about 12, he whistled a header past the post and it came straight for me and knocked me off my feet. People had to pick me up, but that was the power he could get. In those days, the ball was like concrete as well."

Davies was not simply worshipped in the usual way that supporters treat their best players. His talents were so unique that the appreciation somehow ran deeper. He radiated a certain presence and fans, team-mates and, possibly even opponents, were in awe.

Peter Osgood reckoned Davies could hang in the air for "about five minutes". According to Saints fan Jack Halford, "Ron Davies was the finest header of a ball in the world and that included the great Pelé", while fan Jim Chamberlain says, "he was the greatest centre-forward of that generation and one of the best in the world. Manchester United wanted to pay £200,000, but it shows you what Saints thought of him that they fought tooth and nail for him to stay. In this day and age he would have gone".

Those who knew Davies also paint the picture of a somewhat bohemian figure. He liked a drink and legend has it that he would pay the staff at a Southampton nightspot called 'Skyways' a healthy tip to ensure he got back to his car where he sometimes would sleep until the morning. He was certainly one of the 'Ale-House' crew in terms of his capacity for drinking, although it was also not unusual for him to disappear from the group and be found sat sketching away. Davies' drawings were so good that he would have a regular slot in the local newspapers while at both Norwich and Southampton for his caricatures of team-mates.

His good looks and Herculean physique also made him something of a sex symbol and, although his fame was concentrated in the Southampton area, there is a legitimate comparison with George Best in this regard. In one newspaper, he was compared to a pop-star and he was photographed with the actresses Jenny Hanley and Julie Edge in 1970 for a publicity photo-shoot. Hanley had a role as a 'Bond girl' in the 1969 film *On Her Majesty's Secret Service.*

DAVIES' PLACE among the best, most popular and enigmatic Southampton players is clearly beyond doubt. Yet, after severing his ties with football over the past eight years, would he want to talk? My first telephone conversation with his wife Chris ended with her saying that she would ask Ron and explain that I wanted to feature him in this book. When I called back a few days later, she repeated the problems Ron was having with his health and said that he would call the following weekend. Two weeks passed and I heard nothing. At this point, I thought it would be better to write to him so that I could at least set out in my own words exactly what the book was about and why it would be incomplete without Ron's contribution.

Around a week later, I received an email from another family member on Ron's behalf. It explained that Ron had not been in the best of health and that his medical bills were a cause for concern. It said that my request had surprised Ron. It went on to say that Ron had always helped with interviews in the past and was still willing to cooperate, but that a small contribution to his medical bills would be appreciated. There was also something of a carrot being dangled. Apparently Ron might be prepared to reveal the secrets of his heading ability. All in all, it seemed a reasonable request.

I then spoke again with Chris and explained it would be possible to make a modest contribution to Ron's health bills and that, perhaps more significantly, I would also see what the possibility was of staging some sort of benefit match or other function in his honour. Initial conversations with some of the representatives of various Southampton fans' groups had indicated that there would be considerable support for such an event. I explained to Chris that I would ideally like to come out to New Mexico to meet Ron in person for the interview. She said that this would be "no problem".

An email the following week, however, said that Ron would rather speak on the phone. When I spoke again with Chris, she thought it would be okay for me to visit and that "this weekend" should be fine. I was about to book my flight when I made a last call to check whether it was convenient. It wasn't. She said that Ron would prefer to speak on the phone initially and that he would "definitely" call on Sunday. There was also the suggestion of a video conference call.

Sunday came and went and I heard nothing. At this point, I had decided that I would not be calling again. Although no-one had said so, it seemed that Ron simply did not want to be interviewed. Then, out of the blue the following Tuesday, Chris called. "I'm so sorry," she said, "we tried to call on Sunday, but the network was down because it was Mother's Day. I'll have Ron call this Sunday." To be honest, my hopes weren't high. But, on Sunday evening and slightly earlier than arranged, the phone rang and it was Chris again.

"Jeremy," she said, "here's Ron."

RON DAVIES speaks with a curious accent. You can certainly tell that he is Welsh, but also that he has spent the better part of 30 years in the US. Most pleasing, however, is that he sounded extremely upbeat, despite his hip problem. Throughout our conversation, which lasted about 45 minutes, he was both funny and friendly. He asks how I am, congratulates me on writing a book, apologises for the delay in getting back to me and then inquires after most of his former team-mates.

"Denis Hollywood," he says, "we used to call him 'the silent assassin' and how are Jimmy Gabriel and Hughie Fisher? Terry Paine, what a player he was, the best crosser of a ball I ever saw. And what's Mick Channon doing now?" I explain that Channon is still training horses and Davies replies: "I thought he would be, we are actually surrounded by horse trainers out here on the RV site. They are really interesting people. Our neighbours are extremely friendly and we are baby-sitting their dog today. We love animals, we had two dogs in Florida which died and we have a beautiful cat. The dog and the cat get on great."

Although he was looking forward to the 2006 World Cup, it's clear that Davies has made no effort to keep up to date with football and he has no knowledge of recent results in the English leagues. "I fancy Argentina to do well in the World Cup, but the Americans don't really like soccer so it's hard to know what is going on," he says, "they don't give it any coverage, it is all baseball, American football and basketball out here. I enjoyed coaching soccer, one guy was so impressed he gave me a Cadillac – he said, 'that is yours'. I felt like I was the Prince of Wales when I was driving it. I was coach for 15 years and we won three trophies. The American women are superb at soccer, they won the World Cup. The girls have a much better attitude than the men. In California, the men would miss training because they would prefer to go surfing. It was a joke. I still sometimes coach privately now with individuals, but not with teams as I'm not really mobile enough – I can't really swing my hips and it hurts to walk.

"The doctors have said the rest of my body is fine. I suppose I shouldn't be surprised. At Southampton, the doctors told me that I'd have problems with my hips – it's due entirely to all that jumping. What people sometimes don't realise is that I used to go in the gym as well in the afternoon and get the youth team lads to cross it for me and I was up and down on that hard floor. They did warn me, but when you are that age, you think you are indestructible. Unfortunately I wasn't, but I'm still slim – and I think I'll be around for a few more years yet."

Even when he was in his prime, Davies appeared to be a somewhat reluctant celebrity and he once said that a reason for moving to the US was because he was not recognised there. But he is happy to talk openly about where he lives and what he is doing. His main work is for the firm Duncan Constructions. "I can build a house," he says, "I do landscaping and it is so interesting. It is great, in a way I don't want to give it up, but my hip hurts, so I can't really enjoy it. I go out at 5.45am and finish at 4pm and the people I work with are really nice. We have been in Albuquerque for three years and we love it here. It never rains and they are building like crazy here. We are 12,000 feet up in the mountains and it is wonderful."

Davies is at a loss to explain the various rumours about what he has been doing over the past few years, but admits that he is shy of publicity and speaking about himself. "Some people like looking backwards and talking about what they have done," he says. "I can't be bothered with that, I haven't got any ego. Anyway, you've got to go forward, you've got to get on with life, haven't you?" That has certainly been his outlook in recent years, but, for a short while, he is happy to reminisce.

RAISED IN the small Welsh town of Holywell in north Wales, Davies always had talent, but equally possessed a single-minded determination to realise his ambition.

"My parents didn't think I would be a professional," he says, "they thought it was risky because I might not make it and I wanted to prove them wrong. I used to practice all the time on my own. I would always carry a tennis ball around with me and I would practice and practice. I had it in my heart to be a professional footballer. To really make it you have to give it 100%."

Chester City were the club to spot his potential when a scout saw him score six goals for his village side at the age of just 13. "I still remember my first day at Chester as a boy," says Davies, "my mum had given me sandwiches and I left them on the chair, I'd gone into the referee's room and, by the time I had come back, they were all gone. There was a guy called Tommy Gardner and he said, 'I didn't touch them'. There were bits of paper underneath the chair and it went towards the bathtub. He said it was mice or rats, but I just thought they were winding me up. Anyway, they set a mouse trap and left a piece of bread on it. Within five minutes it went 'bang' and there was this huge rat – it was the size of a cat. It was massive and we caught five of them that day. I said, 'I heard that soccer was a rat race, but I didn't expect this'."

After scoring 44 goals in 94 league games for Chester, he moved to Second Division Luton Town where he notched up another 21 in only 32 league games during the 1962/63 season. It was enough to persuade Norwich to buy him and, during three years at Carrow Road, he scored a further 66 goals. Even now, he remains among the highest goal-scorers in the history of Norwich as well as Southampton and, along with Mick Channon, he was voted into Norwich's 'hall of fame' for their 100 greatest players at the turn of the century. There was an outcry locally when he left.

Ted Bates, though, had earmarked Davies as the man who could make Saints a force in Division One and his goals during the 1966/67 were to keep Saints alive as they finished fourth from bottom in their first season in the top-flight. In all competitions, Davies scored 43 goals, including an incredible run from September to November when he scored in ten consecutive league matches. By the end of the season, he had scored three league hat-tricks, including a four goal haul against Aston Villa on the concluding day of the season. In local paper reports, Davies was described as, "a player The Dell crowd have certainly taken to their hearts". By February 1967, his popularity was such that a fan club had been formed in Southampton.

Over the 1966/67 season, he scored 12 more than Jimmy Greaves and 18 more than Denis Law. Davies was aged just 24 and it had been an unparalleled debut season in the top division of English football. In an interview that summer, it was clear that he had already become something of a celebrity. "I really cannot go far in the locality without being recognised and it does mean that if you want a quiet day or two you have to get well away from Southampton," he said.

Davies started the 1967/68 campaign in similar fashion with nine goals in five games to take his tally to 52 goals in his first 52 league and cup games for the club. It was stunning stuff, particularly in a team fighting relegation. By the end of that 1967/68 season, Davies was joint top-scorer in the First Division with George Best. Both had scored 28 goals. Davies contributed another 20 in the league the following season, before his most memorable match when Saints battered a Manchester United team containing Bobby Charlton, Denis Law and George Best by a score-line of 4-1 at Old Trafford. All four Southampton goals were scored by Davies. It is a feat Wayne Rooney has also not yet matched. Davies has not, it seems, kept many reminders of his football past, but he does still have the *Match of the Day* video of that remarkable performance.

"I have got the tape and I've watched it in slow motion," he says, "and when I see the way I could jump in the air, I do think, 'hell man, that was a talent'. People have asked me for years how I did it and it was just a talent I had. My parents were there at Old Trafford that day and it was great. I felt sorry for Bill Foulkes, the Manchester United centre-back, as I don't think he played another game. But the goalkeeper didn't come off his line, so it was like picking cherries off a tree. I must admit, though, that the game now is three times as quick as it was then. You had so much time in those days to do what you wanted to do, but it was nice afterwards when Matt Busby said I was the greatest centre-forward in Europe."

In an interview with Jimmy Hill after the game, Davies describes Manchester United as a "team of individuals", adding, "I always go to the far-post. I don't like going to the near-post, I think it is a lot more difficult to get goals on the near-post". Three of Davies' goals had come courtesy of far-post headers and he had used his strength to out-muscle the Manchester United defence for his fourth. Don Revie, the Leeds United manager, said: "Easily the best performance of the season so far was that of Southampton centre-forward Ron Davies...afterwards, Matt Busby described Welsh international Davies as 'the best centre-forward in Europe' and I would not quibble with such a description. Certainly, I have seen only one player throughout my career who can be classed in the same bracket as Davies as a header of the ball – John Charles."

Earlier in the year, Davies had starred for Wales in the Home Internationals tournament and was again winning admirers. The England manager Sir Alf Ramsey said he scored the type of goals that, "fans would go hundreds of miles to see", while the Southampton manager Ted Bates added, "this only confirms that he is the best centre-forward in the business. The highest compliment I can pay Ron is that I only wish he was an Englishman". Bates, however, would not let other clubs near his prized centre-forward. His standard response was simply: "How can you sell a player who is not for sale?"

At some stage, Davies would have moved from Southampton to Manchester United if it had been his decision, but he accepts that he may have been less successful without the impeccable service of Terry Paine and John Sydenham, as well as the inside-forwards Martin Chivers and Mick Channon. "Busby said to me, 'Ron, I've been after you for years. They won't let you go'," he says, "Ted Bates never let on. It was four years that Manchester United wanted to sign me." Davies was also linked with the top Italian clubs, but is glad that he was never transferred to Serie A. "Jimmy Greaves struggled with it," he says, "the marking is much tighter. I played a game against Italy for Wales and the defender turned and spat in my face – that is what it was like. But I enjoyed my time for Southampton and I was always grateful to Ted Bates for bringing me into the First Division.

"I was just disappointed that we never won anything. I didn't even get to a Cup final, semi-final or nothing. It would have been nice to win something. I scored 43 goals in my first season and we only just stayed up. But, the way I look at it, I could have moved from Norwich to a team who didn't play my system and I would have been a flop. I was playing in a side where the system suited me perfectly. I would have liked to have won something, but I'm still very proud of what I did."

The fact that Davies was Welsh also meant that he had little chance of achieving fame on the international stage. In 1970, he was named in a fantasy British team and admitted a feeling of envy as England jetted off to the Mexico World Cup. By the 1970s, however, Davies was just beginning to slide. Over the next four seasons (from 1969/70 until 1972/73), he remained among the country's best number nines, but his scoring rate slowed. A tally of 49 goals in his final 121 league games at Saints signalled that he was in decline and Bates sold him to Portsmouth for £40,000. Davies did score 16 goals in his first season at Fratton Park in 1973/74, but struggled thereafter before finally getting that dream move to Manchester United in November 1974. But it was a good seven years too late as, by this time, he was past his best and failed to make a first team start.

Spells in the South African League and then in America followed, where he played for teams in Seattle and Los Angeles alongside the likes of George Best and Charlie Cooke. By this time, he had dropped into a centre-back role. Davies was considering a permanent move to the US, although he did briefly return to Hampshire and play non-league football for local south coast teams which included Totton, Dorchester Town and even the White Horse Pub in Ampfield in the Sunday morning Winchester League. Andy Leitch, probably still smarting from being tumbled by that Davies header in the Archers end of The Dell, remembers facing his boyhood hero one Sunday morning.

"I think Alan Ball was running the White Horse team and they managed to get a few well known people in the city to turn out for them," he says, "Ron played mostly in defence, but came up and pushed me out of the way and scored. It was a definite foul, but he did it in such a way that the referee hadn't seen. I told him what I thought, just like I would anybody else, but he completely ignored me. He had put on a few pounds, but there was no doubt that he was still a class act." They do say you should never meet your heroes.

Davies returned to the US with his first wife and their daughters. He later met Chris and they moved to Casselberry on the outskirts of Orlando where he worked as a football coach at the local high school until their move to New Mexico in 2003. His daughters apparently still live in the US.

SO WHAT NEXT for Ron Davies? Will he disappear from view again or will he return to Southampton? It's hard to predict. He certainly speaks glowingly of the Southampton fans and his need for a hip operation means that any testimonial match would be gratefully received.

"The fans were always very nice to me," he says, "they don't forget and I would like to thank the fans. Southampton Football Club wouldn't exist without these people. Micky Channon would sometimes push past crowds of people, but I used to love stopping to sign autographs or going on hospital visits. It would be fantastic if some sort of match or something could be arranged.

"I would like to be able to retire soon and I would love to enrol in Art School at the University of New Mexico. My hip problem means that I can't continue in construction too much longer and I know that I would be bored if I was to retire. I would really like to go to school and learn art. I still draw – but I just taught myself basically."

Chris Davies then takes the phone and stresses that Ron really does need a hip operation urgently. I promise to liaise with supporters' groups about a possible testimonial event. "Thanks," she says, "it's been a long time, you know, since Ron has talked about soccer."

Ron comes back to the phone to say goodbye. "I like you Jeremy," he says, "the trouble is I've had reporters who've let me down. If you could help with a testimonial it would be a great help, but don't worry if it's not possible. If you are ever in America, give us a call. It would be good to meet you. I miss the pubs in England, it's such a friendly atmosphere. It's not the same here. The climate is great, but I'll tell you something – American beer sucks."

BRIAN O'NEIL

1970-1974

SAINTS CAREER

Games	173
Goals	19
Caps	0

MAGIC MOMENT

Attempting to play on, whilst prone on the ground in agony, having torn a cartilage

'BUDDHA'

'Brian O'Neil was the best footballer in mud there has ever been.'

Ron Davies

BRIAN O'Neil can accept Bill Shankly's infamous description of Southampton during the early 1970s as "Ale-House footballers". Yet he does think it is time to set the record straight about the manner of the 1-0 victory at The Dell in 1970 which so enraged the former Liverpool manager. "The 'Ale-House' thing was fair enough because we did drink for England," says O'Neil, "but what Shankly didn't say was that we totally played them off the pitch that day."

If anyone formed the perfect caricature of a pub footballer it was surely O'Neil. With his shirt hanging just above his knees, his socks rolled down to his ankles, no shin pads and odd boots – yes odd boots – Brian O'Neil looked as if he had accidentally landed on grounds like Old Trafford and Anfield on the way to the local park. Not only that, he drank and played pranks like a pub footballer and revelled in every minute of the whole shebang. Yet O'Neil also performed consistently well on the pitch for a Saints squad which, for three years between 1970 and 1973, arguably contained Cult Heroes from number one right the way through to number 11.

Martin, Kirkup, Fisher, Gabriel, McGrath, Walker, Paine, Channon, Davies, O'Neil, Stokes, Hollywood and Steele; the names trip off the tongue like a Who's Who of the most legendary drinkers, hard-men and characters in the club's history. Amongst their number there were also some very good players, but Southampton's reputation as the most sociable football club in the country was well earned. "Even now when I'm sitting at home I'll have a chuckle to myself sometimes at the things that happened," says O'Neil, "they were good lads, the best I have known in football. It was a great bunch and I've been privileged to know them. You couldn't say there was a bad one among them."

IT SEEMS somehow appropriate to be meeting O'Neil in a public house, especially the Cowherds Inn on Southampton Common, which is just a stone's throw from the site of The Dell. O'Neil looks a little different from the man known as the 'Bedlington Terrier' and later 'Buddha', mostly because that messy thatch of dark hair has receded. Yet his face remains instantly recognisable, as does the twinkle in the eye of a player who was among the great characters to pull on a Saints shirt. Even now, former players and friends find themselves in tears of laughter as they reminisce about their favourite Brian O'Neil story. There are literally dozens of them.

The tale which has been recounted most often to me while researching this book occurred on a pre-season tour in Tokyo just a few weeks after O'Neil had arrived from Burnley for a club record fee of £75,000. The full-back Ken Jones and the new northern recruit had been exchanging a bit of banter. Jones was not convinced that O'Neil would be up to scratch when it came to drinking. O'Neil, of course, was more than happy to take up the challenge.

"I said, 'Ken, I'm going to drink you under the table'," says O'Neil, "so we went into a bar and started drinking. It was just beers and I remember drinking so much I passed out and my head hit the bar. Ken said, 'I've won, I've won'. But I came around and I said, 'no, two more beers'. In the end I won and he packed in."

By this stage, O'Neil was slumped at the bar. He still had Jimmy Gabriel and Ron Davies for company. "Jimmy Gabriel loved talking about football and he used to speak to anyone no matter where you were," recalls Denis Hollywood. "Anyway, he gets talking to two American tourists at the bar. He tells them, 'we've just signed one of the best midfield players in the country, this lad here'. He points to Brian and these two Americans look over at Brian. He had been drinking like mad and he was crashed on the bar with his head in his hands. And Jimmy said, 'best midfield player in the country'. You could see these guys looking at each other and thinking 'flippin' heck'. Next he points to 'Big' Ron Davies who is out of it as well and announces, 'best centre-forward in the country, 40 goals last season'. The Americans are totally confused. And then one of them looks up and says, 'what's that noise?' The noise is coming from Brian and they look over and he is peeing himself.

"Eventually Jimmy and Ron drag Brian outside and they are holding him up and trying to flag down a taxi. Of course, the taxis are coming in and looking at Brian and clearing off. So Jimmy says, 'right, I'll hide him in the doorway and Ron, you get the taxi and we'll throw him in'."

As O'Neil was carried back into the team hotel, the rest of the squad were sat around in the hotel bar and began laughing at the state of their new team-mate. The laughter grew louder and louder as they spotted the giant wet patch on his trousers. No-one was enjoying the moment more than the always immaculate Terry Paine. "I came into the hotel staggering and Painey was, 'hey, what happened to your trousers' and he was laughing at me," says O'Neil. "I was rooming with him and what he didn't know was that I had borrowed his trousers. Mick [Channon] turned round and said, 'I don't know what you are laughing at Painey, they're yours'."

As time went on, of course, O'Neil's team-mates got used to his ways, particularly a tendency to borrow things. "He never had any boots and clothes, he would just come in and look through your wardrobe and he would say, 'can I wear that?'" smiles Hollywood.

After proving his credentials as a drinker, O'Neil provided another moment that lingers in the minds of his team-mates on that tour to Japan. "They went to a banquet and everyone was supposed to take their shoes off – Brian had drunk a bottle of Saki [the national drink of Japan] and he wandered off and got everybody's shoes and chucked them out of the window and into a paddy-field," says Hollywood, "nobody had any shoes for the rest of the tour. There were ructions about that."

O'Neil's casual approach to footwear was summed up by the fact that he never once owned a pair of football boots. Team-mates recall how he would be rummaging around the dressing room just minutes before a match searching for some appropriate boots. Sometimes he would end up with boots that did not match and which were different sizes. "In one game, I was late going into the boot room and so I grabbed the first pair I could find," he says, "and they were big John McGrath's. I think he was size ten and I was seven or seven-and-a-half.

"I couldn't kick the ball long in them, but I could side foot it. I didn't bother changing them at half-time and I scored in the second-half. I never had a pair of boots in my life, but it didn't make any difference."

O'Neil was a product of the 1960s, an era in which authority had begun to be challenged and, with the likes of George Best and Peter Osgood around, there was a real accent on entertainment. Yet while football was somehow taken less seriously than it is today, this was a team which would give absolutely everything on a Saturday afternoon. They did the same well into the night in the pubs and clubs of Southampton, but somehow that didn't seem to matter. Drinking had only just become part of British football – Terry Paine says he never touched a drop of alcohol until he was 28 in 1967 – and this Southampton team were leading the charge to the bar.

UPON MEETING O'Neil, who is now 62, the first surprise is perhaps that he opts for an orange juice. He says he no longer drinks and his days are filled spending time with his two grandchildren, Tilly and Luke, whom he clearly adores and who constantly crop up in conversation. Indeed, it is the first thing he tells me. "I take my grandson to school and then pick him up," he says, smiling. "Tilly is 15 months and Luke's just coming up for seven. He plays football after school and I took him to Lanzarote last year at Easter. I think it was the best week I've had. That's my life now, my grandkids. I see them every day and they're great."

In arranging an interview with O'Neil, I spoke to his daughter Jenny and then to Michael Channon Jnr, and apparently he is constantly out buying presents for the younger members of the family, whether it be replica Saints kits or model dinosaurs from a charity shop. After growing up on an estate in Bedlington, a small town around ten miles outside of Newcastle, O'Neil is delighted to see his grandchildren have things his own family could not afford.

"We had enough money for a house, so I never felt sorry for myself," he says, "my father went down the pit and there were seven of us. Whenever someone killed a pig on the estate, you would get the bladder of the pig and blow it up, tie it up and kick it about until it burst. That was how I started playing in the early 50s. We were all well fed as kids, but never had stuff like proper footballs." O'Neil was spotted while playing for Bedlington School and promptly took his place in a Burnley team that was among the very best in British football. Indeed, in O'Neil's first full season after turning professional, Burnley narrowly missed out on a league and Cup double under their manager Harry Potts. Yet after Potts left in 1970, O'Neil says that some of the magic followed.

"We had a chairman called Bob Lord, he ran Burnley at the time," he says, "I went in training one morning and he said, 'O'Neil, you come with me' and I said, 'yes, Mr Chairman'. I jumped in his Rolls Royce and we headed right out along the moors. And a little fella got out of a car and it was Ted Bates and he said, 'do you know who that is?' I said, 'yeah, it's Mr Bates from Southampton'.

"So Ted said, 'I want to sign you'. I just said, 'yeah, I'll come down tomorrow', and I jumped in the Rolls Royce with Bob Lord and I said, 'yes, Mr Chairman, I'm going tomorrow'. He was a hard fella, but he must have sensed I was on my way. He had a tear in his eye and he said, 'bloody hell O'Neil, you have been the best for Burnley'."

At the time, Bates said: "He is a dynamic, industrious midfield player with First Division authority. He has always given us plenty to think about." O'Neil says he never had more fun in his football career than during those first three seasons with Saints from 1970 until 1973. Bates had a deft managerial style and he would happily turn a blind eye to the antics and drinking habits of his players provided they worked hard in training and produced for him on a Saturday. In turn, the players appreciated their manager and, while they would have great fun dodging his attempts to impose curfews, they would, in the words of O'Neil, "run through a brick wall for him".

The connotation of Shankly's description of Southampton as 'Ale-House footballers' may have been prone to exaggeration, but there was certainly some truth to it. Mick Channon says it became a source of pride to the players while Terry Paine simply admits: "We all had our moments," before adding, "Saturday, after an away game, you had five minutes to wash, change, get on the bus and get to the railway station otherwise you couldn't get home and then on the train we had the buffet services and we would go to the bar and have a drink."

After home matches the routine would be a few pints at the Gateway pub and then on to either the After Eight Club in Shirley or the Magnum Club in Southampton. "Our drink in the early days was lager and lime, not whisky, vodka or champagne, we didn't have the money for that kind of thing, but it was part of our lives," says Paine. "It was a poor man's game when we started. We earned just £10 a week in the summer, £17 in the season, £2 for a draw and £4 for a win. You were not going to get leathered on that kind of money.

"Obviously things changed with the maximum wage [being lifted in 1961] and we were the path finders for what they are today. It never struck me that there was a big problem with drinking at the club but new people coming into a club can always look for something to sort out and put right. I've been both sides so I understand where it has come from, but you take it with a pinch of salt."

Things had already begun to evolve from those lager and lime days by the time O'Neil arrived at The Dell in 1970. The wages were now £60 a week plus a £60 win bonus. Ron Davies would drink bacardi and coke, while O'Neil's tipple was always vodka and water. He would drink it until he fell asleep, wake up, drink some more and fall asleep; continually repeating that cycle as the evening went on. "We never caused any bother, just to ourselves," says O'Neil, "I wouldn't go home until Sunday morning. It was a good spirit in the team, all good mates, all good company."

Sundays were also usually a drinking day and the players would get together to talk over the previous day's match. From Monday, it would then be quieter in the build up to a match – Paine says that he still regards drinking after a Wednesday as taboo – although O'Neil was part of a group which would sometimes have a few beers after training. "You could have a drink as long as you trained hard," says O'Neil. "Beer never used to hinder you. If you get into wine or shorts it might. We would have the shorts at weekends, but just beer doesn't do you any harm in the week.

"You'd run it off and you'd have a sauna. Having said that Denis [Hollywood] once thought it would be funny to piss on the coals. It absolutely stank in there."

YET IF weekdays were quieter, end of season tours were the opposite. They were worse than Saturday nights and Hollywood remembers a typical story on one trip to Copenhagen. "One of the directors was a guy called Basil Bowyer who was also a director for a brewery. He arranged for a trip around the Carlsberg factory for anybody who wanted to go and we were leaving at 9am in the morning. The night before we went out and we all ended up in nightclubs. Over there, they were open until 6am, so we just went to the nightclub, had a bit of breakfast and trooped in to the hotel.

"Basil was collecting his party in reception and when we walked through he thought we were all up for this trip. He was 'morning lads, ready for the trip?' And we just looked at him and said, 'good night Basil'."

Bates' attempts to stem the players' socialising were often ignored and he would some-times attempt to get members of his coaching staff to impose some discipline. Hollywood says: "I remember we had a midweek game and Batesy had given us a curfew of 11pm the night before. 'All back or you're fined', he said.

"We agreed we weren't going along with that and we'd all come back together. Jimmy Melia never usually came out, but we made him come with us that time. He was in the nightclub and dying to come home – he was tired and bored. Jim was asleep on a seat and we were all using his head as a table for our paper plates and eating chips and burgers.

"We got back to the hotel at about 3.30am. It was a revolving door and we pushed him through first and I remember there was George Horsfall [the coach] stood at the stairs. He had been stood there for hours and he was noting down the times that we all came in."

The man regarded as the most fearsome drinker, however, was not O'Neil or Hollywood, but the big Scottish centre-half Jim Steele who produced a man of the match performance in the FA Cup final of 1976. Steele, who now runs a pub in the Cotswolds, and the goalkeeper Eric Martin, who now lives in the United States, also apparently sometimes played together in a darts league.

It would be wrong, however, to presume that all the shenanigans were fuelled by alcohol. O'Neil giggles to himself as he remembers Bobby Stokes once staying at his house. The young Stokes was hungry and O'Neil said he would see what he could find. "I looked in the cupboards," says O'Neil, "and all I had was a tin of dog food, some eggs and a tin of beans. So I shoved it all into a saucepan, heated it up and brought it in for Bobby. I told him that it was stew and he ate it all up and said that it was lovely. I never did tell him the truth."

Denis Hollywood recalls having to endure a short spell at the bungalow where O'Neil lived. "He was an incredible character – I used to cry laughing at the things he did," he says. "He had an old dog. It was a lovely little dog and we had to sleep in the double bed; me, him and the dog in the middle.

"He would only have two or three hours' sleep and then he was up and about. If you had a party the night before, you might go to bed at 3am and at 5.30am the hoover would be going. He had a big upright hoover and he wouldn't stop [Hollywood stands up to demonstrate]. He would go up the sofa and down and then come up all in one motion.

"One time I woke up and the dog was next to me and Brian was there as well and do you know what he was doing? He was spitting on my back and the dog was licking it off and he was just sat there killing himself laughing."

Francis Burns briefly lived next door to O'Neil and legend has it that he left because he got sick of the fish and chip wrappers that kept being thrown onto his garage roof.

O'NEIL'S OUTGOING nature was also evident come match-day and, not surprisingly, he became a firm fans' favourite. Nick Illingsworth, who runs the *Ugly Inside* webzine, became a regular at The Dell during the early 1970s and revered O'Neil. "He was the scruffiest man on the pitch," he says, "he had odd boots, his socks were rolled down so that they would be coming over his boots and he was as hard as anyone I've ever seen play for Saints. He played with a smile on his face and looked like he had just been working at the docks or on a farm or something."

Another fan, Dave Collins says: "There was nothing better on a wet winter night at The Dell than seeing O'Neil walking off after a match covered from head to foot in mud. If you didn't know who he was, you wouldn't have a clue who he had been playing for. But he would put his head where some players feared to put their foot."

O'Neil once jogged out for a match wearing a battered old trilby on his head: "I did it for a bet with Mick's [Channon] mate Stan, but I never did get the fiver", he says. Supporters also still remember the moment when he suffered a torn cartilage in his knee, yet lay on the ground still trying to kick the ball, as well as the opposition player. He says that he never really felt pain on a football field.

His spell in South Hants Hospital having a knee operation provided several other stories which are still recounted. "There was a lovely nurse out there," says O'Neil somewhat ruefully. "Me and Mick [Channon] had a racehorse at the time and I said, 'do you like horses?' She said, 'I love horses' and I said I would take her to see the racehorse. I had done all this and I thought 'I'll see her again', but one of the other lads ended up with her. I just laughed."

O'Neil's team-mates would regularly visit him during his stay in hospital and managed to smuggle in bottles of vodka and cans of beer. "I was on the end of the old people's room," says O'Neil, "and this old girl came walking in and we got talking and I said, 'do you want a drink?' She was in her dressing-gown and we had a couple of small vodkas. She hadn't been very well and she died a few days later, but the nurse said she had thoroughly enjoyed herself for that bit of time."

Hollywood remembers that on one visit the players even managed to sneak in a dog to see him. "Brian loved dogs and someone had the idea we would take it in to see him and cheer him up," he remembers, "I put it under my coat as we went in and Brian was chuffed as anything to have this little dog on his bed and running about the place. The nurse saw and was okay about it, but then the sister came in and we ended up hiding this dog in a wardrobe."

Of course, there will be those who hear stories of the 'Ale-House' team and frown at the perceived unprofessionalism of it all. Yet that would be to misjudge the characters which Ted Bates had brought together. This was a team of big, strong personalities and the spirit within the camp was second to none. It was also, arguably, among the best in the history of the club.

ALTHOUGH SHANKLY'S exact description was of Southampton simply as an "Ale-House" team, the tag became embellished to 'Ale-House Brawlers'. Bates had deliberately signed some tough characters as he tried to shore up a squad which, with the likes of Terry Paine, Mick Channon and Ron Davies, contained considerable quality and was always capable of scoring goals. O'Neil had the reputation as one of football's toughest players as did Denis Hollywood, Jimmy Gabriel, John McGrath, Jim Steele and Hugh Fisher. Yet they have maintained that there was a significant difference between being hard and being dirty.

The incident which really upset Shankly involved the centre-back McGrath who collided with Alun Evans. The Liverpool and Wales centre-forward swallowed his tongue and was left unconscious, yet few who were there say there was any real malice in the challenge. 'Big Jake', as McGrath was known, would apparently head-butt the dressing room wall three times with considerable force before stepping out for every match. McGrath died suddenly in 1998 at the age of just 60 but remains fondly remembered.

Saints fan David Cross said: "Many people thought Ted [Bates] had bought a 'dud' to start with. Although only 6ft tall, John looked much larger, partly because of his broad shoulders and the size of his thighs that resembled oak trees. He was solid muscle and people told tales of how he ate raw steak and it showed in his performances.

"A tower in defence, his heading ability was legendary. On one occasion the opposition had a free-kick just inside the Saints half and the kicker thundered the ball into the Saints penalty-box. The ball was met with full force by 'Big Jake' and he headed the ball back up-field and over the astonished kicker's head."

Cross was at The Dell for the Evans incident which so upset Shankly. "McGrath was the last man back in our half and he set off to intercept the youngster [Evans] who was flying down the right wing. It takes time for a man of McGrath's size to gain speed but, as he drew level with Evans, he looked like a rather fast moving tank.

"He was never going to be able to tackle Evans, but in the last few yards 'Big Jake' threw himself at the lad who literally bounced off his chest and fell in a heap, unconscious on the pitch. Shankly was furious and ranted and raved from the touchline as young Evans was lifted onto the stretcher and carried off the field. My abiding memory is of Alun Evans being stretchered off with his arms and legs dangling over the sides of the stretcher – like Pinocchio with his strings cut." Evans did fully recover from the incident.

On this one incident the legend of the team who took no prisoners was born, yet Paine, who played with all the hard men of the late 1950s through to the mid-1970s, maintains that no-one in the 'Ale-House' team could have matched Cliff Huxford. The signing of O'Neil, however, was certainly because Bates wanted to add some presence to his team. "Ted wanted to toughen it up a bit," says O'Neil, "I came in, Jimmy Gabriel, Jim Steele, John McGrath and Dave Walker. I had played against Southampton many times for Burnley and they used to play us off the park in the first-half, but we used to get stuck into the second-half and we would normally get a point."

Once at Southampton, O'Neil used to make it his job to look after his younger friend Mick Channon. "I'll always remember playing Tottenham and I knocked the ball around Mike England and someone scythed me," says Channon, "I took a bad knock and the first person over was Brian O'Neil and he just said 'what number?' He wanted revenge – he wasn't bothered what state my leg was in." Even as he approaches pensionable age, O'Neil still looks out for Channon. "Mick had a hell of a touch for a big fella and if someone got him I would be, 'I'll sort you'," he says. "Even if he had a bit of strife now, if anyone was going out the way annoying him, I'd sort them out."

O'Neil remembers how Bates would encourage him to make his presence felt in the centre of midfield. "He called me in before we played Sheffield United and he said, 'you are playing against a bloody good player tomorrow – Tony Currie', who was on the verge of England at the time. I said, 'I've been thinking about him all week Ted, you don't have to remind me'. Ted just said, 'feel him out early' – I knew what he meant.

"We had just kicked off and the ball went to Tony Currie and he must have gone over on his ankle. But the stretcher came on and carried him off. I looked over to the dugout, more or less to say it's not me, and Ted stood up and gave me a thumbs-up with both hands."

O'Neil also recalls holding the psychological edge over Liverpool's Emlyn Hughes. "I used to say to Emlyn Hughes, 'if I don't get you on the pitch, I'll get you in the tunnel, don't worry, I'll get you'," he adds, laughing, "Emlyn would shit himself." O'Neil never wore shin-pads. He says it was because there was a level of understanding between professionals which meant that he never worried about being injured. "In those days we had respect for the other players and they had our respect," he says, "they wouldn't go over the top on you in the tackle." Denis Hollywood, whom O'Neil considered the hardest player in that team of the early 1970s, also stresses that he would never go over the top of the ball in a tackle. "I never tried to injure anybody," he says, "all I wanted to do was win."

Whatever their intentions, O'Neil and Hollywood racked up enough bookings to be dished out nine and seven week suspensions from the FA in 1971. For O'Neil, it was a record for English Football at that time. The style of the Saints team certainly sat snugly with the 'play hard, work hard' philosophy of the players. But, if anyone was not pulling their weight, there was a dressing room full of players who would let their team-mates know about it. And so would the crowd. Southampton fans have always expected maximum effort from their team and they would not tolerate paying to see a side who had left their performances inside a pub.

"They were great fans if they knew you were having a go and doing your best," says O'Neil, "and I would always do that and we all would. Mick might sometimes make a couple of good runs and he would be knackered, but it would be, 'c'mon you, back here, get your bloody self back, pull your weight Mick'." Channon says that those players of the early 1970s always had a "first class" attitude to training, although he remembers that O'Neil's usual contribution to any half-time team-talk would be something along the lines of, "let's get our sleeves rolled up and steam into these buggers".

DESPITE ALL the stories and shenanigans, it would be unfair to pigeon-hole O'Neil as simply a tough-tackling midfielder. He drove the midfield forward and could pass the ball. He is rated by Paine among the very best midfielders during his two decades at The Dell. O'Neil also represented the Football League team and Bates felt he was worth serious consideration for England honours in 1971. It would also be wrong to place too much emphasis on the 'Ale-House footballer' tag when analysing this team. Although there were relegation battles in 1969/70 and 1971/72, when they suffered maulings of 8-0 and 7-0 at the hands of Everton and Leeds United respectively, Saints finished seventh in 1971 and 13th in 1973, with O'Neil extremely influential in central midfield.

The arrival of Lawrie McMenemy in the summer of 1973, however, seemed to signal the beginning of the end of O'Neil's Southampton career and also perhaps the excesses of a certain off-field culture at The Dell. O'Neil probably needed a laid-back manager to bring out the best in him. His relationship with McMenemy was tested when he once arrived for training smelling of manure in a tractor and Wellington boots. "I had a bit of a farm out at Waltham Chase," explains O'Neil, "about 8am in the morning, I was doing an electric fence for a mate of mine. I was running a bit late one morning, so all I had was a pair of wellies, my jeans and the tractor and I went into The Dell. McMenemy saw it and he said, 'if you ever come in like that again, that will be it'. I was covered in shit and everything. The lads were like 'the bloody smell in here!'

"McMenemy did crack down a bit. He tried to make everyone wear suits, but me and Mick never took any notice. As long as it was done on the pitch, what did it matter? You had to be reasonable, I suppose. You are representing Southampton, but we'd sooner be casual. Lawrie wanted collar and tie. McMenemy was a good manger, some say the best because he won the FA Cup, but I thought Ted Bates was the best."

O'Neil was almost 31 when he left Saints and continued his career at Huddersfield Town before moving to Taunton, Salisbury City and then played locally for Bishops Waltham. He began working for a civil engineer, doing what he calls "grafting, digging holes, pipes, drainage, that type of thing". In the late 1980s, he then moved to Newcastle where he helped train racehorses, but was involved in a somewhat mysterious assault in 1991, when he was reportedly attacked with a fireplace poker. It left him in a coma for three weeks. It is an incident which he clearly doesn't like talking about and, for the only time during our drink together, he clams up somewhat.

"I don't know what happened to this day, but I wasn't too good," he says, "the nurse told my sister that I wouldn't last the night. I've got an idea, but I don't know what happened. I'm a bit one-sided now, but there are a lot of people worse off."

O'Neil certainly still looks in pretty good health, ever-so slightly unsteady on his feet sometimes, but his footballing memories remain vivid. He is still a regular at St. Mary's for Saints home games and that sunny and generous outlook on life shows no sign of dimming. "I always wanted to be a footballer," he says, "and whatever people say about this, that and the other, I can honestly say that I've had a bloody good life.

"My memories keep me going now – well, that and my grandkids."

BOBBY STOKES

1966-1977

SAINTS CAREER

Games	264
Goals	55
Caps	0

MAGIC MOMENT

That left-footed shot which won the 1976 FA Cup for Southampton

'LITTLE BOBBY'

'Better to be a king for a night than a schmuck for a lifetime.'

Robert De Niro in "King of Comedy"

"A lovely guy, always ready to have a chat." Customers at the Harbour View Café in Portsmouth during the early 1990s still fondly remember the small, smiling middle-aged man who would always make them welcome on an otherwise miserable morning. He spoke with a local accent and looked like the sort of chap who had been serving fry-ups all his life. It was a far cry from the hallowed turf of Wembley, but a café in Portsmouth was where he worked. He was comfortable exchanging stories and passing the time of day with the customers who ranged from dockers and lorry drivers to local white-collar workers and tourists.

Yet away from work, he lived a somewhat lonely life. He had split from his wife of 18 years. He was smoking and drinking too much. Indeed, his health had not been the best for some time. When he could only manage two holes at a charity golf event, he put it down to a bad cold. Friends were concerned and attempting to rally round.

Just two days later, Bobby Stokes was found dead. He was only 44. His death certificate describes the cause of his passing as bronchopneumonia. Some of those closest to him say he died of a broken heart. "Bobby Stokes had dozens of friends and thousands of admirers, but died a sad and lonely man," wrote Brian White in his *Echo* obituary, "he would drop everything to attend a charity event or bring a smile to the face of a sick child. The only person he was unable to help was Bobby Stokes."

STOKES' LIFE was a tale of triumph and tragedy. His and Southampton Football Club's ultimate moment of triumph came at 4.38pm on May 1, 1976. Jim McCalliog had looked up, shouted the words 'go Bobby', and threaded a pass beyond the Manchester United defence. Stokes timed his run perfectly and then, with one immortal sweep of his left foot, directed the ball past Alex Stepney. One-nil to Southampton and one of the greatest upsets in FA Cup history. It is a moment that has never been bettered before or since by anyone in a Southampton shirt.

Yet it is also possible that the path to a tragically early death was laid on that unforgettable May afternoon. For the next 19 years, not a week went by when Stokes was not asked about that goal. Or, to put it another way, for almost 7,000 consecutive days, it was all most people wanted to talk to him about. Not that Stokes minded. Not consciously at least. "I am a lucky man because I did something that people will remember me by," he said shortly before his death. "They will say Bobby Stokes – he was the man who scored the winner for Southampton against Manchester United in the Cup final. I travelled to a lot of places and met a lot of people and it always came up in conversation. I'm flattered that so many people remember me."

For all the plaudits, however, there must have been an inescapable feeling that a great future already lay in the past. After all, how would a player who struggled to command a regular place for Second Division Southampton ever better the achievement of scoring the only goal in a Wembley FA Cup final against Manchester United? It was the realisation of a dream, yet perhaps it all came too soon. The manager Lawrie McMenemy correctly summed up the impact that Stokes' moment of magic had on the people of Southampton. "Bobby's goal at Wembley changed a lot of lives," he said, "all those connected with the club and a lot of people in the area." The irony, of course, is that the life which changed most was that of Stokes. Yet it says much for what a genuine and down to earth character he was that it never changed him as a person. Denis Bundy is a regular Master of Ceremonies at sporting events around the south coast and became good friends with Stokes.

"He never understood what all the fuss was about," he says, "I used to compère at The Dell and I would pick him up from Pompey a few times a year. He had such modesty and he was genuinely puzzled by the reception he would get. We used to be in the car park and little kids who never saw him play would come galloping across and want to get his autograph. They would ignore the current players if he was around because they all knew the name Bobby Stokes.

"He loved it and would sign autographs until his hand fell off. He never stopped being who he was from the day he was born until the day he died. I don't think he ever had to buy a drink after the Cup final. He couldn't walk into a bar anywhere in town without someone buying him a drink. He was a heavy smoker too, and I really think it all took its toll on Bob."

Bill Ellerington was on the coaching and scouting staff throughout Stokes' time with Saints. "He always had a smile on his face, we used to mess around and spar together," he says, "I was just so pleased he got the goal, but then I wished that he hadn't scored. He suddenly had to go to all these dinners and had drinks bought for him constantly. He was just a normal working class lad and then 'bang', everything changed. It broke my heart when he died, he was a lovely lad."

The fame associated with an FA Cup-winning goal was also not embraced by Stokes' family and they have remained out of the limelight. The name Bobby Stokes, however, remains inextricably woven into the fabric of Saints. In 2001, with the move from The Dell to St. Mary's, a supporters' poll decided the names of the five suites in the new stadium. Bobby Stokes joined Ted Bates, Terry Paine, Mick Channon and Matthew Le Tissier to be honoured at the new ground.

Yet of all the heroes in the club's history, it is Stokes who remains the most unlikely. He would, after all, never be selected in anyone's all-time Saints XI as a player or manager. An FA Cup-winning performance at the age of 25 should have signalled the start of a great career, yet his form was to plummet and he never again appeared in the top division of English football. After that 1-0 win against Manchester United, he spent the rest of his career moving from the lower leagues to the United States and then non-league. For a fleeting moment in 1976 he stood taller than anyone in Southampton's history, yet he was finished as a professional player by the age of 30. So just who was Bobby Stokes? And what explains his rise and fall as a footballer?

BORN IN Portsmouth on January 30, 1951, Robert William Thomas Stokes was brought up in the tough Paulsgrove area of the city and went to Hillside Junior School where he began playing football at the age of nine. In his first season for the school he registered 53 goals and then moved on to Paulsgrove Secondary School and quickly broke into the Portsmouth and Hampshire Schools teams.

His dream was to play for Pompey. "When I was a schoolboy there was no other team for me but Portsmouth," he later admitted, "Saints were the arch-rivals and I hated them." At the age of 14, Stokes went for a trial at Fratton Park, but he was not selected from a group of 200 and continued to play as a centre-forward for Portsmouth Schools. He recalled his "despair" at being overlooked by his home-town club, but his desire to play professionally burned strongly and it was Tom Parker who spotted Stokes and invited him to join as a Southampton apprentice in 1966, just a few months after England had won the World Cup. A young Stokes had been captivated by the nation's triumph, particularly the exploits of Alan Ball. Like Ball, what Stokes lacked in size he compensated for in his bravery and effort. A huge reservoir of energy was one of his great assets and it was said of him that, "you could wind him up in August and he would still be going in May".

In an early interview in 1969, Stokes admitted that his best chances for success might be a midfield role. At only 5ft 7ins and ten stone, he feared he would struggle as a striker and had hopes of emulating Ball's midfield style which had made him such a key member of the World Cup-winning team.

Stokes gained England youth honours and by 1969 – at the age of 18 – he was pushing for a place in a Saints team which had contained fierce competition up front between the likes of Ron Davies, Mick Channon and the recently departed Martin Chivers. Bates initially saw Stokes as a striker and his chance came on Easter Monday in 1969 against Burnley when he replaced Channon, who had been temporarily struggling for goals. Stokes' shyness was evident in his immediate reaction to being picked. "My first feeling was of embarrassment and I couldn't look at Mike [Channon]," he said, "I just didn't know what to say, but then the excitement bubbled to the surface. Strangely enough, I wasn't very nervous."

Two goals on that debut in a 5-1 win meant that he kept his place until the end of a season which saw Saints finish seventh in the First Division. It was the club's highest league finish to date and, with only one club per city allowed into Europe, it also meant a place in the Inter Cities Fairs Cup. Stokes featured in the first Saints team to play in European competition against Rosenborg, but his place in the side was far from guaranteed. Channon and Davies – two of the club's greatest ever strikers – were never going to be easy to displace and he also found himself utilised as a makeshift midfielder in making only 17 league starts during the next two seasons.

From 1971 until 1976, however, Stokes became a regular in Saints' teams under Bates and then Lawrie McMenemy. His energy continued to be his main strength. Terry Paine, who commanded the right flank for almost two decades, said: "He could run all day. We used to joke that he used to do my running as well. He was one of the greatest team players to pull on a Southampton shirt. Unselfish, totally committed. A small man with a big heart." According to Paine, he was also a better player than many people realised. "He was instinctive, the longer he dwelt on it, the worse player he was and he was a good finisher," he says, "he could score goals. He was one of my favourites and he loved the banter. A lovely, little chirpy character."

John Mortimore, who was the assistant to Bates when Stokes was breaking into the team, pushed for his inclusion. "I thought Bobby was a good mobile player and I wanted him to play," he says, "he was a tough, strong little player. I thought he was a good finisher and I remember we put him in after a meeting with Ted. The Cup final goal was brilliantly taken, but he would put his head in where it hurt as well."

By 1974, Peter Osgood had replaced Davies up front alongside Channon and the charismatic former Chelsea star was to have a big influence on Stokes. They became room-mates and continued to speak regularly until Stokes' death. Osgood was to become the second member of the FA Cup final team to pass away in March 2006 and I talked briefly with him about Stokes just six days before his sudden death. "He was a great lad, brilliant to be around, always smiling and he deserved the goal," said Osgood.

IN THE months preceding the 1976 FA Cup final, however, Stokes was not having the best of times. Indeed, he came within a whisker of being sold. McMenemy had agreed an exchange deal for Stokes with the Portsmouth manager Ian St John which would see him depart and Saints get the defender Paul Went. At the time, McMenemy said: "We believe both clubs and players will benefit if the exchange comes off. If it doesn't then the players will lose out." It seemed as if the deal was a *fait accompli*. After all, Stokes had admitted in April 1975 that he might move on.

Yet, as the deal was set to go through, Stokes changed his mind. The reason why was something of a mystery and remains so to this day. "I just did not think it was the right move for me," he said. Something felt wrong. It proved to be an inspired change of mind. For once McMenemy had got it wrong, but who could have predicted what lay ahead?

As a mid-table Second Division side being rebuilt following recent relegation, Saints entered the 1976 FA Cup with little real expectation. A third round meeting with First Division Aston Villa seemed likely to signal the end of any Cup ambitions and, with Saints fourth in the table at the time, would mean they could concentrate on getting back into the First Division. Odds of 100-1 to win the FA Cup underlined the feeling that it would be a short campaign for McMenemy's men.

Certainly that appeared to be the case as Villa held a 1-0 lead with 89 minutes on the clock. One final opportunity came when David Peach launched the ball into the box. It fell to Pat Earles and then Mick Channon, who laid the ball back to Hugh Fisher to shoot through a crowded penalty area and earn a replay.

Stokes had another relatively quiet game at Villa Park as McCalliog struck twice to secure a place in the fourth round. Blackpool were then comfortably seen off 3-1 at The Dell with Stokes scoring an opportunist goal by converting a miscued Osgood shot. The Hawthorns and West Bromwich Albion lay in wait and again Saints found themselves a goal down with less than half of the game remaining. Channon and Stokes had woke that morning suffering from food poisoning, but were declared fit enough to play and combined to keep the Cup dream alive.

Just as against Villa in the third round, Channon was the provider as he laid it back for Stokes to place his shot past John Osborne. Cup fever was now beginning to take hold of the city and a crowd of 27,614 were at The Dell for the replay. Within a minute, Saints had taken the lead when Stokes and Channon again combined with a one-two which the latter deftly finished from a tight angle. Paul Gilchrist made it 2-0 with a strike described in *Match of the Millennium* as "one of The Dell's all-time great goals" as Saints eventually ran out 4-0 winners.

Saints were on a run of 16 unbeaten in the league and Cup and a feeling was beginning to grow that anything was possible. A 1-0 win against Bradford City followed and, although league form was to slip, it was still an era in which the FA Cup was seen as one of the ultimate football prizes. Domestically it was on a par with winning the league. There were not the millions of pounds on offer for being in the Premiership in 1976 and, consequently, the priority was making the most of this opportunity. It had, after all, been 74 years since Saints had reached an FA Cup final.

The sense of anticipation was only heightened by the avoidance of First Division Derby County, Manchester United or Wolverhampton Wanderers in the semi-final draw. Instead, Saints were drawn to face Third Division Crystal Palace at Stamford Bridge. It prompted the United manager Tommy Docherty to say: "This is the first time a Cup final will be played at Hillsborough. The other semi-final is a bit of a joke, really."

Saints duly completed a 2-0 win and so it was Manchester United and a first trip to Wembley in the club's entire history. The build-up to the match was intense, yet the media attention was to focus almost entirely on the big personalities in the Saints team. Channon was an England regular at the time, while Osgood, a previous FA Cup winner with Chelsea, was also nationally well known. Few outside of Southampton had heard of Stokes, yet he was integral to McMenemy's plans.

Just four days before the final, McMenemy was asked to assess Stokes. "Tends to get over-shadowed by being the local boy among a lot of big names, but is always respected by those he plays alongside because of the help he gives them," he said, "a tireless worker over the years, Bobby doesn't believe in himself as much as he should, but he has made goals for other people and has scored some vital ones himself."

Those words sound almost prophetic now. At the time, though, it was Channon and Osgood who were reckoned to pose United the greatest threat. In the days leading up to the final, Saints got away from the pressures by staying at a 100-acre Surrey hotel complete with an 18-hole golf course, tennis courts, a swimming pool, sauna and croquet lawns. With the industrious Nick Holmes and Paul Gilchrist in midfield, the plan was to utilise the craft of Jim McCalliog by getting the ball forward to Peter Osgood with Mick Channon and Stokes running on to the play.

THE SOUTHAMPTON team were interviewed as they made their way onto the Wembley pitch more than an hour before kick-off as the atmosphere grew. McMenemy was asked how he felt and he pointed to the massed Saints fans and said: "Look at that bonny lad, that's how we feel. It's magic." Stokes was also uncharacteristically forthcoming. "I'm still confident of getting a hat-trick, it's nice to be here and I feel great," he said. In the BBC studio, Bobby Charlton was predicting a clear Manchester United victory, while Frank McClintock said that there was "no way Southampton will win".

As the teams emerged to an almighty cheer, the diminutive figure of Stokes continued to look the most unlikely of heroes. He was third from the back and almost anonymous. It was the last FA Cup final to be attended by the Queen and she looked on in a blue suit and bobble-hat from the royal box as *Abide With Me* and *God Save the Queen* rang out. The Southampton fans sang their hearts out, causing Jack Charlton in the ITV commentary box to remark: "I've never heard it sung with such gusto." The Duke of Edinburgh then met the teams and Stokes, furiously chewing gum, nervously exchanged handshakes and muttered a few words. Saints made their way to the end where most of their 30,000 fans were situated. It was a sea of yellow and blue and red and white.

Only in the early minutes of the match did Saints look uncomfortable, but as the game wore on, Manchester United looked less and less of a threat. Stokes was increasingly dangerous as the second half unfolded and twice went close from outside the box with decently struck shots. He was getting his range and, on 83 minutes, came the chance and the goal for which he will be forever remembered.

The goalkeeper Ian Turner launched a long ball which was well won by Channon. His header found McCalliog, who breached United's defence with a perfectly weighted lofted ball. Stokes, who found himself just in front of three United defenders, took it in his stride and adjusted his feet to get the ball under control. But, rather than take a touch, he immediately unleashed a low, left footed 22-yard shot which travelled with pin-point accuracy into the corner of the net, taking United 'keeper Alex Stepney by surprise and rendering his late dive all the more clumsy.

Saints were in dreamland. They had won the FA Cup for the first time in their history. Stokes looked almost embarrassed when he was interviewed on the final whistle. "It was a good ball, it just bounced up right for me," he said. "It's a fairytale." Indeed, it was. Yet his goal was also far better than he would ever admit. McMenemy said it was crucial that he shot so early. "It was going away from him and he hit it in the opposite corner," he said, "it was a very good goal, good technique."

There was, however, some controversy. To this day, some Manchester United players and fans will claim that Stokes was offside. The television replays are inconclusive. Initially, Stokes does look offside as he is clearly ahead of the two Manchester United players in view. Yet, as the action continues, it is possible to see Martin Buchan level with Stokes. Buchan is not in view at the precise moment McCalliog plays the ball forward, but, as he and Stokes are moving in opposite directions, it seems certain that he had played the Southampton forward onside.

Almost 19 years later, however, when Stokes' testimonial committee was in contact with various companies, it became clear that Buchan had not forgotten. The committee's letter began: 'At 4.38pm on May 1, 1976, Bobby Stokes, gliding past the Manchester United defence, ran on to a through-ball from Jim McCalliog to score the most important goal in Southampton's history'. A reply from the sportswear company Puma explained that it was unable to help as it had already used up its budget for the year. The letter ended by saying, 'this is nothing to do with the fact that at 4.38pm on May 1, I was one of the Manchester United defenders waiting for an offside flag that never came'. It was signed by Martin Buchan, promotions officer.

The final word on the offside debate, however, goes with the referee Clive Thomas who wrote in his autobiography, *By The Book,* "when Stokes…had the ball at his feet, he appeared to me possibly to be offside. I looked quickly to my linesman…and the flag stayed down. Another split-second and I saw another Manchester United defender playing Stokes onside. Then the players were jumping for joy, the supporters were going berserk and Southampton had won".

Another misconception concerning Stokes' goal was that it was somehow lucky. Some have even claimed that it was miss-hit. Those who trained regularly with Stokes, however, had seen him produce that sort of finish time and time again. The captain Peter Rodrigues said: "He was one of the best strikers of the ball at The Dell at that time." Channon goes even further and, considering the international company he kept, pays Stokes a big compliment. "He was probably the best volleyer of a ball I ever played with and was a great finisher," he said. Stokes, himself, always points to the image of the ball bouncing out of the goal with as much pace as it went in. "I hit the ball with my left foot and, to those who claim I miss-hit it, I can only say the ball hit the back of the net and came out again. They don't do that if you miss-hit them."

McCalliog, the man who conjured the pass to Stokes, said: "He [Stokes] wasn't just a worker, he was a skilful lad. The way he took the goal really impressed me. I had played for United before moving to Southampton and I got to know one or two of them pretty well including the 'keeper Alex Stepney. He was a hard man to beat, but Bobby hit his shot perfectly into the place where Stepney couldn't get to it. In the heat of a tense Cup final, it was a terrific piece of finishing."

As Thomas blew the final whistle, the collective sigh of relief could have blown a tidal wave up the Solent. Channon was the first to embrace Stokes and the little man's arms were raised towards the air as he gave a wonderfully innocent gap-toothed smile. His life was about to change. But for now it was time to celebrate.

Rodrigues collected the trophy from the Queen and a joyous lap of honour followed. The display on Wembley Stadium's electronic scoreboard read: 'Congratulations Southampton: 1976 FA Cup winners. Hard luck Manchester United.' As Jim Steele, Mel Blyth, Peter Osgood, Peter Rodrigues and Mick Channon led the way around Wembley, Stokes trotted along some-what anonymously at the back with Nick Holmes. "The big 'uns came up trumps and carried the younger ones," said McMenemy, "Mel Blyth and Jim Steele were terrific at the back and Ian Turner was keeping it out with his kneecap and heel. There wasn't a weak link in the team."

A street party took place that night outside Stokes' home at his parents' house, but he joined the rest of the team as they went out in London. McMenemy recalls receiving a call of congratulations from the losing United manager. "Tommy Doherty said he was just ringing me up quietly to say 'well done' and he said, 'I'm crying when I'm ringing you'. I said, 'I hope you win it next year' and they did." Doherty always showed grace in defeat and was a special guest some 30 years later at the dinner to commemorate the 1976 final.

AFTER SPENDING the evening at the 'Talk of the Town' club, most of the players later headed for bed, but Stokes joined Jim Steele, Mick Channon and Peter Osgood to find another nightspot. "I think it was called 007," he remembered. "When we got inside, it was full of Manchester United fans. You can imagine what sort of reception we got!" Stokes might have been a quiet man, but he was often one of the last home after an evening out. "He loved being around footballers, he loved being around the Peter Osgoods of this world," says Nick Holmes. "Him and Peter Osgood were great, great friends until the end. Pete would always say that Bob would come to life when he was around footballers and around his friends."

His former team-mate Denis Hollywood agrees, saying Stokes was one of the most sociable characters at Saints. "I remember one time when we were getting the train back from the game, the lads were giving me a load of stick about a new coat I had," he says. "It was a bit of an Inspector Clouseau job. Anyway, I made the mistake of leaving it in the carriage when I went to the loo. I come back and all the lads were killing themselves laughing because Stokesy has opened the window and let go of it – apparently it sailed off like a parachute. Anyway, the following week, a parcel arrives at The Dell and it's my coat! Someone on the train had seen what happened and went and found it for me the next day.

"But he was a smashing lad, I've even seen him thump 'Big' Ron Davies. We had all been out drinking and Ron had been on at Stokesy all day and he had just had enough and smashed Ron on the chin! It was funny because it was unlike Stokesy – no-one ever had a bad word to say about him.

"I remember I was playing for the ex-Saints in a game and Stokesy was watching and I hadn't seen him for a while. He was shouting at me, 'Den, Den!' I carried on playing and then Ian Turner wandered out and says, 'Den, Bob wants a word'. I said, 'I'm playing a game'. In the end I wandered over when the ball was up their end and he lent over and he said, 'you okay, Den?' And I said, 'yeah' and he said, 'good'. And that was it."

SOUTHAMPTON CAME to a standstill immediately after the '76 Cup final and, over the weeks that followed, the various honours and prizes were to flood in for Stokes. He received the 24-carat gold-plated boot worth £1,000 as the scorer of the winning Cup final goal and was made an honorary vice president of the Southampton University Students' Union. He was also presented with a Granada Ghia 3-litre car worth £4,500. The great irony being that Stokes was the only non-driver in the team, despite also being offered free lessons from the Bitterne Park Academy of Driving.

The car was eventually shared between the team and Stokes continued to live in Cosham with his parents until his marriage the following year. "I am not a great socialiser," he said in an interview just two weeks after the Cup final. "I mostly go out with the girlfriend and have a game of darts. More often that not I sit in and watch the television. When you're a striker and you're playing in the Cup final, scoring a great goal is something you think about. But I never dreamed the reaction would be like this if it happened. There have been hundreds of letters from all over the place and the kids from three complete classes at schools – one at London, one at Portsmouth and one at Southampton – have sent me letters. I want people to know that I'll treasure those letters.

"I reckon I could go to ten different functions every day for months and still not be able to say 'yes' to all the invitations. It's a problem sorting out which are the most worthwhile causes and it's going to take some time."

Another person who was already making plans, however, was McMenemy. Despite the wonderful achievement of lifting the FA Cup, he had come to a decisive conclusion about the victorious team. In his view, although this Saints side had the quality to match any team on a one-off basis, it lacked the attributes to consistently grind out results and win promotion back into the First Division. Indeed, in an ITV interview just 20 minutes after winning the Cup, his thought process was already clear. "We have a good blend of people," he said, "it's not good enough to get out of the Second Division, but good enough to play in the First Division."

Apart from in the Charity Shield, the FA Cup-winning team was never to play together again and Stokes was among the first casualties. He started only eight league matches of the 1976/77 season, scoring just one more goal and, during the summer of 1977, was given a free transfer to play in the US with old mates Jim Steele and Eric Martin for the Washington Diplomats. McMenemy had signed Ted MacDougall and Phil Boyer and was taking the team in a different direction as he sought promotion.

It was an era in which many former Dell greats could be found playing football in the US and Stokes spent several summers playing for the Diplomats. His career in England, though, was spluttering to an end at the age of just 26. Not even a move to home club Pompey could revive him and he had a short, but unsuccessful spell at Fratton Park during the 1977/78 season.

Explaining Stokes' rapid decline as a footballer is not easy. By the age of 27, he was virtually finished by English league standards. "Washed up? Never," he said in an interview in

1979 while still with Washington. "Most players would give their right arm for what I'm doing now. I'm playing alongside Johan Cruyff against the likes of [Johan] Neeskens and [Franz] Beckenbauer. So, I'm hardly a failure, am I?" The difference, however, was that the likes of Cruyff and Beckenbauer were into their 30s and consciously winding their careers down while Stokes should have still been in his prime.

Some believe Stokes' lifestyle may have been to blame for his failure to continue at the highest level, but the most persuasive argument is that, having reached the pinnacle in 1976, his hunger deserted him. How else could such an accomplished footballer be playing in the Southern League by the age of 29? Stokes was unable to ever really explain his early exit from football, but joked: "It's because I used to do all of [Terry] Paine's running for him that I ran out of steam early."

AFTER FOOTBALL, Stokes became a publican before working in the Harbour View Café. But he found it hard to adjust to life away from the dressing room and the buzz of being around his team-mates. "Sometimes it is very difficult to leave football," says Nick Holmes, "not so much playing, but the camaraderie of the dressing room. You have done it for 20 years and had the same old banter, the same old stick. Bob had been with us for a long time and it never really happened for him when he finished for Saints."

Friends say he only really regained his sparkle at social functions when he was back in the company of the likes of Osgood and Channon. His old team-mates did, however, do their best to get Stokes out as often as possible. That he never drove was obviously a problem, although Channon's son, Michael Jnr, became a self-appointed chauffeur.

"I was 17 or 18 when I started driving and Bobby needed lifts," says Channon Jnr, "Peter Osgood was organising days and he would arrange for me to pick him up, usually it would be a cricket do or a golf day. Bobby was a reluctant hero, but Ossie would get him out and he was great fun.

"I would collect him in my little Fiesta and I used to just gaze at his Golden Boot. He lived for the lads and he was just 'Stokesy' to us. Everybody loved him and appreciated him, but I don't know if he really appreciated himself as much as he should have done. I don't think he ever realised how much he was loved.

"He ended up in a café, but he was not a tragic figure. He was ordinary in the nicest possible way. He couldn't believe what he had done and he was only happy when he was with the lads. I guess it must be difficult to replace the dressing room and maybe he couldn't handle being treated as a legend."

A fervent Saints fan himself, Channon Jnr remembers taking Stokes back to Wembley for the final of the Zenith Data Systems Cup in 1992. "It was unbelievable," he says, "he was coaching some inner-city kids before the final and he was stood right near the spot where he scored the Cup winner. I remember at one point he said to them loudly, so that Bally [Alan Ball] and Ossie [Peter Osgood] could hear, 'you have got to hit the target from there. I hit the target from back here with my left foot!' Bally and Ossie were cracking up.

"There was also a little game played before the final and he was supposed to play, but when it came to it, he just whispered to me, 'I've failed a fitness test. I've had my day in the sun, now you go and play'."

While a lot of happiness left Stokes' life after he had walked out of the dressing room for the last time, he had no ego problem about dishing up fry-ups. By 1994, however, his health was deteriorating and it was known he was not well-off financially. McMenemy was by now the director of football at Saints and put it to the board that a testimonial by held in honour of the FA Cup final hero.

"Like a lot of people who have become famous, I think Bobby had hit harder times and with the help of many people he was getting himself sorted out and we were pleased to help," said McMenemy. "Bobby didn't want handouts. I can see him with his best suit on and with his briefcase in his hand. He was prepared to work very hard on his testimonial. But that's how he was in his football life."

Denis Bundy was actively involved with organising testimonial events. "It was my dream to make him a lot of money," he says, "we were going to auction a few things as part of his testimonial and it could have given him a better quality of life. His marriage broke up and he was also drinking. He was still fit, he didn't put on weight, but I worried about him smoking. Ossie used to give him a right bollocking about smoking. But it was just impossible not to like him, he would do anything for anyone and he deserved that year."

Some of the items that may have been auctioned included the shirt he wore for the FA Cup final as well as the Golden Boot. They would have surely each attracted bids of at least several thousand pounds. After Stokes died, the shirt was returned to the family, but the whereabouts of the boot has become a mystery.

"He gave me the shirt with the number stitched in, the badge stitched in and all the grass-stains and I remember once I asked him for the Golden Boot and he didn't have a clue where it was – the same with his Cup winner's medal," says Bundy.

"Eventually we found it and it was under the stairs with a load of crap – it was all dusty, but that was Bobby. He just looked up at me and said, 'don't worry nipper, I'm not fussy'. But then the boot disappeared and what happened to it is still a mystery. There are only 10 of those boots and no-one knows where Bobby's is. We had done a dinner at Shooters in Southampton a few months before he died. Ossie was there and Lawrie McMenemy was there and some chancer must have nicked it. It was a gold-plated Adidas boot. It couldn't be melted down or anything and, whoever has got it could hardly show it to anyone. It is just a complete mystery."

STOKES WAS never to properly benefit from his testimonial year and Southampton fans never really did get their chance to say 'thank you' and 'goodbye' to one of the club's greatest icons. His death in May 1995 came as a genuine shock to the city, not least his friends and former team-mates.

The tributes poured in and the genuine affection with which he was held quickly became very evident. "I think everybody took a little bit of enjoyment out of knowing him," said McMenemy, "he was always called 'little' Bobby Stokes and his name was always said with a smile." Ted Bates brought Stokes to Saints and pinpointed his popularity within the dressing room. "A great little man for team spirit, you could always have a laugh and a joke in the dressing room with him," he said.

The crematorium in Portchester was packed for Stokes' funeral and, on the gates of The Dell, supporters hung flowers, scarves and left cards in tribute to the man who gave them their outstanding moment. The funeral service began with the hymn *Abide With Me* and concluded with a rendition of *When The Saints Go Marching In*.

"Everyone remembers me for the Wembley goal, but they forget all the times I was kicked up in the air at Newcastle on a raw winter afternoon," he said in one of his last interviews, adding, "even some England internationals fade from the memory. I didn't reach those heights as a player but, through what I did, my name will live on."

He had almost written his own epitaph. It might have taken Bobby Stokes just a fraction of a second to become a Southampton Cult Hero, yet his name may very well be remembered for longer than anyone in this book.

MICK CHANNON

1964-1977
1979-1982

SAINTS CAREER

Games	607
Goals	228
Caps	46

MAGIC MOMENT

His last league goal for the club in 1982; a wonderful volley against Liverpool at the end of a 16-pass move

'WINDMILL'

'It's no surprise he went into horse racing because he could run like he had four legs instead of two.'

John Mortimore

MICK Channon once compared his current job, training around 150 horses and looking after more than 60 staff, to being a football manager. If so, it would appear that Sir Alex Ferguson might be something of a role-model. Channon's stables are set in a stunning location in rural Berkshire. They certainly seem fit for royalty, so it is not a total surprise to hear that the previous owner was the Queen. The sunshine has broken through the clouds on the spring morning when I visit and the horses positively glow in all their glory.

Yet the idyllic feel is somewhat tempered by the constant sound of swearing which booms across the yard. At Manchester United, they call it the "hair-dryer" treatment. At West Ilsley it's just, "Mick being Mick". I'd come fully prepared for Channon's trademark use of industrial language, but it was still difficult not to be slightly taken aback by the ferocity with which it can be delivered. I park up and walk in the direction of his office and the first words which bellow across the yard are: "Oi, not that fucking way round, go through this way." As I nearly jump out of my skin (surely he didn't have eyes in the back of his head), I realise that he was talking to one of the work riders and not a hapless journalist with precious little knowledge of racing and the etiquette that goes with being around horses.

Channon then enters a nearby barn. I can no longer see him, but it is not difficult to guess who is speaking – sorry shouting – from within. His rural Wiltshire accent slices effortlessly through the wall. "What the fucking hell is all this! Fucking sweet wrappers everywhere! I can't fucking believe this! You wouldn't fucking do this in your home! Now clear it up and if I fucking see any of you lot drop a sweet wrapper, you will be out the fucking door!"

He reappears, and somehow communicates through an unspoken medium that now is not the ideal moment to be bothering him. Channon makes no attempt to act differently in unfamiliar company. He clearly has something of a short-fuse, but there is no pretence. What you see is most certainly what you get.

He sits down at his desk and then discusses the day's racing with Sue, who manages the office and seems to know absolutely everything that is happening. It's 10am and Channon has been up working since around 5am. Apparently he is in fairly good spirits because he had two winners and a second at a meeting the previous evening. But you wouldn't know it. The telephone in his office does not stop, and his mobile also rings about every 20 minutes. One call is obviously from a jockey. "Just sit back and let her ride – she's got the ability, no doubt about that," advises Channon.

I have been kindly accompanied on my trip to visit Channon by Brian O'Neil. His former team-mate volunteered to introduce me when I explained, while interviewing him for this book, that pinning Channon down to a time and date was proving difficult. Not wanting to bother him on the mobile, I had phoned the stables about 20 times to be routinely told: "Mick is very busy this week." Although I had spoken to Channon and he said it was no problem for me to visit "anytime", his diary staff had either been told something different or were trying very hard to keep his appointments down to a minimum. When you see him at work, you can understand why.

His son Michael Jnr – himself a passionate Saints fan – has cautioned that it is a particularly busy time of the year, especially with the 1000 Guineas race fast approaching. This is a Classic and one of the most important dates on the flat racing calendar. At the time of my visit, Channon has never trained a Classic winner on English soil and it is his burning ambition to do so. Indeed, you get the impression that filling this hole on an otherwise hugely impressive horse racing CV is becoming something of an obsession. We are less than a month away from the 1000 Guineas and I'm told it's a bit like dropping in on Ferguson just before an FA Cup final.

Channon has twice had the winter favourite for the 1000 Guineas only to be denied by cruel luck on each occasion. In 1999, Bint Allayl broke a shoulder on the Lambourn gallops three months before the race and in 2002, Queen's Logic went lame the day before. When I visit, his hopes are resting with Flashy Wings – the joint favourite. You can sense the mounting tension.

Channon seems pleased to see O'Neil and his friend is known by just about everyone on the estate. "I just go and see him and his mum," says O'Neil, "I often go down to his office and see his kids. Whenever I drive over there, I think to myself, 'I'm going to enjoy myself today'. Mick doesn't change, Ossie [Peter Osgood] never changed, Stokesy [Bobby Stokes], Jim Steele, Terry Paine, those people have never changed. Mick is one of the best blokes you could ever meet." Channon's friends all talk of his loyalty and generosity. It was with O'Neil that Channon first bought a racehorse when he was only 23. 'Cathy Jane' was named after their respective wives at the time – apparently as a tactic to keep them happy with the purchase – and went on to win several races, including at Ascot when O'Neil apparently issued the jockey Willie Carson with the last words, "you're a cowboy, the rest are Indians".

We immediately head to the house where Channon's second wife Jill, eldest children Michael Jnr and Nicola, grandson Archie and mother Betty are all gathered. Channon also has two younger children, Jack and India, but they are at school. As we chat over a cup of coffee, it's obvious that mum Betty is extremely proud of his achievements and she gives a thumbs-up on being reminded of the two winners the previous evening.

The family home – Hodcott House – was designed by Jill after Channon acquired the West Ilsley estate in 1999. It was previously looked after by the Queen's cousin Lord Huntingdon who retired to Australia. The original Hodcott House was mentioned in the Domesday Survey. With around 200 acres of private winter and summer gallops, upwards of 100 boxes, as well as several bungalows and houses, it is, I am told, a racing trainer's dream. Another previous incumbent is the legendary Dick Hern, a former jockey, Derby winner, four times champion trainer and the victor of 16 Classics. Upholding the history of the West Ilsley stables seems important to everyone around the place.

CHANNON HAS certainly been on a long journey since being born in a thatched cottage on Salisbury Plain and then raised in a council house in the small village of Orcheston near Stonehenge. After a glittering football career, he is now firmly established among the very best trainers in the country. In a sport traditionally dominated by the middle classes, Channon has won acceptance among the horse racing establishment.

The BBC commentator Clare Balding was herself a former champion amateur jockey and comes from a horse racing family which runs a rival stables just a few miles from Channon in Kingsclere. Of his status in the sport, she says: "I would say that Mick is among the top half dozen trainers in the country both in terms of ability and size. He has won top class races all over the world. He is a particularly good trainer of two-year-olds – a bit like a teacher excelling with GCSE students – because he seems to have a knack of honing their racing skills much more quickly than anyone else.

"He is a top bloke on the racecourse and at home – even if his language leaves a lot to be desired. He cares about his horses, his staff and his owners. Mick is a huge asset to the sport of horse racing and I, for one, am bloody glad he took up training racehorses rather than footballers."

Two things become quickly obvious while watching Channon at work. The first it just why organising a space in his diary has been so difficult. The second is exactly how he has reached the pinnacle of two completely different sports. The image of some friendly yokel sort of chap, who is always cracking jokes, is largely nonsense. Channon is driven, sometimes frighteningly so. When he says that training horses is "a way of life", he means it literally.

He is now 57, yet the pace at which he works is, if anything, faster than he displayed on a football field. When O'Neil recalls that he was, "so quick, he could catch pigeons", you get the correct impression of his approach to horse racing as well as football. Although he was seen as something of a flair player, Channon's former team-mate Terry Paine makes an observation that is clearly as relevant now as it was when they were players. "He was a winner," says Paine, "he had great heart and great drive within himself."

His son Michael Jnr agrees, but pinpoints a crucial difference. "When he was a player, he only really had to look after himself and he could more or less get by on talent," he says, "it was fun for him, he was one of the best players in the country and, although he was never one for training, he loved competing in games. Now it is different because he is a manager and he has responsibility for everything. He's lucky to have found something he loves, but it's more than an obsession and I'd be the first to admit that he can sometimes be a bit fierce."

Channon looks irritated if he wastes just a few seconds, let alone minutes and is perpetually on the move and seems constantly stressed. The contrast with other retired Southampton players – like, say Matthew Le Tissier or Chris Marsden, who are now largely enjoying life on the golf course – could hardly be more pronounced.

Channon must now be financially secure, yet he is still up at the crack of dawn in the morning and often working until late into the night, usually seven days a week. He is completely hands-on in everything he does at a time when he could surely take a backseat and leave the hard graft to others. Friends and family predict that he will work with horses until the day he drops. "You do what needs to be done – I don't work to any set hours," he says. Balding's observation that football's loss is horse racing's gain is interesting. Had he gone into football management, his passion and capacity for hard work make it odds on that he would have been successful.

AFTER MY brief introduction to Channon, I'm told to wait. The 24-hour horse racing channel is on in his office or I can have a look around the yard. He says that I can come up to the gallops with him in a few minutes and we will speak then. There is a coach-load of French tourists wandering around the estate and peering in at the rows of horses with their long brown noses poking out of the boxes. A couple who own a horse that Channon is training have also dropped by and start chatting. They seem excited to have their horse trained at West Ilsley. "The horses get the best of everything," they say, "you get the feeling that Mick would prefer to go without rather than any of his horses."

Channon deals with everyone in turn and finally gets up and tells me to get into his Range Rover. "Right," he says, "ask me anything you like."

The most obvious question is simple: why does he still do it? Channon looks at me as though I'm a little crazy. "I enjoy training horses, so getting up in the morning is not such a hard thing because I want to win," he says. "It's all about winning, whether it's football or this and the buzz is no different – winning is good for our ego. I want to win and I'm angry when I don't win, especially if I should have won. But that's life, you get on with it and try and win next time."

He seems unaware that he is a particularly driven character. "Everyone has got determination, but you need opportunities sometimes," he says, "a lot of people don't get opportunities. I've been lucky to have opportunities in two sports and I enjoy doing both which is a great help. That's where I have been fortunate with both things. I've enjoyed all of it and I hope I can enjoy it for a few more years. Horse racing was a hobby that has become my job. I didn't plan anything, it was just one of those things that crept up on me." Channon doesn't, however, explain exactly why he still enjoys winning so much despite already having achieved such success.

Upon researching his career, I am struck by a passage in his biography, which was published in 2004, remembering the tragic death of his elder brother in a tractor accident when Mick was just nine. In it, Channon says: "There is never a day passes when I don't have fleeting thoughts of my dead brother, John. We were inseparable as kids and it still hurts like hell that he wasn't able to share in my good fortune. I sometimes think that it was having to listen to my mother's tears night after night for what felt like years afterwards that spurred me on to try to take her mind off the tragedy just a little bit by making a success of my life." As his biographer, Peter Batt, writes: "He has not let her down."

MICHAEL ROGER CHANNON was born in 1948 and showed an early ability with a football at his feet. "I was mad about the game from the moment I was big enough to kick a ball," he says. He and his brothers would play on Salisbury Plain or against a wall in the village and Channon graduated to become the star of the local school team at Amesbury Secondary Modern, where a teacher by the name of Terry Bates played a significant part in smoothing some of the rough edges. In one game, Amesbury won 20-0 with Channon scoring 12 goals.

By this time, he had been taken to his first match at The Dell which was a 1-1 draw with Swindon Town in the old Third Division. "It was that game which made me determined to become a professional," he says. From then on, he and his father Jack would be in the West Stand to watch the likes of Terry Paine and John Sydenham in action.

News of Channon's potential spread fairly quickly throughout Wiltshire, although he was less well known in Hampshire. The Southampton scout Bill Ellerington, however, saw something he liked in a match between Wiltshire and Hampshire schoolboys in Andover. "He would run at people and, if he lost it, he would run at them again and again – defenders hate that," he remembers. Channon was duly signed from under the noses of Swindon Town and he made an immediate impression on the Southampton manager, Ted Bates. "Michael Channon is one of the few people who can get the ball in his own half and produce a goal from it," said Bates. "He can take defences in the last third of the field rather than having to be brought into the penalty area."

In his debut for the reserves, which came at the age of just 15, it was reported that: "He scored the best goal of the match when he beat two before netting with a powerful drive." Channon also marked his full debut with a goal in 1966 when, at the age of 17, he contributed to the promotion to Division One. He admits that he was initially petrified of walking into the first team dressing room and would get more than a little ribbing over that broad country bumpkin accent.

Channon did not regularly establish himself in the team until 1968 when Martin Chivers was sold to Tottenham for a then record-breaking fee worth around £120,000 as well as the services of Frank Saul. Ron Davies and Channon quickly formed a profitable partnership, although there is debate as to how well they were suited. Davies, of course, was formidable in the air from crosses, whereas Channon liked the ball on the ground to run on to. His strengths were his pace, versatility and spirit. Channon had considerable ability, but he would also "have a go" and missing the occasional chance never bothered him.

Paine loved playing alongside him and, while he would feed Davies impeccably in the air, he also knew exactly how to get the best out of Channon. "Micky and I had a telepathy," he says, "whenever I got balls in space, I didn't have to look, I knew he would be on his bike. The greatest asset for any player like me was having someone who is willing to run to get in behind. It's the hardest thing and Mick could do that brilliantly.

"I would get the ball and before I knew it, he would be over the top which is brilliant. He was a rangy player, he could manipulate himself around the pitch with great pace and precision. You knew if he went, he would get it nine times out of ten. If you get a full-back who goes on the overlap for you three times and doesn't get it, he's not going to go the fourth time. Mick was different, he would keep going."

A favourite memory is a spectacular left-footed goal against Liverpool in 1969 in front of The Kop. At the time, Channon said: "I don't think any of the lads at The Dell can beat me over 200-yards. There's nothing between John Sydenham and myself over the first 20-yards, but beyond that I probably just have the edge."

The Southampton president John Mortimore was Bates' assistant manager when Channon emerged as a first team regular. "Mick Channon was just so mobile," he says. "He was quick, but he also had good balance for a big lad. He could start and stop, his change of direction was excellent and he had control of the ball when people were on him. He could slot the ball in and he didn't have to blast it. He also read the situation. He's played wide right, wide left, up the middle. Just off the striker was possibly his best position, but he could play anywhere across the front and still have that composure in front of goal.

"He could check back when he looked in full flight, his change of direction was superb and he could just open up an angle and slot it in. His running frightened defenders because he was quick, direct and could suddenly stop and change direction."

FROM 1969/70 until 1976/77, Channon missed only ten league games in eight years and scored between 14 and 21 league goals in each and every season. It is a record of consistency surpassed only by Terry Paine. Yet while Paine prompted huge respect, there was something in

Channon that guaranteed genuine affection from the Southampton crowd. His accent highlighted his local roots, but it was the enthusiasm and *joie de vivre* which made him so popular. Who else could park themselves on the advertising boards and ask supporters during a game for the horse racing results?

Contrary to popular belief, it was not Matthew Le Tissier who was first credited with divine power. CB Fry's nickname was 'Almighty' and a famous banner at The Dell during the 1970s read, 'Jesus saves – Channon nets the rebound'. Lew Chatterley apparently once had the unenviable task of wearing the number eight shirt when Channon was injured and found himself booed by some Saints fans frustrated their hero was not playing.

Kevin Keegan, who played alongside Channon for both England and Southampton, remembers Lawrie McMenemy preparing a vital team-talk for a game against Manchester United when Saints were near the top of the league during the 1981/82 season. It was just ten minutes before the match and McMenemy went around the players in turn, issuing instructions, but when he got to Channon, there was an empty seat. "The physiotherapist said casually, 'oh, he's upstairs in the players' lounge watching the 2.45pm from Newbury'," said Keegan, "Lawrie stormed into the lounge. Mick just pointed at the television and said, 'have a look at this horse I've got my money on'."

Nick Holmes says that no-one ever saw Channon before a game until ten to three if there was horse racing on. Channon, though, was a player who didn't need team-talks. He was a natural. McMenemy can remember another minor run-in with Channon, although he admits the story may have become somewhat embellished. "I can't remember it that clearly," he says, "but I'm supposed to have been telling Mick off at half-time and he listened and when I drew breath he said, 'gaffer, what you have to understand is that this is my fucking hobby'. Mick played with a smile on his face and free abandon.

"He took horse racing very seriously. It has been proved how much he loved it by him taking a new life. He used to be the footballer who trained horses but now he is the trainer who used to be a footballer. He's now in the top bracket of trainers and he was a good lad for me. On the bus most of the players would look at the papers to see who they were going to back, but Mick was always studying the form – he was into horse racing in a different way."

Peter Osgood would recall how he was amazed upon arriving at Southampton from Chelsea to see the slightly less smart dress code at The Dell and how Channon would arrive for away trips with nothing more than his toothbrush. Yes, Channon was desperate to win during the 90 minutes of a game, but, if he failed, it was quickly forgotten. It's an attitude, you suspect, that he carries into horse racing. There is no resting on his laurels, equally there seems to be little moping around if things don't go his way. "I suppose a lot of sports have become very professional and it is all about winning," he says. "I never had a problem with it, winning is important, but it's not everything. Football has always stirred a lot of emotions, it was important to me when I was playing to win, but once the game was over, I might have a moan and groan, but that was it. You couldn't do anything about it and you have got to get on with life, so you might as well enjoy it. That's always been my motto."

Kevin Keegan has said that Channon is his all-time favourite player because of his approach to football. "When you think of Micky Channon, you think of fun," he says. Keegan tells another story of how Channon, while on England duty, once used the famous detailed dossiers Don Revie had prepared on the opposition as scoring pads for playing cards.

The image, however, that most remember of Channon was him running away from goal having netted the ball and delivering the trademark one-armed 'Windmill' celebration. Osgood claimed that Channon copied it from Pete Townshend of The Who. Channon says it was something that "just sort of happened".

"If I'd done copyright, I would be a rich man," he says. "I think I was so far up on my own it was a long way to run back." It was among the first of the individual celebrations and surely the best. Southampton-born Wayne Bridge ensured that it lived on when he scored a late equaliser in a match at Bolton Wanderers in 2002 and ran the entire length of the pitch with a one-armed 'Windmill'. It was done because his dad, Mick, was such a big fan of Channon's.

HAD HE NOT gone into horse racing, there is little doubt that Channon could have forged a career in punditry. He did work on the panel for the 1982 and 1986 World Cups, where he coined the phrase, "the boy done good". He was, however, ticked off by the PFA after the former Manchester United goalkeeper Gary Bailey complained that Channon had been overly critical of him.

Channon thinks people in football have become too sensitive. When Saints appointed Steve Wigley as head coach, Channon certainly didn't mince his words and all but correctly forecast the relegation of 2004/05. "Coaches are a waste of time – the club needs a manager who will crack the whip and make things happen," he said. "We need someone with a bit of authority, to kick backsides if that is what is needed."

When I visit Channon, the 2005/06 season has drawn to a close with Saints lodged in the middle of the Championship table and Rupert Lowe about to face a challenge after almost ten years as the club's chairman. I don't even have to ask for a view on the situation at the club. He simply commiserates on being a fellow Saints fan, before saying: "Rupert's [Lowe] fucked it up, I reckon. But that does happen from time to time and you just have to pick up the pieces."

It's hardly surprising that controversy has touched Channon on several occasions, not least when he took part in a lucrative trip to South Africa in the late 1970s. Channon, though, defended himself by saying he was opposed to apartheid and that he was involved with coaching in black townships. "I trained barefoot kids in Soweto – and I think that gives me a stronger platform to talk about South Africa than the people who condemn the way things are run there when they haven't been within 5,000 miles of the place," he wrote in his autobiography.

Channon also caused a stir when he admitted that 1976 FA Cup final tickets were sold on the black market by some Southampton players. His defence – that it was a justifiable bonus for players in the days when wages were far lower – may have upset a few supporters, but the vast majority did not begrudge Channon and a few of his friends this perk. Indeed, Channon's openness about any subject has generally only enhanced his popularity amongst fans.

NOTHING, THOUGH, should disguise his quality and durability as a player. He was short-listed for Player of the Year in 1973/74 after scoring 21 league goals in a relegated team and had been attracting the interest of the country's top clubs as well as some further afield including Real Madrid.

Channon still holds the club's all-time goal-scoring record with 228 strikes and, with Terry Paine and Matthew Le Tissier, is generally rated among the top three players in the club's history. There are those who would say that he is the best. "Channon was different class, he was Southampton through and through. He was born down this way and is just a fantastic lad," said his former team-mate Peter Osgood shortly before he died suddenly in March 2006, "I'd put Micky Channon top of the list, then Matt [Le Tissier] and then Terry Paine. That would be my three."

Osgood, however, did not always appreciate some of Channon's play. "Mick was exceptional, but he was a greedy bastard," added Osgood, "and he would say to me in that accent of his, 'Ossie, when I see the whites of those posts you've got no chance'." With his clever flicks and link-up play, Osgood was generally an ideal strike-partner and the duo were, of course, to spearhead Saints' run to the FA Cup in 1976. Channon top scored with five goals in that famous Cup campaign. Nick Holmes recalls how having a player of Channon's international reputation gave confidence to the rest of the team.

"I remember Micky saying, 'right we've made the final now, we're going to win it'," says Holmes, "any doubts I would have had were destroyed and I believed we could do it as well." As a Saints fan, Channon is particularly proud of the legacy which the 1976 Cup final has left and he talks frequently of the club being all about the fans rather than players, directors or managers.

The 1975/76 season was, however, an unsettled time for Channon. Following relegation to Division Two in 1974, he said in a television interview towards the end of the following season that he wanted to leave Saints and play in the First Division again. He made several transfer requests and also relinquished the captain's job for "personal reasons". It meant that it was Peter Rodrigues and not Channon who was to lift the FA Cup at Wembley. "It wasn't my dislike of Saints which forced me to make a transfer request – it was my desire to play in the First Division again," he said.

His testimonial was proof that Channon's desire to leave did not affect his cult status among the supporters. Coming just two days after the FA Cup win, the timing was perfect. Southampton was still a city in celebration and the party continued that night at The Dell. Channon recalls being at the ground early that morning and hearing that supporters had been camped out since 6am to purchase their tickets. There was also the unusual sight of ticket touts doing brisk business at a testimonial.

The official attendance for the match against Queens Park Rangers was 29,508, but most in the ground are confident that there were, in truth, significantly more. Indeed, it may very well have been the highest attendance for any Saints home match. Of that entire weekend, Channon says: "The whole town was unbelievable – sights never to be seen again. Just one of those unbelievable moments in your life that just passes."

Those at the game say it was "bedlam". In *Match of the Millennium*, Dave Juson describes the "Mardi Gras atmosphere" across Southampton for a few hazy weeks. The match stood at 1-1 when Peter Osgood shot towards the goal. But no-one knew whether it actually reached its destination as supporters in the Milton end invaded the pitch.

Channon was to remain for one further season at Saints, scoring four goals as the club reached the third round of the European Cup Winners' Cup which included a brace in a 4-0 win over Marseilles. At the end of the 1976/77 season, he was finally granted his move back into Division One when he was sold to Manchester City for £300,000. He had spent three seasons in Division Two and, although McMenemy maintained that the club had done everything they could to keep him, a parting of the ways had perhaps become inevitable for both sides.

Still, it said much for the strength of both Ted Bates and McMenemy that Channon was the first real star player to leave The Dell since Martin Chivers in 1968. Initially it was a big blow to the supporters. Ted Bates' daughter, Jo, remembers pleading with her dad, then the club's chief executive, to do something – anything – to keep the club's star player.

McMenemy, though, knew what he was doing and brought in Phil Boyer to complement the likes of Ted MacDougall, Nick Holmes, Alan Ball, Chris Nicholl and Steve Williams as promotion back to Division One was secured. Injury and a loss of form ensured that Channon's two seasons at Manchester City were less successful.

THE MOVE to Maine Road was also soon to coincide with the end to his international career. Only Peter Shilton played more often for England while at Saints as for five years and under four different managers, Channon was an England regular. He eventually amassed 46 caps and scored 21 goals, a better ratio than the likes of Kevin Keegan and Martin Peters for the national team.

Perhaps his best international goal came in 1973 against Wales when, lurking in space on the right, he out-sprinted the entire Welsh defence and drove a low shot past John Phillips into the bottom corner of the goal. It prompted him to be briefly dubbed: "The George Best of English football." Channon also captained England when Gerry Francis was unavailable, scoring twice in a 3-2 win against Italy at New York's Yankee Stadium.

The game, though, which still haunts England fans of that generation was the 1-1 draw with Poland in 1973 that denied them their place in the 1974 World Cup finals. The *Sun* covered its front page with the headline 'The End of the World' after a game that England dominated, but could not finish off following the heroics of the Polish goalkeeper Jan Tomaszewski. Channon hit a post that night and also had a goal disallowed for handball by a team-mate.

His international career fizzled out with the emergence of Trevor Francis and it appeared as though Channon's entire playing career was coming to a disappointing end. The move to Manchester City had not worked out and he was out of the England team.

But then Lawrie McMenemy again came calling. At the time, Channon also had the option of becoming player-manager at Third Division Blackpool, but he decided to make a popular return to The Dell. "Lawrie was very good at squeezing experienced players to get something out of them," says Channon.

His second coming at Saints between 1979 and 1982 coincided with Alan Ball and Kevin Keegan and was a great era for the club with consecutive finishes of eighth, sixth and seventh. At this stage, McMenemy began to utilise Channon as a right winger in front of Ivan Golac with the likes of Steve Moran, Phil Boyer, Charlie George and Kevin Keegan playing as strikers.

Channon remained a consistent goal-scorer. Indeed, his last goal for the club was his and perhaps the club's best ever. It came against Liverpool in April 1982 and was the ultimate example of the fabulous passing football that this vintage Saints team, regarded by many as the club's best ever side, were regularly producing. The ball started with Chris Nicholl and then pinged all over the pitch in a wonderful 16-man move which ended with Channon volleying the ball home.

For the record, the sequence of passes went: Chris Nicholl, David Armstrong, Nick Holmes, David Armstrong, Nick Holmes, Kevin Keegan, Keith Cassells, Alan Ball, Keith Cassells, Kevin Keegan, Alan Ball, Steve Baker, Kevin Keegan, David Armstrong, Kevin Keegan and finally Channon. "It was like a pin-ball machine," smiles Keegan. It was the BBC's Goal of the Season for 1981/82. It was, however, also to be Channon's last significant moment for the club as McMenemy decided to part company with one of the club's all-time greats at the end of the season.

MCMENEMY INITIALLY suggested that Channon should go into management, but, at the age of 33 and after 602 starts and 228 goals for Saints, Channon was keen to keep playing for as long as he possibly could. "I'd even be happy just kicking about a village green," he said. He was surprised to be leaving although has never criticised McMenemy. He was on around £60,000 a year, which, as he admitted, could have paid for three other players. Brief spells at Newcastle United and then Bristol Rovers followed.

Channon felt that the end was coming, but a meeting with his old England team-mate Peter Shilton convinced him that there was something left and he was to enjoy three successive years with Norwich City, culminating with an unlikely League Cup triumph in 1985 at Wembley with a 1-0 defeat of Sunderland. Not bad for a 36-year-old veteran.

Channon says he was lucky to have a high level of natural fitness. "Being the super athlete and super fit human being, these things are meant to be," he smiles. "No, actually I was lucky, I was naturally quite fit, slim and tall which certainly helps. It was hard for the lads who had to have sweat suits on every day. I didn't have to do that sort of thing, I could eat what I wanted and drink what I wanted." And of course, as a member of the 'Ale-House footballers' he did sometimes drink what he wanted.

As a player, Channon had obviously changed greatly from the jet-heeled 17-year-old who broke into the Southampton team, but he used his experience to get by. "The best years are sometimes when you know what you are doing and that doesn't happen until the end of your career," he says. "When you have got the experience, you haven't got the fucking legs have you? It's like most things in life, when you know what you are doing, you are too old to get the best out of yourself. Experience is the great thing and the quicker you get it, the more chance you have got of fulfilling whatever your aims in life are.

"When I went to Norwich in the later days I'd lost my pace, but I still enjoyed my football and that to me was what football is all about. It's a hard old game, but football had to be fun for me."

Even after Norwich, Channon was not completely finished as a player and wound down his playing days with his old friend Alan Ball at Portsmouth. The striker Micky Quinn recalls how Channon's presence at Portsmouth made a huge impact on him and the younger players. "I was in awe of Mick then; he would stroll in for training in his cloth cap, his wellies covered in horse shit and with the *Sporting Life* tucked under his arm."

Channon's spell at Portsmouth lasted a year, during which he clocked up his 700th league game. In his entire football career since turning professional, including league, cup and all representative football, he had played in more than 900 games and scored more than 300 goals. A legend, indeed.

AS HE WALKS around the West Ilsley stables, it is obvious that Channon's body has paid a price for all those matches and there is arthritis in the limbs. The mind, though, is probably more focused and intent on winning than ever before. Although he trained to be a butcher and once had an interest in a sports shop and a hairdressers, horse racing was always destined to be his profession after football.

He had four acres of land at Swanmore in 1971 when he bought a horse for the fun of it and then moved to Fair Oak and gradually expanded. His initial aim was to breed a Derby winner, but he became assistant trainer to the late John Baker in Devon and, in 1988, he began working with Ken Cunningham-Brown. After gaining his trainer's licence, he acquired Saxon Gate in Upper Lambourn and gradually built up his string of horses to where he is now after moving to West Ilsley. Since 1988, his yearly tally of winners has risen considerably and stands at well over 1,000 in total. The tally increases just about every week and, at the time of writing, he is near the top of the flat trainer's table for 2006.

As my time on the gallops with Channon is drawing to a close, a batch of about 20 horses come running past. He looks absolutely entranced as he watches them. To the untrained eye, it's simply a load of fantastically fit looking horses. "What are you looking for," I ask. "I want to see their well-being," he says. "They are just cantering at the moment, it's an easy exercise for them, but I know exactly what state they are at because I've been with them every day for the last six months."

"But what specifically are you looking for," I ask.

"I could explain it to you and it would take forever and you still wouldn't understand," he says. Channon can clearly recognise ignorance of racing just as quickly as he can spot potential in a horse.

Eventually the horses slow down and he winds down the window to ask the work riders a series of questions. "Ally, is he all right? Any coughs? He was all right wasn't he?" With that, we are back down to the offices and Channon is off and away to a stud farm. There is barely a 'goodbye' and it is clear that his mind has already switched to his next job before I have even got out of the car.

O'Neil and Michael Channon Jnr are waiting for me and look almost relieved that I have survived about half-an-hour with the main man. Just before we leave the West Ilsley stables, O'Neil pops into the office to ask what is happening today. He is told that Channon has three runners and there are high hopes for all of them.

I listen carefully. Youmzain at Catterick is 5/4, while Airbus and Hanoona are respectively 9/2 and 5/2 at Epsom. I decide to stake £10 on each as well as a £10 treble. Youmzain and Airbuss both come good, while Hanoona finishes second. I've narrowly missed out on winning about £400, but a profit of just over £30 still represents a reasonable return.

Just over two weeks later, however, I tune in to see whether Flashy Wings can, indeed, break Channon's duck in the Classics. Channon's face even before the start of the race tells its own story. Heavy rain has softened the ground and effectively ended his hopes. He was confident of victory if the race been run in dry conditions, but one shower has ruined six months' hard work. Clare Balding tells me that it is inevitable that Channon will eventually win a Classic. "A professional of his class and consistency will get the luck one day," she says.

If he doesn't, it certainly will not be because of a lack of effort.

NICK HOLMES

1970-1987
1988-1989

SAINTS CAREER

Games	**543**
Goals	**64**
Caps	**0**

MAGIC MOMENT

Scoring spectacularly from inside his own half during a 4-0 win against Watford

'THE METRONOME'

IT was the first match of what was to be Saints' best league season. Brian Clough's Nottingham Forest were the visitors to The Dell and the match was 20 minutes old when Nick Holmes' face clashed violently with Viv Anderson's studs. Blood gushed everywhere. Holmes recalls the moment with a grimace. "I wish I had passed out," he says, "the pain was that fierce." He remained conscious, although badly dazed. Slowly, he got to his feet and signalled to the manager Lawrie McMenemy that he could continue.

The date was August 27, 1983: long before the time when a blood injury meant you were automatically taken from the field. The Saints shirt of that season was predominantly white, except for the one worn by Holmes that day. His had become a darker, more crimson colour as the blood continued to flow from his nose. But he completed the match. Saints won 1-0 thanks to a goal from Danny Wallace and it was the future England international who took most of the plaudits. The real hero of the day quietly made his way to hospital and found that he required several stitches on the inside of his nostril.

"Obviously I felt a lot of discomfort during the match, but the main problem was that my nose wouldn't stop bleeding," Holmes says rather nonchalantly. "I felt really groggy, all I wanted to do after the game was sleep." And yet, two days later Saints travelled to London for a match against Queens Park Rangers. Holmes was on the team bus and played the entire 90 minutes at Loftus Road. In fact, he did not miss a single minute throughout a 51-game season which saw the club reach the FA Cup semi-final and finish second in the race for the Championship, just three points behind Liverpool.

"When you talk of bread-and-butter players, he is at the top of the tree," says McMenemy, "a man for all seasons." He certainly was. Holmes missed few matches during the club's golden period between 1975 and 1987. Yet talk about the FA Cup win of 1976 and people think of the likes of Peter Osgood, Mick Channon and Bobby Stokes. Remember the team which got promoted back into the First Division and it is the one touch football of Alan Ball and the goals from Ted MacDougall and Phil Boyer which spring to mind. Reminisce about the League Cup final at Wembley against Nottingham Forest in 1979 and the rampaging Yugoslav Ivan Golac is instantly mentioned. Think back to the side in 1982 which topped the league for the one and only time in Saints' history and it is the performances of Kevin Keegan which stand out. And what of the teams that reached FA Cup semi-finals in 1984 and 1986 and also finished second and fifth in the league? Wallace, Steve Williams, Steve Moran and David Armstrong were the stars.

Through it all, however, there was just one common dominator. Whether as a left-back, a midfielder or a sweeper, Holmes was always there. "The beauty of Nick Holmes came from his versatility – give him a job and he did it. It's as simple as that," says McMenemy. "He is the sort of player you build teams around. If he played in the north, he would be a hero." But not in the south?

Certainly there is a sense that Holmes was once taken for granted by the supporters; rather like that familiar old armchair which was built for durability and always a source of great comfort, but never fully appreciated until it was gone. Yet as the years have passed, Holmes' cult status has grown and grown. Glance at the record books and you will see that only Terry Paine and Mick Channon played more often for Saints. But no-one, neither Paine nor Channon, played more often for a successful Saints team.

Southampton born and bred and as loyal as anyone who played for the club, Holmes is the embodiment of every family value that Saints fans traditionally most love. Yet his cult status remains more retrospective than instinctive. He was always happy to remain out of the limelight in an era when Saints teams were packed with more flamboyant icons. Despite this, a sober analysis of the club's history suggests that few players shone more brightly.

I'M PONDERING all of this as I gaze out across Salisbury City's Raymond McEnhill Stadium. The view over the rolling Wiltshire hills is wonderful. It's 10am on match-day and the anticipation of a handful of backroom staff preparing the pitch, the kit, the programme and the food is tangible. The door swings open and the boss strolls in. Holmes gave up a property business in Florida to manage Salisbury City back in the summer of 2002 at a time when the club was in serious danger of extinction. He has since overseen two promotions. On the day that we meet, Salisbury are sitting at the top of the Southern League Premier Division.

As a player, Holmes was always noted for his fitness and he is clearly still in fantastic shape. He is surely not an ounce over the 11st 11lbs which he weighed as a professional. "I still love training, I can't do so much now, but I love exercise," he says. "Whatever that thing in your body is, it's in me. It's like a drug, if I don't do anything for two or three days my body is telling me that I better go and do something or I might do something stupid."

Playing squash is his main form of activity, although there remains an occasional urge to join in training. "Not too often, though – I don't want the lads laughing at me," he says. The lure of football, however, was strong enough to entice him away from the sun of Florida to a struggling non-league club after 13 years out of the game. "Once the missus agreed I couldn't wait," he says. "I used to watch Premiership games five times a week in the States, but television can never replace the changing rooms. On match days the buzz is similar, although when you are a manager, winning is even more important than when you are a player."

The football bug has been firmly imbedded in Holmes since the age of seven and the memories of his first visit to The Dell remain vivid. "I couldn't see too much because I was too small, but they let me through to the front. You could feel the atmosphere. It was great and was something that The Dell always gave you. I pestered my dad so much he bought us a couple of season-tickets and that was it.

"The 1960s was an entertaining time and I would never miss a home game. We scored goals for fun under Ted Bates in those days with George O'Brien, Derek Reeves and then Martin Chivers. I think we were close to 100 goals in a few seasons. Then Ron Davies came in and became such a massive hero. I marvelled at John Sydenham's pace going down the left and Terry Paine's ability to put the ball on a six-pence, but Ron Davies was my favourite. I wanted to be Ron Davies."

Holmes' chance arrived quickly. A relatively late starter, he broke into the Southampton schoolboys' team at the age of 14 and, by the age of 15, had finished full-time education and accepted an apprenticeship at The Dell. "Once I got into football, all I thought about was football," he says. "Education is now forced on people, but it wasn't so much in those days. My mum and dad had questions – they were obviously concerned. But we all sat down together and the head-master said, 'the lad obviously wants to do this, you ought to let him go and do it'."

Holmes was walking into a dressing room packed full of his heroes. "It was very daunting," he says. "You were told you would be looking after two or three people's kit. I was thinking, 'I hope I get Ron's kit'. As fate would have it, I got Ron Davies, Jimmy Gabriel and Ken Jones' kit. I'd been to an all-boys' school and I really enjoyed it, but it probably gave me more of a sheltered life than other schools. One thing I remember was that I was just astounded at the language which was used. Every other word was a swear word. I just listened and hoped that I didn't say too much when I went home. It was great, the banter that goes around. They took the mickey out of the young boys quite a bit, but I loved it."

As well as the language, the drinking culture which ran right through football surprised Holmes. At the time, Saints had the 'Ale-House' tag. "In the early days there was quite a lot of drinking and that was one of the things I found strange," says Holmes. "You were meant to be athletes, but after training at 12.30pm, the pub was the first place you would go to. I must admit I was never into that. Lawrie was one of those who would initially say 'this has got to stop'. But Ted [Bates] would say it was about performances on Saturday. The blend was quite clever. The drinking was there, but it did become less and less. A winning dressing room, though, is an easy place to be and they were strong enough characters to make sure losses didn't happen too often."

Killing time has long been a problem for footballers. Although Holmes was never one of the big socialisers at the club, his honesty and determination made him a popular team-mate. He remembers joining a syndicate organised by Peter Osgood which bought a greyhound by the name of Daveybreen. He now wonders whether the Portsmouth-based trainer knew it was for a group of Southampton footballers. "We liked the dogs – but I swear that it had only three legs," he says.

THE START of Holmes' career coincided with the end of an era at Saints as first Ted Bates and then Terry Paine departed. Bates, who was the longest-serving manager in the Football League, made a dignified move into the background as chief executive, but the relationship between Paine and the new manager, McMenemy, was more difficult. Paine's last game for Southampton came in April 1974 and, when he was substituted for Holmes, he ignored the 19-year-old as he made his way from the pitch for the final time as a Southampton player.

"It was a big change when Lawrie came in," says Holmes, "I remember Bill Ellerington [the scout] saying to me, 'things are going to be different now' and that was an understatement. The differences in the personalities of the managers were vast. Terry was one of those who couldn't change his ways at that time. His ways suited Ted, but didn't suit Lawrie. It was the last time he played in a Southampton shirt and it was typical of the difference."

As Paine walked off the pitch, he was being replaced by a player who also could hardly have been more different. Quiet and rarely noticeable in a showy or glamorous sense, Holmes preferred to stay in the shadows. He would later become club captain, but was never a dressing room leader in the 'up and at 'em' sense. It is the same when looking back at the 1976 FA Cup final triumph. Holmes appears in hardly any of the pictures, and interviews with him at the time are a collector's item. Of recent players, his persona (as well as the on-field versatility) is similar to that of Paul Telfer. At 21, Holmes was the baby of the Cup final squad and, to this day, he remains grateful for the big influence of Osgood, who deliberately shielded him from the spotlight.

"If there was a group of people, I was always happy to stand in the corner," says Holmes. "But suddenly everything was thrust on us and it was so good for me to have Ossie. He saw that I was the nervous type and he just made a big joke out of everything. I owe him big time in that Cup run. I remember on the morning of the game getting up and having to do the BBC interview as a group, I was thinking, 'I really don't want to do this'. They went through everyone and, when they got to me, I didn't say anything and Ossie said my line for me."

Osgood would joke that Holmes was "my legs" and he was right there beside his nervous team-mate as they met the Duke of Edinburgh just prior to kick-off. "Nicky Holmes, the quiet man of the Southampton team," said the ITV commentator Brian Moore as the camera panned through the team. He was guilty of an understatement. "Wembley was just monstrous," says Holmes. "Yet once you get going into a game you forget about it. I remember having a big scythe at Steve Coppell early on and I settled down after that. We were under the cosh for 20 minutes, but Jim Steele and Mel Blyth were magnificent for us and gradually we became better than them. They ran out of ideas and we killed them off, hence Bob's [Stokes] great goal at the end."

It remains, of course, one of the greatest FA Cup final upsets with Saints, who that year had only finished sixth in the Second Division, toppling a Manchester United team who had finished third in the top-flight. "Lawrie used the older players as his motivational tool," says Holmes. "This was their swansong and he went on about the experience in the dressing room, which far outweighed Manchester United. As a Southampton lad I didn't need any motivating. I would have followed those lads anywhere. If they had told me to run into a tree of roses, I would have run into it for them. Some of the others couldn't do all the running. The Peter Osgoods couldn't do it, but they could do the bits of magic and I was happy to work for them."

The FA Cup triumph sparked a party the likes of which Southampton has never seen before or since. The city stayed alive all night, although the players remained in London. "The evening was shocking," says Holmes. "We went to the 'Talk of the Town' in London. Looking back, I would have loved to have come back to Southampton. All my family told me how good Southampton was and I would have loved to be part of that with the family. But we went to the 'Talk of the Town' and saw Julie Rogers. We were dotted all around the place and then we got together for *Match of the Day*. Jimmy Hill was there and they did a load of interviews – although I managed to stay in the background again."

It became quickly evident what Stokes' goal had meant to the entire city as an estimated 250,000 people turned out on a 19-mile parade on an open-topped bus. 'Southampton in ecstasy', declared the *Echo* as it described the delirium. "The brave and agile clambered up scaffolding, took to the trees, got on top of bus shelters and scaled the ABC Cinema," it said. "They got anywhere, to any vantage spot. A bashful Bobby Stokes was brought into the limelight…King Bobby, the lad with a Golden Boot, and a never-to-be-forgotten joy of a Cup-winning goal at Wembley stood at the front holding the trophy aloft." The reception in Southampton took the players and the manager by surprise. "We realised coming out of London that people were even on the bridges waiting for us and were waving and everyone took turns standing on the front," says McMenemy.

The captain Rodrigues said the sheer numbers of people made it impossible to appreciate where exactly they were in Southampton as the bus parade began. Peter Osgood was driving down separately from London and had to eventually dump his car some miles outside of the city centre and run to meet the bus. What is less well known, however, is how close that Sunday of celebration came to tragedy. "It was unbelievable," says Holmes, "I don't think anyone could ever have thought that could happen. The bus just couldn't move and around West End way they tried to make up some time and our trainer, Jim Clunie, was inches from having his head taken off by one of the over-head wires." Few among the revellers, however, could have realised that the FA Cup team would be broken up within months.

MCMENEMY MAY have built one team capable of the ultimate prize in domestic Cup football, but getting Saints back into the First Division was the club's priority. Reliability, of course, was Holmes' greatest strength and he was to remain a permanent cog as McMenemy constructed something new. "Lawrie learned quickly so he went and saw what was needed to get you out of Division Two," says Holmes. "He was quickly off to change things around a bit. Bally [Alan Ball] came in, Steve Williams and Chris Nicholl had come onto the scene, it was a very a different set-up."

Different, but equally successful as promotion was secured and then a third Wembley appearance for Holmes in just three years following the FA Cup final and Charity Shield of 1976. David Peach was the only other survivor. This time it was the League Cup with Holmes scoring a crucial goal in the first leg of the semi-final at Elland Road as Saints went on to secure their Wembley date with Nottingham Forest. "First half in the final against Forest we played really well, far better than in the final against Manchester United," says Holmes. "But something happened at half-time. Forest came out and dominated us." It finished 3-2 although I have to remind Holmes that he did score one of Saints' goals. It was later described as "the best consolation goal ever seen in a Cup final".

"It was a half-volley, it was one of those half-volleys that sat up nicely on my left foot," says Holmes. "If it had been on my right foot, it would have been over the stands, even at Wembley. It's something that's nice to say, 'I've scored a goal in a Cup final at Wembley'. But I scored better and more important goals."

That was true. Indeed, for someone who played his career in midfield and defence, Holmes' goal-scoring record of 64 in 535 starts is impressive. Easily the most spectacular came from inside his own half at The Dell in a 4-0 League Cup win over Watford. In a newspaper article some years later, the headline read: 'The Saint who out-shot Le Tiss.'

"Mick Channon went in on the 'keeper who mis-kicked the ball along the ground and it came to me about three or four yards inside my half," he says. "For some reason I was over on the right of the pitch and it landed on my left foot. I hit it first time and it flew in without even bouncing. It was just one of those amazing things. Nowadays there seems to be a television camera at every game, but in those days there weren't, so not many people saw it." For those who didn't, it was every bit as good as David Beckham's more celebrated strike against Wimbledon in 1996.

THE EARLY 1980s were Holmes' favourite time as a footballer and he wonders if the midfield of that period was the best in the club's history. "Stevie Williams had all the audacity and skill I would have loved to have and Alan Ball was the most infectious footballer I have ever played with," he says, "Bally insisted the best out of you. Effort, skill, it was a joy to play with Alan and Steve Williams. We had a good contrast as a midfield three. That was the time when

I enjoyed my football as much as I ever could and ever did. I just felt that we had such balance in midfield. It was bom, bom, bom, all one touch. It's a shame nothing lasts – I think it's probably as good a three as we ever had at The Dell."

Ball appreciates the compliment. "Nick was a real good player, incredible energy, what people didn't understand about him was that he had this real desire to win," he says, "he didn't go about it like me in a loud way – I was as daft as a brush. He would do it in a quiet way, he would go about his job and you could rely on him on that left-hand side."

Holmes considers the second place league finish of 1983/84 as the best achievement. By that time David Armstrong had come into the midfield alongside Williams as Holmes shuffled between left wing-back and sweeper. "We had lost Keegan, Channon and Ball, but we still had star names," says Holmes.

Frank Worthington was one. His reputation was that of a playboy, but Holmes says he saw few players who trained harder. "Frank was a different class – he loved Elvis and he loved smacking balls in the back of the net," he says. "He scored that famous volley for Bolton all those years ago and he would do that on the training ground all the time. He'd flick it over his head and he'd bop it in." It would be difficult to find a greater contrast than that between Holmes and Worthington, yet both captured the hearts and minds of a Southampton fan-base who have generally valued honesty and loyalty just above flair.

When it came to the love of being out on a training pitch, however, Worthington and Holmes were kindred spirits. Holmes puts his consistency over the years down to his fitness and enjoyment of training. "I never missed training for 15 years, I never missed anything and I would do extra if I could," he says. "I would come back in the afternoons when other people were not there and maybe coach some of the youngsters, I just loved it so much."

Holmes was only 30 at the end of the 1984/85 season and looked poised to give the club many more years of good service. At this stage, he had already played virtually 500 games and it was conceivable he could challenge Terry Paine's all-time record of 815 club appearances. Jimmy Case, for example, was one year younger than Holmes and joined Saints around this time and played 272 matches for the club.

Holmes, however, was less fortunate. A pelvic injury nagged away for two frustrating seasons before Chris Nicholl took what he described as the "the saddest decision I've had to make" in giving Holmes a free transfer. "When I hit 30, the wear and tear on the pelvis just caught up on me," says Holmes. "It's like a toothache, just there all the time. Even now I can't play squash two days in a row."

Rest sometimes created the false hope of a fresh dawn. After being out for three months early in the 1986/87 season, he returned at 24 hours' notice to score a crucial goal against Manchester United. But his body would no longer stand up to the regular demands of football at the highest level. "Dropping down a level and not tearing around was much easier," he says. "But the intensity and work-rate needed in the First Division was too much."

Holmes gamely gave it one last go when he returned for pre-season training in the summer of 1987. "I came back and I was better than any of them running wise on the first day. The second day was fine and the third day was fine. Then, on the fourth day, I did a hard run and it was there again. I just thought, 'I can't do this'. Some other clubs were offering me decent wages, but I would have been going there and taking their money and I didn't want to do that." One of the best Saints careers had come to an end.

"A year later, I came back and did the reserves and did some scouting, but I could have played reserve team football just once a week without training and helped the youngsters on," he says. "The lads coming through were the Shearers, Le Tissiers, the Kennas. I think I could have brought them on a bit quicker and I wish I'd had that chance."

Holmes, however, had other priorities. A young family needed supporting and the money that is now in the game was simply not available in the late eighties. He was to finally leave his spiritual home. "It was heart-breaking to make the decision that I had to find something else," he says. "For ten years I ran a village store. It was extremely hard work and extremely long hours, but financially it got me what was necessary to look after the kids."

An average day at the Winterslow Village Stores in Wiltshire would see Holmes begin at 5am and work through until around 7 or 8pm. He had come full circle and became a season-ticket holder again, although that did cease during the Ian Branfoot managerial era. "I like Ian Branfoot," says Holmes, "but the football at the time wasn't great. We were working hard all week and we wanted to be entertained."

AFTER SIX YEARS in Florida, Holmes is now happy to be back living in the south of England and involved with football. "Being in charge at Salisbury is as good as it gets for me now," he says, "you have a dressing room, you have a backroom staff and you talk football. You don't stop talking about football. It's a terrible thing, but when you start talking about football nothing else in the world matters. Football is your life, doesn't matter whether it's the Premier League or the Southern Premier League."

Holmes has been enjoying considerable success at Salisbury. In 2003/04, he led them into the first round proper of the FA Cup for a tie against Sheffield Wednesday and, after our interview, Salisbury clinched the Southern League title of 2005/06 to win promotion into the Conference South, just two divisions below the Football League. His beloved Saints were finishing second in the same competition exactly a century earlier. The likes of Alan Ball have since put Holmes' name forward as a prospective future Southampton manager. Holmes, though, plays down that particular comment and his dislike of the limelight perhaps means he is happier at a club like Salisbury.

"To be realistic, it is not likely to happen and I am happy here," he says, "there are no big egos, it is a friendly club and we all work together. I admire what the players do – they have full-time jobs – and I can associate with them." There was a lovely moment at the end of the 2005/06 season when his Salisbury team was on the pitch celebrating their league title and Holmes declined to be photographed with the players and simply walked off the pitch leaving them to soak up the glory. He remains a model of substance rather than self-promotion.

SO JUST WHERE does Nick Holmes stand in the pantheon of Saints greats? And exactly what was his status as a Cult Hero? As a player, he is clearly up there with the very best. The one and only Southampton born and bred member of the FA Cup-winning side, he was an integral part of teams during the early 1980s which can justifiably claim to be the finest the club has known. "I took it as a compliment that Lawrie and Ted saw in me someone who would just be there," he says. "It's not that they would build teams around me, I would be the one who was quite often moved around. But Lawrie realised that at the top level you had to get the blend of the ability and the work-rate and I was the latter.

"One good thing I had was my left foot and I worked hard all the time. It kept me going and got me through. I know teams inquired about me, but playing for Saints was all I wanted to do."

Holmes admits that he did once carry an uncharacteristically militant attitude into a contract negotiation with McMenemy. He laughs at the memory and says it lasted for about five seconds. "I had been there quite a few years – I had missed a few games through injury, but I hadn't been dropped," he remembers. "Usually he would say, 'right I'm going to give you this' and I would just say, 'yes, fine' and sign it. But I thought I would go for a bit more. I went through the records and worked out how many games we had lost when I played and how many games we had won and lost when I wasn't playing. It looked good for me.

"So I went in there with this bit of paper and Lawrie said, 'what have you got in your hand?' He took it off me and said, 'you don't need that, now sign this'. I just said, 'okay'. I wasn't a great one for bargaining but, to be fair, what I got paid to play football was decent. It might not have been as high as internationals, but I had no delusions of grandeur or anything. I was where I wanted to be, I had enough money to look after my family and I was playing first team football, so what was the problem? They were golden years for Saints and I was lucky to play with some of the great names."

Holmes' modesty and lack of international recognition, however, should fool nobody. Those statistics which Holmes almost brought into that contract talk with McMenemy would have made for impressive reading. Saints won more games than they lost whenever he played during this period, but the opposite was true when he was absent. It couldn't all have been a coincidence. Holmes was always there, always involved, always working, scurrying, tackling, passing and even scoring.

Yet Holmes' demeanour and playing style meant there were times when he certainly did not get anything like the recognition that he deserved. He was never voted Player of the Year in his time at Saints and his testimonial in 1987 attracted a disappointing crowd of 7,264 which made him just £20,000. Holmes had been unfortunate in several respects. He had hoped to stage his testimonial in both 1984 and 1986 after the FA Cup final, but the plans were scrapped after agonising semi-final defeats. The Charity Shield was also on the same day. What's more, some supporters may have been turned off the idea of testimonials after an admission around that time from Mick Channon that players from the 1976 FA Cup final team had made money by selling tickets on the black market. Holmes was not implicated in this, but damage had been done. The manager of the time Chris Nicholl said: "Those revelations didn't help football in general and they certainly didn't help Nick. He deserved more than the number who turned up. He has been a great servant of Southampton, a superb professional."

Holmes was magnanimous about the whole affair. Speaking straight after the match, he said: "I was more than happy that 7,000 came. They are the real hard-core fans and I was touched by the reception they gave me." It had been the most exciting and glamorous period in the club's history and the fans were perhaps caught in the moment.

Not now, though. With time to reflect on past heroes, the appreciation of Nick Holmes' contribution to Saints has widened and deepened. "The three players that I've always had fond memories of are Nick Holmes, David Armstrong and Phil Boyer," said Tony Whatley, a long-standing Saints fan. "None of them were particularly 'stars', but players that gave everything in every game. Out of the three Nick Holmes is, I think, our most under-rated player."

CB Fry had an aura which made him the most celebrated and popular sportsman in Britain in the late 1800s and early 1900s. His dashing style also made him something of a sex-symbol

Fry is considered by many to be the finest ever all-round sportsman. He played for Saints and England at football and was a genuinely world class cricketer and athlete

Ted Bates the player appeared for Saints in 216 first class games, plus 181 war-time matches

Ted Bates and wife Mary, who was assistant secretary at Saints from 1945 until 1958. "I was trying to put the men in their place and I did that eventually," she says

Ted Bates and grandson Steven close the gates of The Dell for the last time as Saints prepare to move to St. Mary's in 2001. The Dell had been Bates' spiritual home since 1937 when he arrived as a player

Charlie Wayman presents new manager Sid Cann with a lucky black cat in 1949. Luck, however, had been in short supply in the previous season when Saints missed out on promotion to Division One despite leading Division Two by eight points with only seven matches remaining

Charlie Wayman sniffs out a chance at The Dell during a 3-1 win against Bradford Park Avenue in December 1949 as Ted Bates looks on. That season was Wayman's last with Saints and he left with a phenomenal record of 77 goals in just 107 games

Captain Cliff Huxford shows off the Division
Three championship trophy at the end of
the 1959/60 season. Huxford did not miss
a minute throughout the entire campaign

Saints announced their arrival
as a force in English football during the
1960 FA Cup when they thrashed
Manchester City 5-1 at Maine Road.
Cliff Huxford is congratulated
by manager Ted Bates as his
team-mates celebrate

Terry Paine heads home the goal against Leyton Orient
which effectively secured promotion into Division One for the
first time in Saints' history. The year was 1966 and Paine
would later help England to win the World Cup

Terry Paine and Lawrie McMenemy, arguably Southampton's greatest player
and manager, talk tactics. They spent just one season together

After holding the all-time record for Football League appearances,
Terry Paine has moved to South Africa where he is now the face of football
on the television network Mnet SuperSport

Ron Davies' heading prowess was phenomenal. He developed an ability to leap
and hang in the air by training in heavy army boots when he played for Chester City

Ron Davies is also a talented artist and hopes to enrol on a course
at the University of New Mexico in retirement

With his socks rolled down and odds boots, Brian O'Neil looked like a pub footballer. But he drove the Southampton midfield during the early 1970s

Brian O'Neil on his wedding day flanked by best man Mick Channon. O'Neil made it his business to protect Channon on the football field

Bobby Stokes' shot nestles in the corner of Alex Stepney's net and the Saints no.11 turns to take the adulation of the crowd. His life was never the same again

Stokes enjoys the cheers of the crowd during the triumphant victory parade after winning the FA Cup for Southampton

It is estimated that 250,000 people lined the streets of Southampton during the club's 19-mile victory parade

The opposition are appealing but Mick Channon is already celebrating with his trademark one-armed 'Windmill'. It remains the ultimate individual goal celebration

Mick Channon's testimonial came just two days after the 1976 FA Cup triumph. Ecstatic fans surged onto the pitch in the closing moments to acclaim their hero

Mick Channon's passion is now horse racing and he is one of the
leading flat trainers in the country

Nick Holmes salutes The Dell crowd. Holmes was the one regular throughout
the club's most successful era under Lawrie McMenemy

Nick Holmes is pictured with the FA Cup as manager of Salisbury City after guiding the club to the first round proper in 2003 and a match against Sheffield Wednesday

Lawrie McMenemy was one of the first managers to become a celebrity in his own right. He is pictured after the 1976 FA Cup semi-final win against Crystal Palace

Lawrie McMenemy is joined by predecessor Ted Bates as they celebrate the 1976 FA Cup triumph

Yugoslav full-back Ivan Golac
became the first foreign 'import'
to appear in a Wembley domestic
final when he helped Saints reach
the 1979 League Cup final
against Nottingham Forest

Ivan Golac with wife Bratislava –
"my boss" – he calls her

Lawrie McMenemy sent shockwaves throughout the entire footballing world
when he unveiled Kevin Keegan to a stunned but elated Southampton in February 1980

Kevin Keegan was a double European Footballer of the Year and at his peak as a player when he signed for Saints

Danny Wallace defied multiple sclerosis to complete the 2006 London Marathon. He rates the achievement as equal to anything he achieved with Saints or Manchester United

Happy days for Danny (centre), as he and brothers Rodney (left) and Raymond (right) create history in becoming the only trio of brothers to play together in the same top-flight team in modern times

Mark Dennis puts on an innocent face, but he is in the book again. Dennis was sent off 12 times in his career

A dressing room scrap with Chris Nicholl signalled the end of Dennis' Saints career, but the two old sparring partners are now good friends

Jimmy Case was regarded among the most fearsome midfielders in English football and always particularly relished his battles with the blue half of Merseyside

Case was the complete midfielder. Before joining Saints, he helped Liverpool win three European Cups

Matthew Le Tissier pounces to score the historic last goal at the Dell

Le Tissier celebrates scoring past a helpless Peter Schmeichel during the 3-1 beating of Manchester United in 1996 – the famous 'Grey shirt' match

Le Tissier and his favourite manager Alan Ball. Le Tiss scored 45 goals in just 65 games under Ball; many of them spectacular

No finer proof of a man's Cult Hero status...Saints fans offer their own unique tribute to Francis Benali at the end of the 1993 season

Francis Benali and son Luke. An iconic image of a classic Cult Hero

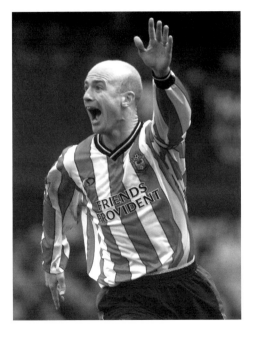

The delight is written all over Chris Marsden's face as he celebrates a memorable individual goal against Ipswich Town in 2002

Captain Chris Marsden and manager Gordon Strachan reflect on what might have been after the 2003 FA Cup Final

Antti Niemi demonstrates the athleticism which has convinced many fans that he ranks alongside the legendary Peter Shilton as the club's finest ever goalkeeper

Niemi sealed his Cult Hero status against Fulham in 2003, when he dramatically blasted a shot against the cross-bar which led to an injury-time equaliser

I LEAVE Salisbury's stadium determined to set the record straight and to ensure Nick Holmes gets the credit that so many of the Saints' faithful would now like to see. As I make my way into the car park, he tells me how much he enjoys chatting about the "good old days" and asks when I first saw Saints play. "1983," I reply. "We beat Liverpool 3-2."

He smiles. "I scored two in that game," he says.

"Really?" I feel slightly embarrassed, but not entirely convinced. Surely I would have remembered the player who scored two goals? I go away to check the records and, sure enough, he did score twice in a memorable victory over the champions-elect. What's more, one of them was apparently a spectacular effort from 30-yards out.

I think back and can clearly remember seeing the likes of Mark Wright, Steve Moran, Peter Shilton, Ian Rush and Kenny Dalglish in action. Yet there is still no recollection of Holmes, the match-winner. Typical really.

LAWRIE MCMENEMY

1973-1985
1993-1997
2006-PRES

SAINTS CAREER

As manager

Games   606

MAGIC MOMENT

Unveiling the double European Footballer of the Year Kevin Keegan to a shocked Southampton public

'BIG MAC'

'He could enter any walk of life and motivate the people around him.'

Nick Holmes

THERE is no such thing as a typical day for Lawrie McMenemy. But, I suspect, this rather random assortment of events and guest appearances is somehow not unusual. I had called him about a football fan who has had an extension completed in the basement of his house. You must enter the basement via a turnstile that was once part of The Dell and inside is a huge room. The room is decked out with all kinds of pictures, programmes and Saints memorabilia and is large enough to also contain a snooker table and a plasma-style screen. But it gets better. For the icing on the cake is the fact that the seating for the television is contained within the former dugout of The Dell. Yes, all 12 square metres of it.

The Dell dugout was one of hundreds of pieces of Saints history that were sold off when the club moved from the old ground in 2001 and the proud owner of an item that would have once accommodated Brian Clough, Sir Alex Ferguson, Bill Shankly, Bob Paisley and most managerial legends you can think of is the Southampton season-ticket holder Richard Prosser. The names Clough and Ferguson, however, mean little to Richard. In his opinion, the greatest of them all is a certain Lawrie McMenemy.

That's right, the manager who guided Saints to an FA Cup triumph, three finishes in the top six of the league and enticed the likes of World Cup winner Alan Ball, European Footballer of the Year Kevin Keegan and goalkeeping legend Peter Shilton to The Dell. All that is more than enough evidence for Richard and a generation of Saints fans who lived through the magical McMenemy years of the late 1970s and early 1980s.

Richard wants to invite the former Saints boss to his house for the grand opening of what has been named the 'Lawrie McMenemy Suite'. I had informed McMenemy and the response was positive. "No problem," he said, "I'm presenting prizes for the Rose Road Association on Tuesday morning. Come and meet me there at the Bradbury Centre, we can have a cup of tea and I'll drive us after lunch."

I duly arrive at the Bradbury Centre and McMenemy is in full flow. The prizes he is handing out are for children who have recently completed a literacy course and he is being swarmed by admirers. Many of them think they might be able to get free tickets to watch Saints and all are sent away with various pearls of wisdom. "Keep working hard", he says, "listen to your teacher. I'll be back soon so make sure that project is finished."

The children hang off each word he utters and follow him everywhere he walks as if he's some sort of latter day Pied Piper. It is not only that he is 6ft 4ins tall, but also something in the way he carries himself. McMenemy – even at 70 – is a formidable presence. He is a natural in this sort of situation and it is obvious that all the staff love him. McMenemy is an active supporter of many charities and, when he was awarded the MBE in the 2006 New Year honours list, it was in recognition of this as well as his football accomplishments.

Next stop, though, is Richard's house. The basement is a shrine to Saints. Upon entering, there is a red plaque with the words 'Lawrie McMenemy Suite' and a ribbon ready for the grand opening. A photographer is on hand to capture the moment for the local press and all present raise a glass of champagne to the guest of honour. Some of Richard's family and friends – all Saints fans – are on hand for the opening ceremony and stand quietly as McMenemy stops for around half-an-hour and perches on the end of the snooker table delivering stories and anecdotes about his career in football.

We depart, leaving Richard and his guests suitably impressed and head back to Southampton – although not before McMenemy has been accosted in the street by an elderly lady who wants his autograph for her husband. She tells him a story about how she once met him at some event and McMenemy nods knowingly. "Oh aye", he says. He signs a card and strolls in a statesman-like fashion back to his car. Another function probably awaits…

WHEN I DO arrange to interview McMenemy for this book, it is several months later and we meet at a local hotel. He has recently returned from a holiday in Florida to attend the funeral of Peter Osgood – his first major signing for Saints. He remarks that he needs a secretary, but that he has no intention of slowing down as he gets older. "You've got to keep busy lad," he tells me.

McMenemy's connection with the Southampton public is extremely strong and, despite severed links with the football club's hierarchy between 1997 and 2006, he has become an ambassadorial figure in and around the city. Indeed, within days of Rupert Lowe's departure as chairman in the summer of 2006, McMenemy had agreed to return as a director on Saints' football board. It is his third stint at the club and it was no coincidence that season-ticket sales received an immediate boost.

At the time we meet, however, Lowe is still chairman and McMenemy is remaining diplomatic in public about the political situation at the club. In the following months he was to declare his support for the leading individual shareholder Michael Wilde in his ultimately successful attempt to topple Lowe. It was a significant move as, although the animosity between McMenemy and Lowe was hardly a secret, it was the first time he had spoken of his opposition to the former chairman. His words were clearly carefully chosen. "My attitude is, I definitely think there has to be a change from the present regime," he said. "They cannot argue that they have not had every chance in nine years. What I do know is that if the current regime [Lowe] wins the EGM then the last person to leave St. Mary's should, it's sad to say, turn off the lights, lock the door and throw away the key for good. I once famously said that after we had reached the semi-finals of the FA Cup, that people would be dancing in the streets if this was up north. A lady sent me a letter saying, 'we are just as proud of you as anyone in the north would be, we just prefer to dance in the kitchen'. At the moment the natives are not dancing in the kitchens, they're dancing with their feet."

McMenemy did not mention Lowe by name, but his intervention, while not the decisive nail in a partially self-made coffin, was another sizeable nail nonetheless. Some might now dismiss him as "old school", but the fact remains that McMenemy brought unprecedented glory to Southampton Football Club and is still very influential. He is a personality who can galvanise Saints supporters and his inclusion on Wilde's new board along with Mary Corbett – the daughter of the former president John Corbett – were appointments which warmed the hearts of supporters and added to a feeling of optimism around the club.

Throughout most of the past decade, though, McMenemy was conspicuous by his absence at the club's home, whether it be The Dell or St. Mary's. He had left Saints with Graeme Souness in June 1997 after spending just over three years as the director of football. McMenemy felt he was not welcome at St. Mary's under Lowe and he made just a handful of appearances at the ground between 2001 and 2006. Lowe has suggested that McMenemy's exile was self-imposed. Whatever the rights and wrongs of what was a rather sad stand-off, there is little doubt that McMenemy's achievements – particularly the 1976 FA Cup final victory – merited significant commemoration. Equally, it was hardly surprising that he clashed with Lowe. While they are hardly similar, both do have strong personalities. McMenemy can be superb with people, but his career in football has also contained some notable fall-outs and it would be hard to ever imagine him compromising a strongly held view in the interests of diplomacy. That imposing character, though, was what made him a great manager – a man who brought a level of glamour, kudos and success to Southampton that now seems almost unimaginable.

LAWRIE MCMENEMY was born in Gateshead in 1936, but spent his pre-school years in Bournemouth before returning to the north east. He is of Irish ancestry and was the eldest in a family of eight with five brothers and two sisters. Like many of the best managers, he was brought up in a tough, working class area of the country and McMenemy's book, *The Diary of a Season,* outlines how his father worked as a caretaker at a community centre and the family lived in a terraced house which had an outside toilet and two bedrooms.

McMenemy was a bright pupil and did well enough at his junior school to win a place to attend the St. Cuthbert's Grammar School in Newcastle and his aim was to become a journalist. It was, in many respects, an ambition he has come to fulfil. As his career in football unfolded, McMenemy demonstrated an acute sense for media management and public relations and he was also a television pundit. He continues to write a weekly column for the *Echo* and – having liaised with him over it on several occasions – I can testify that, unlike most sporting personalities, it arrives so well crafted that the ghost writer is effectively a copy-taker.

Of the 'O' Levels he got at school, it is not surprising, therefore, that one of them was in English. Football, though, was the dominant force in Newcastle and he would play long into the evening with his friends on the cobbled streets around his house. They would apparently use a tennis ball and the lamp posts would be makeshift goals. Upon leaving school at 16, he became a junior clerk in the local education department and was signed on schoolboy forms by Newcastle before being loaned out to Gateshead.

McMenemy was then called up for National Service and spent two years as a guardsman with the First Battalion Coldstream Guards, patrolling Buckingham Palace, St. James and the Bank of England. It was a job which gave an edge to his reputation in football. He had a certain fear factor over even the most unruly of characters, as Mark Dennis testifies. "He had that aura about him as a former Guardsman, he loved discipline," he says, "to get one over the gaffer you had to get up very early in the morning. Very few people crossed him and if you did cross him your days were usually finished at the club. He was very similar to Brian Clough like that."

McMenemy's playing career ended prematurely following a foot injury while with the Army and he took on a coaching position at Gateshead, where he passed his coaching badges, before moving to Bishop Auckland and helped them to the league, the cup and the county cup in the same year. He was then offered a job as a coach at Sheffield Wednesday by Alan Brown and, in 1968 at the age of 32, became manager of Fourth Division Doncaster Rovers. They were promoted in his first season, but relegated two years later and he was sacked.

He was soon back in work as manager of Grimsby Town in 1971 and also took them to the Division Four title. Three decades later, his contribution was enough to prompt them to name a new restaurant in his honour. "I did my apprenticeship in non-league," says McMenemy, "and was quite enjoying it really. I was young, married and had a young family. It was a big decision to go full-time as coach at Sheffield Wednesday, but we took it and went from there." After Grimsby, McMenemy was offered the job of 'team manager designate' to succeed Ted Bates at Saints who was planning to retire after his 18 years at the helm.

DESPITE HAVING no league experience as a player, it had taken McMenemy just five years to reach the First Division of English football. Although he was only officially given the title of 'manager' in November 1973, when Bates became chief executive, he stresses that he was in sole charge from the off.

"Ted came in and he said 'welcome back' to the players, and finished off by saying, 'this time, I don't want anyone coming back in the afternoons with alcohol on your breath for pre-season'," says McMenemy, "and then he said, 'over to Lawrie, your new manager'. I said, 'that's a good joke' and they all looked at me as though I was barmy and I found out just how true those words were."

Initially, however, all appeared rosy and there was briefly the hope of a European place as Saints reached fifth in the table by the middle of December. McMenemy, however, felt he had a team with too many "high fliers" and "drinkers". Indeed, he later wrote that he had inherited a dressing room with "so many gangsters that Al Capone would have struggled to get a game". The degree to which there were problems is, not surprisingly, disputed by those in the dressing room, but, some 33 years on, McMenemy remains adamant he was faced with significant issues.

"It was a dressing room which basically needed sorting out," he says, "there were some good players, but ill-disciplined. Because of that I found it quite a difficult job to start with. I was having to adjust to a higher level and also come to terms with what was going on in the dressing room. There were some players who were really strong, working hard behind the scenes and quite a bit of disruption went on. I never minded rascals, it's villains I didn't want.

"They resented change, they resented someone coming in. That was the general feeling. Mick Channon was never a villain, but he is very strong-minded with strong opinions and I don't think Mick rated me at all when I arrived. He had been with one manager who had signed him from school and there was a terrific bond – and so there should have been. But it wasn't my fault that Ted left and, very unusually, I didn't take over from a manager who was sacked. I think Mick looked at me and thought, 'who's he, where's he from'. They don't know where Grimsby and Doncaster are. Mick had played for England and these were probably little Fourth Division clubs to him. I had to win them over."

Saints' post-Christmas decline meant that the club was relegated back to Division Two in McMenemy's first season as manager. Terry Paine was also substituted in three of his last ten games and then allowed to leave the club. It was a bold move, particularly with the club struggling, but McMenemy, even at a time when his back was against the wall, was showing that he was not a manager afraid to make difficult decisions.

The likes of John McGrath, Brian O'Neil, Joe Kirkup and Eric Martin were also soon gone as McMenemy placed his own stamp on the club. He is happy to take the blame for relegation, although he does point out that the circumstances were unfortunate. In the first season that three clubs were relegated, Saints went down as the third from bottom team with a tally of 36 points which would have ensured safety in any of the club's preceding seasons in Division One. "We went to Everton on the last game and I left Terry Paine out for the first time and we won 3-0," says McMenemy, "but we needed Norwich, I think, to win at Birmingham. Amazingly at half-time, we learned they were winning. They used to put the numbers on the boards [to show the half-time scores], but the fella had put them the wrong way round. We still thought they had won at the end, so it was a double-whammy...

"I really, really blamed myself for relegation although when I looked into it, I realised that we had more points than in three of the seven seasons before. A couple of directors had said to me that I needed to sort the discipline out – George Merrick said that would be my big job. Because they knew how difficult the dressing room was, they [the directors] stood by me. I brought rules in the players had to adhere to. They were characters, some didn't live anywhere near the ground, there was a lot of sorting out to do. I was told to get on with it and I think I repaid them by getting us back where they wanted to be and by winning the FA Cup."

Bates admitted that McMenemy's contrasting personality had been one of the reasons for him being appointed. "I thought he was right [Lawrie] for the club," he said, "he was more outgoing, I was quieter. I thought a change like that would be good for us." Clearly mistakes were made in that first season and, while there were times that McMenemy did suffer booing from the crowd, his job was never seriously in jeopardy, thanks partly to the support that Bates gave him.

McMenemy's self-confidence appeared undiminished and he came to national prominence during the summer of 1974 as a pundit during the World Cup. Nick Holmes was signed by Bates, but played most of his Southampton career under McMenemy and says he was quick to adjust to the demands of the job. "It just goes to show that in this day and age and, especially at Southampton recently, he would probably have been sacked after a few months," says Holmes. "He took a long time, the same as Alex Ferguson at Manchester United, but when he did get it right they didn't look back and that was what happened with Lawrie.

"He wasn't naïve, but he was new to it and the one thing with Lawrie was that he learned quickly. If he made a mistake, it never happened again. What Lawrie did was amazing, but it didn't happen straight away. He would move on quickly, all the players that were bought were basically older players with experience that could get us playing."

EVEN IN relegation, a sign of things to come was the capture of Peter Osgood in 1974 for a club record £275,000. Here was the first proof, in the words of Holmes, that "Lawrie could sell anything around the club".

'The King' of Chelsea was 27 at the time and should have still been in his football prime. But McMenemy was able to convince him that The Dell, rather than emerging Stoke City's Victoria Ground alongside his best buddy Alan Hudson, who had also been banished from Chelsea, was the place to be. "Lawrie told me about his ambition and how he wanted to encourage skill and flair," said Osgood, who also claims he was locked in McMenemy's house until he agreed to sign. Upon Osgood's sudden passing in March 2006, McMenemy said that he had been his most significant signing because he was the first of the superstar names that would come to transform the image of the club. "I will always remember the day I signed Ossie because Terry Paine turned to me and said he never thought he would see the time when Southampton signed a player of the quality of Peter Osgood." Unfortunately, the arrival of Osgood came just too late in the relegation season. "He was not match-fit – he had been in dispute at Chelsea, which was how I got him – and the only time I got him fit was the end of the season," says McMenemy.

A rebuilding period was necessary and McMenemy was evolving the squad by bringing in players like Jim McCalliog, Ian Turner, David Peach, Peter Rodrigues and Mel Blyth. He had constructed a team of what he called "road-sweepers and violinists" that would be capable of lifting the FA Cup. Osgood was the first of the "violinists" and the likes of Alan Ball, Charlie George, Kevin Keegan and Frank Worthington were to follow, but not together.

"If they had, we wouldn't have had a ground big enough," says McMenemy, "the football would have been terrific, one touch, half a touch, we would have played the best football going, had the best social life and we would have also got relegated because we wouldn't have won an away game. Nobody would have got the ball. Ideal teams are made up of road-sweepers and violinists, they were all lead violinists, but you have to have a blend and that to me was the fascination of management. We had to blend them with the youth policy we had which was terrific. They gave the legs to the older players and the older players gave them the brains and the experience.

"Over the period you would probably find that I had five teams. The one I inherited which got relegated. The one I got together for promotion which actually won the Cup. They then found it difficult as Cup winners, and I built a third team which got us promoted, the fourth team allowed us to stay up there and the fifth team pushed up towards the top. I never had big squads and that was a strength and we always developed wonderful team spirit."

Just as he did with Worthington during the 1983/84 season, he also built the attacking dimension to his Cup final team around the clever flicks and touches of Osgood. McMenemy and Osgood had their disagreements, however, particularly after the FA Cup semi-final victory over Crystal Palace when the flamboyant striker joined Jim Steele and Jim McCalliog on an unscheduled drinking session.

It was a story that was headline news at the time but, according to McMenemy, fondly recalled as many of the 1976 FA Cup team gathered after Osgood's funeral. "After the funeral was the sort of event Ossie would have loved," says McMenemy, "we shared happy memories and they all remembered the time when we had to play Portsmouth after the Cup semi-final. On the journey back from winning the semi-final we stopped off at a pub and they let their hair down over the weekend. I got them in on the Monday night and we trained in the gym at The Dell to get a good sweat.

"I was taking them to a hotel, which you wouldn't normally do to play Portsmouth, but I just wanted to get them settled after the Cup game. I had booked a hotel at Hayling Island. One car didn't arrive, I didn't know until I went out to dinner, but it was Jim Steele, Jim McCalliog and Ossie, bless him. After I had the meal I went to my room and told the doorman to shut the door if they were not in by a certain time. Of course they weren't back in time, but they bribed the doorman.

"Next morning I said for them to come to my room. It didn't matter what time it was because they had been in the wrong. They came in sheepishly and I said, 'bye-bye boys, off you go to The Dell'. They couldn't believe it and I said, 'go and run around the track'. Then

I brought over Steve Williams and some other players. The happy ending was that we still beat Portsmouth 1-0. I would never go ballistic publicly, but within the four walls I let them know where they stood."

The three rebels were back, however, before the Cup final. Indeed, McMenemy would treat the older players with respect and he allowed the likes of Peter Rodrigues and Jim McCalliog just a few lagers on the Thursday before the FA Cup final to help them calm any nerves. It was not all iron discipline and he still smiles at the now famous story of Osgood stealing the FA Cup after the team had been treated to a night out at a Southampton casino.

"The next morning I was woken by the secretary who said, 'the Cup's missing'," says McMenemy, "I went 'what are you talking about?' He was really upset. Then the chairman rang me and whenever he said 'manager' I knew I was in trouble and he said, 'manager, where's the bloomin' Cup?' I said, 'don't be daft'. The players were starting to come in and I heard the outer door open and a clanging noise. By the time I got to the door, the Cup was lying on its side. I heard footsteps and I picked the Cup up."

It turned out that Osgood and Jim Steele had stolen the Cup in a bet for a bottle of champagne with Rodrigues and ended up drinking coffee and tea out of it with the locals at a burger van next to Southampton's Guildhall.

THE FA CUP triumph was essential in giving McMenemy credibility. "I remember a significant thing at Wembley," he says, "Jack Charlton was at the game and he walked in the dressing room, he stood and talked to me. Mick Channon walked by and he started singing a verse of the Blaydon Races. In a little way that was Mick saying, 'you've arrived'. He had accepted me. Mick was the sort that if he had a problem he would come straight out with it. It wouldn't fester and I didn't mind that."

That Saints were still in the Second Division did not seriously dent McMenemy's authority and he was well regarded enough nationally to be interviewed in December 1977 for the England job along with Brian Clough. At the time, McMenemy felt the interview "went as well as any interview can go", but, in their wisdom, the FA opted for the 'safe' option of West Ham's Ron Greenwood. Of more importance to Saints, the team was again reshaped after the FA Cup triumph. The likes of Peter Rodrigues, Mick Channon, Mel Blyth, Jim McCalliog, Paul Gilchrist, Bobby Stokes and Peter Osgood left over the next three years and, in that same period, Chris Nicholl, Phil Boyer and Ted MacDougall arrived.

But the key to promotion back to the top-flight was the moulding of what was arguably Saints' finest central midfield pairing. In Steve Williams, Saints had a former trainee with the hunger and desire to become one of the best midfielders in the country while Alan Ball was a World Cup winner and a player of pure class. Of all McMenemy's famous signings, the £60,000 that was spent on the influential Ball from Arsenal was perhaps the wisest.

Ball arrived in 1976 at the age of 31 and he inspired an upturn in form and a promotion push in 1977/78. A natural leader, a hard worker and someone with a burning desire to succeed, Ball was voted Player of the Year as Saints finished second and secured their long-awaited promotion. He was McMenemy's leader on the field and also in the dressing room.

Saints made their way into the top three by the beginning of January and remained in a promotion position throughout the rest of the season, although missed out on winning the title by a single point when they were held to a goalless draw at The Dell in the final game of the season against Tottenham Hotspur. That, though, hardly mattered and with an FA Cup win behind him and a place back in the First Division, McMenemy was firmly established.

By now, he had total control and authority over every facet of the football club and his position was beyond question. Primarily, of course, this had been achieved by virtue of results on the pitch. Saints' reputation as an emerging and fashionable club was underlined by another appearance at Wembley for the League Cup final of 1979 against Nottingham Forest. The scenes on the final whistle at The Dell at the conclusion of the second leg of the semi-final against Leeds United, as McMenemy was mobbed by ecstatic supporters as he made his way triumphantly down the touchline, confirmed he was equally as popular as any of the players. It's not often that a manager is held in such high regard as those heroes out on the pitch but three Wembley visits in three years after no cup finals since the nascent years of the century was a powerful aphrodisiac for the growing cult of McMenemy.

But it was not just within Southampton that McMenemy was held in high regard. His charismatic personality and skill at promoting the club meant that he was becoming a national and, to some extent, even an international figure. That fact is underlined by Ivan Golac, who joined Saints from Partizan Belgrade in the summer of 1978 and later said that the two managers in the English game most admired abroad were Brian Clough and McMenemy.

The persona and success of McMenemy meant that he was constantly in demand and he became one of the most recognisable personalities in football. Although his profile has inevitably lessened in recent years, he was one of the first of the managers to become something of a celebrity in his own right. In 1980 he appeared on *This Is Your Life* and, as well as the interview for the England job, McMenemy was, at different times, linked with Nottingham Forest, Newcastle United, Sheffield United, West Bromwich Albion, Middlesbrough and Birmingham City. There were official approaches for his services from Leeds United and Sunderland in 1978, and then Manchester United in 1981 as the replacement to Dave Sexton. Ron Atkinson was later offered the job. McMenemy considered each of these positions, but, in the end, showed considerable loyalty to Saints.

The size of The Dell was a frustration, but, overall, he was happy and confident that he could achieve further success. "The board loved what was happening, but couldn't understand all the extra fuss and attention we were getting," he says, "I called them the china tea-cup board with the genteel atmosphere. The board meetings were a social gathering for these gentlemen and it was very civilised. They were wonderful, wonderful characters. At the end of the meeting, they would have another drink. They let me manage completely and that was their strength. They trusted me because they had done their homework."

In 1981, after turning down the Manchester United job, he said: "Ipswich have given us a reminder of what we can do and our objective is to win the First Division and we can do it. It is everyone's ambition to either play for Manchester United or manage them. But in their own way, Southampton are now as big as Manchester United."

As it turned out, Saints finished in the top eight of the First Division on five occasions in six wonderful seasons between 1979/80 and McMenemy's final campaign as manager in 1984/85. The peaks were a ten match period on top of the table in 1982 and finishes of second in 1984 and fifth in 1985. To this day, McMenemy maintains that he did genuinely believe that he could win the league with Saints.

SO WHAT made McMenemy the club's most successful manager? The most obvious quality was his persuasive personality and record in the transfer market which saw already well established players like Charlie George, Dave Watson, Alan Ball, Ivan Golac, Mick Channon (who returned), Kevin Keegan, Peter Shilton, Mick Mills, Frank Worthington, Joe Jordan and Jimmy Case sign for him. Keegan admits that McMenemy's reputation was significant in his surprise choice of Southampton after leaving Hamburg in 1980.

"If you were naming your top four managers in the country, Lawrie would have been one of them," he said in his autobiography. Few who held talks with McMenemy ever made the decision not to come to Southampton and his motivational capacity was also a strength. The former Benfica boss John Mortimore was McMenemy's assistant from 1979 until 1985 and, although the difference in personality with the former manager Ted Bates was vast, he says they shared an ability to make players want to give their absolute best.

"Lawrie was very strong," says Mortimore, "you knew where you stood with him, he would call a spade a spade and get on with it. He didn't have the football background that Ted had. Lawrie had to come in and establish himself and he did very well. It couldn't have been easy to follow Ted. The players would have no-one else to compare with. No-one could remember the manager before Ted, so Lawrie had to make his own standing there which he did and he had the respect of the players.

"People could say towards Lawrie, 'what's he done in football?' But he had man-management as a strength like Ted, but just in an entirely different way. Lawrie got good players in and could handle them in his own way. He had that skill and ability to bring in big names to the club. It's hard to say Kevin Keegan was better than Ron Davies, but Lawrie had people with bigger reputations."

Nick Holmes was the one player to remain a regular during McMenemy's entire 12-year reign and also highlights his charisma. "He had the gift of the gab," he says. "The team was like a Who's Who of footballers in the 1980s and that was down to Lawrie." I ask McMenemy about his ability to sell Southampton to so many great players and he simply shrugs: "It was just something I was able to do. Players talk and word gets around. Signing Ossie changed the course of things."

Yet if it was McMenemy's personality that attracted some of the biggest names in football, his strong discipline ensured the younger, less famous players also blossomed. McMenemy could generate a certain fear factor and the likes of Mark Dennis and Danny Wallace still talk about him in a reverential way. When I ask Wallace whether he was scared of the manager as a 16-year-old breaking into the first team, he responds emphatically.

"Scared!?" he says, "we were all frightened to death of Lawrie. I think I was about 5ft 3ins at the time and he was about 6ft 6ins. He was the kind of manager you looked up to and I had the greatest of respect for him. He would always look out for his players and I'm pleased to have him as a friend." McMenemy liked to see players wearing a collar and a tie, he disliked jeans and, although it was the fashion in the 1980s, was not keen on permed hair. An exception, it is presumed, was made for Keegan.

His man-management acumen meant that he knew how to handle certain incidents for the benefit of the greater good and he has a sense of humour. Osgood told a story of when McMenemy found him and Alan Ball drinking a bottle of champagne in a sauna. "'If you can't beat 'em, join 'em', he grunted and shared the bottle with us without even loosening his tie," said Osgood. "As we sat and talked, the perspiration formed in a puddle around him."

Channon remembers a time he was let off travelling on a promotional club trip to the Middle East because it came right in the middle of the Cheltenham Festival. McMenemy would also occasionally join the older players for a day at the races and would, invariably, finish the day better off than any of them by sticking to his totally random method of picking winners. "They famously took me to Plumpton and I backed more winners than those lot together," laughs McMenemy, "they were foaming at the mouth."

Golac and Ball both repeatedly use the word "shrewd" to describe McMenemy and he was clever in the way he organised the club and recruited backroom staff who would compliment his own abilities. He continued to utilise Ted Bates as a sounding board and also realised that, as well as the high profile signings, it was imperative to have a thriving youth policy. He placed great emphasis on the scouting network and was alive to the possibility of young talent.

That was underlined when McMenemy was at a local youth match supporting his sons when he spotted Steve Moran. "I noticed that the young centre-forward kept falling over," says McMenemy. "I asked the manager what was wrong and he said that the lad needed new boots, but that his mum was a widow and they couldn't afford them. At half-time while the team was standing around drinking their Oxo, I called him over and said that if he scored a hat-trick in the second half I would get him some new boots. He put the Oxo down, picked up the ball then ran over to the centre circle and waited for the rest of the team to join him for the kick-off. When the ref blew for the restart, the kid proceeded to score the quickest hat-trick I'd ever seen."

A key appointment in boosting the club's youth structure was the addition of the former Burnley centre-back Dave Merrington, who had been working with young offenders. "Lawrie recognised that I was technically a very good coach and that I also had the ability to work away from the field as well in terms of their education and it was a double-barrelled job," says Merrington. "He had the foresight to recognise that the game was changing and he wanted to change with it. It was modern thinking from Lawrie.

"He was very bright in that he was selective in personnel. When I met him, he was very charismatic and he has got a powerful personality. He felt if he could get round pegs in round holes, he could get elements of the job done through other people. He was never frightened to spend big money, but he wanted quality at the top end and at the bottom end."

McMenemy feels it is wrong to pigeon-hole him purely as a man-manager and, although his trusted assistant Lew Chatterley would do much of the coaching, he says that he was also comfortable with that element of the job. "Like Cloughie I was classed as a manager not a coach, but we could coach when we had to," he says, "I brought in the sweeper system, I was the first one to employ it and it was successful."

The blend of players got better and better and McMenemy managed the arrival of the big names carefully. Rarely did he have more than three or four of the 'stars' in any one team, always mixing them with a conveyor belt of home-produced players like Steve Moran, Danny Wallace, Steve Williams, Nick Holmes, Steve Baker and Malcolm Waldron. It was a recipe which worked and, as Saints were finishing in a position to qualify for Europe for the fourth time in five years in 1985, it appeared that he might go on to surpass Bates' reign of 18 years as manager. Tensions, however, were brewing behind the scenes and McMenemy resigned in June 1985. To the fans it came as a bombshell. McMenemy was later to point at problems in his relationship with the chairman Alan Woodford and said that the "tingle" had gone.

"The sad thing about my time at Southampton was the longer I was there, the better the results got, but the smaller the capacity [of the ground]," he says. "It's a pity it couldn't keep pace because whatever the crowd was we could have filled it. When I first came the capacity was nearly what it is now [32,500], but it came down in that period. One of the most significant changes in football was when you stopped getting a percentage of the gate when you were away.

"Overnight that changed and our ground was getting smaller. It meant that the big got bigger and we were up against it. If anything, I pride myself on being runners-up in the league at a time when the capacity was down. We weren't paying big wages, big transfer fees, but I was producing home-grown players and the art for me of management was to match them with the senior players I was hand-picking, who were great players and who had been greater players."

Rather like Sir Alex Ferguson at Manchester United, McMenemy's style brought success, but there were conflicts along the way. His relationship with Kevin Keegan had faltered and there was the famous 'shower' incident with Mark Wright when, so legend has it, he ended up in a bath-tub following an argument. He also clashed with Frank Worthington. It says much for McMenemy's self-confidence that he never shirked from recruiting controversial personalities, but Worthington lasted less than a season. The parting of the ways apparently came after McMenemy caught Worthington in another hotel room the day before a match. Worthington later claimed that he was simply sharing a cup of tea with the two ladies in question.

AFTER SAINTS, McMenemy returned to his native north east, but his 22-month spell as the Sunderland manager proved disappointing. McMenemy negotiated a deal which apparently made him among the highest paid football managers in the country. Yet it was to become a noose around his neck as the club finished 18th in the Second Division during his first season at the helm. The patience that had been shown to him at Southampton was not forthcoming and, after taking a voluntary pay-cut, the supporters turned as results remained poor the following season. He left in April 1987 and Sunderland were later relegated to Division Three.

McMenemy then took a break from football and eventually became the assistant England manager to Graham Taylor in 1990. His role also involved coaching the England Under-21s, but he offered his resignation alongside Taylor in 1993 after the failure of the full team to qualify for the 1994 World Cup. That era has come to be remembered for the infamous *Do I Not Like That* Channel 4 documentary which showed a sinking Taylor sometimes struggling to balance the magnitude of the job. Perhaps sensing the football disaster that was unfolding, McMenemy rarely figured in the fly-on-the-wall documentary. Indeed, his most memorable contribution is a huge cry of "howay the lads" before one of the games.

His status in Southampton, however, remained untouched by set-backs with England and Sunderland. With the club struggling and the fans suffering under the more direct style espoused by Ian Branfoot, McMenemy was invited to be a 'football director' on the board in December 1993. The Messiah had returned and it was big news which commanded the front page of the local paper. Gates had dropped to around 10,000, but just the presence of McMenemy attracted several thousand extra supporters and his return was greeted with a great swell of enthusiasm.

Within a month, Branfoot had departed as manager with McMenemy becoming the director of football, while his old captain Alan Ball returned as the manager. When McMenemy addressed fans at a forum he was greeted with a standing ovation. "I left for various reasons, but probably should have taken three or six months off and then come back again," he told them, "I should not have done what I did, that's for sure."

The 'little and large' partnership of Ball and McMenemy was an instant success. The threat of relegation was averted and, with Matthew Le Tissier at his peak, the club finished tenth in 1994/95. Yet, while stability had previously been such a strength under McMenemy, it was not the case at Southampton Football Club any more. Ball departed for Manchester City in the summer of 1995 and then Dave Merrington succeeded him only to be sacked the following summer.

Although good friends, Ball has admitted that he was sometimes irritated by McMenemy's presence and his desire to know what was happening. Ball has since said that he never wanted to leave Southampton and that he felt let down by the chairman Guy Askham, who gave him permission to speak with Manchester City. Ball's move had been largely finalised while McMenemy was on holiday. After guiding the team to safety on a shoe-string during the 1995/96 season, Merrington was then greeted with his P45, although McMenemy was again distanced from this decision.

The arrival of a manager with a higher profile in Graeme Souness was to be followed by news that Saints were joining the Stock Market after a reverse take-over of Secure Retirement. The club's parent company was named Southampton Leisure Holdings. The new team of Souness, McMenemy and Rupert Lowe did not last long with the manager quitting after one season because he felt the club did not match his ambition. Having been instrumental in the Souness appointment, McMenemy felt he should also resign. McMenemy was sold shares prior to the stock market floatation and, in 2006, he gave the voting control of these shares to the Hampshire businessman Michael Wilde who was to succeed Rupert Lowe as chairman of Southampton's football board.

MCMENEMY IS somewhat less expansive when it comes to discussing some of the challenges he encountered in football after that wonderful first stint at The Dell. Once the interview is finished, however, he stops and chats for another hour or so and we order more refreshments. He tells me a few fantastic anecdotes about his time at Saints. I suspect he is cute enough to save most of them, though, for when he decides to publish his own memoirs about a roller-coaster ride in football which has contained more highs than lows. McMenemy is a great raconteur and it is a treat to listen to him in full flow.

It is a shame that his presence at St. Mary's has been limited in recent years, although he is now making up for lost time and remains rightly revered for his record between 1973 and 1985. Ted Bates was the most wonderful servant imaginable to any football club, but McMenemy consistently inspired Saints to even greater heights and surely deserves to be recognised as, quite simply, the finest manager in the club's history. Younger Saints fan need only flick through the history books to confirm the unlikely level of success and fame he brought to The Dell. Older fans, though, are blessed with the memories of probably the best moments in their lives as football fans. To them, Lawrie McMenemy doesn't need a suite named after him in the basement of a fan's house. His achievements are what count – and they may never be matched.

IVAN GOLAC

1978-1982
1983-1986

DRAPER TOOLS

SAINTS CAREER

Games	197
Goals	4
Caps	4

MAGIC MOMENT

An unstoppable 25-yard half-volley in a 2-2 draw against West Brom in 1981

'THE CLAW'

THE evening of Tuesday August 22, 1978, was like a blind date for Ivan Golac and the fans of Southampton. The venue was The Dell and, although they had never previously set eyes on each other, it would have been understandable if there was a degree of mutual suspicion.

The manager Lawrie McMenemy had signed a Yugoslav full-back at a time when foreign players in English football were virtually unheard of. Golac, meanwhile, had been with Partizan Belgrade for the past 16 years and was prohibited from playing football abroad until the age of 28. He had spent his entire life under the Communist leadership of President Tito who ruled Yugoslavia from 1945 until his death in 1980. These were the days of a divided world between East and West and Golac had limited experience of the other side of the Iron Curtain. He could barely speak a word of English.

Yet all that was irrelevant in his new home. All that mattered was the way he played football. And, within minutes of his debut against Bolton Wanderers at The Dell, it became clear that it was a case of love at first sight. The timing of Golac's arrival as the first overseas player to join Saints was ideal for a match made in heaven and his affair with the Southampton supporters continues.

Even today, if you say the name 'Ivan Golac' to any Saints fan above the age of 35, the instantaneous reaction is a big smile. The feeling is mutual. That much is clear as we spend two hours together drinking coffee in a hotel overlooking Hyde Park. "Beautiful football, beautiful supporters and beautiful days," says Golac at the mere mention of Southampton. "From day one, from the very first kick, I could sense a connection with the crowd. They were terrific."

I'm fortunate to catch Golac on a brief visit to London. He now spends his time between Vienna and Belgrade, where he owned a chocolate factory, and he is rarely back in England. But he is on a two-night break with wife Bratislava which includes taking in an international match in west London at Loftus Road between Trinidad & Tobago and Iceland.

Bratislava ('my boss' as he calls her) has clearly been promised time in the shops, but Golac's enthusiasm for talking about his Saints career ensures that her patience will be tested. You get the impression she is used to it and has already factored in the probability that her shopping time will come under threat. There was no stopping Golac when he was in full flow on the pitch and nothing, it seems, has changed off it over the past two decades. He still looks in good shape and his greying hair is the only definite sign that he is now into his mid-50s.

INTERVIEWING GOLAC is easy, but hardly an interactive experience. There is no real need to ask questions or even prompt his memory; he simply begins to reminisce, pausing only for breath or interruptions. His face is fixed constantly in a huge smile and there are also times when his eyes go misty at the thought of a particular recollection.

He still keeps in touch with Phil Boyer and Alan Ball and hasn't forgotten the hospitality their families showed when he first arrived in England. Golac also asks after just about every other member of the team and laughs out loud at the mention of Mick Channon. "That bloody old bastard!" he cries. Channon apparently took it upon himself to teach Golac how to swear in English and he hasn't forgotten. There could have been no better tutor.

Golac was a swashbuckling full-back who played every game with a sense of unpredictable adventure and boldness which suggested he was having the time of his life. It was an infectious enthusiasm which lifted everyone around him, most noticeably the crowd. But the wonderful thing about meeting him is the realisation that this is probably how he lives his life. Ivan Golac was not acting. His style on a football pitch was an extension of his huge personality. This carefree right-back, who in the 1979 League Cup became the first foreign 'imported' player to appear in a domestic Wembley final, is every bit as engaging and entertaining over a warm drink as he was on many memorable cold nights at The Dell during some of the club's finest years.

He is also something of a philosopher and the conversation constantly drifts off at tangents as he explains the ways in which football is a metaphor for life. "I don't like to compare yesterday with today because today is the best," he says, "I was happiest then, I'm happiest today and I know I will be happiest tomorrow."

Yet nothing can hide the fun he had at Saints. "It was like a dream," he glows. Golac's style was simple: all-out attack. The crowd adored him for it, but there were many occasions when team-mates were reduced to screaming at him as he stood and admired a great pass or shot. "English football suited me so well, I always loved attacking, playing aggressive football was my nature," he says, "I loved to go forward, to tackle and go into every game to win. That's what I found in England."

Golac was one of the first 'over-lapping' full-backs and he is credited with changing the way many players in that position have since approached their football. The most memorable example of Golac's style came when he cemented his place in the hearts and minds of the Saints faithful with one swing of his right foot.

The opponents? West Bromwich Albion. The date? February 21, 1981. The venue? The Dell. Only 12 minutes had been played when the ball fell to Golac and he produced an unstoppable half-volley from 25-yards out which powered straight into the top corner. The manager Lawrie McMenemy later described it as "the sweetest strike anyone had ever seen...like Concorde taking off".

Does he remember that goal? "Of course," he says, "Alan Ball was with Blackpool and soon after he rejoined Southampton, the first thing he said to me was, 'it was a good try to cross it, Ivan!' It was outside of my foot, top corner. After the game Ron Atkinson came out and applauded. It was very simple. I just came from deep. Kevin Keegan was inside, you could see on the slow motion, he was about to shout, 'you greedy xxxx' and when the ball flew in he was happy. Ha! A good goal."

IF EVER Golac was suited to any team, it was surely alongside the likes of Ball, Keegan and Channon. His capacity for entertainment was the equal of those illustrious team-mates and the quality of football is widely regarded to be the best produced by a Southampton team. Golac, who had the experience of those 16 years with Yugoslav giants Partizan Belgrade, believes it was a team which had the capacity to reach even greater heights than those they achieved.

"We had a smashing triangle, Channon, Bally and myself," he says, "Lawrie created a team that was a thrill to watch and it was a thrill to play in front of such a great crowd. Every year we were improving and improving and in the season 1983/84 we were just three points behind Liverpool. If we had to play Liverpool to decide the title, I think it would be ours.

"We could play against anybody, it was the kind of football that every club would like to see. We had a great privilege to play in front of such great supporters and they had a great privilege to watch such a good team."

With characters like Golac about the place, the Saints team believed they could defeat any opponent, particularly at home on a one-off basis. Consistency, however, was a problem and, while major scalps were common, Saints just missed out on silverware. Golac says he often ponders what might have been possible had the team of 1981/82, which contained players of the quality of David Armstrong, Steve Williams, Nick Holmes, Chris Nicholl and Steve Moran as well as Channon, Ball and Keegan, come together just a few years earlier in their careers.

He weighs up the achievements of Nottingham Forest and Liverpool and concludes that Saints would have been champions not just of England, but of Europe. "In a way, it was mission accomplished," he says, "but I think if we had two or three years to work more together, if we had met slightly earlier, we would have won the European Cup. I was into my 30s, Bally slightly older, [Mick] Channon was over 30, Kevin [Keegan] was getting a bit older. We had a small amount of time. Just a bit earlier and it won't be a problem for us to beat anyone in Europe. Still, it was a great time, maybe the best in Southampton's history."

Golac is known for his confidence and a tendency to exaggerate the capabilities of those teams he played for or managed. But perhaps not on this occasion. When I ask the World Cup winner Alan Ball if he agrees that the Saints team of the early 1980s had the ability to conquer Europe, he replies: "Yes I do. We had a real good team all the way through for a number of years. Chris Nicholl and Dave Watson at the back and then we had people who could score goals. It went from Peter Osgood to Ted MacDougall, Phil Boyer, Steve Moran and then Kevin Keegan. It felt like the Golden Boot was constantly in Southampton. It's something people don't forget – the Southampton fans have been used to watching that calibre of player."

When Lawrie McMenemy thinks of Golac, he instantly remembers the Yugoslav's sheer joy at taking part in training, most notably the five-a-side sessions that used to be held between the ten outfield players in the gym on a Friday morning before Saturday's game. On one occasion, Golac was suspended for a match and McMenemy remembered how he looked heartbroken to miss out on that particular session. It was for first team players only.

Golac purrs at the thought of those indoor training matches. "Oohh," he says, "it was fantastic – half a touch football! I think only Liverpool could play the football Southampton were capable of. We loved football, we loved those training sessions and that is something we always transferred onto the park on Saturdays. Alan Ball, Mick Channon, Kevin Keegan, Charlie George, Phil Boyer, myself, we could close our eyes and play football together – we knew so well where the other would be. We just knew what the next movement will be. Those things don't happen every day.

"You would need 100 years for a new team to be like that and opponents couldn't catch us. Sometimes I'm going right and looking that way [he stands up and gestures to his right], but Bally knows I will go left. Or Channon is dropping in and you know Kevin Keegan will be into the space. You are playing the ball by heart, you know. You don't even think, we were like one."

Golac smiles. "One team, one brain," he says.

"And the best you ever played with?" I ask. "There were a lot of great players at The Dell," he says, "but in my opinion Alan Ball is very, very special." Another huge smile and Golac adds: "As Mary Hopkins said, 'those were the days'."

GOLAC REFERS constantly to English music and says it was even a factor in his ambition to play football in England. He was the son of a soldier who served in President Tito's guard, but, as a teenager growing up near Zagreb in Yugoslavia, he would listen to Western music. By the time he came to England, he had collected some 4,000 albums.

"As a very young kid from the age of ten, England was the country I really wanted to play," he says, "as a young boy, I supported Partizan Belgrade. When I was three or four my dream was to play for them and it was a dream fulfilled. But in 1960 when I saw the game which was played at Wembley between England and Yugoslavia [a 3-3 draw], I said, 'that's the only country I want to play football'.

"Then the Beatles came along. As a kid I had long hair and I knew all the groups and all the songs. My groups were The Rolling Stones, The Kinks, The Long Faces, The Who, The Troggs from Andover in Hampshire, Spencer Davis Group, Dave Clark Five, Status Quo, The Byrds and The Beach Boys, all terrific groups. I knew all the songs and all the words and it helped me learn English. I always knew my destination was England."

But Golac's dreams of Wembley and English football had to wait. The rules in Yugoslavia did not give him freedom from his contract until he reached the age of 28. He had been signed by Partizan Belgrade when he was 12, playing more than 400 games as they won the Yugoslav Championship in 1975/76 and 1977/78. His daughters now live in Belgrade and he is still a legend in the city. Lawrie McMenemy met him by chance in what is now the capital of Serbia in 2005 and said that Golac was stopped by just about every other person as they walked up the street.

"The Yugoslavian League was one of the best in the world," he says, "every game was really tough, even against the Second and Third Division teams. It was a kind of war because there was a lot of talent and ambition. We had a very good crowd for all the games and more or less all the clubs, especially Partizan Belgrade, Red Star Belgrade and Dinamo Zagreb. You could put them among the ten biggest derbies in the world and we would play in front of crowds of 90-100,000."

Golac, though, was counting the days until he could play football abroad. His free spirit, straight talking and rebellious edge brought him into conflict with the Yugoslav football establishment and it remains a mystery that he was only ever to win four caps for the national team. During our conversation, his happy face drops only once and that is when discussing his omission from the Yugoslavia team, particularly the World Cup squads of 1974 and 1982.

It is now difficult to assess what competition there was around him in the 1970s, but it seems highly improbable that there were superior right-sided players in 1982, when he was among the best in that position playing in English football. "They didn't like me because I was a rebel," he says, "I have always been the same, if I think something, I will say it. There were a few strange people and a few things were happening. It was very tough and I played four times which is a joke. I should have played more – a minimum of 50 or 60 games – with the way I was playing and my ability."

Golac wishes that he had considered taking out British citizenship. He briefly played alongside Mick Mills at Saints who was the England right-back of the time and, with characteristic confidence, says: "I felt part of England, everything so normal and spontaneous. I could have played for England, no problem." But if Golac feels angry about his international exclusion, it doesn't last long and he soon slips back into philosophical mood. "One of the biggest media people in Yugoslavia once said to me, 'I don't think you should be sorry because you have done more than all of them put together who have played 60 or whatever times for the national team'," he says, "nothing in life is an accident. God makes our lives and our stars and I know that it was destiny to get to England."

IF GOLAC was, indeed, destined to play in England, fate certainly waited until the last possible minute before intervening. He and his family were in Istanbul and he was ready to join Galatasary when he was informed by the Yugoslav embassy that Lawrie McMenemy wanted to sign him for Southampton. By the next day, the Golac family had flown into Heathrow via Belgrade and were poised for the start of their great adventure.

As ever, at this time, the reputation of McMenemy had helped persuade Golac he was making the right decision. Golac had become Southampton's first foreign player, but, with the likes of Ossie Ardiles and Ricky Villa also arriving in the summer of 1978 at Tottenham Hotspur, the government rather inexplicably imposed a temporary ban on overseas players. The justification was that "we have to pull the drawbridge up", while the PFA's Cliff Lloyd summed up the rather short-sighted thinking by saying, "when you are representing the interests of a group of men, you cannot encourage people to do their jobs…it could spread like a forest fire. It will be a great relief to me now if a ban is introduced".

This meant that Golac missed the first game of the season, but McMenemy used all his cunning to find a way around the rules and simply signed his Yugoslav full-back as a non-contract amateur. Confirmation that this was possible only came less than an hour before the match against Bolton, but, once the good news arrived, a delighted Golac gave his new manager a spontaneous hug. "It was a Tuesday night and I didn't know until 7pm if I was going to play or not," he says, "we drew 2-2, I played against Willie Morgan, I did okay, it was no problem at all. I played quite a few nice balls passing and I could feel straight away a great connection between myself and the supporters and that's how it happened.

"The next game we beat Middlesbrough 2-1 and we beat Wolverhampton 3-2. We had the two boys up front – Ted MacDougall and Phil Boyer – who needed good crossing and they were never short of crossing from the right-hand side." McMenemy's initial assessment of Golac was positive and he had also quickly won the respect of his team-mates, particularly the captain Alan Ball.

After spending just over a month living in a hotel, Golac, Bratislava and daughters Andrijana and Ivana, who were both still toddlers, moved into a house. He also finally got his work permit. Golac and his wife gradually learnt the language, although Ball recalls how his wife Lesley would take them to the butcher's shop and had to make animal noises so they could identify the different meats.

If adjusting to England was taking a little time, there were no such problems from a foot-balling perspective and Golac was an immediate regular in the Saints team. It was a satisfactory first season back in Division One for the club. Relegation was comfortably avoided, but once again it was in the Cup competitions that Saints made their mark. Wins over Birmingham City, Derby County, Reading and Manchester City in the League Cup meant a two-legged semi-final against Leeds United, the club that had wanted McMenemy as manager earlier in the season.

Saints found themselves 2-0 down after 50 minutes of the first leg, but recovered brilliantly with goals from Nick Holmes and Steve Williams to level at 2-2 ahead of the deciding leg at The Dell. For this match, McMenemy produced something of a masterstroke when he unexpectedly selected Manny Andruszewski for the specific task of a marking job on the Leeds danger-man Tony Currie. The tactic worked to perfection and Saints held on to a Terry Curran goal in the 11th minute for a second major Wembley final in just three years. For Golac, it was a dream come true.

"I was always part of big crowds, but there are a few places in the world where you always want to play and the most important one was Wembley," he says. "That was my priority and second was Hampden Park. Those two places are above any other on this planet. We had a terrific run in the FA Cup that season as well. We were very unlucky to lose to Arsenal in the quarter-final when we were 1-0 up. We played very well against Forest, who were twice European Champions [in 1979 and 1980], but I think if we met Forest probably a year after we would have beaten them. There wouldn't have been problems. We beat them 4-1 the next season in the league."

Saints were defeated 3-2 by Forest in the final, but had still acquitted themselves well against a team that were also the reigning English champions. And, as Golac says, Saints were on the up and poised for an era of wonderful football as the likes of Dave Watson, Mick Channon and Kevin Keegan would be added to a nucleus of quality which also included Alan Ball, Steve Williams and Phil Boyer.

THE CULT STATUS of Golac had also become assured and his initial popularity continued to snowball as The Dell crowd saw more and more of him over the next three seasons. The BBC presenter and lifelong Saints fan Tristan Pascoe rates Golac among his all-time football heroes. "He was not only a brilliant player, but also something of a hard man," he says, "I still vividly recall him being taken down by a terrible tackle, yet he was straight back on his feet and limped over to the dugout where he found the 'magic spray' or whatever it was, adminis-tered it himself on the injury and then turned and limped back into action."

As well as his flair, passion and impulsive personality, Golac was also popular in the dressing room. His various antics made people laugh. He was nicknamed 'The Claw' because of his brilliant crossing ability, although some also called him 'Homer' because there was a feeling that he had a tendency to "go missing" in matches away from home.

"You couldn't play Ivan away from home," says Mark Dennis, "at home he was a joy to play with, but something of a liability away from home. Yet he was a great player, he whipped those balls in and played the game the right way. He always played it to feet, wanted it back and never kicked the ball up in the air."

Mick Channon, who often played in front of him on the right, would joke that Golac was the "best right-winger the club ever had". The implication that he sometimes neglected his defensive duties is refuted by Golac. "I know there is a job behind and it was never a problem to sort out the player you are looking after," he says, "my philosophy in life is always, 'okay I'll stop them, but he has to think about me. I want them to think about me'. One of my favourite songs is by the Dave Clark Five and it is *Catch Us If You Can* and that is what I said to my opponent."

There is a great story about the time when Saints had lost badly in one particular match and McMenemy was reading the riot act to the players. As the manager was in full flow, legend has it that Golac simply got up and made his way into the shower. McMenemy asked him what he thought he was doing and Golac turned around and simply said, 'my man, he no score'." I repeat this story to Golac and he nods knowingly, adding, "they used to say I left a space behind and I used to say, 'no, I disagree'. Because my man is chasing me forward – so who's going into that space? A ghost? Nobody. If I get a job to look after a man, he won't kick a ball".

Golac also took on the mantle as one of the senior pros in a team that had outstanding youngsters breaking through like Danny Wallace and Steve Moran. "We used to take the pressure on ourselves," he says, "Danny Wallace was 16 when he played Manchester United at Old Trafford, imagine how many kids have been in such a position? Steve Moran was almost top-scorer in England when he was 20. Wayne Rooney is a good lad, but not as many goals as Steve Moran. It was a great spirit among us, everything was a dream. It was a club you would like to lead as a manager and that's why I would put Lawrie [McMenemy] beside Brian Clough as the best."

Despite Golac's protestations, he and the team did produce his most memorable performances at The Dell. The intimate, atmospheric surroundings seemed to bring out the best in him and he questions conventional wisdom that says it was a progression for the club to move to St. Mary's. Golac believes The Dell was a huge advantage to the team and points to the relegation of 2004/05 as evidence that extra seats and higher revenue do not necessarily equal more points at the end of the season.

"We used to be the best home side in the country – better than Liverpool or any of the big boys," he says, "I think you have to keep what you are. The Dell has gone and it was such a big part of Southampton history. The roots have gone and now you feel like a little bush in the Sahara and a slightly stronger wind can blow you away.

"I don't think a new stadium is going to improve your game. It's better to put some money to refurbish everything and in the youth policies. I think the best part of the game has disappeared and that is when they brought in the rules from the Taylor Report [to phase out standing terraces]. At Liverpool, when you see The Kop and at Leeds United you see the waves of people. The same in Belgrade when you see 90,000-100,000 people. It's the best part of football."

Despite all Golac's positive talk about his time at Saints, it was a dispute over his contract which eventually led to him leaving for the first time in 1982. At the time, McMenemy said that the club were "unable to meet his requirements". Golac was back almost 18 months later to play an important part in the conclusion to the successful 1983/84 season. But he was now into his mid-30s and struggled to get past Mick Mills and Mark Dennis in the full-back positions the following year. His popularity, though, remained and when he was substituted against Coventry City in the penultimate game of the season, the crowd booed the decision.

McMenemy was to leave that summer and Golac started the first nine games of the 1985/86 season before the curtain came down. The manager Chris Nicholl felt the pace of the game had become too much, but said: "Ivan has been a great friend of Saints." Golac accepted this assessment and says: "Last game we drew 1-1 at The Dell against Coventry and I said to Chris, 'I've finished nicely'."

FOOTBALL, THANKFULLY, was not about to see the back of Golac and he moved straight into management, taking with him his positive outlook on life. Shouting and screaming at players would never be Golac's style and he made it his mission to transmit the sort of relaxed adventure which had so characterised his own style.

"Nothing changed in my life," he says. "My message to the players was always, 'I'm going to take the pressure because I never feel pressure'. My self-belief is immense, I feel very confident in life whatever I do. So what I'm trying to do first is to create that atmosphere in the dressing room. As a manager your priority is to relax the boys."

The results of Golac's unconventional approach were, on occasion, spectacular. He was a coach at Partizan in 1989 when the manager was taken ill and he had to take charge of a major European Cup Winners' Cup tie against Celtic at Parkhead. Prior to the game, he spoke with McMenemy who recounted the story. "When he rang me I said, tongue in cheek, 'I suppose it will be attack, attack, attack', which he loved to do down that wing for us from his full-back position, giving me the odd rise in blood pressure. He said, 'of course it is, boss'. I couldn't wait to hear the final score.

"I started to nod as the reporter said, 'Celtic five…' but nearly fell off my chair when I heard that Ivan's team had scored four [which was enough to get them through on aggregate]. When I eventually contacted him to congratulate him I could imagine his lovely broad smile as he said, 'it was no problem, boss. No problem'."

Several years later in 1993, Golac was appointed manager of Dundee United as successor to Jim McLean, who had spent almost 22 years at the helm. The contrast between the moody, calculating McLean and the carefree Golac could not have been greater. Golac quickly became as revered in Dundee as he was in Southampton. Even the journalists loved him and stories of his time as manager are still told with great relish. "Jim McLean would have a press conference with them on the stairs – two minutes, three minutes," says Golac, "I invited them in my office, 'just relax yourself boys, what are you drinking, tea, coffee, whisky, wine?'"

The day he left his job after almost 20 months as Dundee United manager is remembered among journalists who were sent to his house and feared they would find the now unemployed Golac in less than accommodating mood. From outside they could see his feet resting on a chair. He was laid back on the sofa, sipping wine and watching ski-jumping on television. The journalists were immediately invited in to join him for a glass or two. It was mid-morning.

In a television interview just outside his house, he was asked for his reaction to the board's decision and replied: "I feel great. Nothing will change, wherever I'm going, I will take the sun with me." As a manager, his usual reaction to a heavy defeat apparently went something along the following lines: "Hey, boys, it's a beautiful day. Why the long faces?"

His two big triumphs as Dundee United manager, however, have gone down in local folklore. Rangers managed by "dull Walter Smith", as Golac calls him, were the victims on both occasions.

The first great victory was in the league. "We destroyed them 3-0 at Ibrox," says Golac, "I said before the game 'this will be the biggest earthquake happening in Britain and we are going to destroy them, just roll over them'. The press were 'who the hell does he think he is to say such a thing?' The next day I was waiting until the last minute to come out and, at five to three, I came through the tunnel and 55,000 people were pointing at me and booing. Ha! The game started and we were winning 3-0 with about 20 minutes gone.

"After the match it was the shortest press conference in the history of the game. It was the biggest result and biggest defeat for Rangers in a few years. I walked in and they asked if I wanted to take a seat and I said, 'no. I'll be very short'. Ken Robertson [a journalist] said, 'everything you promised, you delivered?' And I said, 'yes and you listen better next time' and I walked out."

Yet the feat which really secured Golac's reputation as a maverick manager who could sometimes pull off the most unlikely victory came in the Scottish Cup of 1994 in his first season as manager. He led them to the final to play Rangers, who were in the middle of a run of nine consecutive league titles. Dundee United had never won the Scottish Cup in their entire history, while Rangers were going for a 27th triumph. Yet that scenario was perfect for Golac's managerial style. He was completely and utterly relaxed, but supremely confident that his team would prevail.

"When I first met the people from Dundee United, I said, 'what would you like to win?'" he remembers. "They said right away 'the FA Cup'. Six times they had lost in the final. So I said, 'you've got it, what's next?' My philosophy as manager was to relax the players. Tuesday before the final they came in to train and do exercises and I took them for a nice walk. We walked through the golf course, smelt the beautiful flowers, listened to the birds, had a nice cup of coffee and enjoyed it.

"The following day we went to a hotel near Hampden Park and we played five-a-side. My side won – and I scored five goals which was a good omen. The players then asked if it was possible to go to Hamilton horse racing the day before the game and I said, 'of course, how many want to go?' The night before, the TV cameras were at our hotel and the players were laughing and joking, pouring water on each other and singing.

"Hazel Irvine [the BBC presenter] asked me 'who is going to win tomorrow?' I said, 'there is only one winner, it is going to be us'. I said, 'I know that Rangers would fancy to play anyone in the world apart from Dundee United'. My philosophy is 'go there, enjoy yourself and show you are better than them'. I never talk about an opponent. They don't exist to me. I just concentrated on my team, my boys and tried to relax them. That's the way my teams played."

The result? 1-0 to Dundee United and one of the greatest upsets in the history of the Scottish Cup. Given all the managerial changes at Southampton in recent years, the thought of Golac patrolling the St. Mary's touchline is as irresistible as it is unlikely.

HE MIGHT be out of sight, but Ivan Golac has not left the minds of the Southampton supporters. He is surely the greatest foreign import that the club has ever had. Certainly, he is the most popular and, upon canvassing the opinions of fans, there was almost unanimous agreement that he should be included in this book.

Over the last ten years, of course, there has been a huge influx in the numbers of overseas footballers in England and Saints have had their fair share who have also achieved a certain cult status. The most notorious is probably the Senegalese chancer Ali Dia who, incredibly, managed to persuade Graeme Souness to give him a game on the basis of a fake telephone recommendation from someone pretending to be World Footballer of the Year George Weah. He came on as a substitute against Leeds United only to be replaced again 53 minutes later once it became obvious that he was well out of his depth. The 30-year-old Dia was later dubbed "the Jeffrey Archer of Premiership imports".

Another footballing failure who achieved a certain ironic popularity was the Ecuadorian Agustin Delgado. He was the club's most expensive ever forward at £3.5m, but suffered everything from back, calf and knee injuries to toothache. He would also regularly disappear without trace. A dislike of cold weather and Gordon Strachan's intense training programme was perhaps the most truthful explanation for his problems, but his occasional appearances were still treated with enthusiasm as his smiley face and rather vacant expression made it impossible to do anything other than laugh at the whole situation.

Of the successful foreign signings, Marian Pahars, Antti Niemi, Michael Svensson, Ken Monkou, Claus Lundekvam and Ronnie Ekelund stand out, yet none of them could match the combination of Golac's quality as a footballer, longevity and pure charisma. Indeed, his impact went far beyond the south coast and his status as one of the great imports in British football history was underlined by a list in the *Observer* in 2003 which placed him the fourth best – ahead of the likes of Ossie Ardiles, Peter Schmeichel, Dennis Bergkamp, Jürgen Klinsmann, Thierry Henry and Juninho but behind only Eric Cantona, Gianfranco Zola and Patrick Vieira.

You sense that Golac would happily talk about football all day. Yet with the time now pressing on, he understands from the looks he is getting from his wife that he better draw our chat to an end. Yet he is still talking as he stands up and puts his coat on. "I was always an entertainer," he concludes, "I think every game should attract a full house, otherwise there is no point to it. For me, life is all about enjoyment. God has given all people on earth a chance, but if you are negative, God cannot help you. He has made me healthy and happy – so just enjoy the life.

"Everything on this planet is absolute beauty. We have to recognise that and if you have a chance, grab the opportunity. If you get half a chance, you can count yourself a very lucky man, so just grab it." His short speech ends with a flourish. "Do you know something?" he says. "Life is a game, not a fight. Those who fight with life have lost."

With that, Golac realises that Bratislava has lost all patience and he is away, heading off several metres behind her in the direction of Oxford Street. The shopkeepers will have had a fun afternoon.

KEVIN KEEGAN

1980-1982

SAINTS CAREER

Games	80
Goals	42
Caps	63

MAGIC MOMENT

Leading Saints onto the pitch for the start of the 1980 season to a standing ovation

'MIGHTY MOUSE'

I sit with Lawrie McMenemy just a few metres from the scene of one of the great moments in the history of Southampton Football Club. And there is not a blade of grass in sight.

"No-one could believe it," says McMenemy, as he takes a sip from his cup of tea, "it was just in there that we did it." The former Southampton manager is pointing towards the restaurant area of the Potters Heron Hotel on the outskirts of Romsey where staff are still clearing up after morning breakfast. It was the venue for the announcement of what was quite possibly the greatest transfer coup in football history.

McMenemy was known for his ability to attract high-profile footballers to the traditionally low-profile Southampton. Yet he has protested that he was only able to afford great players because they were in the twilight of their careers. "I only managed to get them because they were coming to the end…were half knackered and cheap," he said.

There was, however, one glorious exception: Kevin Keegan, the double European Footballer of the Year, who'd won the league, FA Cup, Uefa Cup and European Cup with Liverpool in the 1970s, and also won the German League title with Hamburg before inspiring them to the European Cup final. He was, at the time, arguably the most famous sportsman in Britain. That McMenemy convinced Keegan to come to Saints and The Dell when clubs like Juventus, Barcelona, Liverpool, Chelsea and Manchester United were all fighting for his signature, says everything about his persuasive genius.

In the club's recent history, Southampton fans have experienced perhaps three events which you could call 'JFK moments'. No-one, of course, will forget where they were at 4.38pm on May 1, 1976, when Bobby Stokes slotted the ball past Alex Stepney. Equally, Matthew Le Tissier's last goal at The Dell is a moment when time seemed to stand still. The news that Kevin Keegan had signed for Saints is another happening when Saints supporters can vividly recall exactly where they were and what they were doing. Indeed, all things considered, it was even more unlikely than those famous goals scored by Stokes and Le Tissier.

McMenemy, Keegan, Southampton and Hamburg had somehow all kept the deal completely quiet. It meant that when the biggest name in European football did stride into that famous press conference, the impact could not have been greater. The Keegan signing was announced on Monday, February 11, 1980.

It was in the days long before the Internet and 24-hour news. Instead, word of mouth ensured that McMenemy's dramatic coup quickly filtered through the factories, shop-floors, offices and precincts in and around Southampton. News spread quickly, but confirmation did not really come until it began appearing on radio bulletins, the television and in the local evening newspaper. Few were satisfied until they had seen, heard or read the reports for themselves.

It was totally out of the blue and the initial reaction was one of complete and utter disbelief. When Bob Brunskell rang back to the *Echo* office with the story that Keegan had joined Saints, his colleagues thought it was a joke. Yes, Saints had signed big names before. The arrivals of Alan Ball and Peter Osgood were huge news locally, but believable because Southampton were an ambitious club and Hampshire was a nice place to see out the end of your career. But players like Keegan went to Liverpool or Manchester United and, only if Saints got lucky, would they come to The Dell once they were into their 30s. Of course, it could be argued that the likes of Ball and Jimmy Case played some of their best football for Saints. But that wasn't the point. When they came to Saints, it was several years after they had been in teams that had won the World and European Cup respectively. "We were called to the Potters Heron and wheeled into one of the back rooms," remembers Brunskell. "There was a little stage and a curtain. Lawrie McMenemy was sat up there, as well as Alan Ball and a couple of the directors.

"And he just said, 'I'd like you to meet our new signing' and out of the curtain came Kevin Keegan. Nobody had a clue that this was going to happen. We were all gobsmacked. He had just had three fantastic seasons at Hamburg and he was the top player in Europe, never mind England. For a week or two, all hell broke loose. The phones were red-hot and we had people calling from all over the world wanting to know how Saints had managed to sign Kevin Keegan."

Kevin McMahon is a lifelong Saints fan. "It still sends a shiver down my spine just talking about it," he says, "I was at King Edward's [school] at the time and I was on my way home on the bus to Thornhill. At the bus-stop, you could tell something had happened because people were all talking among themselves. I listened to what they were saying and it was that we had signed Kevin Keegan.

"He was the most famous footballer in Europe at the time. He was an icon. I just remember I got off the bus and ran as fast I could all the way home. The first thing my mum said to me was, 'we've signed Kevin Keegan'. It was just astonishing. Lawrie McMenemy might have signed some players who you could say did more for the club, but, for that moment of hearing that we had signed Keegan, it was something that you just couldn't top in a thousand, million years."

Even the players were in total shock. "We had a day off and I was playing squash at Abshott Squash Club," remembers Nick Holmes. "A bloke leaned over the top and he shouted at me 'oi, you've just signed Keegan'. I just looked up at him and said, 'no, you must have got it wrong'.

"Anyway, when I got off the court and switched the radio on, it was all over the news bulletins. I couldn't believe it. It was fantastic. We had a couple of years with Kev, when he was at his best. What a good player he was and what a nice, decent, genuine and honest bloke he was too."

THE NEWS that Saints had signed Keegan, who was aged 28 at the time of the announcement, was massive at every level. One newspaper described it as a, "fairytale transfer deal which rocked the football world... and which will go down as one of the greatest transfer bargains of all-time". Season-ticket sales for the following campaign immediately went through the roof, sponsors were queuing up and the buzz around the city was immense.

"The club hadn't altered their season-ticket prices for a while and I think that enabled them to double their prices," says McMenemy. "Everything went up, the price of a programme, everything. But nobody blinked because they were getting value for money. The opposition teams were also getting their best crowd of the season whenever we played them and that was in the days when we got a share of the gate. Everyone wanted to see Kevin and he paid for himself straight away."

Keegan's popularity and marketability was only enhanced by the fact that he had been playing in Germany for the preceding three years at Hamburg. It meant that English football fans had not recently seen much of the country's most celebrated player.

His first appearance in front of the Saints fans came at a question and answer session held at the Southampton Guildhall alongside McMenemy, Jack Charlton and Denis Law. It is a venue which holds around 1,000 people, but McMenemy reckoned they could have sold it out ten times over. Without a football in sight, the Guildhall floor became like a terrace as fans began chanting 'Keegan, Keegan' before their new idol even got on stage. When he did arrive, Keegan was given a standing ovation before McMenemy took the microphone and told the fans, "you have shown more passion here tonight than all season at The Dell!"

Southampton were receiving around 1,500 letters of mail every week from supporters as far afield as Egypt or Moscow and Keegan's fan club had members from Malaysia, Canada, Mauritius, Australia and New Zealand. The transfer was even reported in countries with no real football tradition. "The Keegan thing was in every newspaper in the world," says McMenemy, "NBC in America…half a page in the New York Herald Tribune." It was also the lead item that evening on the national news.

To put it in a modern-day context, it was like Southampton signing David Beckham from Real Madrid.

If George Best was the first superstar of British football, Keegan was his successor and it is arguable whether there has been anyone else in British football with the same ability to transcend the sport until Paul Gascoigne and then Beckham emerged. Hard to believe, but Keegan, who had grown up in Doncaster and was the son of a Geordie miner, was also something of a fashion icon and was even voted Britain's best dressed man in 1980. And yes, the Keegan perm was perhaps as famous as those Beckham highlights. He even turned Brut into a fashionable aftershave.

All in all, it meant that Southampton Football Club was very firmly on the map. True, the FA Cup win in 1976 had earned widespread respect, but having Keegan in the team guaranteed a level of glamour and international fame that the club has not known before or since.

SO HOW on earth did McMenemy succeed in enticing Keegan to Southampton? There are those who look back and say that such a signing could never be repeated in the modern age of football. The financial difference between what clubs like Saints compared to Chelsea or Barcelona could offer, it is argued, would be far too great. Perhaps that is true. Yet it would still be wrong to downplay, in any way, the achievement or magnitude of capturing Keegan.

Most thought such a signing was utterly impossible even in 1980 and it is certain that money was not Keegan's primary motive. "If we were talking about the highest bidder, Southampton wouldn't be talking about Kevin Keegan," said McMenemy. "We couldn't compete with Barcelona or Juventus." What happened was, in fact, a remarkable coming together of circumstance between two strong personalities in McMenemy and Keegan who were very much their own men and never frightened of being a bit different.

The seeds were sown in 1979, when McMenemy called Keegan out of the blue in West Germany and asked for help in getting hold of a wall lamp that he wanted which was made in Hamburg. "We were having this house built and the architect said there was a particular light which would look terrific on the wall, but that they were made in Hamburg," says McMenemy.

"He [Keegan] wasn't a lad I had spoken with often, if at all, but I found his number, probably off a press man. There was a bit of small talk, 'how's the weather', all that stuff, and I said, 'look, I'm having a house built and the light's only available in Hamburg. I wondered if we ordered it if you could bring it over'. He said, 'no problem' and I gave him the details.

"I had been reading that he'd said his time might be up at Hamburg because he signed for a period and had an inbuilt transfer fee when he wanted to move. He was linked with Real Madrid and Barcelona, but of course I had wanted to lead into it, so I said, 'by the way, I heard that you were ready to move?' I went on, 'I hear it might be Real Madrid or Barcelona'. I said, 'young family, haven't you? The problem there is you are a superstar and you've got to have protection'.

"I kept making the calls, dropping in pearls like that, and eventually hit him with the big one. 'Ever fancy coming back and coming to a club like us?' Eventually we organised to meet him in a house in London on a Sunday when he was back. It was kept all private and, halfway through the conversation, Kevin suddenly said, 'have you got a contract?' Fortunately we took one and he signed a blank contract. I just gasped. Then he said, 'I've got to admit something, I forgot to bring your light!' But we got the light in the end and, although it's been taken off the wall in the last year, we've still got it in the house."

Keegan later described one of their conversations in an interview for the *Saints Millennium Video*. "He [McMenemy] said, 'if you ever come back, we'd be interested, Bally [Alan Ball] is here and Dave Watson and Mick Channon' – people I knew from England." The mix of characters appealed to Keegan. He knew the quality of Ball as a footballer and was room-mates with Channon for England when they would play cards together and shared a passion for horse racing. Hampshire and the surrounding environment with the New Forest and the coast nearby was also an attraction, particularly as Keegan wanted a suitable destination for a young family.

He had decided that three seasons with Hamburg was enough and, having negotiated a maximum transfer fee of £500,000 when he moved to West Germany, he was in a strong position to join the club of his choice. Italy and Spain offered the best wages at the time, but the style of football in Spain was not particularly attractive. Juventus were the clear favourites and negotiations were at an advanced stage when Keegan's wife Jean made the decision that she did not want to go to Italy. It was a time when there were many stories about terrorism and kidnappings of prominent Italian personalities and it was enough to put them off.

"I weighed it all up and decided that I did not want to play for one of the big football clubs," said Keegan in his autobiography, "I began to think about how great it would be to win the League Championship with an unfancied club like Southampton. I loved the New Forest and it occurred to me that Southampton could be a nice place to finish my career."

He later joked that McMenemy had locked him in a room until he agreed to join. But no-one could change Keegan's mind once it was made up and he had been sold essentially on the challenge of achieving something special with a smaller club like Saints.

McMenemy had handled him with just the right measure of persuasive talk without being overtly persistent. At the time they were speaking, speculation about what Keegan would do next had not really taken off in the press. There were still several months until the end of the season and there was no particular expectation that any news was imminent. But, with Keegan having made his decision and McMenemy keen to seal the transfer, it was agreed to make the announcement in February that he would be joining Saints for the forthcoming 1980/81 season.

McMenemy was determined to keep everything top secret. There was still the slim possibility that another club would attempt to hijack the deal if news did leak, although McMenemy's primary motive in arranging such a covert operation was probably to ensure maximum exposure. He has a sharp understanding of the media and a press conference was duly scheduled for a quiet time of the week on a Monday when little else would be happening in the world of football.

McMenemy asked the media to be at the Potters Heron in the village of Ampfield, simply saying that he would be unveiling, "someone who was going to play a big part in Southampton's future". McMenemy was already a big name nationally and the major newspapers duly arranged for reporters to travel down from London to Hampshire. At the same time, a private plane had been chartered to fly to the airport at Eastleigh on the outskirts of Southampton. Keegan and his wife Jean were aboard tackling a jigsaw puzzle with their daughter Laura, while Hamburg representative Gunther Netzer also accompanied them.

Keegan arrived at Southampton and no-one guessed what was happening. Airport staff just assumed that he was flying in to do a commercial for one of the companies he worked for. Southampton's assistant manager John Mortimore had been informed of what was happening and was sent to collect the Keegan family. "Kevin came into Southampton and some arrangement had been made so that we were able to go out to the plane in the car," he says, smiling at the memory of an operation which McMenemy had planned with such meticulous care.

For McMenemy, the days leading up to the announcement were nerve-racking and he remembers driving through a red light in Romsey as his mind kept turning to the surprise he had in store. The assembled press had absolutely no idea what they were about to be told. "Some thought I was leaving," says McMenemy, "some thought we were announcing a new ground. I got Bally [Alan Ball] along, he thought he was on *This Is Your Life*." And then, like a magician pulling a rabbit out of the hat, McMenemy introduced Keegan. There were gasps as the European Footballer of the Year dramatically entered the room with wife and baby. Some of the press even began applauding.

Keegan then outlined why he had decided to join Southampton. "Lawrie McMenemy is ambitious and genuine, the right qualities for a manager," he said. "I believe in the man, I believe in what he is doing. He is carrying the club in the right direction. If I didn't feel for him and respect him so much, I wouldn't have come to Southampton. I would never have dreamed of joining Saints a year ago. Even when I first heard of their interest, I was only going to see Lawrie out of respect. But when I saw him, I quickly realised here was a club going places. Lawrie thinks big and he's honest. He won me over."

Keegan was also quick to stress that his ambitions were high. "European football will be a realistic target to aim for next season, well within the club's range," he said. "The main targets will be the league and the FA Cup, but if we can finish in second or third place, it will be a step in the right direction." McMenemy agreed that the club could realistically challenge for the league title. "Our aim is to win the First Division Championship," he declared.

But first everyone had to be patient. There were still six months until the start of the next season and the city of Southampton did little between February and August 1980 but discuss the return of the English game's prodigal son. His former Liverpool manager Bill Shankly accurately predicted the excitement that Keegan was to create, not just among the supporters, but also within the dressing room.

"I was surprised when I heard it was Southampton, but Kevin is a boy always looking for a challenge," he said. "They will find his attitude infectious. He'll be buzzing, a real handful for opponents. He'll be like a breath of fresh air to them. He'll play for them if the other lads play for him. And, if that happens, the whole thing will take off." Shankly was right. Well, almost.

OVER THE NEXT two seasons, Keegan's impact did take Saints onto the launch-pad from which they could challenge the likes of Liverpool and the other top clubs. Whether they could overtake them was a different matter.

For many Saints fans, the two seasons between 1980 and 1982 were the most enjoyable in the club's history. Not simply because Kevin Keegan was at The Dell, but because it was the time when McMenemy had assembled perhaps his most flamboyant team. Whether it was the most effective is another question and McMenemy would later admit: "None of the big names were there when we were second in the league [in 1983/84] and that, if anything, was their best achievement." That didn't matter at the time to The Dell crowd as the quality of the football seemed to get steadily better and better.

It was also an era in which Keegan's fame was at a high. His time in Hamburg had only added to the mystique and, wherever Saints went, they were assured of capacity crowds. That was also true abroad and there were several promotional trips to cities around the world.

On one tour to Casablanca, a crowd of 70,000 packed out a stadium to see Saints. Keegan, though, had picked up a hamstring injury and it was agreed that he would be allowed to rest in a hotel and avoid the danger of worsening it by being barged in and around the ground by excited spectators. At least, that was the plan until it became evident that the fans had not come to see Saints at all, but simply Kevin Keegan. The Moroccan supporters began chanting his name. At first it was enthusiastic chanting, but the mood got more fevered and vociferous. And they would not stop.

It got to the stage where the Saints players began to genuinely fear that they would not escape safely if the crowd did not see Keegan. Eventually, McMenemy concluded that Keegan would have to be dragged from his hotel bed to appear. Nick Holmes actually took the phone off McMenemy and told Keegan that he thought someone would get hurt if he did not come to the ground. Keegan eventually arrived with a police escort and, although he could not run, his appearance prompted a standing ovation and sent the locals home satisfied.

By the opening day of the 1980/81 season, The Dell was awash with expectation as Keegan led his new team out against Manchester City. "He was a fantastic signing and the football was just sizzling," says Brunskell, "the anticipation before he played was just incredible. When he led the team out The Dell just erupted – the whole crowd stood as one. It really was quite emotional.

"It was a time when the crowds were less cynical and there was less booing of opposition players, so the reception he got all over the country was fantastic. Every team we played had sell-outs. On a tour to Holland, there were fans travelling all over Europe to see Keegan and when he returned to Liverpool, the whole of Anfield rose to applaud him.

"I remember getting to Roker Park for a match and the fans were queuing all around the ground at 12.30pm for a 3pm kick-off. The team bus would be mobbed as we approached every ground and, eventually, we had to start flying rather than taking the train because the players just didn't get any peace from interested fans."

The Dell was sold out every week and, even though the capacity of the ground was just over 23,000, Keegan later said that it felt like "the whole world was there" for his debut. Keegan would be playing up front alongside Charlie George, but it was Mick Channon, cutting inside from the right, who scored both goals in a 2-0 victory over Manchester City. A relieved McMenemy said: "I was a little worried that after all the build-up it might fall a little flat, but in the end the result was the right one. It was impossible to keep this game on a normal basis with Keegan returning to English football."

Saints built on that immediate success with three wins and a draw in their opening four games to go second in the table, but Keegan was then struck by a persistent hamstring injury and he missed 15 games over the season and did not return regularly until January. Saints had slipped to ninth without Keegan, but he helped inspire an improvement in form that briefly took the club back into the top three and ended with a sixth place finish only ten points behind champions Aston Villa. Keegan managed 11 goals in 27 league games, but had been out-shone by Steve Moran – his scrabble partner on long away trips – who was the leading scorer with 18 league goals.

He was adjusting, however, to life at Saints and later said that the club at the time should have been called "Southampton Funball Club". As ever, Keegan was putting his heart and soul into his new adventure and his attitude was rubbing off on younger players like Steve Moran and Danny Wallace. "Whatever he's doing at any one time he does to a maximum and in fact I used to worry he'd wear himself out, but he's got that energy – he can't sit still, he's always on the go – and, of course, that rubs off," said McMenemy.

Keegan certainly found some of the training sessions at Southampton a little different to what he was used to at Hamburg and Liverpool. The tradition of the Friday morning five-a-side session in the gym had been established under Ted Bates and had become a legendary fixture in the week. Keegan described it as a training exercise which involved kicking "the crap out of each other". He admitted, though, that he quite enjoyed it.

FIRMLY SETTLED IN Southampton and free of injury problems, Keegan was able to produce his best form during the 1981/82 season. Indeed, Mick Channon, who had played for England over several years with Keegan, says he was never better throughout his career. With attack-minded full-backs like Ivan Golac and Nick Holmes, a midfield of David Armstrong, Steve Williams, Alan Ball and Mick Channon and then Keegan and Steve Moran up front, it was perhaps the most mouth-watering team McMenemy was ever to assemble.

Keegan began by scoring nine in the first ten games and was establishing an almost telepathic understanding with Ball, who had adapted his game to remain just as effective at the age of 36 as he had been throughout his career. "No-one taught me more than Bally," said Keegan. "He had a great philosophy: when he was young, he said, he worked up and down the pitch, but as he grew older he worked sideways across it." The quality of the football was outstanding.

"Bally loved it. He said to Keegan, 'don't come deep looking for the ball just stay up there, look for the ball in the box and it will come to you'," says McMenemy, "it was all one touch and terrific stuff. I liked watching it and the supporters loved it. Most had their best records when they played with me and Kevin Keegan scored more with us than he did for Liverpool. He never asked favours to be off training, to miss this or that and he was terrific. He gave everybody a lift, the whole club and the whole area. He was the Beckham of his time without a doubt. No-one was surprised if there was a helicopter waiting for him at the end of a training session."

Keegan scored the winner away against Middlesbrough on January 30, 1982, and it was enough to take Saints to the top of the First Division for the first and only time in the club's history. Saints were still leading the way at the beginning of April and Keegan was duly named the PFA Player of the Year while Moran picked up the young player's award.

But the teams below Saints had matches in hand and a run of only three wins from March until the end of the season meant a relatively disappointing seventh place finish. Keegan was the division's top goal-scorer with 30 in all competitions and was also the club's Player of the Year.

IN HINDSIGHT, there are those who say that the 1981/82 season was a missed opportunity. Bad luck had certainly played its part in the slip towards the end of the season with Moran missing the run-in through injury. Yet the biggest problem was in defence. By the end of the season, although Saints had scored 72 goals, they had also conceded 67 and had the second worst defensive record in the division. The contrast with the champions Liverpool, who had only conceded 32 goals, was obvious.

The brilliant pairing of the centre-back Mark Wright and the goalkeeper Peter Shilton arrived the following season. Unfortunately, it was a year too late for this particular Championship challenge. It's difficult to be too critical of a season which was among the finest in the club's history, but a sense of what might have been nagged away at the always impulsive Keegan.

He recounts a story of how, over a few lagers, the senior players in the team had told McMenemy on the way back from a game when they were at the top of the table that they needed just one more player to win the league. "We had a real chance with the players we had, we were still hungry all of us," said Keegan. "We had some youngsters around Moran, Williams and Baker, it was quite a nice mixture.

"We had such an exciting side, anyone playing up front or in an advanced position for that side was always going to create chances or have chances created for them. The fans were tremendous with every player who played for Southampton. They demanded – in a nice country way – a performance from the team. When they started singing, *When The Saints Go Marching In,* you had to start marching and you had to start going in.

"We gave them some great nights. I remember us beating Man United, Liverpool and Arsenal and not only beating them, but playing them off the park. Games all seemed the same, we got the ball, we attacked. If we got beat it was either because we didn't have the luck – the crossbar or we wasted chances – or the other team played fantastic. We never put in a poor performance.

"I wanted them to buy players when we were top in January and February, it was like 'this is Southampton and we don't have that money' and you suddenly realised the fairytale wasn't going to happen. You could have a lot of fun, but I still wanted to win things even at a small club and I didn't think Southampton were going to win things."

McMenemy says that he did try extremely hard to add to the squad, particularly to replace the injured Moran. "I went in for Trevor Francis and it was all set up," he says, "John Bond was the manager [at Manchester City] and right at the last minute he said that the chairman Peter Swales wouldn't let it happen. That would have sealed it because he was a quality player. For what I had at the time, he would have been the icing on the cake.

"I had to go to plan B which was a kid called Keith Cassells at Oxford who was the top goal-scorer in the lower divisions at the time. It didn't come off really, although the bonus was that I got Mark Wright chucked in. I was opening some pitches at Bishops Abbey when I saw him training with Oxford. I stood and watched and I kept looking at this tall, gangly, ginger-haired lad and I found out who he was and got the scouts on to him.

"By this time, the thing with Francis had fallen through. I was haggling and having to deal with Robert Maxwell. I had made a bid for Keith Cassells and they wanted more so I said, 'I'll give you that if you stick the ginger-headed kid in there'. In his booming voice Maxwell said, 'this boy will play for England'. I said, 'if you are that good at football you are in the wrong job'. I found out afterwards he was showing off and he was in the boardroom and had our conversation on loudspeaker. The other board members said they were sniggering away because I had put him in his place, but he was right: Mark Wright did play for England."

The arrival of Wright had come just too late that season and a sense of disappointment had begun to fester as Keegan's relationship with McMenemy faltered. There was an exchange after one match when McMenemy had accused the team of not working hard enough. It was heat of the moment stuff, but Keegan apparently took it personally.

Yet all still appeared to be well when Keegan returned from a disappointing 1982 World Cup in Spain with England for pre-season training. However, on the Saints' summer tour, Keegan spoke of wanting a "new challenge" and, while Manchester United, as ever, were interested, that challenge would ultimately be breathing new life into Second Division Newcastle United. The transfer fee was £100,000 and Keegan was apparently offered personal terms of around £3,000 a week.

Keegan still had another year on his Southampton contract and, given that news of his departure only emerged in August, supporters were furious. There was a feeling that they had been sold their season tickets on a false premise. It is an accusation which has always been vehemently denied. Keegan wanted to explain why he was going at a press conference, while McMenemy moved swiftly to calm the unrest and even threatened to quit if the supporters did not accept his version of events. His rather dramatic plea for understanding demonstrates the concern that there would be a serious backlash to losing Keegan. "The news was sudden, like a thunderbolt out of the heavens," said McMenemy.

"I battled to get him here, using every part of my experience and strength to sign him in the face of fierce competition. I used those same strengths to try and get him to stay. I didn't admit defeat until I realised that even my best wasn't enough. Kevin Keegan is unique, more so even than somebody like George Best. When he finds his heart isn't in something, you can't shift him. If we had denied him…he would have turned his back on the game.

"If I cannot be believed and if the public believe that we as a club have conned them over Kevin Keegan, there is no way I would want to carry on the job I started here ten years ago. I would walk out."

KEVIN KEEGAN still returns to the Hampshire area regularly and he was back at The Dell several years later for a charity event organised by the late Steve Mills and then again at St. Mary's for the testimonial of Matthew Le Tissier. He went on to finish his playing career at St. James' Park and then became manager at Newcastle United, Fulham, England and Manchester City. His two year cameo with Saints became very typical of a career in football which was peppered by a wonderfully enigmatic nature. Having arrived as a messiah-like figure to great expectations, Keegan inspired magical moments and was then rather suddenly gone in somewhat mysterious circumstances. It was the same at Newcastle and England.

His most recent job in football was with Manchester City and he has since declined interview requests. When events such as Alan Shearer's testimonial at Newcastle in May 2006, came and went without the public hearing anything from Keegan, it came as little surprise that he was the only surviving Southampton Cult Hero who did not give a fresh interview for this book. Keegan is prone to long periods completely out of the spotlight, before throwing himself into the most high-profile of challenges. Of course, were it not for that sometimes impulsive and unpredictable personality, he would have surely never joined Saints.

Any hurt felt by Southampton fans at his rather abrupt departure in 1982 was quickly superseded by the memories of the excitement he provided. To this day, supporters still regularly talk about 'the moment we signed Keegan' and just the thought of it makes the hairs on the back of their necks stand to attention. They know that it would almost certainly need a cash injection of Roman Abramovich proportions for the club to make a comparable transfer again.

Indeed, when McMenemy unveiled Kevin Keegan at the Potters Heron, he rather boldly declared: "This is Southampton's finest day." For many Saints fans, even more than 25 years later, he wasn't far wrong.

DANNY WALLACE

1977-1989

SAINTS CAREER

Games	317
Goals	79
Caps	1

MAGIC MOMENT

An overhead kick to sink Liverpool in the first live televised match at The Dell

'THE DEPTFORD DESTROYER'

'Danny's a true fighter. He is putting so many able-bodied people to shame.'

Michael Watson

IT'S 9.30am – the time footballers normally arrive for their daily training session. At clubs all over the country, they are pulling up in their jeeps, BMWs, Ferraris and the rest. At about the same time in a street in the suburb of Worsley, just outside Manchester, a 42-year-old former Southampton winger closes the front door behind him and begins his own personal training routine for the day. He will be out for almost an hour and, in that time, if he can cover about one-and-a-half miles it will have been a successful morning's work. After that, he will rest for a few hours and be back out again at around 3.30pm for a repeat effort.

He begins shuffling along the pavement and gradually reaches his top pace. Back in 1979, that would have been quick enough to cover 100m in 11.3secs – marginally faster than Theo Walcott at the same age. Nowadays the equivalent distance will take several minutes to cover.

Danny Wallace was diagnosed with multiple sclerosis in 1997, two years after persistent injuries forced him out of professional football at the age of 31. It is almost certain that he was already suffering from the early symptoms of MS while at Birmingham City between 1993 and 1995 and Wallace is convinced that his debilitating disease was the reason behind four injury prone years at Manchester United, which still sometimes haunt him. In the preceding decade for Southampton, however, he inked his name into the record books with a series of memorable feats and performances.

Yet that was then and this is now. After around five years when he struggled to accept that he had MS, Wallace wants to move on and has spent 12 months preparing for an attempt on the 2006 London Marathon. It is a sizeable challenge for the most able-bodied of people, let alone someone who finds walking just a few hundred metres exhausting and who can, at any time, suffer a paralysing relapse which will leave him bed-bound for up to a week.

MS is one of the most common diseases of the nervous system and it affects people of virtually all ages around the world. The symptoms are wide-ranging. For Wallace, the main problem is with the right-hand side of his body, particularly his back. Walking is difficult and he is fatigued quickly. He also gets pins and needles in his hands and feet.

Following diagnosis, he barely left his house. He began drinking heavily and was depressed. "I had some black days when I was sat indoors not doing anything but just looking at the four walls," he says, "I was more or less wishing my life away. It's been very difficult to come to terms with this bloody disease and I got very, very low. I wouldn't even go out. I was like a recluse. I wouldn't talk to anyone, I wouldn't do anything. I wasn't suicidal, but I was quite close."

Wallace, however, has been on a journey towards accepting his condition and is now keen to get out and about. It is about the fourth time we have met over the past two years. On the first occasion, it was for an interview just prior to his testimonial match in 2004. He had not spoken to any journalists for several years, but had insisted on getting out of the house and meeting me at a hotel in Manchester. His modesty – or perhaps low self-esteem – was then striking and he looked genuinely taken aback to be told that Southampton fans still held him in the highest regard. "Do people really still remember me?" he asked and his eyes seemed to well up when I told him that they most certainly did.

Confirmation of his popularity came just a few weeks later when he was introduced to the crowd prior to a match against Bolton Wanderers at St. Mary's. It was a wonderful moment as he slowly made his way onto the pitch with the help of a cane and chants of 'there's only one Danny Wallace' rang out from every corner of the stadium.

WALLACE HAS just finished his morning walk when we meet for lunch in Warrington. He picks me up from the station and, although we are briefly stopped by the police when he takes the wrong junction and drives up a bus lane, he is in good spirits. It has taken a few tries to arrange our meeting. The previous week, he sent me a text message which read, "Jeremy, sorry, my speech is not too good at the moment. Just had a relapse. But call me next week and we'll arrange something then".

Wallace credits his wife Jenny with helping him come to terms with MS. "A lot of it is down to Jen," he says, "she gave me a lot of confidence. She told me it was time to stop moping around and feeling sorry for myself and to get out and see if I could do something. To tell you the truth, I didn't really want to believe that I had this disease. She told me I had to start doing things and it was hard. I was literally scared to go out. I didn't want people to see the way I was walking."

Wallace likens preparing for the marathon to getting ready for a big football match. He can feel the same nervous tension in his stomach and, just like stepping out onto the pitch, he knows there are no guarantees of a successful outcome. "I'm just trying to build up my legs again," he says, "it's not easy as I haven't really done anything for ten years. But I've been speaking to Michael Watson [the boxer] about his experience of doing it [the marathon] and I'm determined. The concern is if I have a relapse it will take me four or five days to get back on my feet. The whole of my right side locks up, especially around the back area and, if I move, it feels like a metal rod running up my back."

Just getting out regularly, however, is a huge step forward and it is a measure of how far he has come that, after previously not wanting anyone to see him, he is preparing to take part in an event which will be watched by millions. Wallace's previous fear of going out and his depression stemmed not only from the onset of MS and the difficulties he was having with his walking, but also a lingering disappointment at the way his career finished.

After spending more that 12 years with Saints, he had commanded the club's record incoming transfer fee with a £1.2m move to Manchester United. He was 25 and should have been at the absolute peak of his powers. Yet after only 55 starts for United in four years, he was sold to Birmingham City for £250,000.

"I felt like people would have a go at me or slag me off," he says, "they are avid fans in Manchester and I felt ashamed because I had left Southampton in good health and I had gone to Manchester United to win medals. To be honest, I thought I was absolutely shit at United. I didn't want to be walking on the street and have anyone looking at me and saying, 'there's that shit player' or anything like that, so I didn't venture out anywhere."

Wallace's analysis of his football career is often overly self-critical. He is particularly hard on himself about his time at United when his body was probably already suffering with the onset of MS. He also glosses over the fact that he did play a key part in the club's FA Cup triumph of 1990, the first major trophy of the Ferguson era. Ferguson himself certainly does not share Wallace's assessment. Ferguson is selective with his interviews, but his keenness to talk about Wallace before the testimonial in 2004 suggests a genuine appreciation of the role he played in helping him lift a first major trophy at Old Trafford.

"He was a terrific player for me," says Ferguson, "he was one of five players I bought around that time with Mike Phelan, Gary Pallister, Paul Ince and Neil Webb, because I felt we needed to freshen up. Sometimes older players can do it once, but maybe not keep doing it. I felt we needed some young players at the time. Danny fitted into what we wanted at that time and he did a great job for us. I remember him making his debut against Portsmouth. I remember thinking it was quite a place to start, but he scored on his debut and he was terrific."

Having won so many major trophies since, it is easy to forget what a watershed moment it was when Crystal Palace were beaten in the final of the FA Cup following some difficult years in United's history. "He was excellent for us in the FA Cup," said Ferguson, "I remember he scored in the fifth round against Newcastle. It was a fantastic goal. He was just on the six-yard box and he dipped his shoulder and blasted it in the net.

"He also made the winning goal in that game for Brian McClair. Then I remember he made the goal for Mark Hughes in the FA Cup final. We were 3-2 down against Crystal Palace and it was the second period of extra-time and he played a very cute pass. He was very, very influential for us. It was my first trophy for Manchester United and you always remember those ones. He gave us width and speed. He could beat a player, he was a good deliverer of crosses and he could finish. He was also a player who could play through the middle."

Ferguson admits he was quite shaken to hear the news that Wallace had MS and can still vividly recall being told. "I couldn't believe it – it was just like, 'no – bloody hell'," he said, "it came as a real shock, he was such a fit and enthusiastic lad."

Wallace said it was "unbelievable" to play in a winning FA Cup team at Wembley, but his appearances were to become less and less frequent as regular problems with calf, hamstring and groin injuries – usually down the right-hand side of his body – increasingly took their toll. "The first time they won the Premiership that killed me," says Wallace. "To see them win it without me knocked me for six. I knew after that I had to go." Wallace held talks with Ian Branfoot about a possible return to Southampton once it became clear that his Manchester United career was at an end and he now wishes that he had made the decision to go 'home'. Not so much for football reasons, just because he believes it may have been easier to cope with the onset of MS around people like Dave Merrington and Lew Chatterley, who were still at the club.

But, without knowing what was happening to his body, Wallace made the decision to join Birmingham following a loan spell with Millwall. Injuries, however, were to become even more frequent and he managed just 13 starts over the next 18 months. Unaware that he was being affected by MS, he attempted to play through the pain. At Birmingham, he would train for 90 minutes and then often sleep right through to the following morning and the next training session.

"I now believe I had this disease before I left Southampton," he says, "but I just thought I was injury prone. You miss a game, you might make a couple of mistakes and that's when your confidence goes and I could just never get any momentum. From 1990 to 1995 I think I played about 80 games in five years. When I was diagnosed in 1997 I knew it had to be linked because as well as the hamstring, groin and calf injuries, when I was playing at Birmingham, I was getting pins and needles and backache.

"I knew there was something wrong because when I finished a game my back would be in bits and I was struggling to walk. I wouldn't tell them I was injured, I would just go home and rest up. That lasted for about a year, which was crazy. I had lost my pace completely and I had pins and needles in my feet. When I kicked the ball, there was no feeling – it just felt like I was kicking a balloon."

The change in Wallace's physical capabilities had become unmistakeable. While the mind was still willing and his bravery and courage remained beyond question, he was finished as a professional footballer without his speed and touch. It was all a far cry from his debut some 15 years previously when McMenemy gave him an unexpected start at Old Trafford and the name 'Wallace' became synonymous with Saints.

DANNY WALLACE was born in Greenwich in January 1964, the son of Vincent and Joan Wallace. His parents had settled in south London after emigrating from Jamaica. His father worked as a labourer and his mother as an auxiliary nurse.

"We were living in quite a run-down place and it was hard for my parents, especially being black people at that time," he says, "there was a lot more racism around and I don't think it was easy for them, but they worked hard and made sure we got everything we needed. We didn't have much money, but I remember when I got into football, my school – West Greenwich – were really helpful. Getting out of London at that time was probably good for me as a lot of my friends ended up getting into trouble."

In an interview in 1989, his late father Vincent recalled how young Danny became besotted by football from the age of five, despite the fact that he was the first in his family to take any interest in the sport. "His mother would send him to the shops for a loaf and he'd set off with a ball under his feet," said Vincent. "Then he'd come back still with the ball and without a loaf. I asked him what he was going to do in life. When Danny said he was going to be a footballer I said he was too small and he would get knocked about. He just told me not to worry about that."

Cricket was Vincent's passion, but he supported Danny in his dream and he was already causing interest among football scouts by the age of 13. "I played for a Sunday team with Ian Wright – he lived a couple of miles away from me and we had a good team," remembers Wallace, "then I played for the school team and then the district team. My PE teacher Keith Hodder wrote to the club and Bob Higgins [a Southampton scout] came to watch me."

Higgins later recalled the moment he first watched Wallace in action and the lengths he went to ensure that the local London clubs did not beat Southampton to his signature. "I knew I had to act quickly, but the day I decided to sign him as a schoolboy, I found I had run out of registration forms," he said. "I could not believe it, so I cheekily phoned a friend at Millwall, told him I was coming up to London and asked if I could borrow some of his schoolboy forms. I didn't dare tell him who they were for or I would have had no chance. That afternoon I drove to London, picked up the forms and popped round the corner to sign Danny from under the noses of Millwall – and on their forms. They were furious when they found out."

Just like Theo Walcott some 25 years later, it was the pace of Wallace which first excited the Southampton coaches and they quickly realised that the club had unearthed a precocious young talent. At just a fraction under 5ft 5in and less than ten stones in weight, Wallace compensated for his lack of physical stature with a fierce competitive instinct.

For Saints, he was generally appearing in a youth team which played in the Hampshire League, but, despite having played only one reserve team game, McMenemy allowed him to travel with the squad which were facing Manchester United on November 29, 1980. Wallace had no idea that he might play. He thought he was simply being taken along for the experience as a reward for his form in the youth team. Yet with Kevin Keegan already unavailable through injury, McMenemy was short of attacking options. That situation suddenly became a crisis when Steve Moran went down with a stomach bug during the night.

Even then, Wallace had no idea that he might play until McMenemy pulled him to one side just an hour before the game to tell him he would be starting. "Scared," is how Wallace sums up what he felt, although he believes the timing of the team announcement definitely helped him. He had, after all, slept soundly the night before in the belief that there was no way he would be getting his chance. "I didn't know what I was doing," he says, "it was one of those days where I thought I'd only gone up there to pack the kit and clean a few pairs of boots and suddenly I'm going out to make my debut against Manchester United."

From playing at little non-league grounds around Hampshire, he was getting changed in the visitors' dressing room at Old Trafford alongside the likes of Mick Channon, Charlie George, Dave Watson, Nick Holmes, Chris Nicholl and Ivan Golac. The crowd that day was 46,840. Reuben Agboola, who was only 18 at the time, was also given his debut and both teenagers were to acquit themselves admirably as Saints drew 1-1 thanks to a goal from Holmes.

WALLACE WAS only 16 years and 314 days old on his debut and so became the youngest ever to play for Saints. It was a record that was to last almost a quarter of a century until Theo Walcott surpassed it against Wolverhampton Wanderers on the opening day of the 2005/06 season. Comparisons between the two have naturally been made. At the same age, both possessed electrifying pace and were equally comfortable playing on the wing or attacking through the middle. Wallace was arguably the better tackler and superior in the air, although Walcott had the edge in crossing and shooting ability.

Walcott, of course, only stayed at Saints for just five months after making his debut and attracted an unprecedented fee which, with international appearances, could amount to £12m. He may very well go on to great things and become a regular in the England team, but Walcott's achievement in playing at such a young age is perhaps marginally less impressive. Unlike Wallace, Walcott was making his debut in front of a home crowd in the second tier of English football. He was also playing in an inferior Southampton team.

Wallace's debut is a day that he will not forget and there was a nice moment on *Match of the Day* that evening when the young 16-year-old refers to his manager as "Lawrie". McMenemy looks down at him as if he is about to cuff him around the back of the head, before Wallace quickly adds: "Sorry, the gaffer."

The former Southampton manager later explained why he had enough confidence to play Wallace at such a young age. "The lad had excited me in training," said McMenemy. "He lacks nothing in confidence and I wanted to have another look at him in a game."

Wallace was to feature only eight more times in the league over the next two years, although he did enough to make an impression on Kevin Keegan when he came on as a substitute during a memorable 5-5 draw at The Dell against Coventry City. Keegan recalls Wallace storming into the dressing room and then throwing his boots on the floor. As his confused team-mates looked at him, it became clear that he'd lost count of all the goals and thought his team had been defeated 5-4. It was typical of Southampton during the era in which he played. Just like under Ted Bates, McMenemy's Southampton teams played attacking football and Wallace, who had now established himself in the side, was scoring his share of goals.

From 1982/83 through to 1988/89, Wallace averaged almost ten goals a season despite generally playing out on the wing. "Danny has speed, skill and balance," said McMenemy. "If there is one thing a defender finds hard to handle it is pace and Danny adds to that part of his game by being able to cross a ball well. His first touch is good too. Some players have pace, but they have difficulty in bringing the ball under control. Danny can kill it straight away and then be off on a run. His strength lies in his pace. He can go past defenders as though they were not there. He has got guts. When things don't go right for him, he doesn't drop his head and hide. He always comes back for more."

THE TWO GAMES for which Wallace remains best remembered came within just two months of each other in 1984. It was the season that Saints were to finish second in the league and the fixture at The Dell against Liverpool – who would go on to take the title by only three points – was selected for live screening on BBC. At the time, this was unusual and it was moved forward to a Friday night. It was the first time that a football match had ever been televised live at The Dell and Liverpool, who were the best team in Europe at the time, were given something of a football lesson by Saints and particularly a 20-year-old Danny Wallace.

It finished 2-0 with Wallace scoring two classic goals. The first was an acrobatic overhead scissors kick which was to win Goal of the Season, but Wallace still maintains that the second gave him most satisfaction. "That game is what most people seem to remember," he says. "We had a great team that year, absolutely brilliant. I wouldn't say we did better than the 1976 FA Cup team, but coming second in the league, three points behind Liverpool, was a tremendous season for us. I thought we were better than Liverpool that year.

"People in Southampton still always come up and want to talk to me about those goals. For me the header was a lot better. To beat Alan Hansen in the air, I preferred that one, but the other wasn't a bad goal and I can still remember the move clearly. Frank Worthington turned someone and saw Mark Dennis running down the left and he crossed it in. Mark Wright had made a run into the box and he headed it, I was facing our goal and I just thought 'go for it' and I let fly. It was perfect for an overhead kick and, as I was going over, I saw it flying into the top corner."

Wallace's fine form continued and the following month both he and Steve Moran scored hat-tricks in an 8-2 win over Coventry City. The man of the match, though, was undoubtedly Wallace, who provided assists for four of the five goals he didn't score. Left-back that day for Coventry was a novice called Stuart Pearce, but he was given a torrid time by Wallace. It was the most goals Saints have ever scored in a top-flight game.

Yet for all the records they set on the pitch that day, it is the argument in the dressing room between Wallace and Moran over who should have the match ball that both players now remember best. "Because I completed my hat-trick before Danny, I claimed the match ball," says Moran, who has become a LGV driver since retiring from football, "but in the dressing room the players got me to change my mind because it was Danny's first hat-trick and I'd got a few already. So Danny got to keep the ball and they found a spare one which the lads signed for me. Danny was quick, he was exciting and he was unpredictable – a typical winger. He would do the hard things brilliantly but sometimes make some of the easy things look hard."

Wallace's form for Saints was bringing him to national prominence and an England call-up looked inevitable. However, with the likes of John Barnes and Chris Waddle available, a position on the wing was always going to be one of the more competitive places in the team. It was at a time when the manager Bobby Robson was accused of overlooking Saints' finest talent (David Armstrong, Steve Williams and Mark Dennis had all struggled to get into the team), but Wallace made his debut in January 1986 against Egypt.

His inclusion was the result of the unavailability of both Barnes and Waddle, but he scored a 52nd minute volley to help England to a 4-0 win and won praise from the manager. "He took his goal remarkably well and kept battling throughout the game, which I thought he would," said Robson. Wallace, though, was injured at the time the next squad was selected and his England career was to stand at just one game and one goal.

While Wallace's capacity to produce the most thrilling and crowd-pleasing football was unquestioned – as was his effort – he was sometimes let down by a lack of consistency, particularly when it came to his crossing. Having said that, if Waddle and Barnes were understandable inclusions in the England squad, it was difficult to understand why Stoke City's Mark Chamberlain was sometimes preferred.

"He had his favourites like any other manager," shrugs Wallace. He did, however, have some high-profile supporters, including George Best who said: "Danny Wallace is the best winger in England by a long way. Why he hasn't a stack of caps a yard high is beyond me. The way he is ignored by Bobby Robson is criminal. His pace is blistering, his ball skills are masterly and he scores spectacular goals. More importantly he knows he is a great player and that gives him confidence to take others on. If he performed like that for a top team like Liverpool he would be an automatic England choice. He would certainly get into my England team ahead of John Barnes."

A feeling that his career was perhaps being hindered rather than helped by staying at The Dell seemed to increase with the departure of the manager Lawrie McMenemy. Chris Nicholl did a decent job as successor, but the era of regular European football and signings like Kevin Keegan and Peter Shilton were coming to an end. In several interviews during the late 1980s, Wallace's thinking is not difficult to interpret. Speaking in 1987, he said: "With Peter Shilton and Mark Wright gone, Bobby Robson might not come down and look at Southampton. I believe I could stand a better chance if I moved to a bigger club and there is the danger I could get stale if I stayed too long at Southampton."

DESPITE the murmurings of discontent, by now there was the extraordinary situation of three Wallaces pushing for first team places following the progression of his younger twin brothers, Rodney and Raymond. They were almost six years younger than Danny, but both came through the youth system to sign professional forms in 1988. Rodney was a player very much in the mould of Danny with terrific pace and the capacity to score spectacular goals. Raymond was less gifted, but showed determination to become a professional footballer.

It is also a little known fact that Danny's older brother Clive once had a trial as a goalkeeper. Considering that dad Vincent had only followed cricket, and that the age gap meant Danny never really played football with his two younger brothers while they were growing up, it is extraordinary that they all became professionals.

It was on October 22, 1988 that the Wallaces first played together and became the first trio of brothers to appear in a Football League match since the 1920s. All three played the majority of the 1988/89 season with Raymond at right-back, while Rodney and Danny supplied the likes of Alan Shearer, Matthew Le Tissier and Paul Rideout. Saints finished 13th that season with the worst defensive record in the First Division, yet one of the most potent forward lines.

"It was a hell of an achievement to all play together," says Danny, "especially as we didn't play any football together at home. To start with Rodney did not want to play football, but Raymond was all up for it. Rodney saw what was happening and he got interested – I think I got him his first boots. My old man was really proud. He would stop people in the street and talk about his sons playing football. My dad died not long ago and it was great that he could have seen that. I don't think that will happen again – it's amazing to have three brothers playing in the same team."

By this time, however, Danny was aware that he was attracting the interest of some of the biggest clubs in England and had decided that he wanted a fresh challenge away from The Dell. He handed in a transfer request before being sold to Manchester United in September 1989. It was a move, sadly, which was to signal the beginning of the end of his football career.

His two brothers initially remained with Saints and Rodney was arguably to match Danny's level of performance over the next two years, particularly during the 1989/90 season when he scored 18 league goals and helped the club to a seventh place finish. At the time of writing, the club has not since finished higher. Yet with Danny gone, his brothers also became restless and the popularity of the Wallaces was somewhat damaged when Rodney made a total of eight transfer requests over the next 20 months. Eventually he played out his contract and, with Ray, moved to Leeds United in a deal worth £1.7m. Rodney, who is now taking his coaching badges and living in Surrey, went on to win a league title with Leeds while Ray drifted out of the game and now works as a gym instructor in Manchester. It marked the end of an era for Saints too as, for the first time in almost 15 years, they went into the 1991/92 season without a Wallace on the books.

The word 'loyalty', of course, is a strange subject where football is concerned. Because they feel it themselves, supporters have the expectation that their heroes will share a blind devotion to their club. In some instances, most notably in Southampton's case with the likes of Ted Bates, Matthew Le Tissier, Nick Holmes and Francis Benali, that commitment and loyalty is matched. Generally, though, players and managers understandably want to do what is best for themselves, their careers and their families. Danny Wallace has a genuine fondness for Saints, but finds it hard to understand how some fans, who so revered him during the 1980s, felt let-down when, after more than a decade at The Dell, he took the chance to join what is arguably the biggest club in the world. He still remembers an incident in a Southampton restaurant called the Indian Cottage shortly after his move to United.

"I was out with my wife and a couple of friends and a couple of geezers came up to me and started slagging me off," he says, "I got pissed off with it and basically told them to, 'fuck off and leave us alone'. It ended up in a big fight. Jen joined in and broke her little finger and another girl we were with broke her arm! It was a nightmare, absolutely crazy and all because I had joined Manchester United."

In hindsight, of course, it proved to be a fantastic deal for Saints. Danny Wallace had cost the club nothing, they had benefited on the field from his best years as a player and then profited financially when selling him for a club record fee.

ONCE HIS CAREER had come to an end, little was heard from Wallace until 2004 when it was announced that Saints would stage a testimonial for him at St. Mary's. MS had severely restricted his earning potential and he had left football just before the huge salaries came into the game following Sky's involvement in launching the Premiership as a distinctive new brand. Given his service to Saints, Wallace deserved his big night. "It was unbelievable, I was choked up," he says, "a lot of the people hadn't seen me play and it was just an amazing feeling. The fans were like they have always been. Playing at The Dell was such a great feeling. It was such a close-knit family club, you more or less knew most of the fans. They would come up to you and it was great to play for a team like that."

Wallace's testimonial was held on May 17, 2004, and attracted a long list of the club's greatest names as well as some of those from Manchester United. The players included Antti Niemi, Steve Williams, James Beattie, Viv Anderson, Paul Parker, Ray Wallace, Mark Wright, Kevin Moore, Kevin Bond, Russell Osman, Reuben Agboola, Denis Irwin, Francis Benali, Matthew Le Tissier, Jimmy Case, Clayton Blackmore, Tim Flowers, Paul Ince, Gordon Strachan, Nick Holmes, Micky Adams, George Lawrence, Rod Wallace, Mark Hughes, Cyrille Regis, Ian Baird and Steve Moran. Appropriately, the All-Star Saints team was managed by Lawrie McMenemy as Danny Wallace looked on from the stands, enjoying the moment, but no doubt itching to be a part of events on the field. A crowd of just over 13,000 turned out to pay tribute to Wallace and he earned £110,000.

Gordon Strachan, who had recently departed as the Saints manager, remembered the evening fondly. "It showed what a good club it is and what good people there are that support the club," he said. "As a player Danny had a great change of pace and he was brave. There is a physical and mental bravery and he is still showing that mental bravery, which is the hardest one. It [the testimonial] showed everything that is good about the club. The club is not built on bricks and mortar, it is about people."

Wallace looks back on the testimonial as an event which was not only beneficial financially, but also in helping him come to terms with MS and to look positively at the rest of his life. He has since launched the Danny Wallace Foundation, which is a charity to help MS sufferers. "The testimonial really perked me up," he says, "I needed to be out doing something, getting out and talking to people again. It made me realise that people do appreciate what I had done. So many people came up to me and said, 'thanks for being a Southampton player'. That meant the world to me."

AT 5PM on Friday April 28, 2006, Danny Wallace completed the 26 mile 365 yard London Marathon. Waiting for him to present the medal was Michael Watson, who himself completed the marathon in 2003, despite suffering brain injuries in a boxing match with Chris Eubank. Walking between four and five miles each day, it took Wallace six days to complete the course. In that time, he lost his balance and fell over on six occasions.

As Wallace made his way through the streets of Greenwich and then Deptford where he was brought up, an impromptu rendition of *You'll Never Walk Alone* boomed out from an apartment. It reduced his support team, which included wife Jen and former Southampton team-mate George Lawrence, to tears. "It was one hell of an experience," says Lawrence. "The crowds were fantastic and it has been brilliant for giving him something to focus on. Danny knows now that he can be an inspiration to people and he wants to do much more to show others what is possible.

"I've known Danny since we were both about 13 or 14. To see him with MS was hard to start with. Every time I saw him I was in tears. But he feels better about himself and that makes me feel better. He is bubbly now and willing to get out."

For Wallace, the 2006 London Marathon was one of the best experiences of his life. "I got stronger as the week went on and once I got over halfway I knew that I would be able to do it – I was flying," he says. "The reaction was just unbelievable. The cabbies were the best thing, they would be stopping and bibbing their horns. It was definitely on a par with making my debut for Saints or winning the FA Cup. On the night I finished, I slept with the medal around my neck. Since doing the marathon my energy levels are unbelievable. I'm not tired and I'm getting out of bed wanting to do things."

People often say it's so sad when you see the likes of Muhammad Ali, Michael Watson and even Danny Wallace. They say they thrilled millions in their prime with skill and achievement beyond the dreams of the average sports fan and now they struggle with everyday tasks. Meeting Wallace makes you realise this is the wrong way to look at it. Sport came easily to these people – they were naturals. But it shows real courage to confront illness and disease, to open the front-door and step out of the sports bubble. Danny Wallace is doing just that and has become an inspirational figure to people far beyond football. He is now looking for fresh challenges.

"I've got to find something else now," he told me just three days after finishing the London Marathon, before asking, "do you think I could do a sky-dive?"

MARK DENNIS

'PSYCHO'

1983-1987

SAINTS CAREER

Games	129
Goals	2
Caps	0

MAGIC MOMENT

Scoring a spectacular volley in a 4-3 win against Norwich before being hauled up before the FA for an incident involving an opponent during an argument on the way to the tunnel

'You had to handle Mark Dennis like a father, not a Sergeant-Major.'

Jim Smith

MARK Dennis shakes his head at the memory. "I've done a lot of silly things," he says, "but that was my biggest mistake." From an extraordinary life tinged with sadness, glory, three near death experiences, 12 red cards and more trips to FA disciplinary hearings than most of his fellow professionals combined, it's not easy to predict what Dennis will say next.

"Okay Mark, what was the biggest mistake of your life?"

"What happened with Chris Nicholl – what led to me leaving Saints," he replies.

A cloud of mystery has long hung over the events of February 1987. Dennis was established in the Southampton team and regarded by The Dell crowd as the best left-back the club had ever had. Many felt an England call-up was long overdue, although his poor disciplinary record, which led to the nickname 'Psycho' well before Stuart Pearce received the monicker, and colourful off-field antics were holding him back on the international stage.

But that didn't matter in Southampton. As a player, Mark Dennis was in his entertaining prime. A brilliant, rampaging full-back and a key member of the team that finished second in the league in 1983/84, he was the darling of the terraces and looked set to cement his status as one of the club's greatest players.

Saints were hosting Norwich City at The Dell and had lost 2-1. It had been a transitional time for the club following the departure of Lawrie McMenemy. There was little danger of rele-gation, but the days of regular European football were passing and remaining a First Division force was soon to become the priority. The new manager Nicholl was having to establish himself among strong and sometimes difficult characters.

Still, no-one in The Dell crowd could possibly imagine they had just watched Dennis play his last game for the club. What happened next in the dressing room has been the subject of gossip and rumours for almost 20 years, but Dennis is now happy to confirm that a fight did take place between him and the manager. He is also willing to hold up his hands and admit he was in the wrong.

At the time, Dennis was going through a marriage break-up. Having gained custody of his five-year-old daughter Joanne, he was a 25-year-old lone father. He had been out the night before the Norwich game and, when Saints officials made some inquiries into his where-abouts, they found he was at a local snooker club. To make matters worse, his little daughter had been with him, sleeping peacefully underneath the table.

As heated words were exchanged following the Norwich defeat, Dennis was challenged over his activities the previous evening. "I had been out late and my daughter was under a snooker table," he admits, "there was a curfew and I was out with her. I was in the wrong. Thinking about it now, if I was Chris I would have done the same.

"I didn't agree with styles of play, rightly or wrongly, and we had a few words. I said something to him and Chris gave me a real good right-hander. I didn't go down onto one knee which was good and I flew into him. George Horsfall [the reserve team manager], bless him, dived in as did a few others. It was a free-for-all."

Dennis found himself sidelined for the rest of the season and a high profile stand-off ensued between player and manager. There was a wall of silence at Southampton, although the club secretary Brian Truscott issued a short statement the following week, saying: "We look upon this as a domestic matter, to be dealt with internally and not one which is subject to public comment."

It was claimed that Dennis was injured and he continued to be left out of the team. The situation alerted other clubs and Dennis then issued his own statement saying he had been offered better deals elsewhere, but that he wanted to stay with Saints. "I have a number of other considerations to take into account, namely the future happiness of my daughter Joanne, who is settled in Southampton and is due to start school shortly," he said. Another factor was the fans. "The support I have received from them over the last two months has been overwhelming," he added.

"I have received many letters and approaches from them asking me not to leave. I have made it quite clear that I like it here and have always enjoyed playing football for the club. My feelings for the club and supporters will never change."

A reconciliation looked plausible. Five days later and the newspaper headline said it all: 'Dennis gets the sack'. It was April Fools' Day, but this was no joke. Nicholl had taken the decision to terminate Dennis' contract. The final straw was perhaps a newspaper article which quoted Dennis criticising the manager. Dennis had been banned by the club from speaking to the press following another embarrassment earlier in the season.

The sacking hit Dennis hard and he responded by threatening to quit football entirely. "I'm stunned, I feel so disappointed that I'm seriously considering packing the game in altogether," he said, "it's left me completely disillusioned." Of Nicholl and the chairman Alan Woodford, he added: "I can't put into words what I think about the way they have treated me. 'Big' Lawrie [McMenemy] knew how to handle me. I don't know what it was. But he demanded respect and he got it. Nicholl demands respect and gets nothing. I've had 200 really lovely letters from fans in the past month."

At the time, Nicholl said: "You can be sure Southampton Football Club do not willingly lose a player of Mark's ability and no way has this been done without serious thought and very good reasons. For the overall health of the club this had to be done. I take no pleasure in the club taking this measure. I see it as my failure."

SO DENNIS WAS gone. Or was he? The supporters certainly made it clear who they supported. The next match was at home to Wimbledon and the cult status of Dennis among the fans was evident. 'Saints fans say Mark must stay' said one banner, while another read, 'Give Nicholl the sack and bring back Dennis'. The manager was booed loudly and chants of 'Nicholl out, Dennis in' rang out during the game.

Saints fan Tim Mumford explains what made supporters side with Dennis. "Mark was our left-back and left-midfield...come to think of it left-wing also all in one," he says. "He had tireless energy, pin-point passing accuracy, vicious tackling ability and put the fear of Christ into his opponents. 'Psycho' was never beaten for pace and his crossing from deep or wide created numerous opportunities for [Steve] Moran, [Danny] Wallace and [Frank] Worthington. When he played, Saints were completely impenetrable down our left. I cannot remember a player more related to and popular [for an obviously non-glamour position] with the rank and file on the terraces. He was a 'casual icon' and the epitome of a 1980s top-flight cult player. Southampton Football Club has had some fabulous left-backs including Peachy [David Peach] and Bridger [Wayne Bridge]. As much as I love those guys, they couldn't lace Dennis' boots. We'd all just chant incessantly, 'Psycho Psycho Psycho Psycho'."

Dennis eventually had an appeal against 'unfair dismissal' heard by a three man Football League management committee panel and ended up with a partial victory that made him a free agent. There had been talk that he would be kicked out of football altogether, but he joined Jim Smith at QPR, who had managed him earlier in his career at Birmingham City.

When I telephone Smith to talk about Dennis, he responds with a prolonged chuckle. It is a familiar reaction from most people who knew or know him whenever the words "Mark Dennis" are uttered. His behaviour might sometimes have been inexcusable, but he is still held in great affection. "Often silly, but never malicious," says Smith, "and what a character. When I first knew him he was a young lad, away from home and a typical Londoner; cocky, bouncy, bright. If something was ever missing, if there was some trickery or someone had water poured on them or there was some prank going on, you knew that he would be behind it.

"He was one of the best uncapped left-backs. I think his reputation affected him. He was a bit impetuous and rash in the tackle. He was coming towards the end of his career and I needed a left-back. It was as simple as that and I knew what a quality player he was."

Dennis reflects on the turmoil in his life at the time of his move from Saints to QPR and shakes his head once again. He remains an entertaining character, but he is the first to admit that he was, at times, out of control. It is almost two decades since he left Saints and he has become good friends with Nicholl. "We were two different people," he says, "but I get on fabulously with Chris now. We realised we couldn't gel and that was down to me more than him. Too much water had gone under the bridge and I left, but it's great that we are friends and we can move on. We play golf together and I can see now that it was hard for him. There were also people like Mark Wright, Andy Townsend and Peter Shilton in the dressing room at the time and we were not the easiest to handle.

"We still laugh and talk about what happened. In the dressing room things like that do happen and I've still got the scar to prove it on my eye, which is quite funny. It was passion, heat of the moment stuff. I know I didn't portray my life well and didn't look after myself as well as I should. But there is one thing I can say and that is I didn't let the team down on the park. I'm proud of that, but if I had my time again I would do things differently."

As we chat for around an hour in a room at the St. Mary's Stadium, the honesty with which Dennis analyses his life is often startling. Yet, in hindsight, if you track the events in the year leading up to his dismissal from Saints, you have to conclude that it was almost inevitable. He was only 25, but he had become an accident waiting to happen.

BORN IN STREATHAM on May 2, 1961, Mark Dennis was the son of Earl and Sheila. Evidence of Dennis' footballing talent first emerged as a nine-year-old when he starred in the cubs' cup final which was played locally on the ground of non-league Tooting and Mitcham. He briefly stopped playing football, however, at the age of 13 before taking it up again at 15.

He was playing for a Tommy Trinder team against Fulham when he was spotted by the Birmingham scout Don Dorman, who had previously uncovered Trevor Francis. Dennis then spent six years at St. Andrews and developed a close relationship with Smith. "Jim [Smith] was fantastic," says Dennis, "he was a great man-manager, loved his football, passionate. He would lose it in the dressing room at half-time and in them days it wasn't paper cups, it was china cups. You would be ducking everywhere. But it would be forgotten afterwards. He was a great motivator and a players' man."

However, once Smith left Birmingham in 1982 to be replaced by Ron Saunders, it became inevitable that Dennis would move. His disciplinary record meant he was available for a nominal fee, but Lawrie McMenemy had confidence in his judgment as well as his renowned man-management skills and gambled on the south Londoner.

The quality of Dennis as a player was rarely in doubt, but he needed a strong and imposing manager to produce his best. McMenemy's status in the game at the time was beyond question and Dennis can still vividly recall walking into the dressing room for the first time. He says his jaw was fairly close to the ground. "There was Mick Mills, Peter Shilton, Mark Wright, Steve Williams and Frank Worthington sat there. Great, great players. Steve Williams was the best midfielder I ever played with – Jimmy Case not too far behind. They were just great characters and players.

"Shilton for me, with Gordon Banks, is the best goalkeeper ever – it was just amazing. Lawrie McMenemy and Lew Chatterley took me into the dressing room and I think it took me about two seconds to say, 'I'll sign'. Middlesbrough also came in for me and I had spoken to Terry Venables at QPR. Terry was a good friend and a magnificent manager. Lawrie was a man-manager, Terry was hands-on, but I still say to this day that I made the right decision."

Dennis went straight into a team which found itself fighting with Liverpool, Nottingham Forest and Manchester United for the First Division title. "We were exceptional at home," remembers Dennis, "we came second to Liverpool, but we beat them and we thought we were the best side that year. The Dell was a fortress – the press called us a bad red wine because we were bad travellers, but we put a decent run together away from home as well."

Defensively Saints were extremely secure, conceding only 38 times in 42 matches. As well as Dennis, the influence of Shilton was clear, but also the class of Mark Wright at centre-back. Wright and Dennis shared heartache in the FA Cup semi-finals of 1984 and 1986. Many still believe that 1984 was the year Saints should have repeated the triumph of 1976. Dennis says they "battered" Everton, but believes the Merseysiders had their name written on the Cup that year. "We felt we let ourselves and the manager down," he says. Earlier that year Saints had memorably defeated Portsmouth in the fourth round at Fratton Park. Dennis was struck by a coin during the game, but in time added on for that incident Steve Moran brilliantly half-volleyed a David Armstrong cross past the Portsmouth goalkeeper Alan Knight for a famous victory.

Then there was the 1986 semi-final when Wright departed with a broken leg during the first-half against Liverpool. He had collided with Shilton and Craig Johnston and his broken fibula was also to end his World Cup hopes later that year. As the match drifted towards extra-time at 0-0, Dennis found himself in space and fired a powerful long range shot past Bruce Grobbelaar. It seemed destined for the net, handing Dennis a place in the club's history and

Southampton their chance in the Cup final. But late in its trajectory, the ball rose and rose and just glanced the woodwork on its way over. "It breaks my heart remembering it," says Dennis, "I was wheeling away to my daughter, but it hit the post and went out. Unfortunately Kevin Bond made a mistake to let Ian Rush in to score in extra-time and it was agony for us."

It had been the tenth time Saints had reached an FA Cup semi-final in their 100 year history, although the wait for another opportunity was to be another 17 years. The 1986 semi-final, of course, came under the management of Chris Nicholl, but the departure of McMenemy was to gradually affect Dennis.

NO-ONE COULD entirely curb Dennis' wayward side, but it was notable considering his disciplinary record that he was never sent-off during almost two seasons under McMenemy's management. Dennis is convinced that this was no coincidence. "Lawrie was hard on me," he says. "We always muck around now and say we had a love-hate relationship. I loved him and he hated me. I'm still great friends with Lawrie, he did so much for my career. If I'd signed for someone else except for maybe Terry Venables, I don't think I would have been in the game for more than two years because I had a lot of problems.

"My marriage was going downhill and I had a lot of demons that I needed to win over. Lawrie didn't suffer fools gladly, but he knew when I went out for him on the pitch I would give everything. He said to me that I was the first man on the team sheet which was lovely, but he had to watch me off the park. That was the problem in my younger days, but he would come down on me like a ton of bricks."

Dennis believes that having players around him in the dressing room whom he respected was also important. "I had a lot of faults, but I learnt from people like Micky Mills," he says, "he would tell me I was letting the players down and he has had me pinned up against the wall before. I needed players like that to be on top of me. Lawrie was good at getting experienced, world-class players in who could also do a job for him in the dressing room if something needed to be said." There were, however, fewer of those sort of players following the departure of McMenemy. In the year preceding his dressing room fight with Nicholl, Dennis was finding himself increasingly in trouble away from football.

His marriage to Jane had begun to crumble in 1985 and trips to the magistrates' courts were becoming a familiar occurrence. He says the support he received in 1985 from McMenemy and the chairman Woodford was "fantastic" as he fought to gain custody of his daughter. But the following year things began to unravel.

In 1986 he was reportedly fined £400 and £500 for admitting assaults on a policeman and a nightclub owner. There were also suggestions he had threatened his wife. According to newspaper reports, he was told by the magistrate to take the chewing gum from his mouth prior to the hearing over the nightclub incident and it was said that he and Jane left court arm in arm.

They were apparently arrested after a high speed car chase through Luton. Dennis then went missing shortly before pre-season training in the summer of 1986 after contract negotiations had broken down, with Nicholl admitting he had no idea where the player was.

By November, however, there appeared to be some hope that he had turned a corner. He had recently signed a new two year contract and, in an interview, he said he had been "saved by football" and suggested his problems were now behind him. "I could easily have gone under and it was football that saved me," he said, "my marriage had gone wrong, I had problems all over the place and I needed a get out. Football provided that release. It helped get my mind off everything else that was going wrong in my life. When I played and trained I ran myself into the ground just to get things out of my system. I get stick from rival fans, but I can handle that."

Nicholl was also talking in a conciliatory way. "He is trying hard to improve and sorting his home life out has helped," he said. As Christmas approached, Dennis even had a friendly bet with the FA saying he would pay £500 to Children In Need if he got in trouble within a year and they would pay the same if he didn't. The FA were on fairly safe ground.

Within a week, despite the ban on him from speaking to the press, he was quoted at length in a national newspaper detailing a brawl he had with the England goalkeeper Peter Shilton. In it, he said that Shilton got nasty when he was drunk and described how they came to blows during a pre-season tour. He was charged with bringing the game into disrepute, fined £250 and suspended by Saints for a week. The chairman Alan Woodford said: "It has got to stop. We have got to make sure this does not happen again." The manager Nicholl was also furious. "I will be discussing the matter with the chairman," he said, "the article has not helped Southampton Football Club and it has not helped Mark Dennis." Gordon Taylor, the secretary of the PFA, said: "I find Mark's outburst astonishing. It is incomprehensible to me how he can attack his own team-mate in such a way. We have fought long and hard to get freedom of speech for players, but it is not a licence to sling mud."

For him to speak out so openly about a team-mate, particularly one as high profile as Shilton, sent shockwaves through football. Dennis, though, remains unrepentant and, while he is happy to accept the blame for other incidents, he says he did nothing wrong in talking about another side to Shilton's character. "It was a pre-season tour to Athletico Bilbao," says Dennis, "and afterwards we had been in a nightclub and we'd had a few words. Anyway, he came out and butted me and knocked my tooth out and we had a fight in the lift. When you are young, you do silly things, but me and Peter never got on well. I get on great with Chris Nicholl now, but Peter and I never got on. He was a loner. I didn't like his attitude, I loved him for what he could do on the pitch because he was the best, but as people we never gelled.

"He wasn't happy about what went in the paper, but people are never happy when the truth comes out. If it wasn't true he could have sued me, he didn't and it's as simple as that. I think it hurt him to a degree." Chris Nicholl later spoke about his time as manager and the sight of Peter Shilton, Joe Jordan and Mark Dennis all sat in opposite corners of the dressing room.

THE CRITICS were lining up to condemn Dennis and some in the press were even saying that he should face a life ban from football. That clearly hurt. "Some of the papers said they should kick me out of football," he says, "the *Sun*, the *Mirror* and the *Star* – I wouldn't talk to them because they were parasites. I've learnt that you can't beat them, but I wouldn't join them. They still like me to this day because I sell papers. But basically what they were saying was 'take away his livelihood' which is an awful crime to me, especially when you have got a little girl. But the press are like that – they even have a go at the royal family and get away with it."

Dennis remains equally dismissive of what he calls the "FA fuddy-duddies" who were regularly fining him on disrepute charges. As well as the Shilton article, Dennis was also hauled before the FA after being sent-off for an incident in the tunnel after a game against Norwich at

Carrow Road. Earlier that afternoon, Dennis had scored a spectacular volley in a seven-goal thriller, but he was in familiar hot water for a scuffle with Ian Crook during an argument in the tunnel. "Handbags," is his one word analysis of the Crook incident.

"The FA used to remind me of looking at the Muppet Show to be honest," he says, "I couldn't believe how little they knew about the game. They have always liked 'yes' men. They've done it with their managers. They have always had managers they could control and they are the same with players. They never liked me from day one and absolutely hammered me. Other people got into scraps and they would give them a slap on the wrist and send them away with a Crunchie, but not me."

Former Southampton team-mates were sorry to see Dennis leave the club, saying there was never a dull moment when he was around. "Me, Mark and Jimmy [Case] used to go out a lot," says Danny Wallace, "Mark's wife Jane was quite a character. I remember she was on the phone to my missus once saying he [Dennis] had gone out for a paper and hadn't come back for three days. Another time, I remember he came in and he was in bits because he had read about Aids in the papers and Don Taylor [the physio] had to calm him down and tell him not to worry. I got on really well with Mark, I love him to death."

Another great friend was the flamboyant Frank Worthington, who was at Saints during the 1983/84 season and had been with Dennis at Birmingham. The duo apparently spent five days together for Worthington's stag party. "Frank was larger than life, his hero was Elvis," says Dennis. "He had a badge that said 'TCB'. I said, 'what's that Frank' and he said, 'Take Care of Business and I always do'. He was great."

But if Dennis had hoped that his move away from Saints in 1987 would prove to be a fresh start, he was to be disappointed. By November 1987, he had found himself being sent-off for an 11th time in his career and was handed a massive eight game ban which spanned some 61 days. Dennis was photographed leaving the FA headquarters after receiving his ban with a bag of golf clubs as he made his way to Cornwall for an extended holiday.

Yet his problems were still not behind him. In December 1987, he was reportedly interviewed (though not charged) by police during an investigation by police over an incident involving counterfeit money and he was then stabbed in a serious brawl in Croydon. A tabloid report started with the following sentence: "Former Southampton soccer star and football wild man Mark Dennis has had his throat slashed during an ugly street fight."

In December 1988, he faced his sixth FA charge of bringing the game into disrepute following allegations (which he denied) that he spat at an opponent. In interviews, however, he continued to speak fondly of Southampton. "Most players will have a club which is more special to them than others and for me it will always be Southampton," he said. Injuries were beginning to disrupt his career. He moved to Crystal Palace in 1989, but was released and, at the age of only 30, his professional career was at an end.

His private life was also more settled, although he did make the papers one final time for a non-football-related incident when he was accused (but found not guilty) of an assault in Tooting. A member of the public had reportedly called the police after claiming to see him doing squat thrusts in the middle of Mitcham Common while under the influence of alcohol.

When Dennis now looks back at the scrapes he got into during the late 1980s, he is convinced that his relationship with his former wife was a major factor. "I got married at a very young age – I was just over 17," he says, "it wasn't love, it was infatuation, she wasn't the right partner for me and I probably wasn't the right partner for her. It went very bitter. I ended up winning custody of my daughter. I did have to pay up, but it was worth every penny to keep young Joanne. But when I got in trouble it was usually sticking up for her [his wife]. I don't get in any trouble with the police now. I was in trouble five or six times for affray and ABH and every time my ex-wife was there. Ever since we got divorced I've not been in any trouble with the police. I've been married to my wife Nicola for 11 years and with her for 18 years and never had a problem."

Given that his personal life was stabilising, it was sad that Dennis was forced out of the game at such a young age. He now wonders whether his off-field lifestyle, particularly heavy drinking sessions, contributed to his premature exit. Saints fan Eddie Bulpitt recalls how Dennis used to be sat in a local Southampton pub called The Bassett with a pint in his hand within minutes of the match finishing. "No matter how quickly we got to the car and drove to the pub [after a game], there was Mark Dennis, sitting in there with a mate or two, pint in hand," he said, "how he got there so quickly we never found out. But he was always friendly and would always chat, never came across as being aloof."

Dennis, who is now teetotal, smiles at this anecdote. "My mottos were, 'win or lose, have a booze' and, 'you have to replace your fluids'," he says. "But if I hadn't drunk, could I have played a few more years? Would I have got the injuries? You never know."

What is certain is that this attitude, this behaviour and this passion for the game and life, combined with his incredible off-field antics, cemented his place in Saints' fans hearts. For many who watched Southampton regularly during that era, Dennis is the ultimate Cult Hero. Yes, Le Tissier was a better footballer, scored more goals, hit more headlines for his on-field performances, but Dennis had that compulsive element to his personality that meant fans associated with him because he played like they would if they'd been good enough to pull on a red and white striped shirt. To use a modern idiom, he had Simon Cowell's elusive X-factor.

AS A PLAYER, though, during his brief peak, the quality of Dennis goes unquestioned in football. Jim Smith and the then England manager Bobby Robson both agree he was probably the finest uncapped England left-back.

At the time, Kenny Sansom was a regular fixture in the England team. Steady and reliable, he lacked the panâche of Dennis, but he was seen as a much safer pair of hands. Indeed he is almost the exact opposite of the volatile Dennis. "Mark had so much ability and must have been the best player we had at our place never to have got a cap," says Nick Holmes. "If he'd been given a chance, I'm sure he would have made an impression. It's a pity he's not playing now because it's a bit easier to get an England cap these days."

The England question was debated many times and it was generally felt that Dennis was a better tackler and crosser of the ball than Sansom. His skill was best illustrated by a superb individual goal against Newcastle United in 1986 when he cut in from the left and chipped the goalkeeper. Yet unless Dennis was going to automatically play, it is perhaps easy to imagine why his reputation would have made Robson reluctant to take him away on England duty. It should, however, be pointed out that he was a popular team-mate at Saints. "Mark always had a reputation that went with him, but he was a decent lad," says Holmes, "if you'd taken that side away from him, he wouldn't have been such a good player."

Dennis accepts that he sometimes had difficulty controlling his temper on the pitch and fans still reminisce about the almost child-like way he might react if enough of them encouraged him to serve retribution on an opponent. "I've said my ex-wife was there for a lot of the problems I got into away from football," he says, "but on the pitch it was down to me. I played hard and sometimes I was out of order without meaning to be, but I loved the game and I loved playing.

"I got wound up easily by players and I don't blame them, but later on in my career I learnt how to handle it better and it helped when I had the players around me who controlled me like Mick Mills, Ivan Golac and Nick Holmes. The fans could wind me up to get back at someone and sometimes I did do it because I didn't want to let them down, but that's for the wrong reasons."

It was as if gaining immediate popularity with the Saints fans was more important to him than averting an incident which could further harm his international prospects. Dennis, though, rejects any suggestion that he would have ever deliberately hurt another player. In 1986, Liverpool midfielder Kevin MacDonald's leg was broken following a challenge, but it clearly upset Dennis and he later went to see his opponent in hospital. "Kevin MacDonald, God bless him. We both went in high and I broke his leg," he says, "I was upset about that. Kenny Dalglish said we both went in high. I was dreadfully sorry, but if you don't look after yourself, you end up exactly like Kevin ended up."

The appreciation of his footballing ability, however, meant that fans voted Dennis into Southampton's 'team of the century' in 1999 alongside former sparring partner Peter Shilton, Ivan Golac, Mark Wright, Chris Nicholl, Terry Paine, Jimmy Case, Alan Ball, Matthew Le Tissier, Mick Channon and Ron Davies.

DENNIS CONTINUES to live in Southampton and remains a popular figure in the area. He is sometimes a host in the match-day suites at St. Mary's and is a regular figure at Hampshire Cricket's Rose Bowl during the summer, where he indulges a passion for cricket. The affection for his adopted home is mutual. "The people of Southampton have saved my life," he says, "if I had stayed living in London I wouldn't be here now. I call Hampshire 'God's Country'. I've been here 25 years and I love it.

"The youngsters now don't remember, but the mums and dads tell them about me. I was nicknamed 'Psycho', I wasn't actually a fan of Psycho and my mum and dad didn't like it. When Stuart Pearce came along they would say that I was the original 'Psycho' but nowadays people call me 'Denno' – I much prefer that, I must say."

Understanding Dennis' enduring cult status is not difficult. With all his faults, honesty and effort, supporters knew there was absolutely no pretence. With that vulnerability about him, the women wanted to mother him. The men simply revered him as a footballer and as one of the lads. Just thinking about Mark Dennis still makes fans, team-mates, managers and even journalists laugh with a misty-eyed reminiscence reserved only for the true hero. Rather like Brian O'Neil, most have their own favourite story.

"I had a fantastic relationship with the fans," says Dennis, "there were times during my career when I did let them down and I let players down, I paid the price for that and I always said sorry afterwards. But I went out and gave everything. And the thing about the supporters at Southampton was that even if you had a bad game, as long as you gave everything, they always appreciated that. They love loyalty and they love exciting football, movement and good passing. If we lost 4-3 and played tremendous football, the fans were happy."

After retirement, Dennis briefly worked as a postman, before returning to football as the assistant manager with Fleet Town in 2002. He then became the director of football at Eastleigh in 2003, only to resign and then return again after a disagreement with the chairman in 2006. Eastleigh have enjoyed considerable success while he has been at the club.

The Eastleigh manager Paul Doswell has been a Saints fan "since I could walk" and says: "Mark was the most popular player and the chants used to be 'Denno for England' and 'Psycho!' It was a travesty that he didn't play for England and it was because there was that perception about his disciplinary record. The supporters were devastated when he left, he was an icon and it is fantastic now to work with him." Doswell says that Dennis' enthusiasm and passion burns just as strongly from the touchline as it did when he was out on the pitch. "He is very vocal, he gets wrapped up in the game and he wears his heart on his sleeve," he says, "but he is an infectious person to be around. He doesn't accept cheats and he doesn't accept people not working hard. As a person, he is the nicest man you could hope to meet, he will stop to speak to anyone and he is unaware that people are a bit in awe of him."

This archetypal hell-raiser has been fully rehabilitated and now is deeply involved in the fabric of the modern Southampton FC. Indeed, given that the club had banned him from talking to the media as a player, there is a certain irony in the fact that Dennis co-hosts a morning radio-show for the club's *The Saint* station. He is an outspoken pundit. When the midfielder David Prutton was suspended for ten games following a push on the referee in a match against Arsenal at the end of the 2004/05 season, Dennis could sympathise. "It was a case of the red mist coming down," he said, "I thought someone had said something about his missus the first time I saw it."

With his radio show, job at Eastleigh FC and settled domestic life (he has another daughter and grandchildren), Dennis says he has never been happier, particularly when he remembers – in a totally matter of fact manner – that he almost died on three separate occasions. "When I think about my times, I look at the good and the bad and the good outweighed the bad," he says. "There's been three times when I've nearly parted with this world. I got stabbed in the throat when I was at QPR at a London PFA awards dinner at the Grovenor. It was over a taxi and I was lucky on that occasion. I also got stabbed in my shoulder and I lost about three pints. Then, when I was playing in 1985, I had a massive haematoma in my leg down at Manchester United and I stupidly played on. I was rooming with Mark Wright. We beat Manchester United on the Wednesday and we were going on to Newcastle and it just kept bleeding and bleeding.

"I woke up in the middle of the night in agony. Mark called the ambulance and four pints of blood came out. I wouldn't have the blood transfusions because Aids was all around at the time in the papers. I was in hospital for quite a few weeks and I was very ill." According to team-mates, Dennis embarked on an unusual recovery programme. "His missus came to visit him in hospital and took him out in a wheelchair and he got pissed down the pub," laughs Danny Wallace.

"I'm like a cat – I think I've got nine lives – but fortunately no things like that happen now and I'm enjoying my life," says Dennis, "I love my family, I've got my grandchildren and every-thing is rosy."

As he grasps my hand and gets up to return to his radio show, he gives a final shake of the head. "I went to hell and back," he says, "but do you know what? It's been lovely on the way back."

JIMMY CASE

1985-1991

SAINTS CAREER

Games	272
Goals	14
Caps	0

MAGIC MOMENT

Inspiring a 4-1 rout of former club Liverpool in 1989

'UNCLE JIMMY'

JIMMY Case is the most decorated footballer to ever play for Saints. Many would also argue that he was the hardest, certainly of the modern generation. A winner of three European Cups, four league titles, a Uefa Cup and a League Cup with Liverpool, his medal haul surpasses that of Peter Shilton, Kevin Keegan and arguably even World Cup winner Alan Ball.

Yet for all that success at Anfield, it is widely thought that he produced the finest playing days of his career while at Saints. They were certainly the most influential. At a bargain cost of just £30,000 from Brighton & Hove Albion, of all the many famous Lawrie McMenemy signings, Case was the best value. "More a gift than a signing," says McMenemy.

The likes of Matthew Le Tissier, Jason Dodd, Alan Shearer and Rodney Wallace still look slightly awestruck as they remember the man known to them as 'Uncle Jimmy'. "The top man," says Le Tissier, "Jimmy looked after all the lads, like myself, Alan Shearer, Tim Flowers, Rodney and Ray Wallace. Ask anyone about Jimmy Case and they will tell you he was top class."

"Jimmy was the boss," concurs Francis Benali. "He took it upon himself to be almost a minder to the team. He guided us and protected us." Jason Dodd recalls trembling when he first walked into the dressing room and saw Jimmy Case. "I was shaking like a leaf, but I was made to feel very welcome," he says. "People like Jimmy relax you by taking the piss – they called me 'farmer boy' because of my west country accent. Jimmy had done it at the very highest level, but you would think he had just come off the local park after playing football. He hasn't changed at all and that's why everyone takes a shine to him." In his autobiography, *One Hump or Two?*, Frank Worthington says Case is one of the players from his entire career who he would want most in his team, particularly in what he calls the "trenches".

And it is this steel, this grit, this spirit which has made Case one of the biggest of all Saints' Cult Heroes, and who to this very day is greeted with real enthusiasm by fans whenever he meets them.

CASE JOINED Saints at a time when a new generation were just beginning to blossom and he made it his business to look out for them. For the likes of Le Tissier, Wallace and Shearer, it was like starting at a new school with the advantage of knowing your older brother was one of the toughest kids around. Touch any member of his family and retribution was generally swift.

After arriving as a short term replacement to Arsenal bound Steve Williams in 1985, Case played for six seasons at Saints. Even at the age of 37, his release by Ian Branfoot was the cause of huge controversy. Until now, it is something Case has never talked about. It was the first major decision Branfoot made as Southampton manager and, from that day, he faced a losing battle to command respect – let alone affection – from the terraces.

Instead, Case's Saints career coincided almost completely with Chris Nicholl's time as manager and in that period few can recall another team coming out on top in a physical battle.

The likes of Glenn Cockerill, Neil Ruddock, Barry Horne, Jason Dodd and an emerging Francis Benali were also in the team around this time, but the leader of the pack was unquestionably the stocky, menacing figure of Case.

In his autobiography, *Gray Matters*, Andy Gray recalled an encounter. He said: "Undoubtedly the hardest man I ever came across was the Liverpool midfielder Case. He was a real beast, tough as old boots. I'd had a few encounters with Jimmy in the Merseyside derby, but by the time I had my moment of madness he'd left Anfield and was playing for Southampton. For whatever reason I got it into my head that I was going to take Jimmy out…it was master versus pupil, and have no doubt about it, I was the schoolboy. The first chance I got I steamed into Case…but Jimmy had seen me coming and had taken the appropriate measures…I limped around for as long as I could, until eventually the pain got too much and I was substituted.

"If I thought I'd denied Jimmy the satisfaction of knowing he'd put me out of the game I was sadly mistaken. As I headed for the touchline I heard a cry of 'Andy! Andy!' When I looked around there was Case smiling sweetly at me and waving goodbye."

WITH THAT 1980s moustache, just the sight of Jimmy Case was enough to send shivers down the spine of opposition players. The facial hair has now gone. Other than that, he looks pretty much exactly the same as when he was playing. We meet in a Southampton hotel and just about everyone who walks past recognises him and exchanges greetings.

Case returned to the Southampton area after ending his time in league football as Brighton manager and follows Saints home and away with the club's in-house radio station, *The Saint*. His breakfast show on the radio station and weather forecasts became almost a cult item in themselves and he continues to host an after match phone-in for supporters, with his scouse wit raising plenty of laughs along the way.

It has kept Case involved with football, although he remains firmly of the old school. Straight talking, funny and totally down to earth, gimmicky fashion items and the pretentious celebrity image of lesser players could hardly be more alien to him. The contrast between the laid-back Case in retirement and the man who liked nothing better than going head-to-head with the likes of Bryan Robson, Steve McMahon and Graeme Souness is obvious.

"I'm far removed from the aggressive, do or die footballer off the pitch," he says. "But those who don't know me seem surprised when they meet me – as if I'd be biting people's heads off. On the pitch, it was totally different because of that competitive edge."

Case ponders how football has changed in the years that have passed since he hung up his boots and it is clear that he comes from a football culture which now barely exists at a professional level. The changes he finds most disappointing are related. First, stricter rules have meant the decline in what he calls the "art of tackling". Paradoxically, the theatrical reaction to being tackled has heightened beyond all recognition.

Tackling is a subject Case enjoys discussing. It is something he clearly has thought about and it is a topic of conversation on which he is an expert. Like a scientist revealing a rather complex chemical formula, he goes into great detail about how to win a 50-50 challenge. He stands to demonstrate his point.

"There is an art of two decent players going into a tackle," he says. "It's body shape, you lean forward into it and if he just goes back, you have won that tackle and got the ball. It's like when you watch kids, it's the ones who back out of a challenge that always get hurt. If you are standing like this [he rocks backwards] you have got no forward momentum and so you are just taking a pounding.

"You are not giving any force back and so you will get hurt and that has stuck with me right the way through my career. Timing is everything. It's the reading of the body, of the person, the reading of the play. Tackling is an art in itself, but nowadays it doesn't really appear on the main billing. Any foot up, any little bit of aggressiveness and it's a yellow card."

As a tackler, Case was renowned, particularly considering he started out as a winger for Liverpool. At Southampton, he moved into the centre and came to be involved in some notorious incidents. He is open and honest about what went on in those midfield battles, but emphatically denies ever trying to injure a fellow professional. "I've never broke anybody's leg," he says, "and primarily you have got to go for the ball, you can't just go for the man."

"Intimidation" is the adjective Case prefers to use. Often it is in a preventative sense. "Every team has got to have someone with a bit of presence," he says. "You have to make sure that you don't let them intimidate you as a unit. If someone was getting intimidated, young Rodney [Wallace] or even Alan [Shearer] up front, we would make sure our next challenge on that particular person would be a slightly heavier one, if you get my drift?

"You have to get around and protect them by stepping up your game in terms of being aggressive. If you do that the game usually calms down a bit and it stops people. It's part of the game because what they are trying to do is simple – they are trying to stop them from playing."

Having once been the young skilful winger that others wanted to stifle, Case knew exactly what the opposition would be trying to do to his younger Saints team-mates. "If you intimidate a winger by giving them a whack early on, he's frightened to play after that," he says. "A lot of the coaches will say it's worth a booking because you have stopped their main threat because he's hobbling or not wanting the ball anymore."

One of Case's great assets, however, was an ability to step up this physical side of his game, while also persuading the referee that nothing untoward was happening. He could be subtle, hence Joe Fagan's description at the beginning of this chapter. "If you turn around and have lost it and you are shouting and pointing at someone because of a challenge, the referee knows you have got things in your mind you want to sort out," he says.

"So you just got on with it and it might be just in my favour one or two times later on. If it is, then the next one, I'll whack him – meaning you whack him and take the ball. But there are certain other things you learn challenging that after a while become natural. For example, you could go into a challenge and the elbow comes into their ribs or your knee could go in their thigh. I remember doing it to Terry Hurlock. He was down and I've slid in with my left foot going on the ball, but he knows what I'm going to do and 'this one' [the right leg] has swung in and gone right in there on the inside of his leg."

Case says that counter retribution was an inevitable part of the game although there were those who would also back off. "You got a lot of players out there who want to kick the hind legs off you. When you are playing for any length of time you get to know the players. I played against [Graeme] Souness when he was at Middlesbrough, Archie Gemmell, Bryan Robson, a fella called [Ian] Bowyer at Nottingham Forest, Steve McMahon and a young Roy Keane.

"[Allan] Clarke from Leeds would just want to top people all day long. No-one would see it, the ball would still go there, but he would have a few studs on your ankle. There were players you knew would hurt you if you gave them half a chance, but that didn't bother me. That's the territory you are in. It doesn't matter. You live by the sword and you die by the sword."

Live by the sword and die by the sword. These are words which manager Nicholl used when Case avoided disciplinary action following a high challenge on Everton's Graeme Sharp which left the striker needing several stitches in his leg. Case grins at the memory.

"Did you get sent-off?" I ask.

"No, no, he just got carried off," he says. "I've seen Sharpie since and we're fine, but what it was with him, if you went in 50-50 and the ball was on the floor, he would go like this [Case stands to demonstrate and lifts his leg off the ground]. He would be over the ball and right up your leg. So in this challenge we were going for the ball at speed, the ball was bouncing and he was coming across and I knew what he's going to do, but it's all split-second stuff as you impact.

"So I've just gone like that [Case lifts his foot further up], he's gone a bit higher again so at the last minute I've gone whhiiituup [Case's foot comes even higher], right the way up his leg. He couldn't carry on and, as I said, he had to get carried off." Case pauses, gives a mischievous smile and adds the following detail: "On a stretcher." By way of justification, he adds: "But he had probably topped another person on our team in the same game."

Case recalls another incident. This time his opponent was Manchester United's Norman Whiteside. "Norman had hold of the ball and I whacked him pretty hard," he says. "A little while later I was going towards the flank and I knew Norman wanted to whack me with his left foot. I knew he was coming and the next minute, just as he came scything in, I lifted my legs up off the floor and he took the ball as well as me. But I've come down 'crunch' with my elbow right in his ribs. The referee could see the intent was there from him because he was sprinting towards me thinking, 'I'm going to get him', so he's booked Norman for it. As we were running away, Bryan Robson [Whiteside's team-mate] turned to me, shook his head and said, 'you didn't half do him there'."

Case did not always get away with it, however. There was even one occasion when he could claim to have been wronged by a referee after an incident involving Robson in January 1991. The two midfielders were running side by side towards Saints' goal when their heels clipped and referee George Courtney issued a straight red card to a bemused Case. "I shook Bryan's hand and I said, 'it's not your fault' because he knew I hadn't touched him," he says. "George Courtney was the big 'I am' and just dismissed it straight away and didn't even bother looking at the video. I got a three game ban for that and those are three games which you can never get back."

Case discusses these various run-ins with fellow professionals and officialdom in a matter of fact manner, but it must have been a frightening experience to crunch into a challenge with him. He is only 5ft 9ins tall, but it is the sturdy build and natural body strength from the neck down which is striking. More important still, is the look in his eyes. He would never shy away from a challenge.

Case believes he was born with a fairly high pain threshold. "You have a reputation through flying in there and not being worried about getting hurt," he says. "If they've caught you, you have this strength about yourself, a pain threshold, you can stand a bit of pain and some people can't. You have to have an ability to shrug it off and keep focused on what you are doing without getting up and showing it or throwing a punch. If you do that, it's the world's worst because you don't help the side. Neil Ruddock, for example, would be the first person to throw a punch and he's not even in the incident, he's 20-yards away. The secret was never to say anything to another player if he hurt you. I'd just remain expressionless and then I'd quietly catch up with the player later on."

Not surprisingly, Case despairs at players of today who try to get their opponents sent-off. "It would be harder for me now and people say you would be off the pitch every five minutes," he says, "the game certainly has changed, I don't know whether it's for the better. I like a good challenge and I just fear that a lot of the aggression has gone out of the game. There's a good lot of skill in there and pace, but there's also diving now. In my time, rolling around like that would have been taken as a sign of weakness.

"It did creep in when I was playing, but it was only in the penalty box, now it is all over the pitch. They should use the cameras for the fakers. Give them an accumulation of bookings and then ban them for games and you would soon stop it. They are making fools out of referees."

CASE'S TOUGHNESS was a product of his upbringing on a Liverpool estate down by the docks. He idolised Brazilian soccer star Tostao and a school teacher was the first to recognise his talent when he saw him kicking a tennis ball around the playground.

"I was a stocky player – I had a relative bit of skill and good range of passing," he recalls. "I was the smallest kid on the pitch playing in the age groups above, but I was the one that got stuck in. I used to fly in and parents would be looking away. I mistimed one or two, but I was learning because you have got to come up to the standard of those around you."

Case graduated through the school teams then joined a tough dockers team called Blue Union. He still shudders at the memory of the physical nature of matches which clearly had a significant influence on him as a footballer.

"The referees were not the strongest and people were stinking of booze," he says. "I was 16 and I was quick, playing on the wing. We used to play with crowds three deep on the sides and I remember getting taken straight through the crowd with some of the tackles. But I would always get up and I would learn."

Upon leaving school, Case served an apprenticeship as an electrician, even turning down an offer from Liverpool until he had got a trade under his belt. He did, however, play part-time for the reserves and made his full debut in 1975 against Queens Park Rangers. The Liverpool midfield at the time included the likes of Tommy Smith. "All the good sides can play football and pass and move if the opposition wants to do that," says Case. "But if they don't and they want to start kicking lumps out of you, you have to start kicking and we could do that as well."

Liverpool's heady cocktail of toughness, skill and wonderful passing meant a level of domination on the European stage which has never been matched by a British club. There is not a hint of brag as Case recalls those Liverpool years. Indeed, he can't remember exactly everything he has achieved. "I've never added it all up – I've got to do all that, you know, just research myself," he says. "But if you went into world or European football and lined up all the medals, I'd probably be quite a bit up there. Not many have got three European Cups and a Uefa Cup as well."

Case remembers taking his medals home and leaving them with his mum. For many years they were kept up in the loft in a Tesco bag at his parents' house. Today, they are safe in a bank. He smiles: "My dad was getting worried in case the house got broken into. They were good times, but the years at Liverpool went very quick. You thought winning happened every year. I remember we were sitting there one time and had won the European Cup and we were in a hotel and having a beer and someone said, 'it wasn't as good as the first time'.

"The first European Cup win against Borussia Mönchengladbach was the pinnacle. Another season we won virtually everything and only used 14 players. That was what Bob Paisley [the former manager] thought was his best Liverpool side."

CASE LEFT Merseyside for Brighton, helping the Sussex club to reach the 1983 FA Cup final before moving to Saints. At the time, it was a signing which was not met with universal enthusiasm. He was into his 30s and most assumed his best years had passed, particularly as Brighton were happy to sell. "I think a lot of eyebrows may have been raised," says Case. "I remember signing on a Tuesday afternoon. It was March 19 and I had no hesitation signing at all. The club had always been a decent club – a family club. I went for my medical up at the Nuffield in the afternoon and signed at 4pm.

"At the time I had a groin strain, but nobody knew about it. I told a bit of a lie just to sign, but it wasn't any problem. Lawrie [McMenemy] was looking for a stop-gap because obviously Steve Williams had moved on. He wanted someone who could get stuck in and marshal it."

It proved to be an inspired signing. The blend of players like Case, Glenn Cockerill and Colin Clarke worked well alongside the club's emerging talent. In his first full season, there was a 2-0 FA Cup semi-final defeat against Liverpool in 1986 when victory would have made Case the first player to appear in three FA Cup finals with different clubs.

But the highlight of Case's Saints career was unquestionably the 1989/90 season with Southampton finishing seventh and scoring some 71 league goals. The football was up with the best seen at The Dell, notably a 4-1 demolition of Liverpool as Case orchestrated a humiliation of his former club. It was a season which underlined a crucial point in his Cult Hero status.

Yes, Case was one of the more feared midfielders in the league, but he was also a footballer of rare quality. His range of passing was outstanding and there was talk of a call-up to the England squad while he was well into his 30s. Nicholl was one of his greatest advocates, saying: "Jim's job is to make people play and there are not many midfield players who can win the ball and deliver the first time pass as well as he does."

Glenn Cockerill played alongside Case in the centre of midfield for most of his Southampton career. "He has to be the best I've played with," says Cockerill. "People said that me and Jimmy were one of the best pairs that the club had and I learnt so much from him both on and off the field. I was only 26 and he could sit in that holding position and dictate the play which gave me licence to get forward.

"Later on Barry Horne came into the midfield and we had the three of us which gave freedom to the likes of Matt Le Tissier and Rodney Wallace. It didn't matter who they were, you could sense that opposition teams were aware of Jimmy's presence, he had a certain aggression, but he was also dangerous with his passing and could make clever runs forward."

Southampton's midfield of the late 1980s and early 1990s was certainly fairly fearsome and there was a certain 'cult' status to Cockerill with his permed mullet as well as Horne and Case's eventual replacement Terry Hurlock. Anthony Lovell was a particular fan of Horne. "These days, when the epithet of 'hard man' is conferred upon any footballer who appears disposed towards thuggish and confrontational play, it is all too easy to overlook and forget the true galvanisers that stepped onto the pitch," he says. "Barry Horne was one of these. A quiet yet devoted grafter, here was a man who never shirked a challenge, never failed to put his body on the line if the cause demanded it. The moment in his Saints career that springs to mind instantly is his 40-yard artillery shell of a shot to drag Saints back into an FA Cup fifth round replay against Bolton in 1992 which provoked a pitch invasion."

Mark Wood, a Saints season ticket holder since 1990, is an advocate of Hurlock. "He was everything a Cult Hero is about," he says, "he would die for the cause for your club in whichever way possible and he had the demeanour outside of football as being one of us, just an ordinary person doing a day job who would go and enjoy himself when he finished. I also love the stories that he is now just your run of the mill builder and that every now and again you will find him staying in a caravan." When Hurlock signed for Saints from Glasgow Rangers in September 1991, he was apparently missed by the waiting television cameras as he arrived in the back of a friend's white van rather than the customary footballer's BMW.

Yet while the likes of Cockerill, Horne and Hurlock have many supporters, it is Case's class and influence as a footballer which makes him the midfield Cult Hero of his generation. While at Saints he was asked to take on a different job to the wide-right role he had performed with Liverpool and he revelled in the additional responsibility of playing more centrally. "I think I played better because I was more involved," he says, "it's a hard area to play in, but I had quick feet which you need when you have got players coming at you from all over the place."

It also confirmed that Case was a complete midfielder – strong in the tackle, but capable of deft touches and accurate passing over short and long distances. Above all, he could keep a clear head regardless of what scrapes he might have been getting into. "Brian Hall said I was the only winger who could win a 50-50 ball with someone like Kevin Beattie or Terry Butcher, get myself off the floor and get the cross in," he says. "Some of the aggressive players would mess up the pass after they had made a challenge, but I had the ability to be calm and collected even if I had the adrenalin going through me after a challenge."

Not surprisingly perhaps for a player brought up at Liverpool under Bill Shankly and Bob Paisley, he also possessed great vision. "He was a fantastic servant to the club," says Mark Dennis, "I don't think he has ever been replaced. A holding player who dictated the play and could spray the ball around – a truly exceptional player."

There is debate among Saints fans as to the finest central midfielder in the club's history. The names Alan Ball, Steve Williams and David Armstrong would also feature highly in any discussion, but, in some respects, Case was more eye-catching, perhaps because he was in a somewhat inferior Southampton team whilst being used to sharing a pitch with the lavish talent that populated the Liverpool sides he played in. "You needed that bit of vision playing with people like Kenny Dalglish," he says. "For example, I've got the ball out wide on the right and he's just inside on the edge of the box. I'll play it in to him and then I'd run down the flank. He'd go to give it me and then turn to go the other way. Kenny hasn't forgotten me, but the full-back will stop and he will then reverse pass. If I didn't read Kenny, the ball he gives looks a bad one.

"I used to love playing European football because it was different than the domestic stuff. Tactically you had to be aware and the games were so enjoyable, it made your brain work. I enjoyed the challenge of stopping them playing and creating something ourselves. That side of it was unbelievable."

Case's good form meant he was Player of the Year at Saints in 1989/90. At the age of 36, he was still as fit as ever, but the winds of change were about to blow through The Dell.

SOUTHAMPTON SLIPPED to 14th in 1990/91 and Nicholl was surprisingly sacked as manager. Branfoot succeeded him on June 11, 1991. On June 13, the news broke that Case had been handed a free transfer. It was described by the journalist John May as, "a public relations exercise equivalent to shooting Bambi".

Branfoot said that it was purely a football decision. Others felt he was simply scared of Case's popularity. Case was the number one idol on the terraces and many Saints fans had wanted him to be player-manager. At the very least, it was hoped that Case would eventually be given a coaching job at the club when he retired.

That sentiment was underlined some five years after he had left The Dell in 1996 when Dave Merrington was sacked and Case topped every poll of supporters for their preferred choice as manager.

At the time of his departure in 1991 Branfoot said: "He has no experience or qualifications [as a coach]. I bracket him in the same company as Keegan, Channon and Ball who all performed wonders for this club. We will help all we can because of his fantastic record and by letting him have a free [transfer] it gives him the chance to negotiate his own signing on terms."

As he recalls that time a look of contempt crosses Case's face. "What happened was this," he says. "He called me into his office to tell me, and I think he said about ten words to me. I could accept he might have wanted to change it around, but what was really disappointing was that he never talked to me and found out what I was all about.

"I didn't want to be a manager – he was the manager. I just wanted to play and would have played long-ball football if that's what he wanted. I would have supported him. I would rather do someone a favour and I would have been a help rather than a hindrance. He said he was giving me a free transfer, as if he was doing me a favour. But I said to him, 'you are not giving me a free transfer, I have earned that'.

"I was over 35 and had played for more than five years at Southampton, so I was entitled to it. I don't know, but I think people are sometimes scared of having people around who are popular, they think you are a threat."

Cockerill had a spell as captain following the departure of Case, but says that Branfoot made a mistake. "Jimmy should have been given another year," he says, "I think Ian was advised by someone to get rid of him, but he should have given him a chance."

AFTER SOUTHAMPTON, Case joined Harry Redknapp at Bournemouth and proved his point by playing 40 league games the following season. The twilight years went on and on as his career gradually turned full circle. After achieving so much with Liverpool, Brighton and Saints, he was happy to go on playing without great financial reward at a lower level and eventually in non-league. Indeed, with Bournemouth in serious financial difficulty, he was willing to play on half wages rather than have his contract ended.

"The money side of things didn't bother me, I just wanted to keep on playing because when you get older, it's hard to go back if you miss a season," he says. "After Bournemouth, I went to Halifax with 'Big' John McGrath and Frank Worthington, I played there for six months and then I went to Wrexham for six months and they got promotion. Then I went to non-league at Sittingbourne, played there for a month and Liam Brady phoned me up and I went to Brighton as reserve team manager."

Case was soon made manager, but with Brighton in turmoil off the pitch and about to have the Goldstone Ground sold from under them, he only lasted a year, although did continue to play league football into his 40s. "I didn't really want to be a manager and it was the worst time in their [Brighton's] history," he says. "We had riot police in the dugout and the tunnel to keep the supporters from getting at the directors and I had to lock the referee in his room with the ball-boys."

By the time he hung up his boots, Case had played well over 750 matches in a career spanning more than 20 years. Coming from the era he did and given some of the social habits of players from that time, his longevity is surprising. "I never exactly looked after myself in certain ways, but I'm fortunate that I've not been seriously over-weight, I'm not a big eater and I always trained well," he says.

Drink was a part of a footballer's life in the 1970s and 1980s. "When you were on the fringe of the first team at Liverpool you would go out for a couple of drinks with the lads and if you had an orange juice people would say, 'he won't make the first team' and it was a bit like that," he says. "We all used to have a drink, even at Brighton we were successful in the Cup and had a decent team. You've got to have a team building situation, it's looking after each other and when you get that good atmosphere between the players, you can't beat that bit of banter and dressing room humour."

During his short time in management at Brighton and also with the non-league New Forest club Bashley, Case would try to encourage that camaraderie. He was always happy to see the players sink a few celebratory beers in victory. There were also stories of the occasional tipple before the game. Case confirms it was a trick from his early Liverpool days. "I used to have a little bottle of brandy on the table before the games," he says. "It was in an unmarked bottle. If you looked at it you would think it was oil, but that was the brandy bottle. If you took a little sip it got the blood circulating and warmed you up."

He laughs, sensing how it might sound. "You are not pissed," he says, "although there's probably legislation that stops it now anyway."

JIMMY CASE WOULD, of course, be a multi-millionaire had he played in the present day. Yet he is content at the way his career panned out. "I just wanted to play and wasn't interested in chasing money," he says. "I actually feel sorry for the players today because they are analysed such a lot. We could go out and socialise and it wasn't such a problem as it is now."

Case's common touch made him a natural in the era in which he featured. He still works occasionally as a plumber or an electrician, his favourite lunchtime snack is a pork pie (he says he keeps the brown sauce in the glove-pocket of his car – although I can't tell if he is joking) and he is never happier than spending a day fishing with his dad who is in his 80s. At heart, he remains a Scouse football fan who made good. Saints supporters knew that and loved him for it.

MATTHEW LE TISSIER

1985-2002

SAINTS CAREER

Games	540
Goals	209
Caps	8

MAGIC MOMENT

The last goal at
The Dell and his last
for Southampton.
Roy of the Rovers stuff

'LE GOD'

FOOTBALLERS

are usually late, but none so apologetic as Matthew Le Tissier. "I'm really sorry, mate," he says, marching into the reception at St. Mary's with more urgency than I can ever remember him showing as a player. "I was at a function last night, a friend suggested a game of golf and this slipped my mind. I haven't messed up your day, have I?"

But it's not a problem. I've enjoyed a cup of tea while waiting with Le Tissier's mentor and the former Southampton manager Dave Merrington, who, by complete chance, is at St. Mary's for a separate interview. Merrington has been talking to me about Le Tissier.

"You had to find the key to his heart to know what would make him respond and I had the key," he says, beaming with pride. "Some people called him lazy and they were right up to a point. But what they missed was what I loved and do you know what that is?" Before I have a chance to answer, Merrington whispers: "That he was a genius."

It's 10.45am and Le Tissier has already played 18 holes. He's not feeling like a genius today, however. "Bad morning," he says. "I was eight over – and my handicap is up to six these days."

Le Tissier is only 45 minutes late, which is about standard for footballers, although he does have a reputation for punctuality. He looks absolutely thrilled to see Merrington. "I've just been telling him that you were bloody useless," laughs Merrington, as he gives his former pupil a rub on the head. Le Tissier enjoys the banter. He knows what he means to Merrington and, indeed, the rest of Southampton.

A genius indeed. Say whatever you like about Terry Paine, Mick Channon, Kevin Keegan and Ron Davies, but Le Tissier is the club's only player to have a genuine claim to that particular word for what he could do on a football pitch. Southampton will never produce anyone comparable and it is quite possible that the British game will never see another like Le Tissier.

Yet he is something more than a genius. He is also a maverick. In many respects, Le Tissier stood outside of the team. He did not have to be super-fit and was a player from whom less was generally expected in return for the moments when he would produce so much more. And he delivered with such regularity that, for a period during the mid-1990s, Saints were close to being a one man team.

Indeed, between May 1992 and December 1996, they did not win a league football match without Le Tissier on the pitch. He did not have to run, tackle, mark or track back. Instead, he did the difficult things; the mazy dribbles, extravagant passes and goals to dream for.

Footballing mavericks, though, are becoming an endangered species. Just look at Joe Cole. He started out as a maverick, yet what has happened? It's been knocked out of him by José Mourniho at Chelsea. Okay, he has probably become a more effective player, but not nearly as entertaining as might have been the case. Cole has become a team player. The likes of Le Tissier, though, were different and special. At Southampton he was cherished, yet England managers treated him with suspicion. Graham Taylor, Terry Venables and Glenn Hoddle seemed to fear Le Tissier precisely because he was a maverick.

It is an attitude that has been prevalent at international level for many years, but which has also become more common among the club managers. With the likes of Peter Osgood, Stan Bowles, Tony Currie, George Best and Frank Worthington, the 1960s and 1970s was an era for mavericks. Yet this sort of player has become rarer. In the 1990s, you had Paul Gascoigne, Chris Waddle, David Ginola and Eric Cantona as well as Le Tissier. But where are their like now?

The arrival of Gordon Strachan at Southampton, with his emphasis on fitness, was indicative of changing times across football and you have to wonder how Le Tissier would have coped in the modern game. Yes, it is only four years since he retired, but it was back in 1998/99 that he last played more than 20 league games in a season. That's almost a decade ago. And, even then, he had become something of a rarity.

As I briefly explain my theory, Le Tissier nods in agreement. He has had the same thoughts. "There is much more emphasis on work-rate for the team now," he says, "you still get talented players coming through with the likes of Joe Cole and Thierry Henry, but I think the fun has been taken out of it a little bit.

"I used to have a go at referees and linesmen, but I did enjoy my football and I tried to play with a smile on my face and it is noticeable that there is less of that. Joe Cole is doing a fantastic job, but he has had to adapt his natural game to stay in the team. If I was starting out my career it would be a lot tougher for me to get in sides. I got in at a decent time when it wasn't all about doing 100m in 11 seconds and being a highly tuned athlete which is what they are these days.

"I did manage to carry it off. There probably wasn't too many players like me around, I probably got through on God-given ability more than anything. I did work at my game in terms of free-kicks and shooting, but I was never one to be in the gym pumping iron and going on four mile runs to keep fit. But I still think there should always be room in a team for someone who can create something out of nothing and change a game in a flash of an eye."

SO COULD Le Tissier have made it in the current era? He has no doubts – and even reveals that he thought, at the age of nearly 37, he might just have been able to help Southampton get out of the Championship following their relegation in 2004/05. "If I was starting out now," he says, "I would have to adapt because I wanted to be a footballer. I would have had to do what Joe Cole has done basically and got fitter and upped the work-rate although that would probably have detracted a little bit from the other stuff I could have done.

"Not too many know this, but I came in and did a bit of training with the lads in the summer of 2005. It was a bit of fun and I actually seriously thought about doing a pre-season at the beginning of the year. I thought I might get my boots back on and see if my body could take it. I thought playing in the Championship, I might be able to live at that level and I did quite a bit of training at the start of the season, but I kept picking up niggling strains again."

The return of Le Tissier in any capacity would have instantly created an enormous buzz around St. Mary's. There has probably been no more universally popular player in the club's history. That was underlined when he put himself forward with Francis Benali to replace Harry

Redknapp as the manager in December 2005. In a poll in the local paper, the names Le Tissier and Benali streaked ahead of established managers, including George Burley, who was eventually appointed.

"I was serious, very serious," says Le Tissier, "I was quite prepared along with Franny to come in and steady the ship and get us back. To see the club drifting, it was going nowhere and I felt me and Franny could have had something to offer. The chairman [Rupert Lowe] didn't give us an interview really and obviously didn't take it that seriously. But I would have been prepared to do it if he had asked me."

It was probably somewhat unrealistic, although indicative of Le Tissier's self-belief that he felt he could be a serious candidate. Le Tissier has no managerial experience, although he has been taking his coaching badges. He says it is more as a back-up option should his media work fall through rather than because of any huge desire to return to football.

That much becomes evident as he admits that he turned down the possibility to return as a coach at St. Mary's at the beginning of the 2005/06 season. With an eye for positive publicity and the boost it would have given the club, Sir Clive Woodward approached Le Tissier shortly after he began work at Southampton following his switch to football from rugby union. "I spoke to Clive and he wanted to employ a forwards' coach," explains Le Tissier, "we had a few discussions about it and we got down to talking about hours and money and that's where it all stalled. Unfortunately it wasn't really worth my while.

"It would probably have impacted on my television work with Sky. For what they were offering, it would have probably been five or six days a week and I could earn a lot more than that by working six days a month at Sky. It was a no-brainer really. It didn't really get off the ground once I realised what money was on offer for the job they wanted."

Le Tissier's decision was entirely understandable, but also indicative of a side to his character that the most blinkered and romantic supporters would rather ignore. For them he is 'Le God', the man who, in the age of mega-money, chose to show loyalty to their club even if it meant wrecking his chances for medals and England recognition. To a large extent this is true. Le Tissier does very much like the region and his bond with the Southampton supporters is cast iron.

YET AS circumstances meant he would not return as a coach in Saints' hour of need, Le Tissier does not pretend that his decisions to stay at The Dell during the 1990s were fuelled simply by a feeling of loyalty and love for the club. "I stayed for different reasons at different times in my career," he says, "early on, I had the chance to move to Spurs and my wife at the time didn't particularly want to move, so I decided not to go. The Spurs thing went quite a way down the line [wages were discussed]. That was the closest I came to leaving Southampton. I was a Spurs supporter as a kid and that was quite a big thing.

"Then Chelsea came in for me in 1995. But I was having a great time under Alan Ball then, I was enjoying my football so much and I was in the England squad so there didn't seem to be any reason to move on. I loved living in the area. I loved the reception the fans gave me and that also played a part in the decision to stay."

Le Tissier is happy with the decisions he made, although he is certain that they cost him opportunities on the international stage. "Terry Venables was manager at Tottenham and had wanted to speak to me when I said 'no'," he says, "and he became England manager and he put me in and then dropped me. In 1995, Glenn Hoddle was manager of Chelsea and he wanted to speak to me and I said 'no' and then he put me in the England team and then dropped me.

"They were probably not the best career moves in terms of England. I've got no question in my mind that being at Southampton made a difference to being picked for England. If you play for a bigger club you get more chances to play for England and better chances to play for England. That's just a fact of life. I knew all that when I made my decisions to stay. It's not the way things should be done, if you are a good player, you are a good player, and you should get in the England team. It shouldn't matter what club you play for."

Hoddle is generally portrayed as the biggest villain when it comes to the debate surrounding Le Tissier and England. Certainly he did not treat Le Tissier particularly well by picking him for a qualifier against Italy at Wembley and then dropping him after he had unfairly taken most of the flak for a 1-0 defeat. Hoddle then ignored him for the 1998 World Cup despite a hat-trick for the England 'B' team as well as seven goals in his last nine league games that season. Mark Dennis has his own theory on why Hoddle overlooked Le Tissier. "I believe that Glenn Hoddle was jealous of Matty because Matty was a better player than him," he says.

Yet it is far too easy to blame Hoddle for Le Tissier's brief international career. Le Tissier was still a fine player between 1996 and 1999, but he was certainly in decline. No, it was much earlier in his career that Le Tissier was most harshly overlooked. Graham Taylor was England manager from 1990 until 1993 and then Terry Venables from 1993 until 1996.

It was during these two periods, particularly the reign of Venables, when he was arguably the best footballer in the country. Indeed under Alan Ball from January 1994 until the end of the 1995 season, Le Tissier went on a run where he conjured 45 goals – mostly of the spectacular variety – in only 65 games. Perhaps even more remarkable was the fact that he scored these goals as a roaming midfielder behind two strikers.

"It was odd, I was playing the best football of my career and he [Venables] left me out after we played an abandoned game in Ireland," says Le Tissier. "The match lasted 25 minutes or something and I started that game and the next squad was announced and I wasn't even in the 22, let alone the starting line-up. I was playing really, really well. I couldn't quite understand it, but that was his decision."

Staying at a relatively small club and a lack of work-rate were clearly factors in England managers' decisions not to pick Le Tissier, yet the biggest explanation was perhaps the difficulty in finding a position for him without changing the team's system. As Alan Ball found, to get the best out of Le Tissier, you basically had to give him licence to do as he pleased. Within a 4-4-2 formation, that was difficult.

He didn't really cover enough ground to play in any of the midfield positions across a rigid four, meaning he would probably have been best utilised as a second striker. Teddy Sheringham, however, was filling that role for England with distinction alongside Alan Shearer. Le Tissier admits he was at his best in a somewhat unconventional position between the midfield and the strikers.

"I started off on the right-wing, by the time of my mid-20s I was more involved in games and I would always want to drift inside and be part of the game," says Le Tissier. "I played as a centre-forward off Alan Shearer or Iain Dowie quite a lot and then when Alan Ball was manager and I had my best time I played behind the two strikers. We played three at the back, four in midfield and I would play behind the strikers. That was the position that suited my game best without question. I realise that it does put a lot of strain on people around me to work that bit harder to get the ball back, but, as long as I'm producing when we get the ball, then we can get away with it. If I'm not producing then we are in trouble."

Of course, most Southampton fans who had seen the mesmerising quality that Le Tissier could produce would argue that England managers should have been bold enough to build the team around him. Yet while it might be possible to sympathise with the problem of finding a place in the team for Le Tissier, his absence from entire England squads was truly baffling. What an option he would have been off the bench. And how invaluable might his penalty taking have been as England crashed out of World Cups in 1990 and 1998 and then the European Championships of 1996 because of missed spot-kicks?

Le Tissier boasts the finest penalty-taking record in modern football with 47 goals from 48 attempts for Southampton. It was no fluke, for he used to practise his penalties and the number of times he shook the inside side-netting from the spot is testament to his accuracy and power.

Typically, the one penalty he did miss, against Nottingham Forest in 1993, is most remembered and I can still vividly recall my shock, while stood in the East Stand, when Nottingham Forest's Mark Crossley parried the ball away. Le Tissier did, however, partially redeem himself with a screaming 25-yard left foot strike in the same game. Still, a return of eight England caps was scant reward for a player of Le Tissier's quality.

THAT LACK OF international opportunities was particularly galling considering his ice-cool temperament and knack of producing his best when the spotlight was at its brightest. It is a facet of Le Tissier's character that is often skirted over, particularly by those who did not regularly watch Saints. Le Tissier was rightly regarded as a flair player, but the implication of the word 'luxury' meant that he was sometimes perceived as an unnecessary accessory when it really mattered. The opposite, however, was true.

As a match grew in importance, whether personally or for the team, so did the odds of Le Tissier producing something out of the ordinary. A disproportionate number of his goals were scored either in front of the Sky cameras, late in matches or during the relegation scraps of 1992/93, 1993/94 and 1995/96.

"I was quite aware of that," agrees Le Tissier, "I think it boiled down to the fact that I enjoyed the big occasions. I didn't feel any pressure. If it was the last day of the season and we needed a point to stay up or three points to stay up, it never weighed on my shoulders. I always looked at it and my mindset wasn't 'we might get relegated' it was 'I can score the goal that will keep us up today, I can be a hero if I produce the goods'. That is how I looked at it and that is how I produced the best football sometimes in high pressure situations.

"People often say that when you are in a relegation scrap you need people who are going to fight and give you 110 per cent but at the same time you still need someone who will score you a goal and who is brave enough to get on the ball and not be put off by a pressure situation. I remember being a little bit nervous on my England and Saints debuts, but, apart from that, it was excitement more than nerves whenever five to three came and the bell went. My thought was, 'I'm on stage now – let's go'.

"I liked playing in front of crowds and I have an ego. So, for me, going out and entertaining people was a massive buzz and it give me the chance to show off. I knew I could play football, I knew that I was decent and I like showing off in front of people and letting them see what I can do. I scored a few useful goals in training, but the best ones were saved for the real thing."

Le Tissier's favourite manager was Alan Ball. The reason he so flourished at that time was because the 1966 World Cup winner showed such belief in him. There is the famous story of that first training session under Ball who singled Le Tissier out and told him and the other players: "Whether you like it or not he is the best player at this club by a million miles. His goals will keep us up. For him to do that he can't run and tackle because he's useless at that."

Again, it was evidence of the maverick at his best by almost standing outside of the team. The other players at Southampton didn't mind a bit because they knew just how good Le Tissier was. For them, he was absolutely essential rather than any sort of luxury. "We all know about Matt's ability as a footballer, but he is a strong character in many other ways," says Francis Benali, "he would stand up and produce his best when it mattered and that was the sign of a great player."

Ball's quality as a manager in this period stemmed from his willingness to embrace Le Tissier completely, despite his weaknesses. He wasn't frightened or suspicious of a maverick, as perhaps his predecessor Ian Branfoot was. Le Tissier's response was both instant and emphatic.

He scored six times as Saints won three of their first four games under Ball and eventually stayed up by a point at the end of the 1993/94 season. Ball rates Le Tissier alongside the best players he has played with or against, including Pelé. "He wanted so much responsibility and no-one else gave it to him," says Ball. "Not the responsibility where you stick your foot in, but getting the ball in the hard part of the pitch in the bit between the penalty box and the halfway line. He was just phenomenal. He was brave around the goal, brave on penalties and free-kicks late in the game. That was a massive thing that no-one knew. He had the heart of a lion and he would do the hardest thing possible. He kept Southampton up single-handedly for years and I was disappointed in Glenn Hoddle and Terry Venables because he was an international player."

Le Tissier was already a Southampton Cult Hero before Ball arrived, yet it was during this period that his status among fans was propelled to another level completely. A T-shirt seller apparently coined the much loved nickname of 'Le God' and hundreds of supporters began spontaneous bows of worship to him whenever he took a corner. "It was quite weird actually because the first time they did it, I didn't realise where they had got it from, but it was from *Wayne's World* [the cult film of the time]," smiles Le Tissier. "One of the lads had to explain why they were doing it and where it came from. It was nice, it was lovely and it was very flattering."

The whole 'Le God' theme was also taken on by the *Echo*, who had a huge red billboard made on the Millbrook Road – one of the main arteries into the city – which simply said: 'You are now entering God's Country.'

"The 'Le God' thing took off and I got some letters from religious people saying, 'you are not God, could you please go on national television and say you are not God'," he says. "I was just like 'get a life, it's a bit of fun'. It was quite funny and I felt quite proud really – it brings back good memories."

LE TISSIER'S capacity to produce his very best at important moments during his Saints career is best characterised by two examples. The first arrived after Branfoot had controversially dropped him for three matches in favour of Paul Moody, a striker who spent the vast majority of his career in the lower leagues.

"I remember when Ian Branfoot threw Matty back to me and said, 'I'm not happy, he's not working hard enough'," says Dave Merrington, who was reserve team manager at the time. "I said I would do it, but I wanted licence to do it my way and Ian just said, 'do it'. So I brought him back morning and afternoon, but I didn't run him. I brought him back to play football. What I realised very early on with Matty was that you could not run him to fitness with the clock. He did not respond to that. You had to have a form of psychology, so everything he did was with a ball.

"One-on-one, two-on-one, two-on-two with a ball. By the time I had finished with him, he had worked longer and harder than if I had run him against the clock. We got his weight right and he was on song. I think players know how much you believe in them and I think that Matty responded to how I worked with him."

Le Tissier's return from his brief exile was the game against Newcastle in October 1993. For around an hour, he failed to produce and Moody was warming up. "I'm certain Ian Branfoot was thinking to substitute me," he says. A long ball was played forward and Iain Dowie headed it just behind Le Tissier. Yet with a flick of the heel, it was under his control and then guided past Barry Venison. Kevin Scott attempted to cover, but Le Tissier lifted the ball over his head and then wrong-footed the goalkeeper Mike Hooper with a delicate volley. It was a moment of pure artistry. In 1996, Paul Gascoigne scored an inferior imitation of this goal against Scotland in the European Championships. Gascoigne's effort was voted the best ever seen at the old Wembley Stadium.

Le Tissier, though, was not finished on that particular day. Newcastle had pegged Saints back to 1-1 with just a few minutes remaining, but it was time for another moment of magic and my own personal favourite among Le Tissier's vintage collection. This time Neil Maddison headed the ball to him 25-yards from goal and, using his thigh to control it, he twisted in one movement and produced a breathtaking dipping volley which flew both over and past Hooper. It was the certain match-winner, but Le Tissier showed virtually no emotion and simply turned and walked away with his left arm raised above his head. Point proven and two mesmerising knockout blows in any bout with the manager. "It was one of the favourite matches of my whole career, but also a pivotal moment," he says.

Le Tissier does not say any more, but the implication is that he may have been forced to leave had those goals not gone in and Branfoot continued not to pick him. "Different managers have different views, I just needed someone who wanted someone like me in the team," he says, "Ian Branfoot tried to change me. He wasn't keen on the way I played football. He was about knocking the ball into the channels and chasing after it. That wasn't suited to me at all. He was probably the worst out of all the managers for trying to knock out of me the way I played and it was a nice way to respond. Alan Ball was completely the opposite. He had as much belief in my ability as I did in my own, he just brought the best out of me, he built the team around me and I rewarded him with the best football of my life."

Indeed he did. The quality of the goals he scored throughout his career were staggering, but in the Ball period they literally seemed to be flying in virtually every week. *Match of the Day's* 'goal of the month' competition became the Matthew Le Tissier show. There was the incredible strike past Tim Flowers against Blackburn, which Le Tissier rates as the best of his career and won Goal of the Season in 1994/95, the extraordinary free-kick against Wimbledon when the ball was rolled back and he flicked it up for himself and volleyed it into the top corner, a rasping half-volley after 25 seconds against Liverpool and an injury-time, curling free-kick to beat Aston Villa.

That Villa free-kick brings back personal memories. It was a Monday night and I watched the match with a group of about ten friends and can vividly recall a living-room being wrecked amid the celebrations. Of course, there were many other incredible goals and moments; the chip past Peter Schmeichel, the 30-yard shot that left Steve Ogrizovic stranded as well as some of the early efforts which tended to highlight Le Tissier's dribbling skills, such as the 1990 waltz past most of the Norwich team.

Perhaps the footage is not there for the likes of George Best and Pelé, but it's hard to think of another footballer who has scored so many classic goals. What's more, Le Tissier scored such a variety, whether from long range, dribbles, deft touches or sheer power. His right foot was like gold, but the left foot produced goals superior to the average professional. There were also a good number of headers, free-kicks, assists and, of course, plenty of penalties.

I mention the likes of Best and Pelé and Le Tissier simply says: "I would be quite happy to pick my best 30 goals and put them next to the best 30 goals of anybody and I think they'd rank up there." Those who think all this might sound somewhat exaggerated need only purchase a copy of the *Unbelievable* video or Le Tissier's own compilation of his 50 greatest goals.

THE OTHER GAME which so underlined Le Tissier's big match temperament came in the last competitive fixture at The Dell. Even when he was a shadow of the player he once had been, it showed that his quality with the ball at his feet remained permanent. Arsenal were the opponents and it was quite an occasion. The best, some might argue, in the history of the old stadium.

After 103 years, the bulldozers were poised to demolish a venue of so many great memories. Former legends were introduced before the game, although with Saints limping somewhat to the end of the season following the departure of Glenn Hoddle, it promised to be a nostalgic and historic affair without any real fireworks. There are those who now say it was somehow inevitable that Le Tissier would score. But that's nonsense. He was without a league goal for more than a year and, whatever the former manager Stuart Gray says, sentiment was surely the main reason for him being on the pitch.

With 17 minutes remaining, Le Tissier ambled on. He was no longer in the best of shape – a look at the team photo that year suggests Glenn Hoddle, Rupert Lowe and Stuart Gray were all carrying less around the mid-rift – and he looked somewhat out of place among a field of athletes. Being a little different, though, never did bother a maverick. And the genius hadn't disappeared either. So, when the ball broke in the penalty box in the 89th minute with the score-line at 2-2, there were still few more dangerous. His back was facing the goal, but he spun perfectly on his right foot, twisted into the shot and did exceptionally well to get round and over the ball sufficiently to strike it into the top corner. Technically, it was a good goal, particularly with his wrong foot. Emotionally, it was a fairytale.

Le Tissier says that he knew from the moment it left his boot that it was heading for the back of the net. "I would spend ages practising shooting with both feet," he says, "my left foot wasn't very good when I started, but towards the middle to end part of my career I was fairly confident if it fell on my left foot outside of the box as well. It was something I worked on and it paid dividends that day. The whole lead up to the game was a frenzy for the fans, so many people were looking forward to the game. I knew I was going to come on as a sub, but who could have thought it would have ended that way? I knew exactly where it was going and I was away to where my son was. It was a perfect ending to the day."

The Dell's league finale ranks alongside the great moments in the club's history. No doubt diehards will frown on my commitment as a Southampton fan when I say that I was in France that particular weekend. Indeed, without a mobile phone which worked abroad in those days, it was not until I found an Internet café on the Sunday morning that I read what had happened. I had not expected Le Tissier even to play and I vividly remember having to read and re-read the article several times before I could fully comprehend what had happened. The studious looking Frenchman sat adjacent must have wondered what tragic event I was studying as my eyes moistened over. Yet that was the effect Le Tissier was to have on Southampton fans. He was a symbol of the football club and someone who made you proud among supporters of other teams.

LE TISSIER says he can remember quite distinctly when he first realised that he possessed a talent which was out of the ordinary. Growing up in Guernsey playing sport with older brothers Carl, Mark and Kevin clearly accelerated his progress. "I played in the school Under-11s seven-a-side tournament when I was eight," he says, "they picked me in the team and I scored two goals to win the final. At that point, I remember thinking, 'I'm playing against 11-year-olds here and I still scored two, maybe I'm quite good at this'.

"My brothers were good footballers, my dad was a good footballer and it helped a lot. Kevin was offered a pro contract at Oxford when he was about 19, but he didn't want to leave home and Carl was offered an apprenticeship at Southampton before me but he didn't want to leave either.

"That was their decision and they have both done okay for themselves. It was a wrench for me at 16 as I had hardly been off the Island at that point, but the desire to be a footballer was so much in me that I knew I had to leave."

As a schoolboy, Le Tissier's team was Vale Recreation and his goal-scoring feats were exceptional. In one season, he scored more than 150 goals. Le Tissier first came to Southampton's attention while touring Hampshire with an Under-15s team from Guernsey in 1985. Lawrie McMenemy was still manager at the time. "The schoolmaster was taking his team around Fratton Park and he rang the ground and asked if there was any chance they could look around The Dell," says McMenemy, "so I got one of the staff to show them around. The teacher was so grateful and wrote to me and said, 'if ever I can help you, let me know'. I said to him, 'if you see any good kids, let me know'. We must have given them a better welcome than Portsmouth and he recommended Matthew Le Tissier."

Le Tissier signed as an apprentice in May 1985 and it took just a few months before he realised that his talent could make him stand out at any level. "When I came to do my first pre-season training it was a struggle," he says, "I was behind in terms of fitness with the other lads. They had been at Saints for a couple of years and their fitness levels were so much more than mine.

"I had never done a pre-season, all I had ever done was play two or three matches a week. I don't think I'd ever been on a pre-season or a six mile run or anything like that so it was a bit of a shock to the system. But once the season started, I started flying in the youth team and I realised that I could cut it at this level and still stand out and score goals in this kind of company."

Le Tissier made his mark at senior level in the League Cup in November 1986 when he scored two goals in a 4-1 win over Manchester United which hastened the sacking of Ron Atkinson. Later that season, he scored a hat-trick in what was only his fifth league start in a 4-0 win over Leicester City. He continued to impress while in and out of the team over the next few years before really arriving in the 1989/90 season with 20 league goals. He was voted PFA Young Player of the Year and Saints' seventh place finish was to be their highest in Le Tissier's entire career.

He scored another 19 league goals the following season, but the sacking of Chris Nicholl and the arrival of Branfoot seemed to stall his career somewhat. After the profitable Alan Ball-era, Le Tissier was also the club's leading goal-scorer in the league campaigns of 1996/97 and 1997/98, the latter a season which proved to be the last in which he managed double figures.

Although in range of Mick Channon's all-time goal-scoring record of 228, Le Tissier was to add just 11 more goals from the beginning of the 1998/99 season. Indeed, he scored only nine goals for Saints once he was beyond the age of 30. A final tally of 209 puts him second in the all-time list, 19 behind Channon, albeit from 140 fewer first team starts. He says it was the biggest disappointment of his career that he was never able to overhaul a record that had once appeared well within range.

LE TISSIER is happy to shoulder some of the blame for the somewhat premature decline of his career, but points out that, just as he was blessed with wonderful football skills, he was not born with the sort of natural fitness levels of a Francis Benali or Paul Telfer.

"There was a realisation as I got to 33 that my body would not be able to do it anymore and I had about five separate calf strains in the last year," he says. "But something people don't always realise is that there was a long time in the 1990s where I was playing in the side not 100% fit. I would play carrying injuries because the team needed me out there. I was under quite a bit of pressure from several managers to get out on the pitch even if I wasn't fully fit.

"I reckon out of 540 games, 30% were played when I wasn't fully fit and I think that took its toll later in my career. But, yes, I was never a fitness freak and it was something I found really hard. I would do all the pre-season training that everyone else did, but I did find it more difficult than anyone else.

"It was something I just wasn't born with naturally. I didn't have naturally high fitness levels and it was a real grind for me. I've never seen a man who can motor like Paul Telfer could for the distance he would do. I just wasn't capable of that – whether it is a mind thing, or a physical lung capacity thing, I don't know, but that side of it just wasn't easy for me."

It was at the end of a reserve team match in 2001/02 when Le Tissier had again broken down through injury that he made the decision to end his career. "I knew when I came off that would be it," he says. "The manager [Gordon Strachan] came into the changing room, he sat next to me and I went, 'you know what I'm going to say, don't you?' He nodded his head and said, 'I know'. That was it. I knew at that moment. I had made up my mind. Even before that game I was 85 per cent certain I would retire.

"We had a little chat and he then left me on my own in the changing room to think. He said some nice things to me about, in this day and age, the whole of my career has been recorded on video, so I will always have that to show my children, and I could be proud of what I had achieved in the game. I had a bit of time to myself, took a bath and left the stadium."

How Strachan and Le Tissier would have gelled as player and manager is a fascinating thought. They clearly respect one another greatly and it is possible that Strachan might have been the ideal sort of mentor to get Le Tissier much fitter earlier in his career. Perhaps he would have made Le Tissier even better. Alternatively, Strachan's emphasis on fitness and pragmatic approach to football might have provoked a clash.

Strachan is certain it would have worked. "Tiss understands what he is and he understands what other people are," he says. "He is not 'this is the way I play and everyone should play like this'. There are special ways of dealing with special players. You have to make your own rules for some players. There are exceptions and I think you will get that in the game – you have people like Tiss, [Brian] McClair, [Kenny] Dalglish, Willie Miller – they just go through training. I think we both understand that there are different types of players. We used to communicate well together. I got on great with him and I think he is a fantastic fella."

Le Tissier knows it would have been tough. "I didn't do a pre-season under Gordon," he says. "But I remember speaking on the phone to Doddsey [Jason Dodd] and Franny [Benali] and he had them running on the beaches in Scotland and they just said, 'you are so lucky that you have retired'. I would have struggled so badly with that."

FOLLOWING A 32,000 sell-out crowd for a testimonial which attracted the likes of Paul Gascoigne, Chris Waddle, Kevin Keegan, Alan Ball, Peter Beardsley, Ian Wright and Alan Shearer, Le Tissier has continued to live in the Southampton area and has been the recipient of many impressive honours as well as some unusual acts of respect. Most notably, he followed in the footsteps of former Prime Minister David Lloyd George in being awarded the freedom of the city.

He has also been an ambassador for Saints, guest of honour at an England international at St. Mary's and is the proud holder of an honorary degree from the University of Southampton. Le Tissier was even nominated in a poll of greatest living southerners alongside the likes of Jane Austen, Florence Nightingale and Isambard Kingdom Brunel. All that, and he has had a pub, a road and a racehorse named after him.

In retirement, there have been a few business ventures and he has caddied for Hampshire gold professional Richard Bland. His main job, however, has been on the *Soccer Saturday* show on Sky Sports. The presenter Jeff Stelling reckons that Le Tissier is a natural and compares his laid back style with the tendency to come out with a classic one-liner to his footballing skills. "I had a great testimonial in the last game of my career, which meant I didn't have to seek work straight away," says Le Tissier. "I could pick and choose what I wanted to do and the Sky work came up and I really enjoy it. It's taken off from there really.

"All you have to do is keep up to date with what is going on and basically it's like sitting with your mates and having a chat about football. We have a few debates and people have different opinions. We have quite heated debates sometimes, but once the subject is finished, everyone has a laugh and forgets about it.

"I try not to give too much criticism to players although there was a period with [Mateja] Kezman at Chelsea and I just happened to be watching him and he was having this nightmare and Jeff [Stelling] kept asking me and in the end I said, 'I'm sorry, but he's rubbish'. We were talking about the England manager and he asked me about Steve McClaren and he knows I find him boring and I said, 'the England manager needs to have presence and charisma, but Steve McClaren has got neither'. Maybe that was a bit harsh, but they pay you for your opinion."

Le Tissier is also something of an ambassador around Southampton. "I try and stick to the local charities and try and make a difference down here," he says, "I'm a vice president of the Wessex Cancer Trust, which is something I have supported for a long time. There's the Wessex Heartbeat and Barnardo's and it's just nice to give something to this community because I've been living here 20 years now."

AS THE INTERVIEW is drawing to a close, Le Tissier regularly uses the words "no regrets" when assessing his footballing career. It strikes me that he has obviously been asked so many times about a lack of silverware and international honours that he has become instinctively defensive about his achievements. A runners-up medal in the Zenith Data Systems Cup is hardly an accurate reflection of his career, yet those many moments of magic and the accomplishment of keeping Saints in the Premiership most certainly are.

At the time of writing, Saints have only played 35 seasons in the top-flight during the club's 121-year history. Le Tissier played in 16 of those campaigns – a span at that level which is matched only by Jason Dodd, who featured three years later from 1989/90 until 2004/05. Only Terry Paine, Mick Channon and Nick Holmes have played more matches for the club than Le Tissier, but no-one has played more often in the top-flight.

And with more than 50 of Channon's league goals coming in Division Two, Le Tissier holds the distinction of being the club's leading scorer in English football's top division. He is also one of a select group of players to have reached the landmark of 100 Premiership goals. Whatever anyone says about what might have been, that's not a bad list of achievements for a player once described as having, "eyes for the impossible and a body for darts".

Le Tissier says he is most proud of the part he played in keeping the club in the top-flight and upsetting the likes of Liverpool and Manchester United. "As much as the chairman [at the time Rupert Lowe] will hate me saying this, we are a small club," he says, "we only recently got the stadium. At The Dell we were getting crowds of 15,000, so it was an achievement to stay in the league. It might have been relegation fights, but we were battling the odds and, for all of the 1990s, we won.

"For me, the matches that stand out are when we gave the big clubs a bit of a hammering. In 1989 we beat Liverpool 4-1 when they were one of the top teams and it could have been seven or eight because we battered them that day. And then there were the games when we beat [Manchester] United 3-1 and 6-3 in consecutive seasons."

Supporters of Saints rightly feel blessed to have had a Matthew Le Tissier at their club. He was so good that even opposition fans would often applaud his goals, none more than those in The Kop at Anfield. They appreciated genuine footballing class.

"No man has given me greater pleasure," says the Southampton historian Duncan Holley. "No man has made me catch my breath in absolute awe at some of the things he has done. He was a player from a different age, he is player who can bring a tear to the eye with some of the things he does. I don't think you can replace that."

It was Danny Blanchflower who famously once said: "The great fallacy of the game is that it's first and last about winning. It's nothing of the kind. The game is about glory. It's about doing things in style, with a flourish, about going out and beating the other lot, not waiting for them to die of boredom."

I believe Terry Paine was the most effective Southampton player. But the most magnificent, the most glorious and the man who delivered most entertainment? Well, there's really no contest. Matthew Le Tissier; a footballing genius and the last of the great mavericks.

FRANCIS BENALI

1983-2004

SAINTS CAREER

Games	389
Goals	1
Caps	0

MAGIC MOMENT

Launching John
Fashanu into orbit
as a fresh-faced
21-year-old

'FOOTBALL GENIUS'

THE walk from his home in Portswood to junior school in Southampton used to take Francis Benali about 15 minutes. And, every day, twice a day, he would follow the route that took him past The Dell. A large metal gate stood between Benali and, what to him, was a theatre of dreams. But he would always pause and peer through the bars in the hope of catching a glimpse of a legend.

The World Cup winner Alan Ball, the double European Footballer of the Year Kevin Keegan and the England striker Mick Channon were at Saints during this time. To a young Francis Benali these men were superstars and the gates to The Dell were the entrance to a whole different world. Somewhere distant, magical, but probably inaccessible. Everyone, though, has dreams. Benali's was that one day he would become a professional footballer. Not uncommon, although Benali was a little bit different. Liverpool, Manchester United or England were never in his sights. It was Southampton. Always the Saints. In his mind, it was them or nothing. He must have walked past The Dell about a thousand times as a schoolboy and every journey only reinforced that feeling.

His attachment to Southampton Football Club was evident some 25 years later as he watched helplessly from the stands during the sad relegation season of 2004/05. Matches were being thrown away from winning positions and a lack of backbone was evident throughout the team. It was two years since Benali had last played competitively, but he watched what was happening out on the pitch and felt the urge to return. When he retired from playing, Wayne Bridge had established himself in Benali's favoured left-back position. Bridge had become an England international and Benali had been told straight by Gordon Strachan that his first team days at the club were probably numbered. Yet Bridge was to move to Chelsea in the summer of 2003 for £7m and Benali was left wondering what might have been. He was now 36, but still as fit as ever.

He pondered the situation over the summer and decided to get in touch with the then manager Harry Redknapp. "No promises," said Redknapp. "But you are welcome to join in with pre-season training." Benali jumped at the chance to see what he had left.

"It was hard work, I hadn't trained or played day-to-day for two years," he says, "and I had no idea where I'd be fitness wise. It was just something I thought 'maybe it could happen'. If it had suited all parties then great, I'd have loved to have done it. I don't think there have been too many people, if any, who have been out for two years and gone back to it. I would have enjoyed that prospect if it had come off."

Redknapp admitted that Benali was still as "fit as a fiddle" and gave him a run out in a pre-season friendly against the non-league team Eastleigh. In a twist of fate, Matthew Le Tissier was a guest player for Eastleigh, although he only played a few minutes at the end of the match in front of a crowd of several thousand.

For Benali, the game appeared more serious and he put in a decent performance. Some of his passing was characteristically wayward, but the commitment and sharpness was there.

So was some of the tackling and he certainly provoked a few cheers with one rather high and reckless challenge which left a hapless opposition striker requiring treatment. Redknapp's face after this incident was a picture as he first grimaced and then began laughing. It appeared Benali might have done enough for Saints to take a gamble.

But there was no news and several weeks later Redknapp confirmed that he would not be signing Benali. "He's a terrific character and I wouldn't like to say he couldn't play at this level," said Redknapp, "I'm sure he could play at somewhere like Bournemouth, but if he can't play for Southampton, I don't think he wants to play at all."

Benali was disappointed. He wondered whether his return was blocked because it would have been seen as a rather desperate measure. "Maybe people would have viewed it as panicking to a degree after relegation," he said. "I could understand that for the club to sign a player who hadn't been playing for a couple of years would be unheard of really, but I felt I was up there with the guys still. I was a bit rusty in a few areas, but hopefully that would have come back over the weeks and months. It was a shame it didn't come off really – I would have loved the opportunity to have pulled the shirt back on."

Physically, you would have to think that Benali would have been capable. As we sit and chat over a tea in the living room of his Southampton home, it is clear that he has barely gained an ounce in weight since his playing days. He is dressed in tracksuit bottoms and a T-shirt and has just been out running in preparation for the 2006 London Marathon, which he went on to complete in an impressive 3hrs 31mins.

Yet nothing can replace playing for Saints. Other football options were available to Benali below the Championship and several local non-league sides would have jumped at the chance to sign him. But no. "It was Southampton or not at all," he confirms. "Maybe I should have gone on and continued playing football. It would have prolonged my career. It's difficult, but my love for the game was so much that I was very serious about it. I devoted myself to it, in preparation and in the way I trained and played. If I played on a part-time basis I just don't think I could devote myself as I would want to unless it was for Southampton Football Club.

"Maybe I'm wrong to think like that, but that's how I feel. I do feel very proud and honoured to have represented this football club especially as a Southampton boy." Represented is a word Benali uses frequently when he looks back over his playing days. There is a definite sense of duty in what he did. The pride he felt at pulling on his hometown shirt was like that of an Australian cricketer donning the baggy green cap.

Southampton supporters recognised that in Benali's performances. Their affection was shown many times over the years, although most humorously in 1993 when, as an end of season tribute against Oldham Athletic, they donned false moustaches, sunglasses and wore head-scarves. The sight of Benali look-a-likes all over Oldham certainly lightened the mood that afternoon on the team bus. "All the lads were looking and pointing and kept shouting 'there's Franny'," says Benali, "no, no, there's Franny!"

He understood the humour; after all he was one of them. He can recall the excitement in Southampton in 1976 when the FA Cup was won. As a schoolboy, he would stand on the terraces at the Archers end and watch his heroes in action. Remembering that feeling, he says: "I used to think it was such a great pitch. I used to just look at it and think how fantastic it would be to play on there. It's a memory – that first impression when you see a stadium, the pitch, the lights and the fans. It is a magical moment. To see the people you had seen on television in the flesh was amazing. It was a dream world, I couldn't have dreamt of anything better as a boy."

BUT WAS THAT young Francis Benali good enough? Early on, there was, with the benefit of hindsight, a far-fetched hope that he would eventually follow in the footsteps of the club's great strikers. Benali was an early developer and schoolboy photographs of him confirm the arrival of that trademark moustache. He was quicker and stronger than most footballers of his age. These qualities allied to his determination and above average talent made him a prolific goal-scorer as a schoolboy.

He played in the local Tyro Youth League and progressed to the England schoolboy team, scoring on his debut against Northern Ireland and going on to play at Wembley among his nine international matches. "As a boy growing up and a teenager, I was pretty much the size I am now," he says. "I was a handful for other lads my age and like most kids growing up I had dreams of scoring goals. I was always kicking the ball against a wall or at the park with my mates having a kick about. All I can ever remember wanting to do was play football and whenever I picked up a football I found myself as a striker."

Benali was one of the intake of apprentices in 1985 along with Matthew Le Tissier. He was signed as a striker. Yet, when he hung up his boots 18 years later, he had managed just one goal for the club in some 389 appearances.

He did, of course, end up playing the vast majority of his career at left-back, but the goal remains a treasured memory. It came in December 1997. Leicester City were the victims and, fittingly, the provider was Le Tissier whose free-kick found Benali for a powerful header into the top right-hand corner. "With my goal-scoring record, Leicester probably weren't bothered about picking me up," he says. "They probably thought, 'it's only Franny'. I was really chuffed it was Matt who passed it because we had both been at the club so many years. I was pleased the goal was at The Dell and it was something that always sticks in people's minds.

"When the ball went in, my mind just went blank. The lads said I just stood there and screamed and then I set off on a run. But I did not get too far before they all jumped on me. Funnily enough the day before the match I stayed behind for some extra shooting practice."

Benali watched the video of his goal over and over that week and said it put him in a "dream world" for a few days. The goal also proved to be the decider in a 2-1 win, although wife Karen, who had always loyally backed her husband to score with a £1 bet, missed out on her one and only pay out because it was not the first goal of the match. The odds were 66-1. Still, his goal did make someone a few quid as for the next few weeks the inevitable 'I was there when Franny scored' T-shirts did a roaring trade.

The decision to move Benali from his original position as a striker was, in truth, one that gave him a chance to realise that dream of playing with Southampton at the highest level. Once in senior football, Benali was no longer unusually quick or strong and lacked the touch to become a successful striker at the highest level. His fiery on-field tempera-ment was also better suited to not being the target of fierce tackling. The new manager Chris Nicholl and the youth team manager Dave Merrington, however, had seen enough to want to persevere.

"We have moved him to a role where he doesn't have someone up his back kicking and frustrating him," said Nicholl at the time.

"He is a player who will go in where it hurts and that sorts out the men from the boys," added Merrington.

Benali willingly accepted the change of position. "I did find myself getting in confrontations with defenders when I was a striker," he says. "I used to react and they thought I would be better without defenders whacking me from behind. My strengths were in defence. I was at my best making tackles, winning the ball and keeping it simple after that. I enjoyed the challenge of coming up against people like Alan Shearer, Eric Cantona and Ian Wright. I liked the challenge of stopping someone from playing."

The positional change had no impact on that ambition to succeed and a willingness to work as hard as he possibly could to make the best use of his talent. A major influence was Merrington, who was responsible for schooling the club's finest crop of young players. A committed Christian who also worked with young offenders after his playing career, Merrington saw it as his job to instil standards of discipline and respect in the players as well as mould them into top class footballers. The 'Merrington stamp' remains obvious in the likes of Benali, Matthew Le Tissier, Alan Shearer, Jeff Kenna and Jason Dodd.

Benali says it was a "great grounding" and describes Southampton at the time as being like a "factory" in producing quality players. "I don't think anyone who worked with Dave would have a bad word to say about him," he says. "He had that fear factor, but also respect. He prepared you for the games both physically and mentally. You got an education in life as well as football and he was a hard task-master. If the toilets weren't cleaned right, if the training rooms weren't tidy or the kit wasn't done right, we got punished for it and the footballs would be thrown to one side. One of Dave's sayings was 'if you can't do it right, we will put the footballs away and we will run'. You soon got the message." It instilled a streak of toughness, togetherness and, most importantly, a willingness to take responsibility in difficult situations. These characteristics formed the core of the team during the 1990s.

FROM 1991/92 until 1999/2000, Saints finished 16th, 18th, 18th, 10th, 17th, 16th, 12th, 17th and 15th. The fact that there were 22 teams saved them in 1993 and 1994, while 1996, 1997 and 1999 were also years when survival was only secured on the final day of the season. As David Bull remarked in *Match of the Millennium:* "The 'Great Escape' became part of the lexicon, not to say the mentality, of Southampton fans in the 1990s – so much so that we can still debate which was the most tense final countdown."

Two things kept Saints in the top-flight for so long. The first, obviously, was the goals of Matthew Le Tissier. The second was a fighting spirit which was epitomised by the likes of Benali and also Jason Dodd. "We had characters who could stand up for themselves," says Benali. "Tough, strong characters and good people as well."

Dodd captained Saints throughout much of this period, eventually clocking up more than 400 appearances for the club in a highly distinguished career. "It was drummed into you that you were representing the club and for the younger lads, like myself, Franny and Matt, our early days at the club were life-building as much as football building," says Dodd. "We proved everyone wrong. Every year we were favourites to go down and we would be 'fucking hell, we are favourites again' and it would just be funny. We had a small stadium and squad and we were down near the bottom every year and I guess someone had to be tipped to go down. But we always believed in ourselves and you had eleven players together in it for each other."

The former striker Iain Dowie also highlights that spirit within the club. "We had big characters there at Southampton," he says, "we had Terry Hurlock, Micky Adams, Tim Flowers, Neil Ruddock, Glenn Cockerill and Ken Monkou. We had big leaders about the place and a lot of tenacity. You could look around and think there were enough people who were going to go to war with you. We also had people with the strength of character to cope with the situation."

It certainly was a team packed full of 'personality' if not always quality. Indeed, the likes of Cockerill, Dodd, Hurlock, Ruddock, Dowie, Adams, Monkou and Flowers, all have a certain Cult Hero status in their own right. "We had that confidence in one another," says Benali. "We were such good mates as well off the field that we would fight for one another. The team was full of very competitive characters and it used to sometimes end up with dust-ups on the training ground as well, but that's the sort of people you wanted. I would look around and just think 'we're fine here'. You knew they were people who would back you up in any situation and they were people who you could rely on."

That great team spirit resulted in some memorable victories. There was the FA Cup win on penalties over Manchester United at Old Trafford and a 6-3 drubbing of United in 1996. Yet it was the performances under the pressure of relegation which were most vital.

Like in April 1994, when Saints fell behind three times and trailed 3-1 with 35 minutes to go, but still defeated Norwich City 5-4 at Carrow Road. It was a season in which Saints were never out of the bottom three between September and January under Ian Branfoot. Alan Ball inspired an improvement in form, but Saints were still left potentially needing a result on the final day of the season against West Ham United at Upton Park. Ipswich Town, Sheffield United and Everton were also all competing for the final relegation position, but a 3-3 draw meant survival.

In 1996, Saints also produced a draw on the final day of the season – this time against Wimbledon – to secure their Premiership status, although it was their form during April which laid the foundations for survival. On this occasion, it was the battling qualities of the likes of Benali which proved vital with Le Tissier scoring less goals, although producing the goods at important times. Merrington had replaced Ball as manager that season and the sweetest victory came with a 3-1 win over Manchester United at The Dell which was best remembered for Sir Alex Ferguson's complaint that his players had difficulty seeing one another because of their grey shirts.

Another memorable run-in was 1999 under Dave Jones when consecutive victories against Leicester City, Wimbledon and Everton in the last three matches safeguarded the club's Premiership status. They had spent from August until the end of April in the relegation zone. At the time, Benali summed up the fear of relegation. He said: "It dominated every waking thought, the fear of failure drove us on. I wanted my children to have a Premiership club and to be able to watch games in a superb new stadium."

With strikers and attacking midfielders, there are always goals to mark those magic moments that pass into folklore. But for a defender like Benali, who only had that one strike to celebrate, it was the 1998/99 relegation battle which produced a classic moment which helped earn him the undying devotion of Saints fans. Needing to win at fellow strugglers Wimbledon in the penultimate game, 14,000 Saints supporters travelled to the game at 'Dell-hurst Park'. With the score still at 0-0 Benali produced a dramatic goal-line clearance from Robbie Earle to keep Saints in the game. They went on to win 2-0 and Benali was the hero. By now Saints were renowned as the survival experts and it was no coincidence that the departure of major characters like Benali, Matthew Le Tissier, Jason Dodd and Chris Marsden was to precede the rather feeble exit from the Premiership.

It's often said that a mark of a team's toughness is the ability to perform away from home. That Saints lost 13 out of 19 away from St. Mary's in 2004/05 said it all. They were short of street-fighters.

IT IS A CLICHÉ, but also a truism to say that whatever Benali lacked in skill, he made up for in heart and spirit. Often, though, it over-spilled in the wrong way and Benali had a poor disciplinary record. Yet, like Mark Dennis, it was an element to his character which somehow cemented his cult status among Saints fans. Within football, however, he developed what they call "a reputation".

Speaking in September 1989, Chris Nicholl's words were spot on. "He has got to make sure he calms down and controls his aggression because he has the makings of a good player. But he cannot afford to get a reputation." At times, that reputation was well earned. Benali was sent-off on 11 occasions for Saints. Some of the incidents have gone down in folklore on the terraces. The journalist Graham Hiley was on hand for each of them. He described a high tackle on Nick Barmby which "almost took his head off" in a televised 4-2 defeat at White Hart Lane and, of a challenge on West Ham's Paolo Futre, he wrote that Benali, "virtually launched him into row F of the main stand".

The incident, though, which is best remembered was his tackle on John Fashanu. The Wimbledon striker had the reputation as one of the hardest, most physical forwards in British football, but a youthful Francis Benali was undeterred. He was only 21 at the time and had established himself in the first team. "He launched John Fashanu so far into the air that he almost came down with ice on him," said Hiley.

It is an incident fondly recalled by supporters. "It was an incredible sight," said Mike Tanner. "Fashanu had this reputation as one of the tough guys in football and little Francis Benali left him a crumpled wreck on the floor." Memories of the tackle were recently posted on the *SaintsForever* supporters' message board. "I was sitting in the front row of the main stand at Plough Lane that day," wrote one fan, "and about two minutes before that incident Fashanu had sent Benali into the dugout with a tackle. As Franny climbed back up Fashanu stood over him and shouted, 'let's see if you're brave enough to come back for more you little ****'. Had I not heard the previous conversation I would have been livid with Franny for making us play with ten men, but in light of Fashanu's comments I just had so much respect for him."

Benali laughs at the memory. "He was a big guy and played on his 'Fash the Bash' reputation," he says, "it was mis-timed a bit, but it looked quite spectacular the way he went up and over and landed in a heap on the floor. I think maybe I endeared myself to a lot of fans with that one incident and it was the turning point in the game itself. We were losing the game at that point, but Matt scored a hat-trick." Saints drew the game 3-3, after trailing 3-1 at the time of Benali's 59th minute dismissal.

Of the Barmby incident, he says: "Nick Barmby was down to frustration – we had conceded three goals in a short period of time and I lost my head."

But there are plenty of stories of Franny taming football's elite. On another occasion, David Beckham refused to shake Benali's hand after coming off second best in a challenge with him. The incident happened just in front of Gavin Wingfield. "Beckham, in his prime, climbed on Benali to reach a header," he says, "Franny dropped his shoulder and with it

Beckham onto his head. Benali shrugged his shoulders in a 'what happened there sort of way' and looked at me with a cheeky grin. Still grinning he went over to see if Beckham was okay, or was it to tell him not to try it again? Whatever, Beckham had at least five minutes of treatment right in front of me and suffered non-stop abusive singing from me and my friends. He looked at us at one point and shook his head."

Benali, though, was never a malicious player in the sense that his bad tackles or challenges were planned. Usually it was a genuine case of the 'red mist' descending. It was a weakness that successive managers tried to remedy and, as the years went by, Benali was slightly less prone to making a reckless challenge. "A lot of sending-offs I have deserved to go, but there were some where I felt a little bit hard done by, none less so than my old mate Graham Poll who sent me off about three times I think," says Benali. "I never intentionally meant to hurt anyone. At the time I was giving it everything and I had the attitude that if you are in the way, you are going to get hit as well.

"Sometimes it was a tactic if you came against someone who was that quick or that good that maybe you'll try and give them a whack. You do try to have that intimidation or that fear factor over them. A lot of time I will see the challenge on TV later and think 'that was stupid', but I don't think anyone was seriously injured.

"Fans and players enjoy that physical element of football, but I can see a day when tackling will be taken out of football. It will become like basketball, a non-contact sport, which would be a crying shame."

Benali's motivation for trying to curb his disciplinary problems was two-fold. From a professional point of view, it was putting his place in jeopardy and it was also costing him money in fines. Yet there was also a personal standpoint. He was becoming genuinely concerned by his image. After a sending-off for the reserve team in 1997, Benali spoke of his concern. He said: "After I got back from Reading I went up to see the kids who were asleep. I just looked at them and thought, 'what have I done?'

"I don't want them to hear bad things about me when they go to school or for them to grow up and think that their father was a nasty player. And when I come to the end of my playing days I don't want to be remembered for the number of times I have been sent-off. I hate it when people sympathise with Karen for being married to me."

The great irony, of course, is that away from football, Benali is one of the nicest, most laid-back people you could hope to meet. "I was worried about my reputation," says Benali. "If you spoke to fans from other teams they probably would have said I was dirty. They saw an image on the football pitch and I did use to change when I walked out on that pitch.

"I did become a different person. People found that hard to understand unless it was someone I knew or got to know. A lot of the people I've met in the past thought I would be the same person off the pitch as I am on it."

IN ASSESSING BENALI AS a player, it would be unfair, however, to dwell solely on his disciplinary record. His style was certainly raw and his crossing was sometimes frustratingly wayward. Yet there were few fiercer tacklers and opposition forwards did not enjoy playing against him. As Lawrie McMenemy summed up: "He is very popular with the crowd who have probably moaned on occasions when he has landed the ball on their heads instead of the centre-forward's, but he has always bounced back to help the cause."

There were many times during Benali's career when it appeared his time at the club was coming to an end. Replacement left-backs were regularly brought in, but he had the knack of constantly bouncing back. And, when it mattered most during a relegation scrap, managers invariably turned to him.

Dave Jones felt the side missed his "influence, grit and fire" when he was not playing. Lee Todd, John Beresford, Patrick Colleter, Graham Potter and Simon Charlton were all brought in at different times as potential replacements, but Benali saw them off. Glenn Hoddle was the one manager least convinced and Benali spent his one and only spell away from the club on loan at Nottingham Forest while the former England manager was at Southampton.

Whilst at the City Ground Benali added to his cult status on the south coast. In a match against Portsmouth, legend has it that he even wore his Saints top beneath his Nottingham Forest shirt. Benali returned once Hoddle had departed for Tottenham, but the emergence that year of Wayne Bridge was to signal the end of his playing career. Bridge was of international quality and did not miss a league game from March 2000 until January 2003.

Benali could have moved on during this period, but made the decision that he wanted to end his career where it had all started. "I was fit and young enough to keep on playing, but we had a great player and a lovely lad like Wayne Bridge coming through who had taken over my position," he says. "If it was going to be anyone, of all the people I saw off over the years that were signed to take my place, eventually I was pleased that it was a local boy and someone like Bridgey who took my position in the end.

"Gordon Strachan came to me and said, 'with the emergence of Bridgey, if you want to get regular first team football it's not going to be at Southampton'. I was faced then with a decision that if I wanted to continue playing on a regular basis it would mean leaving Southampton. When I sat down and really thought about it and discussed it with my family, I made the decision that I didn't want to leave Southampton Football Club.

"I've got a happy and healthy family who I adore and, as much as I enjoy football, family has always come first. The personal and family happiness has always been paramount to me, I'm quite a home bird and wouldn't make decisions just for me. I've grown up among family and friends over the years and I didn't want to uproot. My wife Karen is a local girl, the city is perfect for us and you just can't put a price on personal happiness."

Yet again that loyalty that Southampton Football Club so often engenders rose to the surface and yet again the tug proved too strong for one of the club's great Cult Heroes to ignore.

WITH HIS CONTRACT due to expire at the end of the 2003 season, it appeared that Benali's career would gradually fade away. But then came an unlikely finale. After a then record-breaking 113 consecutive Premiership appearances, Bridge picked up a calf strain in a 1-0 defeat against Liverpool. Saints were facing Millwall the following week in the FA Cup fourth round and manager Gordon Strachan had a decision to make.

Benali was now 34. It was three years since he had featured regularly and he had not played at all for the first team in 16 months. Strachan admits he was initially in two minds about what to do. He considered reshaping the team or even moving Rory Delap from midfield to left-back. He was weighing all this up when there was a knock on his office door. It was Francis Benali.

"I just wanted to let him know that I felt ready and I wouldn't let anyone down," says Benali. "I knew he was thinking of playing other people in that position. I thought I should at least let him know that I wanted to play and that I was up for the challenge."

Any doubts in Strachan's mind disappeared and Benali found himself back in the team to the delight of the supporters. He played in the two Cup matches against Millwall and also in a 1-0 win over Sunderland and a 2-0 defeat against Manchester United – ending his top-flight career by marking David Beckham. "It was a nice bonus to play in the Cup run," he says. "I put the ball into the box when Beatts [James Beattie] knocked it down for Kevin Davies and I cleared one off the line, so I played a part. It was a nice reward as there were long months where it took a lot of dedication and strength of mind to stay as fit as I could in case the call did come."

It was the year, of course, that Saints were to progress through to the final. "I thought it would be a lovely way to sign off if we could achieve an FA Cup winners' medal," he says, "if there is one regret, it is that we never won any silverware in all the time I was playing." Benali travelled to the FA Cup final as part of the squad, but was not selected among the substitutes. Yet the depth of feeling towards him in the dressing room was summed up by a gesture from Danny Higginbotham. The runners-up medals had been presented and there were only 16, meaning that Benali had missed out.

"I was sat near Danny in the changing room and he just looked at me and he said, 'Franny I want you to have this'. It was his medal. He said, 'you've been here a long time, you deserve it more than I do'. He was serious and he meant it. I said, 'no, don't be stupid, you've played your part and that's yours'. It quite choked me up that he was prepared to give away a Cup final medal." The following day, however, the Football Association sent Saints three extra medals and Strachan was delighted to present Benali, Kevin Davies and Saints' other long-serving stalwart, Jason Dodd, with a runners-up medal.

Although he took on a coaching job with Saints in 2003, Benali left within a year after deciding to pursue various business interests. His dream was to manage Saints, but the realisation that he might have to drag his family all around the country in order to move up the ladder was not appealing. An application to return in tandem with Matthew Le Tissier in 2005 was not seriously considered by the board of directors.

"I loved the idea of coaching and even managing," he said. "I would take little bits and pieces from each of what was good and add them to my thoughts. Dave Merrington was a massive influence as a youngster, Alan Ball was great, Gordon Strachan was right up there as well. If there was one name I couldn't really take to, it was Glenn Hoddle. His tactics and knowledge of the game go without question, but his man-management skills left a bit to be desired. It worked both ways because I wasn't the sort of player that he took to either."

BENALI WAS AFFORDED the chance to say a final goodbye when his departure coincided with the staging of the inaugural Ted Bates Trophy friendly match in January 2004. In many ways it was fitting that Benali should bow out in a match being played in tribute to Bates. It would be hard to imagine two people who have cared more about Southampton Football Club.

A near-capacity crowd saw Saints take on Bayern Munich with Benali coming on as a substitute with five minutes to go to a standing ovation. "It was an emotional night because that was the occasion when I thought to myself 'this is the last time I'm going to appear in front of a crowd in a Saints shirt'," he says. "It was a strange afternoon. I spoke with Gordon Strachan and he said, 'I think it's right that you have a little run out this evening'."

Strachan also recalls the ovation, saying: "It was priceless. You can't put money on that – it will stay with Franny for the rest of his life." Strachan, of course, faced Benali as a player for Leeds United and smiles: "He gave me the biggest bruise I have ever had. He kneed me up the backside and I have never seen a bruise like it. It went from my bum to my shoulder blades!"

BENALI'S RELATIONSHIP with the supporters during the 1990s is perhaps matched only by Le Tissier. Jason Dodd was, of course, another revered player, yet Benali's local roots and perhaps more limited ability made him all the more a hero on the terraces. Who else would have part-ownership in a local Indian restaurant? Not surprisingly, Kuti's is among the most popular restaurants in the city among fans who sometimes used to sing 'let's all have a curry' at the part-owner as he gave his all for them in a red and white shirt.

Benali's testimonial came in 1997 and The Dell was a sell-out as he walked onto the pitch with his two children. Amazingly, he even managed to score a goal. Alan Shearer was certainly impressed. "Franny's goal was unbelievable," he said. "Tim Flowers said he tried his best to reach it, but he won't sleep at night now." The manager at the time was Graeme Souness and he was struck by the show of passion from the Southampton supporters. He said: "The warmth from the crowd was wonderful – it was as good as anything I have known in football."

"It was an occasion that will live with me forever," says Benali.

As a player, few have been such a part of their local community as Benali and he continues as something of an ambassador for football in Southampton at numerous events for friends and various charities. "I think it is part of your responsibility," he says. "I saw myself as one of the fans. Just because I played professional football I'm no different to anyone else really, you do see certain characters who think they are a bit special. I enjoy getting out into the community and meeting people."

It's somehow reassuring to meet a footballer who so appreciates his life. Benali has a scrap-book of his career which wife Karen has meticulously kept. Lawrie McMenemy sums him up: "He is like a stick of rock – if you cut him open there would be Southampton FC running right through him. By his own admission he is not blessed with the ability of Le Tissier, but there are few with a bigger heart."

Benali appreciates the tribute. "I've been very fortunate," he says. "I feel quite privileged to realise a lot of my dreams and I'm extremely proud when I look back. It goes very quickly, but I did something I loved, in my home town with everyone around me. I wouldn't change a thing and, if I could do it all again tomorrow, I would."

If only, Franny, if only.

CHRIS MARSDEN

1999-2004

SAINTS CAREER

Games	152
Goals	8
Caps	0

MAGIC MOMENT

Maradona, Ricky Villa and John Barnes all rolled into one when Marsden scored a miraculous solo goal against Ipswich in 2002

'MARSDINHO'

> ## 'The FA Cup final is a great day - and to win it is the greatest day of your life.'
>
> ### Sir Bobby Robson

Abald Englishman takes his seat at Aces Cocktail Bar in Paphos, south west Cyprus. It's the sort of place that will be packed to the rafters with English tourists come June, but in the winter months it is altogether more civilised. The locals enjoy a few pints as they gather for their Saturday afternoon ritual while matches from the English Premiership flash from every television. In all, there are seven screens simultaneously showing different games.

The bald Englishman is now 37 and shakes his head as he watches Thierry Henry deliver yet another master-class. "He must be the fastest footballer ever," he says. Henry plays like he is from another planet and the locals also look on in wonder at his pace, skill, balance and finishing power. They all dream of producing just an ounce of Henry's quality during their weekly five-a-side matches together.

There is little to suggest that the bald Englishman is different to anyone else in this group of awestruck football fans. Yet he would be instantly recognised by any Saints supporter. For the bald Englishman is Chris Marsden and it was only three years ago that he was proudly leading Southampton at Cardiff's Millennium Stadium as his team did battle with Henry and Arsenal in front of millions of viewers across the entire globe. Some in the bar were sat in exactly the same seats as when they watched that match.

The only people to recognise him as the captain of the only Southampton team to reach the FA Cup final in the three decades since 1976 are the few regulars who know him best, as well as the occasional football anorak who notices even the more obscure ex-Premiership player.

Few realise they are sat with someone who went toe-to-toe with the dazzling Henry and played in teams which defeated Arsenal, Chelsea, Manchester United and Liverpool in the past five years. Although Marsden has changed little physically since he last played for Saints, he admits he sometimes forgets that he was once rubbing shoulders with the best footballers on the planet. Yet at the end of the 2003 FA Cup final, the television cameras capture a lovely image when Marsden congratulates Thierry Henry with a prolonged handshake and a pat on the cheek. There is a brief look of mutual respect and, for that moment, they were equals.

"I have to pinch myself to be honest," he says, "especially when I see Henry – he is just incredible. He has got to be the best player in the world. I know Ronaldinho has got all those tricks, but I don't think he can influence a game in the way Henry can. My lad has the Fifa computer game and he says, 'you played against him, didn't you dad?' It all seems a bit strange."

It is a comment which is typical of Marsden. Unfashionable and unfancied for most of his career, he was what people would describe as "a journeyman" professional. Yet for five years at Saints – and particularly two under the management of Gordon Strachan – he was hugely influential in some of the club's best seasons in recent memory. Indeed, if anyone reflected a

Southampton team which, under Strachan, achieved more than even the most optimistic supporter could have imagined, it was surely Marsden.

Through a combination of effort, will power and sheer hard work, he squeezed the absolute maximum out of himself and was to enjoy the sort of finale to his career which must have seemed impossible after 12 years spent plying his trade in the nether regions of the Football League. After a brief spell in Korea and then back with his home-town team of Sheffield Wednesday, he retired from football and opted for the superior climate of Cyprus and a way of life that he has taken to his heart. Several holidays while he was still playing convinced Marsden that it was where he wanted to be.

"It's great, the school starts at 7.30am, so I'm up at the crack of dawn with my son Matthew to take him to school," he says. "It's red hot by about 1pm and everyone has a sleep and everything shuts down and then reopens again at 4pm. You really try and get everything done by about 1pm in the summer. I'm playing plenty of golf and my handicap is down to five, I'll pick my lad up from school and I seem to be busier than when I was playing football. They have a great attitude to children here, you are outside most of the time and you don't feel like you have to be watching them all the time."

Marsden looks lean and fit and admits that he still runs regularly and plays those five-a-side football matches with a group of friends. "I can't run like I used to, but occasionally I still take it round them all and score," he says, "I had 20-odd years as a professional and I'm happy with that. I always wanted to be a footballer and I've played about 500 games so that's not bad."

Unlike many players who have recently retired, it seems that Marsden is not missing football. He asks after the latest gossip at St. Mary's, but does not seem particularly interested in hearing about the soap-opera that has taken place behind the scenes since he and then Strachan left in quick succession. Indeed, Marsden appears content to have ended his day-to-day involvement with professional football and is just delighted to have so much quality time available to spend with his family.

There is no desire to get into coaching and he sees no reason to return to England. In any case, he does not want to move while his son Matthew, who is nine, is completing his schooling. He is generally far more interested in what he will do tomorrow than what he did yesterday. Yet what of those marvellous memories of his time at Saints? "Oh yes," he says, "of course I still think about them."

IT IS NOT surprising that Marsden can reflect on his Southampton career with such pleasure. In many respects, his story was a fairytale. He arrived at The Dell the wrong side of 30 and left five years later having proved himself at the highest level. He had also established himself as a lifelong idol to a generation of Saints fans.

To Gordon Strachan, helping someone like Chris Marsden to realise his footballing dreams was as satisfying as any of the medals he won as a player or manager. But how did it happen? How, at the age of 30, did Marsden go from an unknown player who had moved around the lower leagues to one of the stars of a Premiership club that suddenly found themselves reaching a Cup final and qualifying for Europe?

First and foremost, credit must go to Dave Jones who had managed Marsden at Stockport County. They had spent 18 months together from January 1996 until June 1997 and, after Marsden failed to really settle at Coventry City, Wolverhampton Wanderers or Notts

County, Jones was a manager he particularly respected. "I think a lot of the players owe him a lot," says Marsden, "obviously myself and Paul Jones in particular as he knew us from Stockport, but he also got in Beatts [James Beattie], Marian [Pahars] and brought through Bridgey [Wayne Bridge] and converted him into left-back."

When Jones went looking for added steel and character in his Saints team prior to the conclusion of the 1998/99 season, he turned to Marsden, a player he admired for his quality on the ball as much as the combative streak that he became better known for. Marsden admits that early in his career, particularly during almost six years with Huddersfield Town, he regarded himself as something of a flair player in the centre of midfield.

That self-assessment changed very quickly, though, once he arrived at Southampton and saw what the likes of Matthew Le Tissier and Marian Pahars could do on the training ground. "I thought I was a decent player, but instead of poncing around I realised I had to run around," says Marsden. "Running around a bit more seemed to help. I thought I was quite a good foot-baller and then I played with some of the Premiership players and you see what they can do when they control it and pass it and I realised that I would have to adapt.

"I was not as good as I thought I was. I just thought, 'bloody hell, these are good players', but I adapted and, by increasing my work-rate, I became a better player and could do a job at the higher level. Matt Le Tissier was just dipping a bit, but to see the things he could do was amazing. That was sheer ability, you could not teach that and I soon realised my place."

Although eyebrows were raised at the sense of purchasing a 30-year-old from Birmingham, Marsden quickly proved to be an important signing for Saints. He arrived for £800,000 in February 1999, with the club having been rooted in the bottom three of the table all season after losing their first five games. A wonderful finale, however, which included three wins and two draws in the last five games pulled Saints one place above relegation.

Marsden also made an early impression with a thundering headed goal in the draw against Blackburn Rovers and then repeated the feat in what was a crucial win against Leicester City. Survival in 1999 was paramount in safeguarding the move to a new ground at St. Mary's, but perhaps also important in allowing Marsden to believe that he belonged in the Premiership.

"Staying up by the skin of your teeth is as good as winning anything," says Marsden. "You don't enjoy all the pressure at the time, but when you look back, it really is sweet. After that Glenn [Hoddle] took over, things improved and it was unfortunate that it didn't work out for Stuart [Gray]. But with the move to the new stadium and then when Gordon Strachan became manager, the whole concept of the club changed."

WHEN THE TOPIC turns to Strachan, it is noticeable that Marsden becomes more passionate and talkative. He had held his own in the Saints team under Jones, Hoddle and Gray, but with Strachan he was transformed to a level where, alongside the likes of James Beattie, Wayne Bridge and later Antti Niemi and Michael Svensson, he was among Saints' best players. "Gordon was an inspiration," he says.

We are talking the day after Strachan has guided Celtic to the Scottish Premier League title at his first attempt and Marsden is not at all surprised. "People talk about players, but a lot is down to the manager," he says, "Southampton had the same type of players after Gordon left and everyone knows what happened. It makes a big difference who is steering the ship."

Fitness was famously the priority for Strachan and, even if he did not have the most talented squad of players in the Premiership, the new manager set out to ensure that no team would work harder and cover more ground during a game.

He introduced regular sessions of what he called 'character running'. I once asked Strachan what he meant. "That's running so hard that it makes you sick," he said, "I like to see when the body collapses first, that's character running. Footballers when they get to 30, they think they are near the end. But I think you can be at your most influential because you know more about the game, you know more about life, you know about your job and what you are supposed to do. Years ago the bodies were packing up at 32, now their bodies are as good if not better than they were at 18 so they should be more influential. Marsden was the most influential in his 30s."

What Strachan wanted from his team was made clear on the first day he walked through the door. "Normally they come in and have a light one and I made sure that, from now on, Monday will be a hard day as well and I blew people away," he says, "I joined in to make sure it looked like I could do it as well."

The players were suitably impressed. "Some people say they need more rest when they are older, but Gordon Strachan said, 'you have got no bloody chance' and made a valid point when he said you have to work harder as you get older," says Marsden. "You have to earn your place. The likes of me, Francis Benali and Jason Dodd probably worked even harder than anyone. Of course we moaned, although no-one did as much as Jason Dodd! But the thing with Gordon was that as soon as he said anything, we seemed to reap the benefits. We didn't win at home for a few games, but we were quickly playing much better and it felt like we had turned the corner. That was important because if someone comes in and says 'do this' and we get shafted there is a problem. But what he said worked.

"He has fantastic authority and one hell of a presence. He is a fantastic coach – he is a witty little bastard as well and it was a fun place to be. The other thing I liked about him was that he would speak to you like a man if there was a problem. There would be no snide remarks, you knew where you stood and he would have it out with you if it was needed."

For Strachan, those first few weeks of his reign as manager at Saints were pivotal not only for the club, but also for his own career. Despite four good years at Coventry City, the Sky Blues had been relegated in 2000/01 and he was later sacked. It was clearly risky to then take charge of a team that were 19th in the table. "I put my neck on the block," he says. "But I wanted to take the gamble and sometimes fortune favours the brave. The start wasn't easy." Strachan eventually steered Saints into the middle of the table by the end of that 2001/02 season.

He made several changes, but the most significant tactical adjustment was the decision to switch Marsden to the left of midfield. "I think I had played in left-midfield maybe once before in my life when I was 18 and I think I was subbed that day," says Marsden. He was now 33, but with Wayne Bridge behind him at left-back, he was to produce the best form of his entire career. Bridge liked nothing better than to gallop forward, meaning Marsden could tuck inside and even switch to left-back as cover for his partner. Marsden, himself, had a sweet left foot and rarely let anyone down with his own crossing and, for the next 18 months, Saints had one of the most effective left flanks in the entire Premiership.

Strachan explains his thinking. "I felt Bridge was getting blocked off by people in front of him and I saw Marsden as a tucked in guy," he says. "The stringent four with a wide man in front of Bridgey wasn't allowing him to come through on the overlap with the ball or without it.

So we played Marsden another 15 yards inside and from then on we had five midfield players with him [Bridge] coming through. There was suddenly a gap in front of him where there had been a brick wall. It was brilliant – it was a great left side. Bridge and Marsden were great for each other."

Marsden made it his job to look out for Bridge and their partnership benefited both players. "Having Wayne Bridge obviously helped me," says Marsden, "it's no coincidence that when you have got an England left-back next to you, you are bound to look a bit better. He is a fantastic player and that made a real difference. I like to think I helped him. He is someone who would listen to anything you would say. Bridgey wasn't just a full-back, but a left winger as well. He was one of those rare breed of players who could be defending one second and, within the blink of an eye, could be up the other end crossing it."

While playing as a tucked in left-midfielder, it was in the latter half of the 2001/02 season that Marsden really began to cement his cult status among the fans. He was as fit as any of the younger players, while his work-rate and appetite for success became infectious. He brought an extra element of steel and leadership to the team. His range of passing was also decent and, although not the quickest, he had become the team's midfield driving force. Marsden produced a series of influential performances before topping everything with a virtuoso individual goal in a 3-1 win against Ipswich Town. Marsden later joked that it was, "Maradona, Ricky Villa and John Barnes rolled into one" – and he wasn't far wrong.

It began when he deceived Matt Holland and dropped his shoulder to turn inside. He then ghosted past Jermaine Wright and Titus Bramble, totally wrong-footed Hermann Hreidarsson before rounding Andy Marshall to send the ball into an empty net.

What Marsden remembers best about the goal is running away from Gordon Strachan who had surged down the touchline to offer his congratulations. "I didn't score many goals and when it went in, I saw Gordon doing a Barry Fry running down the touchline and I thought 'fuck that', so I ran the other way and left him stranded on the touchline on his own! I'm not sure what happened, I just kept on going. I think I'd still be going now if I hadn't have scored."

Marsden's sometimes talismanic performances during that season were enough to persuade fans to make him Player of the Season. It followed a tribute to him in 2000, when fans sported swimming caps in impersonation of his bald head. Nicknames included the 'Bald Beckenbauer' and 'Marsdinho'.

YET IF 2001/02 had finished sweetly, things got even better the following season as Saints recorded their best Premiership finish of eighth, reached the FA Cup final and qualified for Europe for the first time in almost 20 years. The start to the 2002/03 campaign was actually slow, but once Brett Ormerod and then James Beattie found their goal-scoring touch, Saints enjoyed a wonderful run of form from November until January which saw them unbeaten for almost two months.

St. Mary's had become a fortress and, between January 14, 2002 and January 17, 2003, they lost just one home match. "The crowd was coming, Bridgey was coming through and everything James Beattie touched was turning to gold," says Marsden.

"We had so many people in good form at the same time and that obviously helps. Look at Fabrice Fernandes, he was unbelievable. He could do anything with the ball not only in training but in games as well. You think you are decent and you see a proper player like that.

"There was Michael Svensson, no-one was going through him, he brought out the best in Claus [Lundekvam] and then Antti Niemi came in and in the middle we had [Matthew] Oakley, [Rory] Delap and Anders Svensson. People talked about the fitness, but when things are going well you can run that extra two or three yards. The only one we didn't have who could have made a difference was Marian Pahars, who is an unbelievable talent.

"Everyone was playing well and there is nothing better than having a settled side. You will always get people unhappy with one thing and another, but basically 90% agreed with the manager and what he was trying to do and appreciated what he wanted to do. It was fantastic, we thought we would win against anyone and we knew James Beattie would score."

Beattie finished behind only Thierry Henry and Ruud van Nistelrooy in the race for the Premiership Golden Boot. Marsden says that Beattie was often playing through injury. "Beatts would go the whole hog for the manager", he says, "he would play with injuries and a strapped up leg and still go out for the boys. People didn't see that."

Despite a solid league campaign, it was the FA Cup which was to dominate the season. The club captain Jason Dodd had been in decent form at right-back in the run up to Christmas, but was cruelly sidelined with an ankle injury and was to miss the entire Cup campaign. As one of the most loyal and dependable players in the club's history, it would have been a fantastic reward towards the end of his career to have led the team out in Cardiff.

In Dodd's absence, Strachan turned to Marsden. Dodd and Marsden were room-mates on away trips and close friends and the former captain continued to play his part behind the scenes throughout the campaign. "I was gutted for Doddsey not playing in the Cup final," says Marsden, "he was the captain of the team and my friend. He'd been there for years and done a lot for the club and deserved to play." Dodd, however, still regards the FA Cup of 2003 as one of the highlights of his Saints career. "The Cup final was a high point even though I didn't play," he says, "it wasn't great that I wasn't playing, but Gordon Strachan did what he could to keep everyone involved."

The road to Cardiff began in spectacular fashion with what was probably the finest performance by a team under Strachan with a 4-0 demolition of Tottenham. It tasted all the sweeter to the fans for Glenn Hoddle's presence in the opposition dugout. Saints faced four teams from what was the First Division (one league below the Premiership) on their run through to the final. It was a good draw, but no-one who had been at the club over the preceding two seasons needed reminding that the FA Cup can be a great leveller. In 2002, Saints were humbled 2-1 by Rotherham United and the previous year they lost an incredible match against Tranmere Rovers. At half-time the score was 3-0 to Saints, but by full-time they had succumbed to a 4-3 beating. Wayne Bridge, Claus Lundekvam, Paul Jones, James Beattie, Jo Tessem as well as Marsden featured in both that match and the 2003 FA Cup run.

For different reasons, those defeats at Tranmere and Rotherham were experiences which helped in 2003. "Anyone who played against Tranmere would have remembered it and it was a lesson that you can't take anything for granted," says Marsden. "The only thing that didn't happen that day was that the plane didn't crash on the way home." The Rotherham defeat was also significant for a conversation between Strachan and Marsden when they resolved not to allow the pressures of the Premiership to impact on the club's performances in the Cup competitions the following season.

A late equaliser from Kevin Davies was needed to keep Saints alive against Millwall in 2003 as two goals from Matthew Oakley in the replay ensured a fifth round meeting with

Norwich. Marsden was outstanding in this match and was involved in both goals as Anders Svensson and Jo Tessem wrapped up a 2-0 win. The quarter-final against Wolves pitched Marsden and Saints against their former manager Dave Jones for the first time since he had left the club in 2001. The opening goal always looked crucial and Marsden broke the deadlock and produced another Man of the Match display as Saints eventually eased home 2-0. His volley took on the stuff of legend within hours of the final whistle.

"By 10.30pm that night it had turned into an overhead scissor kick of Ronaldo proportions," remembers Marsden. "To be honest, I don't even know what I was doing there and I just hooked it back in. Beatts took an initial swing at the ball and it seemed to put the 'keeper off and lollipop in. It's true that I didn't know it was my goal straight away. I just ran away in delight and I think it's the only time I've ever been quicker than Bridgey."

The semi-final against Watford was a wonderful occasion. "It was just an amazing weekend," remembers Marsden, "when we got to our hotel on Saturday night there were fans waiting outside and that's the first time I have witnessed that. When we got off the coach there was a huge cheer which sent a great tingle up my spine. The gaffer was very calm and just explained to us the importance of the situation and told us to enjoy the experience."

The game followed a very similar pattern to the victories over Norwich and Wolves as Saints gradually ground down their opponents, thanks more to their superior work-rate than any major advantage in quality. Marsden was again influential as he and Wayne Bridge caused numerous problems down the left. The breakthrough came just before half-time when Marsden crossed the ball for Brett Ormerod to put Saints ahead. From there, the result was rarely in serious doubt and Saints were in their first FA Cup final for 27 years.

Marsden vividly remembers receiving congratulations that evening from his former managers Dave Jones, Stuart Gray and Graham Taylor. "They didn't have to do that, but that is the bits of camaraderie you get in football," he says. "There are some very genuine and nice people in football, but it is the idiots that sometimes get the headlines."

AND SO TO Cardiff and the club's second post-war FA Cup final appearance. The build-up in and around the city was phenomenal with posters, scarves and shirts seemingly hanging from every other window. Shops were closed on the day of the final and banners seemed to hang from most bridges on the M27, M3, A34 and M4 en route to Cardiff.

The players had new designer outfits for the big day. As they tried their new suits on, James Beattie casually strolled past the cameraman in his sunglasses and said simply, "nice fabric". Marsden was asked his thoughts and replied, "I just wear what I'm given". Beattie and Marsden were both extremely popular players, but it was a moment which somehow summed up the captain's appeal to the average football supporter. Does he still have the suit? "Of course," smiles Marsden, "and the shoes as well, what do you expect? I'm a Yorkshireman." Strachan joked that he had jumped around in his bedroom before the match to be sure that the suit could withstand his animated touchline demeanour.

Marsden was, however, struggling with a knee injury in the weeks leading up to the final and it was arguable whether he was fully fit. He trained on the Thursday before the match and only passed a fitness test on the Friday. Strachan, though, wanted his leader on the pitch and his importance at that time to the team was summed up by the BBC pundit Peter Schmeichel. "It is not a gamble because he is so instrumental," he said, "if he had just a medium game by his standards it will be worth it." Marsden got through the 90 minutes. He performed reasonably, although was not as influential as in the earlier rounds. That may have been because of the quality of the opposition as much as his knee.

Aware of the threat posed down the left by the likes of Robert Pires, Ashley Cole and the drifting Thierry Henry, Strachan had opted for the more defensive combination of Chris Baird and Paul Telfer on the right as Fabrice Fernandes found himself on the substitutes' bench. The game-plan was primarily designed to stifle Arsenal and the debate will rage forever as to whether Saints should have been more adventurous.

Just ten days before the final, Saints had been beaten 6-1 by Arsenal and Strachan's thinking was clear when he said that he still thought his team could win, but that he would have to pick players who could tackle. "Manchester United adjusted their game for Arsenal – if they have to then we have to," said Strachan at the time.

Arsenal were without both Patrick Vieira and Sol Campbell and had been somewhat fortu- itous to get past Sheffield United in the semi-finals when David Seaman had pulled off a wonderful late save after his team had taken the lead with a disputed goal. With Saints having scored in each of the three previous encounters between the clubs, Strachan clearly felt confident that it would be possible to create something.

The priority, though, was nullifying the flair of Wenger's men. In truth, to remain in the game with a chance of glory throughout the entire match perhaps represents ample evidence that the tactics paid off. Arsenal might have contrived to lose the league that season to Manchester United, but at that moment in time they were the best team in the country and the gap in quality with Saints was sizeable. Arsenal had begun their record-breaking run of 49 league games undefeated with that 6-1 defeat of Strachan's men and finished some 43 points ahead of Saints the following season as they regained the Premiership title.

Arsenal also had the advantage of experience. Nine of their team had played in an FA Cup final compared to no-one for Saints. The bookmakers made Saints 11/2 to win – a shorter price than the 7/1 they were in 1976, yet still definite outsiders.

There was almost a catastrophic start when Claus Lundekvam tugged Henry back inside the penalty area after only 23 seconds, but Saints could be thankful that the Frenchman stayed on his feet and was denied by Antti Niemi. Saints largely contained Arsenal before falling behind to a Robert Pires goal just before half-time. They then only really threatened late in the game with Brett Ormerod forcing David Seaman to make a good save after he ran on to a flick from Jo Tessem. Then, in the 96th minute, James Beattie headed Matthew Oakley's corner past Seaman only for the left thigh of Ashley Cole to come to Arsenal's rescue. It had been a spirited effort, but the dream was not to be.

The captain's initial feeling was of intense disappointment. "I don't feel like I've achieved anything – I expected us to win," said Marsden. Three years later and he is more philosophical. "It was special, but it would have been nice to have won," he says. "We were just not good enough on the day. It took me a long time to watch a video of it. When I did, I thought Henry was the difference."

Strachan would not change anything about the tactics he employed that day. "I thought our plan was decent, we hoped to stay in at 0-0 or 1-0 with 20 minutes to go and I knew our fitness would be good," he said, "we had some good chances at the end. Telfs [Paul Telfer] had a header, Brett [Ormerod] had one and Beatts [James Beattie] had a good chance, so there were three decent chances and I fancied us if it had got to extra-time. We were giving away greater individual skill, greater strength, greater speed and greater experience of those occasions. We had to do what we were good at by working hard and by having huge hearts and that's what we did. We needed a bit of luck to have won, and we didn't get that."

Strachan's words were perhaps proved right just a few months later when Saints beat Manchester United in the league with a last minute James Beattie header after largely playing to contain the Champions. On that occasion, it worked. In the Cup final, it went the other way. For everyone connected with Saints, however, the highlight of the day was provided by the magnificent support and conduct of the fans.

As the teams made their way onto the pitch – with Saints led by Strachan and Marsden – the sea of yellow and blue and the sight of thousands of balloons and scarves was simply breathtaking. The BBC's veteran commentator John Motson was even taken aback. "Just look at those flags and scarves," he said, "I don't think I have ever seen it so colourful."

Rain and a newly laid pitch meant that it was the first FA Cup final to be played beneath a closed roof and this only amplified the explosion of noise which greeted the teams. The Arsenal end looked subdued in comparison. It was the difference between supporters complacent with success and those determined to make the most of what might be a once in a lifetime experience.

Even in defeat, the Southampton supporters remained for the presentations and applauded Arsenal as well as their own Cup final heroes. It was a gesture that was appreciated and noted throughout the football world. "They were a credit to Southampton, a credit to football, a credit to the FA Cup and a fabulous example to the watching world – it just made me happy and proud to be one of them," said the former manager Dave Merrington.

MARSDEN WAS TO finish second behind James Beattie in the Player of the Year poll for 2002/03. His Cult Hero status was again in evidence when he began writing a popular column for the local *Echo* newspaper called 'Life on Mars'. In a change of tack from the often banal opinions of footballers, he was willing to speak out on all manner of issues. Marsden generally showed great sympathy with the average 'working man' and many of his columns could have come straight from the comment pages of the *Sun*.

Amongst other things, he called for passports to be taken away from football hooligans, the England cricket team to boycott Zimbabwe as well as better pay for fire-fighters, teachers, nurses and soldiers. He also criticised the Government's treatment of pensioners, saying, "these people have worked hard all their lives, some of them even fought for this country in a world war and now these taxes go up yet again". Marsden did, however, support the controversial decision to go to war with Iraq. "Our armed forces are going to be giving freedom to ordinary citizens in Iraq who don't have that option," he said.

His political views generally seemed to flow from a feeling that money was being wasted and he delivered a classic column on the state of funding in higher education. "If people want to get themselves educated then they shouldn't have to pay for it," he said. "What I think should happen is that they should stop the grants for living costs and let the students find themselves accommodation and get a part-time job to pay for it…personally I don't understand the need for so many people to go to university. Plenty of people have useless degrees, but if you want to find an electrician or plumber it's almost impossible." You could almost sense the entire Northam end at St. Mary's nodding in agreeement.

As well as politics and a bit of football, there was also plenty of humour as Marsden kept Saints fans updated, among other things, with his golf, his gardening, his admiration for the actress Halle Berry, his delight at the return of Dirty Den to *EastEnders* and the constant abuse he suffered in the dressing room on account of that bald head. Strachan once even jokingly blamed Marsden's head for failing to beat Newcastle when a late header seemed to slide agonisingly wide off his scalp.

Marsden says his popularity was simply because supporters could appreciate he was doing his best for their team. "The fans in Southampton aren't stupid," he says, "they know if you are trying for them. It's not cheap to watch football – what is it? £100 to take a whole family. When you are a fan, you know some are better than others, but all you want to see is people trying their hardest."

After the Cup final, Marsden hoped to play for another two seasons and was optimistic that the club could continue to challenge for silverware. Yet, in the words of Gordon Strachan, "a little bit of Mars died" following the departure to Chelsea of Wayne Bridge in the summer of 2003. To a certain extent that was true, although he still played his part in a strong start to the 2003/04 season as Saints reached fourth in the table by Christmas.

Marsden had contributed to victories against Manchester United, Liverpool and Portsmouth but was becoming concerned by the failure of the chairman Rupert Lowe to offer him another year on his contract beyond 2004. It was a difficult situation as Lowe knew that Strachan was planning to leave at the end of the season to take a break from football.

The loss of Bridge was one thing, but the knowledge that Strachan would depart probably hit Marsden even harder and, despite his manager advising him to see out the season, he decided to leave during the January transfer window. "Gordon was going to leave, I wasn't going to get a new contract so I left, simple as that," he says. He felt he was worth another season and had options to remain in English football or play in Russia, the United States or Korea. "I could have gone to another Premiership club, but what for?" he adds. "I had a fantastic time at Southampton and it wouldn't have been the same."

And so it was that Marsden and family jetted off for Korea and a bizarre stint with Buscan Icons that lasted just two matches. "Lovely people, but it didn't work and we just didn't settle," says Marsden. He returned to England and played a few games for Sheffield Wednesday before persistent injury forced his retirement from football just prior to his 36th birthday.

BACK IN Aces Cocktail Bar in Paphos, and there are numerous photographs of various football celebrities pinned all over the walls. Among pictures of Ronaldinho, Henry and Rooney, there is the familiar face of a bald Englishman. "The FA Cup is designed for players like Chris Marsden and Brett Ormerod," says Gordon Strachan. "They're unlikely to play in the Champions League or win league titles, but in the FA Cup it was the chance for them to be legends or champions for the day."

Marsden takes a glance at the picture of him captaining the Southampton team and nods in agreement. "I was never going to be a superstar," he says, "but I had my big day and it is something I will always remember."

ANTTI NIEMI

2002-2006

SAINTS CAREER

Games	123
Clean Sheets	38
Caps	64

MAGIC MOMENT

Smashing a shot against the bar which led to a dramatic late equaliser against Fulham in 2003

NIEMI

1

'ICEMAN'

SWEDEN in the summer of 2004. James Beattie wanders by, smiles for a few photographs, happily obliges with some autograph requests and exchanges small talk with some of the youngsters who hover below him. Kevin Phillips and Graeme Le Saux are also quickly recognised and afforded the same treatment as they gently trot towards a training pitch on the outskirts of a small town called Boras near Gothenburg. The first team coach Steve Wigley takes the players through some gentle warm-ups while the manager Paul Sturrock is slumped in the dugout, looking on.

The real action, however, is taking place on an adjacent and smaller training pitch. "C'mon Antti!" yells the Southampton goalkeeping coach David Coles. "It's the final minute, Alan Shearer's headed it. C'mon, c'mon, make it!" Antti Niemi scrambles back, leaps through the air and tips the ball onto the cross-bar. "Great save!" cries Coles. "Now once more – get up, c'mon, c'mon, it's Michael Owen!" Niemi springs to his feet, flings himself back into the air and makes another breathtaking save. He then collapses into the goal. He is exhausted.

Coles sees me watching and ushers me closer. "It's okay," he says, "you can stand next to me if you want. Antti doesn't mind people watching. It makes him concentrate harder."

"Right," says Coles, turning back to Niemi. "Quick rest, then three more sets."

Niemi gives the Southampton goalkeeping coach a long, cold stare, before smiling: "Can we at least wait until my heart-rate gets below 180?"

Coles laughs, but ignores him. "In the goal," he demands a few seconds later. "Now touch your left post before every save. And it's 15 press-ups for every one you let in." Coles then proceeds to kick shots out of his hands from a distance of ten yards as Niemi flings himself to keep the ball out, before scrambling to his feet, touching the far post, and pulling off yet another amazing stop. Three go in, but Coles accepts he 'went early' once. This means the shot was impossible for even a superman goalkeeper to save.

The duo settle on 30 press-ups. Niemi mutters a few choice words about his trainer, pretends he is not going to do them, before completing the punishment. But they're not normal press-ups – Niemi does his with hands balanced on a pair of footballs.

Every Premiership fan can recall a Niemi 'wonder-save'. But the privilege of watching him train makes you realise that he actually produces dozens of similar or better stops every day in preparation for what might be a single, sudden moment in a 90 minute match. "There is never a day when I don't think 'wow, how's he got to that'," Coles says. The training I watch is apparently Niemi's weekly 'hard' session. What he does is physically quite frightening, with an emphasis on producing and reproducing explosive power.

As they are drawing to a close, the chairman Rupert Lowe appears, fully decked out in training kit with the initials 'RL' emblazoned on his top. He looks a bit out of place, but, in fairness and contrary to what is sometimes said or written, he has only even taken part in training on one morning a year during the more relaxed pre-season environment. On this occasion his role basically involves a bit of running, collecting some balls that have gone into the woods behind the goal and accompanying a rather reluctant Sturrock for a jog around a nearby lake. "I could have kept running, but had to slow down for Paul," he announces when they return.

As Lowe bounds over in the direction of the goalkeepers with an enthusiastic look on his face, it appears that he fancies a few shots. "Who's going in goal?" he asks. Niemi doesn't move a muscle from where he is sat, while Coles, who also appears somewhat unwilling, eventually takes up position for Lowe. The chairman is having a lovely time and smashes a few penalties in his direction. He scores more than he misses.

As it has just been his most gruelling session of the week, Niemi then sits out the practice match which concludes the morning's training. It means Coles and Alan Blayney take up position in goal for the two teams. Niemi sits on the touchline and looks oblivious to the action, except for what is going on in one goalmouth. Kevin Phillips descends on goal, but Coles pulls off a fine point-blank stop. A genuinely excited Niemi rises to his feet to cheer. "Well done Colesy, great save," he shouts.

As Coles makes his way off the field, he is congratulated by Niemi and the duo walk off the pitch and get into the bus together. They are virtually inseparable all week. Indeed, anyone spending time around Saints from when Niemi signed in August 2002 and then left for Fulham in January 2006, could not have failed to notice how closely he worked with his trainer.

COLES WAS SACKED as the club's goalkeeping coach just two days before Christmas 2005 and you hardly had to be a conspiracy theorist to wonder whether it played a part in Niemi's decision to leave just a few weeks later. At the time, Niemi pointed to the lure of playing in the Premiership as his motivation for departing and, while that was the most important factor, he admits that the treatment of Coles did play a part.

"David Coles was huge for me, as a goalkeeper you can't ask for more," he says, "and what happened with David Coles did make it [the decision to leave] a bit easier. I just couldn't understand how they could treat him like that. For him to be sacked on the eve of Christmas knocked me sideways. I had never met anyone so hard-working in football. He had spent seven years doing 12 hour days. It just annoys me when people talk about family clubs and loyalty because it doesn't work all ways. Football can be very ugly."

Coles was part of a complete clear-out in the club's first team coaching staff when Sir Clive Woodward and George Burley teamed up as the director of football and the head coach. The new goalkeeping coach Malcolm Webster has followed Burley throughout his recent managerial career. In many respects, the departure of Coles signalled the end of an era for Niemi before he actually left Southampton, although the duo remain in constant contact.

"It was the first time I got the sack and it hurt quite a bit," says Coles, "I had to go home and tell my wife and kids two days before Christmas that the old man had got the sack. That day, Antti came around my house and we sat, had a coffee and we both looked really despondently at each other. We didn't know what to say to each other. But the fact that he was there and he cared made a big impression on me.

"The day he signed for Fulham he came around to my house with about four cases of red and white wine. I do miss him. We have such a close bond. I probably won't work with anyone like that again. I speak to him every day. There's not a day goes by when Antti doesn't ring me or I don't ring him. We've always got something to say to each other – it might be just to have a laugh and a joke. We developed that friendship through hard work together. He's been fantastic. I admire him as a person and I admire him as a goalkeeper. There's not much more compliment I can pay."

Despite his sadness over Coles' departure, Niemi stressed that he left Southampton on good terms and with some wonderful memories. "I hoped we would be in with a stronger chance of reaching the play-offs [of the Championship]," he says. "If we were fighting for the top four, it would have been a more difficult decision. I thought George Burley was a great choice as manager, but at my age [33 at the time] I had to look at the bigger picture. It wasn't about money – I had an offer from another Premiership club with higher wages – but mostly about testing myself in the Premiership. Fulham is a good club and it is a nice part of London.

"When Southampton sold me, I had a chat with the chairman [Lowe] and thanked him. I had a fantastic time and I am grateful for the opportunities I had. There was always speculation about me, but I never had any direct contact with Manchester United or anyone else and had never wanted to leave. It was all just paper talk, you get linked with different things, but the only club that came in for me while I was at Southampton was Celtic in the summer of 2005 and the chairman didn't let me go. That was it."

With Saints having slipped down into the bottom half of the table, there was no hope of a return to the Premiership until 2007/08 at the earliest and Niemi would have been 35 then. The fans understood and most were grateful that he stayed at the club after relegation despite his status among the very best goalkeepers in the English game. They were also pleased that he decided against joining Portsmouth (who also wanted to sign him), despite the fact that such a move would have meant no personal upheaval for Niemi as well as the chance to work with Coles again.

The reaction to Niemi's departure was indicative of the huge affection with which he was held among the supporters. He was perhaps Southampton's highest quality player since Matthew Le Tissier and those God-like worships were often re-created behind the goal in the Northam end for Niemi's saves. 'We've got the best 'keeper in the world,' was the chant – and the supporters truly believed it of a player who was honoured on the last day of the 2003/04 season by the travelling fans who all donned blonde wigs and waved Finland flags during the match against Charlton.

CHOOSING THE ULTIMATE goalkeeping Cult Hero for this book, however, was still a difficult task. There are so many outstanding candidates throughout the club's 121-year history. For sheer excellence, the legendary Peter Shilton as well as Thomas Allen and George Clawley can justifiably claim to be the best.

In terms of pure personality and eccentricity, it would be fair to say that the likes of John Robinson, Eric Martin, John Burridge and Bruce Grobbelaar are fairly unbeatable. And what about Ian Turner, who played so well in the 1976 FA Cup final, or Tim Flowers?

Southampton have been blessed with many great goalkeepers, going right back to the earliest days in the club's history when Robinson played such a part in three Southern League titles and reaching the FA Cup finals of 1900 and 1902. As well as his outstanding perform-ances on the pitch, he achieved notoriety for punching a spectator in the face during a 2-1 win at New Brompton in October 1902. Robinson played between George Clawley's two stints at The Dell. Clawley was at Southampton from 1896 to 1898 and 1903 to 1907 and played for the winning Tottenham Hotspur side in the 1901 FA Cup Final, the last team from outside the Football League to win the trophy.

The next great Southampton goalkeeper was Allen, who was probably the finest to grace The Dell until the arrival of Shilton in 1982. Allen played during the successful 1920s when Saints first entered the Football League. He continues to hold the club record for appearances as a goalkeeper (323 matches) as well as the lowest tally of goals conceded in any league season with just 21 in 42 games. That mark was set in 1921/22 on the way to promotion to Division Two and also stood as a national record for some 60 years.

Indeed, in five seasons between 1920 and 1925, Saints conceded only 156 goals in 210 league matches. It is a record which compares favourably with Shilton's five year stint at The Dell, although Saints were then in the top-flight and renowned for their more attacking football. Shilton's incredible record of 125 international caps and over 1,000 league appearances means that he is certainly the most famous goalkeeper to have played for Southampton. Another with impressive statistics is the Scotland international Ian Black who, between 1947 and 1950, actually conceded fewer goals (95) than the number of league games he played (97).

Of the characters, it is the antics of Martin and Burridge which stand out most. With his flowing locks, Martin – or 'Harpo' as he was nicknamed – was a definite folk hero during the late 1960s and early 1970s. His tendency to come rushing off his line is still fondly remembered as well as the interaction with fans during the pre-match warm-up. A favourite tradition was when he would throw the balls from distance into a sack held open on the touchline by one of the coaches.

However, when it came to crowd-pleasing antics, it is doubtful that anyone could really compare with Burridge. His stay at Saints lasted only two seasons, but, just as he did at more than 30 different clubs where he was a player, coach or manager, he endeared himself to the fans. 'Budgie' would do hand-stands before matches and, legend held, would apparently even sleep in his gloves. Chris Marsden, who played with Burridge at Sheffield United, remembers how he would dive around the dressing room catching oranges. Yet, for all his extrovert behaviour, he was perhaps years ahead of his time in terms of his training and diet. He was also into self-hypnosis and set a Premiership record when he appeared for Manchester City at the age of 43. He now lives in Oman where he has coached the national team.

So how does Niemi fit into this assortment of personalities? And what makes him my chosen Cult Hero? Without the available footage, it is impossible to compare him to Allen from the 1920s, but he is surely superior as a goalkeeper to anyone else with the exception of Shilton. As a shot-stopper, Niemi possibly holds the edge over Shilton, although the commanding presence of the former England captain means that he can make a convincing claim to be the finest goalkeeper Saints have had.

Niemi's popularity, however, surpasses that of Shilton. Whereas Shilton was hugely respected for his professionalism, efficiency and brilliance, he was somehow not quite loved on the terraces in the way Niemi was. Largely that was to do with the way the Finn carried himself and also the era in which he played.

With Saints settled into their St. Mary's home and, at the time, becoming well established in the Premiership under Gordon Strachan, the crowds were able to flock to see the club like never before. Indeed, between November 2002 and August 2004, attendances of more than 30,000 were registered at every home league game. With football itself booming, the popularity and excitement around Saints was as high as it had been since the early 1980s.

However, with far more women and families coming to watch football, it is questionable whether even the teams of the 1980s would have attracted such consistently high numbers. The fans' three favourite players at this time were Chris Marsden, James Beattie and Niemi. While Marsden tended to be most popular among the traditional supporter and Beattie with the new type of fan, Niemi was idolised by a cross section of the club's support. With his bleached blonde hair and appreciation of the crowd, he stood out in an era of often dull and insular football players.

His popularity was obviously driven by his performances on the pitch, but also a level of modesty and intelligence. He understands what football is and cuts straight through the hype which surrounds his profession. "My happiness doesn't depend on football," he says, "sure, football means a lot to me and it can take a few days before I get back to normal if I make a mistake, but there really are more important things in the world."

He values his strong relationship with supporters, but the cult of celebrity does not sit easily on his shoulders. An unflappable character on and off the field, Niemi gets mildly agitated just once during our chat and that is when discussing the impact fame sometimes has on footballers.

"It's nice to give autographs to kids, that's no problem, but there's a lot of things in football I don't like," he says. "I like talking to fans, but I just think there are so many more important jobs in the world. You get people who think they are special just because they are footballers. You get a young boy who is suddenly earning a lot of money and gets big-headed and you think 'so what, you can play football'.

"If I was a doctor or something I would be proud of myself, but being a footballer? What is that? Don't get me wrong, I love the fans and it's brilliant. It's a lovely feeling, it's fun and it's a big sport, but there are so many more important professions in the world."

NIEMI CAME TO the Premiership relatively late in his career, joining Southampton at the age of 30. He had earlier spent six years at HJK Helsinki before shorter spells with FC Copenhagen, Charlton Athletic, Glasgow Rangers and then almost three years for Hearts in the Scottish Premier League. Niemi was a player already known to Gordon Strachan as he had previously tried to sign him in 1997 when he managed Coventry City. Interestingly, however, it was Lowe who pushed for Saints to sign Niemi in favour of the Croatian Stipe Pletikosa who had been closely watched by Strachan and the goalkeeping coach Coles.

The fact Strachan had shown such interest previously in signing him was a factor in his decision to move south. "The key reason was that I wanted to test myself in the Premiership against the best players in the world," says Niemi, "I just wanted to improve as a goalkeeper. I had spent five years in Scotland, I had been to all the grounds quite a few times and, although I loved it in Edinburgh, it was the right time for me.

"Gordon Strachan was trying to sign me at Coventry and that made a difference to me, it's nice to know someone believes in you. But I only really left for sporting reasons, I liked it in Edinburgh and the contract terms were not a great deal different. I felt I was doing well at Hearts, I was making good saves, but I wanted to find out if I could do it in England."

Initially, however, Niemi had to be patient. At a fee of £2m, he had clearly not been signed simply as a reserve. Paul Jones had been the first choice Southampton and Wales goalkeeper since 1997, but doubts had presumably crept into Strachan's mind. By this time Jones was 35 and, while his kicking had always been somewhat erratic, the occasional mistake had also crept into his game. But Jones was still a goalkeeper of Premiership class and, with Niemi arriving just after the start to the 2002/03 season, the Welshman initially produced some impressive performances to stay in the team.

What can only be described as a howler in the 1-0 defeat against West Bromwich Albion, however, gave Niemi his opportunity. He literally grasped it with both hands in a goalless draw with Charlton, which included an outstanding save from a Claus Jensen free-kick. For the next three-and-a-half years, Niemi was Southampton's first choice goalkeeper. "When I first joined the club Paul Jones was playing out of his skin," says Niemi, "he was making fantastic saves against teams like Chelsea and all the big boys.

"He was playing really, really well and I was thinking, 'I'm never going to get a game – how am I going to top that?' Fortunately, though, Gordon Strachan had plans for me. But I looked up to Paul Jones and he gave me good advice. I had never played in the Premiership, he had played a few hundred games and he was always very nice to me. I've never had any problems with other goalkeepers at any club I have been at. I think there is a certain understanding between goalkeepers because it's such a specialist position."

Both Jones and Niemi certainly showed a great deal of class in dealing with the situation so well, although, as time went on, it became evident who the first choice goalkeeper would be. Jones was the equal of anyone as a shot-stopper, but the level of calm and consistency exuded by Niemi made him impossible to dislodge. It is something his team-mates quickly sensed. "Antti Niemi is really a quiet man," says the centre-back Claus Lundekvam, "he doesn't say much, but he has got great presence about him that is very reassuring."

The step up to the Premiership was not problematic. "It sounds weird, but in a way I found it easier in England than in Scotland to start with because the players are doing the right things," says Niemi, "the midfielders and strikers are doing the correct things. If you give them a chance they are more dangerous, but you are also playing with better defenders in the Premiership."

The Swedish centre-back Michael Svensson had also been signed for £2m during the summer. Paul Williams made way as Svensson and Niemi provided the sort of injection in quality that would have improved any team in the Premiership. With Wayne Bridge outstanding at left-back and Jason Dodd or Paul Telfer extremely solid at right-back, Saints were able to establish one of the finest defences in the entire Premiership. It formed the foundation for some notable success.

DURING THE 2002/03 and 2003/04 seasons, only the top five teams at the time (Arsenal, Chelsea, Manchester United, Liverpool and Newcastle United) could boast a superior defensive record to Southampton. It was something which the players rightly took great pride in and, there is a hint of regret, as Niemi recalls those partnerships. He wishes they could all have played together for a few more years.

"I was over the moon after my debut against Charlton," he says, "it was a quiet game, but it was one of the best feelings to play on such a big stage – it was the biggest stage I had played on. We seemed to gel extremely well together. We all complimented each other quite well. Claus Lundekvam is a very good player, extremely elegant. He keeps the game simple and he is very laid back, but he needs someone who is aggressive like Michael Svensson to play with him and we hardly conceded any goals. It was rarely more than one in a match.

"It was water-tight at the back and the three of us all got on really well off the pitch. We are all from the same part of the world, we had this unbelievable understanding and looking back we were all playing well. Outside of the top five or six, we were the most difficult team to beat in the league. Jason Dodd is obviously not the quickest, but he is defensively very good. We had Wayne Bridge and he's a fantastic player."

Lundekvam has been at the heart of the Southampton defence since 1996 and has little hesitation in saying that Niemi is the best goalkeeper he has played alongside. "He is still one of the best in the Premiership without a doubt," says Lundekvam. "We had two years where we all played really well together at the back. I think at that time we had a very good spine to the team. Myself, Michael Svensson and Antti Niemi were playing together almost every week and it provided a very good platform for the team who also did well."

The 2002/03 season, of course, was to see Saints finish eighth in the league and reach the FA Cup final. Niemi was in outstanding form throughout, producing countless wonderful performances. The most memorable was perhaps a triple save to deny Patrick Vieira in a 3-2 win against Arsenal. It came shortly after half-time at a vital moment with the game still level at 1-1. "A bit lucky, he should have scored," is his understated assessment.

But there were many other jaw-dropping moments over the next few years: a one handed reaction stop to deny Szilard Nemeth at the Riverside, a double save from Kevin Phillips against Sunderland, a brave block from an Alan Shearer pile-driver, acrobatics to deny Jay-Jay Okocha and afternoons of almost lone resistance against Aston Villa and Everton. Perhaps his best game was Paul Sturrock's first match as manager when he almost single-handedly denied Liverpool in a 2-0 win which included a penalty save from Michael Owen.

Strangely, though, it was not a piece of goalkeeping for which Niemi will be best remembered among Southampton fans. He cringes somewhat at the memory, but the moment which will always stick in people's minds came at Loftus Road against Fulham in March 2003. Deep into injury-time, Saints were trailing 2-1 when Niemi came forward for the first corner of his life.

There was a deflected shot, a bit of a goalmouth scramble and then the ball flew in his direction. Yet, rather than panic, Niemi calmly controlled the ball on his chest and then smashed a volley onto the crossbar from which Michael Svensson headed home the equaliser. As unlikely as it seemed, it was a moment which summed Niemi up. Whatever the situation, whether having to head clear a defender's mis-hit back-pass or go eye-to-eye with the best strikers in the world, he seemed able to produce the goods. To borrow a phrase from the darts commentator Dave Lanning, Niemi is 'cooler than a refrigerator in an igloo'.

Niemi's mental strength is something highlighted by Coles. "He is like a hawk during a game – he never takes his eyes off the ball," he says, "you have to be mentally strong and he is the strongest I've ever come across for preparation. Most goalkeepers nowadays can make saves. The mental preparation is as important as the physical side. In training he was phenomenal. It was an ego thing to him. He really believed he shouldn't let in goals.

"Yet if he did, he has got that mechanism to say 'that's gone'. He doesn't get bothered by anything, he just gets into what else he should be doing. His strength is his fantastic shot-stopping, but he also worked very hard on crossing and dealing with back-passes. He is also very quick from his line, he supports the back four and anticipates things very quickly. He's got a presence – he's laid back, but works very hard."

By the end of the 2003/04 season, Niemi was generally regarded among the best goalkeepers in the Premiership. He was regularly linked with both Manchester United and Arsenal and there seemed little doubt that he could potentially improve either team, who at the time had Jens Lehmann and Tim Howard as their number one choices, but Niemi was perfectly happy at Saints while they were in the Premiership. Much like Matthew Le Tissier, why should he even contemplate moving?

IT SEEMED unthinkable after five consecutive finishes free from the fear of relegation that the 2004/05 season would finish with the club bottom of a league table for the first and, so far, only time in its entire history. In all, it was the third time Saints have been relegated since they joined the Football League in 1920. It highlighted several truisms of football.

The first was the delicate line between success and failure. All may have appeared rosy from 2002 until early 2004, but Saints had been struggling for goals and a real creative spark. Niemi's heroics in goal had often masked some weaknesses elsewhere. In a league where there was very little between those teams aside from Manchester United, Chelsea, Arsenal and Liverpool, small cracks always threatened to develop into gaping holes.

When the problems arrived, they did so both on and off the pitch. Off it, the departure of Gordon Strachan as the manager in February 2004, had an enormous effect. The high standards of fitness and work rate, which had underpinned the excellent defensive base, seemed to slip and his successor, Paul Sturrock, appeared to have difficulty commanding respect from the players and staff at the club. Where the blame lay for that problem is difficult to judge.

Results, however, had remained reasonable and it came as a considerable shock when it was announced that Sturrock and Saints were parting company by mutual consent following a win against Blackburn Rovers in August 2004. By this stage it appeared that Lowe was already considering his 'master-plan' of having a head coach work alongside a director of football – with the rugby union World Cup winner Sir Clive Woodward poised to give up his job as England coach.

Sturrock's title was bizarrely changed during the summer from 'team manager' to 'head coach'. The Scot, however, was more of a traditional manager and was rarely a huge presence on the training ground. In short, he was the opposite of what Lowe seemed to want. Steve Wigley, however, was a track-suited coach who would train the team while issues relating to the 'bigger picture' could be looked after elsewhere.

Given that Woodward had already made visits to the training ground at this stage and, later admitted, that he signed his contract to join Saints as early as November 2004, it is safe to assume that he was taking a close interest in developments at St. Mary's. Sadly, however, the results under Wigley were poor and he was sacked at the beginning of December with Saints in the relegation zone.

After Wigley, Lowe was overruled by the board who collectively decided to opt for Harry Redknapp. If there was a manager less suited to Lowe's grand vision for the club than Sturrock, the directors had perhaps found him in Redknapp. It was another surprising appointment, which brought some improvement in performances, although a 2-1 defeat by Manchester United at St. Mary's sealed relegation on the final day of the season.

Redknapp was also gone by December 2005, meaning the players had been managed by six different people – Gordon Strachan, Paul Sturrock, Steve Wigley, Harry Redknapp, Dave Bassett and George Burley – in less than two years. It was an extraordinary turnover. Niemi has said that the club had got itself into a "mess", likening the situation to being aboard a "bad rollercoaster ride".

He believes it did have an impact on the players, but says responsibility for relegation should be shared. "I think Gordon Strachan made a big difference," he says, "he was a good manager and got the best out of players and everybody. He had a lot of charisma, he worked as hard as anyone and, when he said something, everybody listened. After he left, we had a few managers in a short period of time. It was unsettling and it gives a football player an excuse to get away from responsibility. Obviously it didn't help and someone got it wrong." The fall out from the off-field problems continued in the months after Niemi's departure, culminating with Lowe's resignation as chairman in June 2006.

Niemi, though, prefers to concentrate on matters on the field when discussing Saints' relegation. Naturally he focuses on the defence and says that losing Michael Svensson to a long-term injury which ruled the Swede out of the entire 2004/05 campaign was crucial.

Lundekvam agrees: "We lost Michael Svensson and a few others like Chris Marsden and James Beattie and when you lose those sort of players, you will feel that." Niemi adds: "It was sad for two years to be one of the best defences and then see what happened in the last year. When Michael Svensson got injured that was when the problems started. The contrast was so huge. Nobody was playing well, we looked around and we were not trusting anyone.

"From being a really, really solid unit, players got scared of making mistakes. There was the Portsmouth game and I blame myself for that. But it got to the stage where you were almost expecting someone to make a mistake and that's when you overdo it because you get too pumped up. I felt I had a lot of games where I didn't do anything wrong, but didn't make any good saves or really help the team."

In fairness, Niemi had another decent season personally, although that was marred somewhat by the 4-1 defeat against Portsmouth when he uncharacteristically rushed from his goal to deal with a through-ball, only for Lomana LuaLua to pounce. It was hard not to feel some sympathy, however. With centre-backs Claus Lundekvam and Andreas Jakobsson constantly backing away, Niemi was simply trying to do something about the shell-shocked defending that was going on under his nose.

But it was not just a fragile defence and lost confidence which cost Saints. Since the departure of Wayne Bridge to Chelsea in July 2003, a lack of pace had been an obvious deficiency in the team. The absence of a creative spark from midfield dated back even further. Yes, the likes of James Beattie and Brett Ormerod were hard workers, but, even when the club reached the FA Cup final, Saints were a team better at stopping their opponents from playing rather than creating too much for themselves.

A tally of 43 league goals in 2002/03 (23 of which were scored by Beattie) was an indication that there would be problems if the defence faltered. Indeed, it is worth noting that Saints scored two more (45) when they were relegated than in the season when they had recorded their highest Premiership finish. Prior to the 2004/05 season, Niemi and others in the team were hoping that money would be invested in the sort of midfielder or striker with the pace and skill to unlock defences of the highest calibre. No such player arrived and there was a predictable and plodding feel to a midfield devoid of pace.

"The balance of the team wasn't right," says Niemi, "there was something missing. At Fulham, we have had players like Steed Malbranque or Luis Boa Morte who make things happen and we have always got a chance of winning games. You need those sort of players, but it takes a bit of money from the board to get them."

The club captain Jason Dodd was disappointed that he was not utilised by Redknapp, particularly in the closing weeks of the season when the team appeared to lack strong characters. "It was horrendous," he says. "Up until Christmas I probably didn't deserve to play, but for the last three months I was fit and I thought I was going to get a chance after being called back from loan. Of course, it might have been worse, I don't know. I wanted to play, but Harry Redknapp had his ideas and we will never know."

As Saints attempted to rebuild following relegation, Woodward arrived as first the technical director, then the performance director and, following the appointment of George Burley, became the director of football and later the technical support director before he departed in August 2006. "I only met Clive Woodward a few times," says Niemi, "I can only speak about my personal experiences and I got a good impression of him. There was a lot of negative stuff in the papers, but, in terms of fitness and making the training ground better, there is no reason why his skills cannot be transferred."

AS WITH SO many of Saints' Cult Heroes, Niemi has left a little piece of himself in Southampton and cannot really bring himself to completely leave. He continues to follow Saints from afar and has been seen at matches when he is not playing for Fulham. That, of course, reminds fans what they are missing and keeps him fresh in their minds, but he is in no way a posturing footballer, returning to the site of his former glories to gloat. Niemi is genuinely fond of the club which brought him into the top-flight of English football. And the fans are more than fond of him. Since leaving Saints, he has received hundreds of emails from fans thanking him for his contribution to the club. He replied telling them that he had enjoyed his best days as a footballer with Southampton.

"What really stands out from my time at Southampton are not the games, the goals or any of the saves," he says. "What I really remember was the FA Cup final and walking out onto the pitch for the warm-up. I looked at the Arsenal end and it was still empty and then looked up to our end and there was just this sea of yellow and blue. It was unbelievable. That to me sums up Southampton Football Club. That is the real loyalty in football."

Bibliography

Alan Ball: Playing Extra Time
(Macmillan 2004) by Alan Ball

The Alphabet of The Saints: A Complete Who's Who of Southampton FC
(ACL & Polar 1992) by Duncan Holley and Gary Chalk

By The Book
(Willow Books 1984) by Clive Thomas

CB Fry: King of Sport
(Metro 2002) by Iain Wilton

CB Fry: The Man and His Methods
(JW Arrowsmith 1912) by A Wallis Myers

Chambers Biographical Dictionary
(Chambers 1990) by Magnus Magnusson (editor)

Charlie George: My Story
(Century 2005) by Charlie George

Cricket: Batsmanship
(Eveleigh Nash 1912) by CB Fry

Danny Boy: Life, Football & Multiple Sclerosis
(Highdown 2006) by Danny Wallace

Dell Diamond: Ted Bates's 66 Seasons With The Saints
(Hagiology 2004) by David Bull

The Diary of a Season
(Arthur Baker 1979) by Lawrie McMenemy

The English
(Penguin 1999) by Jeremy Paxman

El Diego
(Yellow Jersey 2004) by Diego Maradona

Football League Tables 1888-2001
(Soccer Books Limited 2001) by Michael Robinso

Full-Time at The Dell: from Watty to Matty 1898-2001
(Hagiology 2001) by Dave Juson and David Bull

Gordon Strachan: The Biography
(Virgin 2004) by Leo Moynihan

Gray Matter: Andy Gray, The Autobiography
(Macmillan 2004) by Andy Gray

In That Number: A Post-War Chronicle of Southampton FC
(Hagiology 2003) by Duncan Holley and Gary Chalk

Kevin Keegan: My Autobiography
(Warner Books 1998) by Kevin Keegan

Le Tissier
(Thomas 2005) by Jeremy Butler

Life Worth Living
(Eyre and Spottiswoode 1939) by CB Fry

Looking for Eric: In Search of the Leeds Greats
(Mainstream 2000) by Rick Broadbent

Man on the Run
(Arthur Baker 1986) by Mick Channon

Match of the Millennium: The Saints' 100 Most Memorable Matches
(Hagiology 2000) by David Bull and Bob Brunskell (editors)

Mick Channon: The Authorised Biography
(Highdown 2005) by Peter Batt

My 1998 World Cup Story
(Andre Deutsch 1998) by Glenn Hoddle with David Davies

One Hump or Two? The Frank Worthington Story
(ACL & Polar 1994) by Frank Worthington

On the Edge of Reason
(Paper Plane 1997) by Dave Jones

Ossie: King of Stamford Bridge
(Mainstream 2002) by Peter Osgood with Martin King and Martin Knight

Saints: A Complete Record of Southampton Football Club 1885-1987
(Breedon Books Sport 1987) by Gary Chalk and Duncan Holley

Saints v Pompey: A History of Unrelenting Rivalry
(Hagiology 2004) by Dave Juson with Clay Aldworth, Barry Bendel, David Bull and Gary Chalk

Soccer: The Hard Way
(Pelham Books 1970) by Ron Harris

Strachan: My Life in Football
(Time Warner Books 2006) Gordon Strachan with Jason Tomas

Tie a Yellow Ribbon: How The Saints Won The Cup
(Hagiology 2006) by Tim Manns with David Bull

Tom Finney: My Autobiography
(Headline 2004) by Tom Finney

Who Ate All the Pies? The Life and Times of Mick Quinn
(Virgin 2004) by Mick Quinn and Oliver Harvey

VIDEOS, DVDS AND AUDIO

Charlie Wayman interview
(David Bull 1998)

Dream Fans: The Spirit of Southampton
(Javier Igeno Cano 2005)

Matt Le Tissier: Unbelievable
(REB Productions 1995)

The Saints Millennium Video
(Route One Broadcasting 1999)

Southampton vs Manchester Utd: 1976 FA Cup final
(ILC Sport/ITV Sport 2004)

Southampton vs Arsenal: 2003 FA Cup final
(BBC Sport 2003)

Taking Le Tiss: Matt's 50 Greatest Goals...In His Own Words
(Natter Jack Productions 2004)

Subscribers

Dawn Adams	Mark Dennis	Graham Heal	Matt Le Tissier
Stephen Aldridge	Matt Le Tissier	John Hibbert	
Bob Amey	Terry Paine	Paul Hickey	Francis Benali
Phil Andrews	Matt Le Tissier	Derek Hicks	Antti Niemi
Norman Bainbridge	Terry Paine	Derek Hindle	Matt Le Tissier
Brian Barendt	George Ephgrave	Lewis Hodder	Matt Le Tissier
Andrew Beach	Chris Marsden	Steve Hopgood	Matt Le Tissier
MJ Bennett	Francis Benali	Rob Horne	Matt Le Tissier
Kevin Bills	Matt Le Tissier	David Howard	Terry Paine
Stuart Bishop	Matt Le Tissier	Peter Humphries	Mick Channon
Robert Bradshaw	Gordon Strachan	Nick Illingsworth	Matt Le Tissier
Nick Brice	Mick Channon	Mark & Carole Judd	Mick Channon
David Brindley	Mick Channon	Cliff Keith	Mick Channon
	& Matt Le Tissier	Andy Kershaw	Matt Le Tissier
Adrian Brown	Matt Le Tissier	Mervyn King	
Stephen Brunsdon	Mick Channon	Ian Knight	John McGrath
Terence Bruty		Pete Lacey	Mark Dennis
Michelle Bunten	Lawrie McMenemy	Keith Legg	Steve Williams
Nigel Burgess	Francis Benali	Adam Leitch	Chris Marsden
Tony Butt	Nick Holmes	Malcolm Lewis	Matt Le Tissier
Graham Cabble	Mick Channon	Amanda Liford-Symonds	Mick Channon
Javier Igeno Cano	Matt Le Tissier	John Lilly	Ron Davies
John Caws		Barry Richard Lock	Matt Le Tissier
Stephen Cheffy	Mike Channon	John Lovelock	Terry Paine
Jim Clarke	Matt Le Tissier	John Lovelock	Terry Paine
John Clements	George O'Brien	Neil & George Marriott	Mick Channon
Nigel Cleverley	Matt Le Tissier	Colin Martin	Terry Paine
Christopher Collins	Matt Le Tissier	Dave Masters	Mick Channon
Jeff Colmer	Matt Le Tissier	Chris Matthews	Ron Davies
Graham Comfort	Peter Crouch	Donald McAllen	Charlie Wayman
John Connaghan	Claus Lundekvam	Nigel McAllen	Mark Dennis
Marisa Cooper	Danny Wallace	Andrew Mengham	Ivan Golac
Lee Curtis	Mark Dennis	Michael Mengham	Mark Dennis
Peter Day	Mick Channon	Tom Mitchell	Matt Le Tissier
Tristan Daynes	Francis Benali	Andy Moisan	Matt Le Tissier
Trevor Defferd	Matt Le Tissier	Andrew Moncrieff	Matt Le Tissier
Garry Denton	Matt Le Tissier	Andrew Moriarty	Matt Le Tissier
Ian Donaldson	Matt Le Tissier	Martin Murray	Brian O'Neil
Robert Donaldson	Mick Channon	Raymond Mursell	Charlie Wayman
Dave Dudman	Eric Martin	Dave Newell	Terry Paine
Jo Dunsford	John Sydenham	Matthew Norton	Matt Le Tissier
Robert Elliott	Terry Paine	Barry Osgood	Matt Le Tissier
Johnnie Fanning	Mark Dennis	Gordon Parrish	Matt Le Tissier
George Farmer	Terry Paine	Ray Peacock	Alan Shearer
Norma Farminer	Matt Le Tissier	Paul Pearce	Matt Le Tissier
Joy Faulkner	Terry Paine	Alf Peckham	Bill Ellerington
Dianne Fenwick	Terry Paine	Trevor Penton	Mick Channon
Mrs Foster	Matt Le Tissier	David Pepper	Matt Le Tissier
David Freemantle	Ron Davies	Paul Pinchbeck	Matt Le Tissier
Simon Green	Matt Le Tissier	Nick Powell	Peter Wells
Sean Hammerton	Matt Le Tissier	Phil Rawlings	Mick Channon
Alan Harfield	Matt Le Tissier	Dan Reeves	Matt Le Tissier
Daniel Harris	Matt Le Tissier	Louis Reeves	Tim Flowers

Marcus Reeves	Francis Benali
Neil Reeves	Matt Le Tissier
Jamie Richmond	Matt Le Tissier
Andrew Roberts	Peter Crouch
John Robins	Matt Le Tissier
Dennis Robinson	Ron Davies
Gary Rogers	Mick Channon
Steve Rogers	Terry Paine
Mark Rooke	Matt Le Tissier
Robert Rooke	Bill Ellerington
Brian Sandy	Matt Le Tissier
Alison Shephard	Matt Le Tissier
Paul Sheppard	Ron Davies
Mark Sills	Mick Channon
Kevin Slawson	Mick Channon
Brian Smith	Terry Paine
Richard Buckingham Smith	Matt Le Tissier
Phil Snarr	Mick Channon
Derek John Stevens	Mick Channon
Lis Strange	Mick Channon
John Stranger	Matt Le Tissier
Jan Stroud	Matt Le Tissier
James Sutton	Matt Le Tissier
Martin Synan	Terry Paine
Janet Tarbart	Mick Channon
Ted Tarbart	Terry Paine
Ross Taylor	Matt Le Tissier
Ian Thumwood	Matt Le Tissier
Julian Titt	Mick Channon
Glyn Tudor	Ron Davies
Graham Watford	Matt Le Tissier
Nichola Weston	Matt Le Tissier
Brian White	Terry Paine
John White	Matt Le Tissier
Ross White	Jimmy Case
Barry Whitlock	Mick Channon
David Wilkinson	Matt Le Tissier
Glen Williams	Francis Benali
David Willis	Matt Le Tissier
Joyce & George Wilson	Terry Paine
Keith 'Tug' Wilson	Terry Paine
Martyn Wilson	Matt Le Tissier
Malcolm Wing	Mick Channon
David Witt	Matt Le Tissier
Howard Woadden	Terry Paine
Tony Woadden	Ted Bates
Mark Wood	Terry Hurlock
Russell Wood	Danny Wallace
L Brian Woolgar	Ivan Golac
Robyn Young	Mick Channon
Simon Young	Matt Le Tissier

TOP SIX PLAYERS VOTED FOR

Matthew Le Tissier	59
Mick Channon	25
Terry Paine	19
Francis Benali	6
Ron Davies	6
Mark Dennis	6